The Western Abenakis of Vermont 1600–1800

The Civilization of the American Indian Series

The Western Abenakis of Vermont, 1600–1800

War, Migration, and the Survival of an Indian People

By
Colin G. Calloway

University of Oklahoma Press : Norman and London

By Colin G. Calloway

Crown and Calumet: British Indian Relations, 1783–1815
(Norman, 1987)
New Directions in American Indian History (Norman, 1988)
The Abenaki (New York, 1989)
The Western Abenakis of Vermont, 1600–1800 (Norman, 1990)

Library of Congress Cataloging-in-Publication Data

Calloway, Colin G. (Colin Gordon), 1953–
    The Western Abenakis of Vermont, 1600–1800 : war,
migration, and the survival of an Indian people / by Colin G.
Calloway.
        p.   cm. — (The Civilization of the American Indian Series)
    Includes bibliographical references.
    ISBN 0-8061-2274-9 (alk. paper)
    1. Abenaki Indians—Wars.   2. Abenaki Indians—History.
I. Title.   II. Series.
E99.A13C36   1990
974.3′004973—dc20   89-40736
                                                                CIP

Copyright © 1990 by the University of Oklahoma Press, Norman, Publishing Division of the University. All rights reserved. Manufactured in the U.S.A. First edition.
    The Western Abenakis of Vermont, 1600–1800, is Volume 197 in The Civilization of the American Indian Series.

To Marcia and John

Their bodies
have long forgotten the wound's
heat, the sudden fever of smallpox
the ache of starvation.
On these banks their winter camps
abandoned
moulder beneath roots of alder and vine.

And you came here believing
that this was a vacant country.

—Cathy Czapla, "Abenaki Ghosts"

Contents

Illustrations

Maps

Preface

This is the story of the making of a remnant Indian people, the story of two centuries of war and migration during which the western Abenakis of Vermont became scattered across large areas of the northeastern United States and southern Quebec, leaving only isolated enclaves in their original homelands. It is also a story of persistence and survival.

Few Vermonters, and even fewer visitors to the state, think of Vermont as "Indian country."[1] Scholars of Indian history have tended to concentrate their attention far to the west where Indian groups survived intact in greater numbers. The powerful and pivotal Iroquois of New York demanded the attention of contemporaries and have continued to attract the attention of historians. But smaller eastern remnant groups like the western Abenakis seemed too few, too dispersed, and too intermarried with surrounding populations to merit more than passing notice by students of Indian history, and they have often gone ignored by the general public. Moreover, such groups survived for centuries by keeping a low profile and avoiding the attention of non-Indian society.

In recent years, however, these groups, conscious and confident of their Indian identity, have demanded political recognition and attracted public attention. At the same time, Indian historians have begun to call for a rewriting of American history that incorporates the experiences of Native American peoples. Despite considerable headway in the last decade or so, much work re-

mains to be done before the history of the Northeast can be re-
told taking proper account of the Native American presence and
perspective. This book about the Abenakis is a rewriting of one
story in the complex anthology that is the history of northeastern
North America.

The history of the western Abenakis has suffered from the
long-standing notion that their homeland was little more than a
no-man's-land between competing groups before settlement by
European pioneers. The traditional view that the area that became the state of Vermont was uninhabited before to the arrival
of Europeans has long since been discredited, and the western
Abenakis are recognized as the original inhabitants of Vermont,
as well as New Hampshire and parts of northwestern Massachusetts and southern Quebec. But the opinion still prevails that
the Indian inhabitants were few in number and drifted north to
Canada as English settlers pushed up the Connecticut and Champlain valleys. This partial truth obscures the full picture of western Abenaki history. Vermont was neither an empty wilderness
nor simply a flight path for Indians disappearing into Canada.
It was the core of the western Abenaki homeland. Vermont
was Indian country when Europeans arrived and was home to
both indigenous and immigrant Indian peoples. Lake Champlain
(Bitawbagok), the site of western Abenaki creation stories, remained the center of the universe for western Abenakis in Vermont and throughout much of northern New England. The
headquarters of the reconstituted Sokoki-St. Francis Band of
the Abenaki Nation at Swanton stands today near the Missisquoi site that functioned for generations as a spiritual and physical sanctuary and a focus of western Abenaki resistance and
independence.

Direct documentary evidence of the western Abenakis is scarce
in the early historic period. The sources are relatively rich in information about the colonists' dealings with the Iroquois of New
York, the eastern Abenakis of Maine, and the Algonquian peoples
of southern New England. But the Sokokis, the Cowasucks, the
Missisquois and their neighbors appear only fleetingly in the
French and English records, which offer tantalizing glimpses
rather than a composite picture of Vermont and New Hamp-

shire's Indian inhabitants. The western Abenakis adopted evasive strategies in turbulent times and successfully covered their tracks. There are no detailed descriptions of life in western Abenaki villages in Vermont. The problem was compounded by the destruction of French mission records when Rogers' Rangers torched St. Francis in 1759 and by a fire in 1911 at the New York State Archives in Albany that destroyed an invaluable collection of Indian records. But scattered fragments in surviving French and English colonial documents, placed against the historical backdrop, provide a sense of what was going on in western Abenaki country.

This book attempts to reconstruct western Abenaki experiences during two centuries in which war and migration dominated their world. It traces Vermont Abenakis who migrated into surrounding regions, as well as displaced neighbors who moved into the western Abenaki homeland. It shows how Abenaki dispersals in the face of crisis produced a scattering of the people but also ensured the survival of significant enclaves of Abenaki population in their ancestral lands. It would be wrong to think of dispersal as some kind of tribal master strategy. Migrations occurred in family bands, not as a mass tribal exodus. Abenaki leaders exercised a precarious authority limited by their ability to instill voluntary obedience in their followers, and local circumstances and individual decisions guaranteed a variety of responses.[2] Yet in times of chaotic change traditional patterns of life offered security and continuity.

This book concentrates on the western Abenakis of Vermont, but the history of the Vermont Abenakis cannot be told without reference to kindred communities in New Hampshire and Quebec with whom there was extensive interaction. The eastern Abenakis of Maine, who figured prominently in the Anglo-French colonial wars of the eighteenth century, were portrayed in a barbaric role in the histories of that conflict penned by Francis Parkman and other New England historians in the nineteenth century. The eastern Abenakis recaptured public attention in the twentieth century when the Penobscots and Passamaquoddies brought suit against the state of Maine and won their landmark settlement in 1980. They too experienced upheavals and dislocations in the seventeenth and eighteenth centuries, and refugees from eastern villages often relocated to French mission villages alongside western Abenaki migrants. Eastern Abenaki bands crop up in this narrative, but their migrations—well covered in André Sévigny's book *Les Abénaquis: habitat et migrations (17ᵉ et 18ᵉ siècles)*—are for the most part peripheral to the story told here. For the purpose of consistency I have chosen to employ the names of Indian communities as they appear most commonly in the records: St. Francis, rather than the more correct Odanak; Bécancour, rather than Wôlinak; St. Regis, rather than Akwesasne; and Caughnawaga rather than Sault St. Louis or Kahnawake.

This will not, and should not, be the last word on the history of the western Abenakis. It describes and connects some pieces in the moving mosaic of western Abenaki history, but further research and scholarship will no doubt reposition some of these pieces and add new ones to the puzzle. As a more complete picture emerges of the historical experiences of the western Abenakis and other remnant Indian groups, we will be better placed to retell the story of northeastern North America in a way that incorporates all the actors in the drama.

Acknowledgments

Anyone familiar with the literature will recognize my indebtedness to the handful of scholars who have published on the western Abenakis. Without the pioneering work of Gordon M. Day, Director Emeritus of the Canadian Ethnology Service, students of western Abenaki history and culture would still be groping in the dark. William A. Haviland and Marjory W. Power have provided a much-needed synthesis of the archaeology and anthropology of native inhabitants of Vermont, from the Paleo-Indians to the present; Peter Thomas' excellent dissertation gives an in-depth study of Fort Hill and culture change in the middle Connecticut Valley, and John Moody's manuscript and continuing researches on the Missisquoi community represent a major contribution to reconstructing western Abenaki history. The works of Thomas M. Charland and André Sévigny provide valuable views from Quebec. This book builds on, and hopefully complements, the work of these fine scholars.

In addition, I have accumulated ideas and knowledge through conversation and correspondence with many scholars of Indian history. Two years as editor and assistant director of the D'Arcy McNickle Center for the History of the American Indian at the Newberry Library in Chicago gave me the opportunity to rub shoulders with some of the most productive and insightful individuals working in Indian history. Frederick E. Hoxie, Peter Nabokov, and Helen Tanner were particularly helpful in discussing a wide range of issues.

Many individuals and institutions have provided me with vital support in the course of researching, writing, and publishing this book. The Vermont Historical Society granted me its first annual research fellowship in 1984 and further encouraged my work with the award of the Ben Lane Prize for 1984 and 1986. The National Endowment for the Humanities twice awarded me grants for travel to collections, allowing me to visit the Public Archives of Canada in 1985 and the Massachusetts State Archives in 1987. At the University of Wyoming, the late Lawrence A. Cardoso, Chair of the History Department, encouraged me to press on with the book and left me with sufficient time to do so in my first year in Laramie. The University of Wyoming also afforded financial support in the form of a Basic Research Grant from the College of Arts and Sciences, a Faculty Development Award, and a Faculty Growth Award from the Alumni Association. The staffs of the National Archives of Canada, the Newberry Library, the Vermont Historical Society, the Massachusetts State Archives, and the University of Wyoming Coe Library all provided valuable service and proved exceptionally helpful. Julie P. Cox and her staff at the Vermont State Archives provided prompt and expert assistance in response to my long-distance enquiries. I am also grateful to the Vermont Historical Society for permission to reprint portions of my previously published articles listed in the bibliography. Susan Weber deserves thanks for the care with which, as managing editor of *Vermont History*, she worked on those articles. Thanks also to Chief Homer St. Francis for taking time to read the manuscript and to John N. Drayton for providing quiet encouragement from the time I first mentioned the project to him. I am grateful to Dean R. Snow and anonymous readers of the manuscript for their comments and suggestions, and to Sarah Morrison for her thoughtful editing. Betty and Horace Bezanson of Bellows Falls, Vermont, provided a home base and support many times during the years this book was taking shape.

Two people deserve special credit. My wife, Marcia, brought me to Vermont and instilled in me a sense of its unique character. John Moody took an early interest in the project, selflessly shared knowledge and notions with me, and constantly encouraged my endeavors even as he reminded me that there were larger issues than the book at stake here. Without these two friends, this book would not have been written, so it is fitting that they share the dedication.

COLIN G. CALLOWAY

Laramie, Wyoming, and Bellows Falls, Vermont

Chronology of Western Abenaki History, 1600–1800

1600	Western Abenaki population estimated at about 10,000.
1609	Champlain explores Lake Champlain. His Indian guides tell him of rich cornfields on the eastern shore, but report that the inhabitants have withdrawn to avoid the ravages of war.
1616–19	Epidemic disease among the Indians of New England.
1633–34	Smallpox epidemic.
1650–51	Sokokis, Pennacooks, and others join a French-inspired coalition against the Iroquois Confederacy.
1663	Sokokis of Fort Hill disperse under the pressure of Iroquois attacks.
1669	Multitribal expedition of New England Algonquians defeated by the Iroquois.
1675–77	King Philip's War disperses tribes in southern and central New England; Abenaki and Sokoki refugees begin to arrive at French mission villages.
1688–97	King William's War; Abenakis participate in raids on New England
1701	The Iroquois establish peace with the French and their Indian allies.

1702–13	Queen Anne's War; Abenakis participate in raids on Deerfield, Massachusetts, and other settlements.
1723–27	Grey Lock's War
1730–33	Smallpox epidemic in Abenaki country.
1735	Western Abenakis and Sokokis from Schaghticoke sell lands on the middle Connecticut and Deerfield rivers
1743–44	Jesuit mission established at Missisquoi.
C. 1744	Seven Nations confederacy formed
1744–48	King George's War; western Abenaki war parties raid New York and New England.
1748	French establish sawmill at Taquahunga on the lower falls of the Missisquoi River.
1752–64	Governor Benning Wentworth grants townships in the "New Hampshire Grants."
1752–53	St. Francis Abenakis meet with Phineas Stevens in Montreal and at Fort Number Four and forbid further encroachment on their lands.
1754–63	French and Indian War; Abenakis fight alongside the French.
1759	Rogers' raid on St. Francis. Oral tradition suggests an attack on Missisquoi also about this time.
1760	French surrender Montreal
1763	Royal Proclamation affords protection for Indian lands.
1764	Connecticut River established as boundary of New Hampshire.
1765	Governor of Lower Canada recognizes Missisquoi River area as Indian land; Abenaki families lease land on Missisquoi River to James Robertson.
1766	In council with British and Caughnawagas on Isle La Motte, Missisquoi Abenakis reassert that they have occupied their lands since time immemorial.

1770	Controversy over Abenakis who have relocated to St. Regis.
1773	Missisquoi Abenakis complain to British about encroachments on their lands.
1773–92	Allen brothers purchase lands around Swanton.
1775–83	The American Revolution; many western Abenakis relocate on the upper Connecticut River and assist the American forces; St. Francis divided by the conflict.
1777	Vermont declares independence.
1779	John Hilliker and other Dutch settlers rent Abenaki land at Missisquoi.
1783	Britain recognizes American independence and hands over lands south of the forty-fifth parallel without reference to the Indians' claims.
1784–88	Ira Allen and company deny the Abenaki presence and rights despite Abenaki protests.
1790	Indian Trade and Intercourse Act prohibits sale of Indian lands without congressional approval.
1791	Vermont enters the union as the fourteenth state.
1798	First of a series of petitions brought to the Vermont legislature by the Seven Nations, claiming compensation for lands lost in Vermont.
1783–1800	Regular "sightings" of western Abenakis despite reports that all had left for Canada. Abenakis survive by keeping a low profile.

The Western Abenakis of Vermont
1600–1800

Chapter 1

The Green Mountain Frontier:
Conflict, Coexistence, and Migration

Today, it is hard to imagine the tranquil Green Mountains as an historic battleground between competing groups and cultures. Yet, for more than two centuries, Vermont was caught up in a turmoil of dramatic changes that shook the native Indian societies to their very foundations, produced far-reaching migrations, and opened the way for the conquest of the area by English invaders. Conquering the Green Mountains entailed more than simply settling the land; it required the dispersal, dispossession, and expulsion of the native inhabitants.

In the final years of the fifteenth century Europe embarked on a program of expansion which, in the course of subsequent centuries, saw Europeans established in positions of dominance in Africa, India, the Far East, Australia, and the Americas. The North American phase of this process involved the defeat and dispossession of the native Indian inhabitants during some three hundred years of conquest and coercion. These global and continental clashes dwarfed the penetration and occupation of the territory inhabited by the western Abenakis. The apparent sparseness of the native population might suggest that the conquest of Vermont was accompanied by little of the bloodshed and genocide that marked European expansion elsewhere in America: Vermont's "Indian troubles" seem comparatively sporadic, small-scale, and short-lived; however, viewed in a wider context, the Abenaki raids that permeated Vermont's frontier history belong to a continentwide phe-

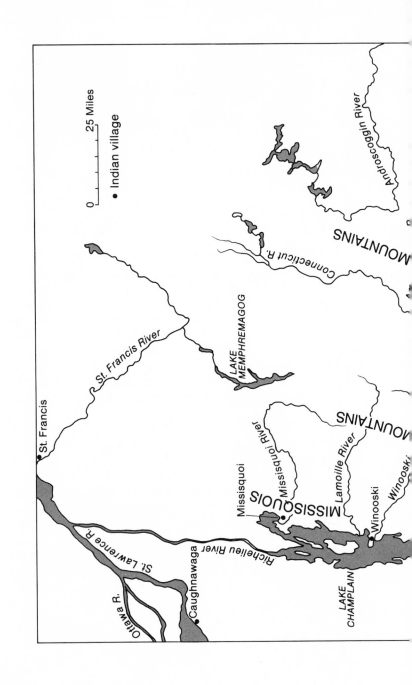

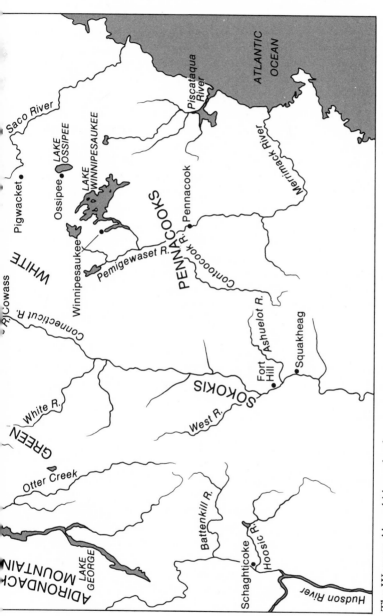

The Western Abenaki homeland

nomenon of European invasion and Indian response. General studies of Indian-European conflict tend to ignore the struggles waged in the Vermont region; local accounts run the alternative risk of losing a sense of the larger picture. Indian-European skirmishes in the Green Mountains were details in that larger picture and governed by scenes elsewhere on the canvas, but they were an integral part of the panoramic clash of cultures on the North American continent. Western Abenaki migrations and dispersals occurred because of forces of destruction that operated throughout North America.

Tribes who survived physical extinction wrought by war and disease faced the prospect of slower demise and cultural extinction. And yet, everywhere, Indian remnant groups managed to survive centuries of chaos, conflict, and acculturation. Faced with invasion and dispossession, Indians had a number of choices: conflict, assimilation, intermarriage, migration, and low key survival in their traditional habitats.[1] Western Abenakis exercised all of those options in varying circumstances; in each case their choice cost them heavily. They fought and coexisted with the Europeans who invaded their lands, and they fled and avoided them. In the course of the two centuries from 1600 to 1800 the forces unleashed by the European invasion scattered the western Abenakis, like Old Testament nations, far beyond their homeland; but, as happened elsewhere in North America, pockets of Indian population survived behind the frontier in Vermont. The Abenaki people survived their diaspora.

Archaeologists are slowly piecing together the evidence of the earliest human occupation of the territory that became *Ndakinna*, "our land," to the western Abenakis. Paleo-Indian peoples were exploiting the Champlain Valley over 11,000 years ago. Living in small groups and hunting with fluted spearpoints, these people subsisted on large game such as mastodons, mammoths, and caribou, as well as the marine mammals abundant in the Champlain Sea. By about 8000 B.C. a gradual warming trend began to produce far-reaching environmental changes. Lake Champlain emerged; new plants and animals appeared, and by about 5000 B.C. the Vermont woodlands had assumed some of the characteristics of today's deciduous-coniferous forests. Archaeological sites throughout the Champlain Valley, as well as at interior lakes and ponds, show that Indians of the Archaic Period (7000 B.C. to 1000 B.C.) depended on a variety of resources; hunting deer, moose, and small game, fishing, and gathering wild plants. These basic settlement and subsistence patterns continued into the Woodland Period (1000 B.C.–1600 A.D.). Heavily used sites in the lower Winooski and Missisquoi river intervales, as well as farther south on the Connecticut River, suggest that the middle Woodland period in western Vermont was one of considerable dynamism. Population increased, pottery developed, bows and arrows replaced spears, and, sometime in the late Woodland Period, Indians in Vermont added maize horticulture to their hunting, fishing, and gathering activities. Indian women began to raise corn, beans, and squash in the Connecticut and Champlain valleys several hundred years before the arrival of Europeans. The Abenakis continued to rely on hunting, fishing, and gathering, and early frosts in the Champlain and Connecticut valleys meant agriculture never assumed the importance it did among the Indians of southern New England. Nevertheless, the comparatively new food sources allowed bands to congregate in greater numbers and settle in one place for certain periods of the year, adding a new dimension to native life. William A. Haviland and Marjory W. Power, in their book *The Original Vermonters,* describe the western Abenaki way of life that evolved over the ages before European contact. After 1600 that way of life suffered wave after wave of unprecedented change and disruption.[2]

By 1600, the western Abenakis inhabited a region from Lake Champlain on the west to the White Mountains on the east, and from southern Quebec to the Vermont-Massachusetts border. The Sokokis and Cowasucks on the Connecticut River, the Missisquois and other bands on the shores of Lake Champlain, the Pennacooks and Winnipesaukees of the upper Merrimack, and the Pigwackets of the Maine–New Hampshire border were all western Abenakis, distinguishable from the eastern Abenakis of Maine as a language group rather than by a distinct geographical boundary. Non-Abenakis who abutted western Abenaki territories included Mahicans from the Hudson Valley, Mohawks from

Table 1: Western Abenaki and Neighboring Groups

Name	Alternative Forms	Affiliation	Location	Principal Villages	Comments
Abnaki, "People of the Dawnland"	Abnaki, Abenaqui, Oubenaqui, Wabanaki	Eastern Algonquian	Maine, Vermont, New Hampshire, Acadia, Quebec	Missisquoi, Cowass, Pennacook, Pigwacket, Winnipesaukee, Norridgewock, Penobscot, Squakheag, St. Francis, Bécancour	St. Francis Abenakis often called Arosaguntacooks
Androscoggin	Arosaguntacook, Amariscoggin	Abenaki	Androscoggin Valley and St. Francis River		
Caughnawaga	Kahnawake, Sault St. Louis	Mohawk	Near Montreal	Caughnawaga	
Cowasuck, "People of the Pines"	Cohass, Coos, Cohassiac, Koes	Western Abenaki	Upper Connecticut Valley	Cowass, near Newbury, Vermont	
Kennebec	Caniba, Kenebeck, Norridgewock	Eastern Abenaki	Kennebec Valley	Norridgewock	Kennebecs often referred to as Norridgewocks
Mahican	Mahikan, Mahingan, Mohican, Loups, River Indians	Eastern Algonquian	Upper Hudson Valley, southwest Vermont, western Massachusetts	Several villages on the Hudson; later Stockbridge, Massachusetts	
Missisquoi, "People of the Flint"	Missique, Missiassik, Mazipskoik, Misiskuoi, Mississco	Western Abenaki	Missisquoi Valley, from Lake Champlain to the headwaters	Overlooking Missisquoi River, around Swanton, Vermont	
Mohawk	Maqua, Agnier, Anniehronnon	Iroquoian	Mohawk Valley		Often simply referred to as Iroquois
Ossipee		Western Abenaki	Lake Ossipee, New Hampshire		

Pennacook	Penacook, Penikoke, Openango	Western Abenaki	Merrimack Valley	Pennacook (Concord, New Hampshire)	
Penobscot	Pannaouamske, Pentagouet	Eastern Abenaki	Penobscot Valley	Penobscot, now Indian Island, Old Town, Maine	
Pigwacket	Pequawket, Pequaki	Western Abenaki	Saco River, White Mountains	Pigwacket, near Fryeburg, Maine	Occupied an intermediate location: other sources refer to them as Eastern Abenakis
Pocumtuck	Pocumtuc	Eastern Algonquian	Middle Connecticut Valley	At Deerfield, Massachusetts	
Schaghticoke	Scatacook, Skatacook	Various: Mahicans and refugee New England Algonquians	Hoosic River at confluence with the Hudson	Schaghticoke	Sometimes referred to as Loups
Sokoki, "People Who Separated"	Sokwaki, Squakheag, Socoquis, Sokoqius, Zooquagese, Soquachjck, Onejagese	Western Abenaki	Middle and Upper Connecticut Valley	Squakheag (Northfield, Massachusetts) and Fort Hill	
St. Francis	Arosaguntacook	Mainly western Abenaki	St. Francis River	St. Francis (Odanak)	
Winnipesaukee	Wioninebesek, Maunbisek (?)	Western Abenaki	Lake Winnipesaukee, New Hampshire		Name came to be applied indiscriminately to all western Abenakis

Note: This table and the Glossary in the back of the book necessarily convey a static and simplified picture of Abenaki locations and nomenclature. In reality, there was flexibility within and movement between groups, and confusing changes in terminology surround the Abenaki and their neighbors.

New York, and members of the so-called Pocumtuck Confederacy farther down the Connecticut Valley. French records of the mid-seventeenth century refer to the Abenaki-speaking tribes and the Sokokis as the "great Nations of New England" and speak of the Abenaki, Sokoki, Mahican, and "numerous other savage nations which are sedentary and have villages of a thousand or two thousand fighting men," indicating communities of 5,000 people and more. The Baron de Lahontan described the Mahicans, the Sokokis, and the Openangos, or Pennacooks, as "erratick Nations" who wandered between Acadia and New England. Mahican, Pocumtuck, Pennacook, and other villages in the south, where agriculture was more extensive, were apparently larger than the western Abenaki villages farther north, but the evidence supports recent estimates that as many as 10,000 western Abenakis inhabited modern-day Vermont and New Hampshire in 1600. In 1614, Captain John Smith heard of at least thirty villages along the Merrimack River, and the Pennacooks alone may have numbered some 12,000 people.[3]

Western Abenakis normally did not operate, nor did they encounter invaders, as a single "tribe." The family band was the basic unit of western Abenaki society and subsistence. Communities were generally seasonal and consensual concentrations of family hunting bands that dispersed throughout the surrounding area during much of the year. Complex social and cultural interactions within tribal groups affected how they lived and how they responded to the intrusion of foreigners. Indians interacted with outsiders and newcomers on the individual, family, and band level, rarely on the tribal level.

Western Abenaki social organization was fluid and flexible, and bands accommodated both separation and integration. Villages fluctuated in character and composition with the rhythm of the seasons and changing social and subsistence activities. Several of the best-documented villages in and around Vermont were in fact postcontact phenomena, although they may have had precontact roots, and postcontact villages on the cutting edge of the colonial frontier were rarely stable ethnic communities. Organization for war and territorial defense required alliances between bands and produced unusual concentrations of population in key locations. As Ted J. Brasser has explained, group identifications along the moving frontier changed over time as Indian sociopolitical units grew larger and their constituents became more heterogeneous. These units were all "phases in a continual process of restructuring the native societies, in response to situations requiring cooperative efforts to reduce internal strain and external stress." Small local groups reassembled into larger clusters, so that cultural distinctions among tribal groups often were lost. In Maine, Harald Prins found that in the process of developing adaptive strategies, "native communities were forced to maintain fluid ethnic and territorial boundaries, allowing a constant merging and fissioning." Some of these communities survived; others proved abortive.[4]

Outside observers often saw only chaos and social fragmentation, but all Indian communities were "intertribal" to some degree. In any village could be found traders, captives, spouses, refugees, and visitors from other groups; and the influxes of newcomers increased dramatically in the wake of European invasion. Abenaki villages in the north absorbed growing numbers of refugee immigrants from the south. Those immigrants in turn helped offset losses caused by disease and war in the northern villages. Numerous small bands utilized Vermont's valleys, rivers, and forests, but by the time the English had penetrated the Green Mountains, key Indian communities were located at Squakheag and Cowass on the Connecticut River and at Winooski and Missisquoi on Lake Champlain. These core communities were the foci for extended networks of family bands, and dispersal into surrounding areas, always an integral part of Abenaki life, now became a vital strategy of defense and survival.

Nineteenth-century historians assumed that the Sokokis lived on the Saco River in Maine and regarded the southernmost Sokoki band at Squakheag as a separate and isolated group. From seventeenth-century French documents, Gordon Day has since shown that the Sokokis inhabited the upper Connecticut River, and the Jesuit Father Gabriel Druillettes spoke of the Connecticut as the "river of the Sokokis."[5] The name Sokoki derives from the term "Sohkwakhiak," meaning "the people who separated," which has prompted various interpretations of their origins as a splinter group from some other tribe.[6] They occupied the region from Squakheag (Northfield, Massachusetts) to the great rapids at Bellows Falls, Vermont, and had locations of special importance at ancient fisheries on the West River near Brattleboro, Vermont, and at Bellows Falls. They, or an earlier people, had inscribed a thunderbird at Brattleboro and etched petroglyphs at Bellows Falls. After they lost some of their original lands in the south, the Sokokis extended their hunting territory to the headwaters of the Connecticut and even to the country south of the St. Lawrence.[7] French records frequently refer to the Sokokis and the Abenakis as separate groups, which may indicate that the French applied the name Sokoki to all western Abenakis to distinguish them from the eastern bands of Maine and Acadia.

Cowasucks

An important Indian community inhabited Kowasek, Coos, or Cowass, "at the place of the white pines" on the Oxbow of the Connecticut, near modern-day Newbury, Vermont. The Cowasucks may have been an upriver group of Sokokis, and the two peoples were closely associated, but their centrally located village, at a crossroads of trails and waterways, brought regular influxes of new inhabitants to Cowass. The oxbow area offered rich soil, game-filled forests, and plentiful harvests of trout and salmon. The first white captives who trudged through Cowass saw cleared and cultivated fields, and early English settlers found the remains of a fortified Indian village there. Indians, French, and English alike recognized Cowass as a place of considerable strategic importance in the eighteenth century. Cowass "was the key that opened the door to, or shut it against the direct communication between the colonies and the Canadas." More important to the Abenakis, it was also sacred land that held the bones of their ancestors.[8]

Indian bands of varying sizes and duration occupied Otter Creek and the Winooski, Lamoille, and Missisquoi rivers, which run into Lake Champlain. Lake Champlain was not only an area rich in resources and a vital waterway, it was also a sacred center of the western Abenaki universe. Eastern Abenakis looked to Maine's Mount Katahdin as the spiritual center

Drawn by A.C.Hamlin.

TOTEMIC DEVICES, WEST RIVER, (Vermont).

Drawn by A.C.Hamlin.

PICTOGRAPHIC INSCRIPTION AT BELLOWS' FALLS, (Vermont).

Petroglyphs at Bellows Falls and inscriptions at West River. (Reproduced from Henry R. Schoolcraft, *Information Respecting the History, Conditions, and Prospects of the Indians of the United States* [1854–60], Newberry Library)

of their world; western Abenakis looked to the Champlain Valley. Here western Abenaki traditions place the exploits of their principal culture heroes and mythic transformers. Here, satisfied with his work after he had dragged himself around forming the hills and valleys of the region, Odzihózo turned himself into a rock—Rock Dunder—where, for hundreds of years, passing Abenakis have left offerings of tobacco. Archaeological evidence from the Missisquoi, Lamoille, Winooski, and Otter Creek valleys testifies to the ancient importance of the Champlain Valley as a center of Indian habitation. The village at Mazipskoik, or Missisquoi, represented the best-known and most enduring settlement. Located at the northern end of the lake in an area of natural abundance, Missisquoi offered a focus for Indian groups in the Champlain Valley throughout historic times and up to the present. Traces of occupation stretching as far as fifteen miles from the mouth of the Missisquoi River indicate a continuous presence at "the place of the flint."[9]

Between the Abenakis of Maine and the Sokokis of the Connecticut River lived the western Abenaki peoples of New Hampshire: the Pennacooks, the Pigwackets, the Winnipesaukees, and the Ossipees. The Lake Winnipesaukee region may have been one of the major population centers in New England, and bands from the Saco and Merrimack watersheds congregated at the lake's outlet at Ahquedaukenash, or Acquadoctan, for fishing each spring. Half a dozen Indian communities nestled on the upper Merrimack River. The principal Pennacook communities were at Amoskeag Falls and Pennacook, although scholars distinguish between the upper Pennacooks around Concord, who were western Abenakis, and the lower Pennacooks, who were also called Pawtuckets. Pennacooks may have had settlements as far north as Cowass: Henry R. Schoolcraft, writing in the nineteenth century, said they "kept a kind of armed possession" of the country that was so vital to communication between the Merrimack and the St. Lawrence, but he exaggerated their power and control. The Pennacooks' proximity to the Sokokis, their western Abenaki linguistic affiliation, frequent interchanges and probable intermarriage between the groups led some writers to confuse the tribes and attribute Sokoki locations to the Pennacooks. Moreover, the French sometimes referred to both Pennacooks and Sokokis as Loups, a name they originally applied to the Mahicans and to other, more distant peoples on the south and west.[10]

At the head of the Saco River in the White Mountains lived the Pigwackets, or Pequawkets, who, despite their intermediate location and the indefinite boundaries between eastern and western Abenaki groups, figure as western Abenakis in this work. Their main villages were near Fryeburg, Maine, with others at Conway and Ossipee. They were in easy reach of the Androscoggin, Merrimack, and Connecticut rivers and could travel the Ammonoosuc River direct to Cowass.[11]

Farther east, the Abenakis of Maine enjoyed frequent contact and communication with their western relatives, although there was no political coordination between the groups and unity of action was rare. Eastern Abenaki groups like the Kennebecs, Androscoggins and Penobscots—often lumped together as "Eastern Indians" in English colonial records—edged westward up their river valleys, and the tendency to follow river courses and trails toward the Green Mountains increased as English pressure from the south and east intensified in the late seventeenth and eighteenth centuries.

South of the Sokokis lived the Pocumtucks. That name has been applied to a single group living near Deerfield and also to several bands extending from present-day northern Connecticut up the Connecticut river to the borders of Vermont and New Hampshire. The so-called Pocumtuck Confederacy was more likely a group of small bands loosely focused around the main community.[12]

On the western slopes of the Green Mountains, the Mahicans occupied territory in southwest Vermont. The Mahicans' villages were concentrated in the upper Hudson Valley, but Vermont historian Walter Hill Crockett suggested that they had settlements at Bennington and Pownal, wintered in the Hoosic and Housatonic valleys, and had campgrounds in the mountain passes near Arlington and Manchester. The height of land probably constituted a boundary between Mahican and Abenaki peoples, but there were clearly zones of overlapping territory where Mahicans and Abenakis coexisted rather than conflicted. The Mahican range was reputedly restricted by a belief that the mountains harbored potentially evil spirits, although Mahican tradition tells of annual spring moose-hunting expeditions to the tops of the Green Mountains. Other accounts place Mahicans as far north as Otter Creek and the head of Lake Champlain, although this is probably to be explained by the Mahicans' own dispersal from their original homeland. Mahicans found themselves under increasing pressure to move farther north and east in the contact period, and the composition of their nation changed as splinter groups amalgamated into larger tribes.[13]

Most accounts treat Lake Champlain as the boundary between the Iroquois of New York and the Abenakis of northern New England, and the archaeological and linguistic evidence supports such a view.[14] Mohawks conducted incursions to the east, but the evidence that they ever occupied the Vermont shore of the lake is unsubstantial. On a couple of occasions Abenaki delegates in treaty councils made the enigmatic statement that the Connecticut River formed the eastern boundary of Iroquois territory, but the spokesmen were eastern Abenakis looking toward the middle and lower Connecticut; no western Abenaki would have conceded the Vermont heartland.[15] The Mohawks represented a significant and often threatening presence on the west, and their warriors, hunters, traders, tribute collectors, and diplomats crossed western Abenaki land. But the Mohawks and the Champlain Valley Abenakis also shared in social and cultural exchanges that were later the basis of close relationships between Abenakis in Vermont and Iroquois at Caughnawaga and St. Regis.

In time, new villages beyond the peripheries of the heartland became important centers of western Abenaki life and movement. By the end of King Philip's War in 1676, Schaghticoke on the Hudson River and the French mission village at St. Francis were attracting substantial numbers of Sokokis, Pennacooks, and other Abenaki refugees. The inhabitants of Schaghticoke eventually filtered north in a steady exodus toward St. Francis, which emerged as the core of Abenaki resistance to English expansion during the French and Indian wars. St. Francis became the major center of western Abenaki population in Quebec and played a significant role in the history of Abenaki communities that remained in Vermont and New Hampshire.

The traditional concept of "frontier" has serious limitations for the study of interactions between Indians and non-Indians. It carries with it outmoded notions about the advance of "civilization" and the conquest of a "savage" and "empty wilderness." The Eurocentric view that sees the early history of Vermont as simply the steady advance northwards of English settlement and the corresponding retreat of the Indians presents a distorted picture of the reality of western Abenaki occupation, neglects other patterns of movement and survival behind the frontier, and ignores alternative sources of conflict and interaction between natives and newcomers.

The Indians' presence and attunement to the environment caused European colonists considerable anxiety and made them conscious of their own vulnerability in their "New World." Survival necessitated adapting European ways to the American environment and adopting Indian methods of travel and subsistence. In an age when European colonies were still thinly populated, survival also necessitated securing the friendship of neighboring Indians who could provide a protective buffer against rival colonies and powerful tribes. The Green Mountain "wilderness" was very much an Indian world and Europeans knew it. When Europeans penetrated that world, they went either as captives, powerless in Indian hands, or as tentative trespassers, armed and cautious. For early New Englanders, Vermont was both a forbidding wilderness and an Indian stronghold.

European "explorers" who ventured into northeastern North America in the early seventeenth century found substantial native populations, functioning institutions, and sophisticated patterns of social and economic activity. Indians fed the visitors from productive agricultural and hunting resources, guided them along established avenues of travel and communication, dealt with them by traditional diplomatic and political procedures, and acted as interpreters of native languages and cultures. Only from a purely Eurocentric viewpoint could the newcomers be considered "explorers," although they came with definite purposes that were to change forever the societies they met. Western Abenakis had felt the repercussions of their coming generations before the first European settlers actually arrived in their country. The European invaders came from rich and varied geographical and cultural backgrounds, drew on different historical experiences, and maintained distinct religious and political affiliations. On the Green Mountain frontier Sokokis, Cowasucks, Missisquois, and displaced Algonquians contended with English Puritans, New England "Yankees," Scots, and French Catholics. The Puritans who founded the first English towns in New England, migrated overland to the Connecticut Valley, and pushed upriver into contact and confrontations with the Indians, came themselves from a broad array of dissenters driven to emigration by economic depression, political unrest, and religious pressures. Accommodation of other Christian groups and growing mercantile and agricultural interests transformed English Puritans into New England Yankees. By the early eighteenth century Scotch-Irish Presbyterians were colonizing the frontiers of Maine, Massachusetts, and New Hampshire, and a broad strain of peoples from throughout the British Isles were reshaping the human geography of northern New England. On the eve of the American Revolution the western Abenakis found themselves on the far edge of a great bulging arc of moving settlement that stretched from Nova Scotia to Florida and was fueled by both the American-born population and a massive influx of emigrants from London, Yorkshire, and Scotland.[16]

On the north, French missionary and fur-trading activities produced interdependence, intermarriage, and a network of relationships with the Abenakis that the English never duplicated or appreciated. By the eighteenth century many western Abenakis had acquired French names and donned French clothes. Many others were baptized as Catholics, wore crucifixes, and were buried in French cemeteries.[17] The multicultural backgrounds of the European invaders are evident in the surnames that survive in Abenaki communities in Vermont and Quebec.

Even the Anglo-French frontier was not clearly defined as Indians traveled and traded back and forth among the French and the English, and the spheres of influence emanating from French missions and English trading posts overlapped in Abenaki country. When New Englanders spoke of Canada, they often indicated merely a vague area north of their farthest settlements, but western Abenakis in the mid-eighteenth century regarded the English frontier as a clear line of encroachment that had advanced no farther than Fort Number Four on the east and Fort St. Frédéric on the west.

The Green Mountain frontier was not just a geographic region where two cultures collided. The western Abenaki homeland was also a cultural meeting ground where Algonquian and English, Iroquois and French, contended and interacted. The pressure of forces in the seventeenth and eighteenth centuries generated wide-ranging and recurrent conflicts among these peoples, but never totally eradicated undercurrents of peaceful interaction. If Vermont was a war zone, it was also a common land and a place of refuge for Indian peoples in time of crisis. Western Abenaki communities dispersed in response to external pressures, but they also restructured and changed in composition as they incorporated Indian refugees from other areas.

The historian can only estimate the early impact of European invasion on the original Vermonters; however, there is no doubt that the western Abenakis felt the effects of the epidemics, wars, and commercial and cultural encounters that occurred in surrounding areas. Historians have persistently neglected communication between non-European peoples, but early colonists in northern New England inherited a network of Indian trails that testified to the range and frequency of travel by the native inhabitants. Well-worn paths connected principal centers of Indian population and linked up with other trail networks. Major watercourses—the Connecticut, Merrimack, Hudson, and St. Lawrence rivers and Lakes Champlain, George, Memphremagog and Winnipesaukee—facilitated material and cultural exchanges within and far beyond the Green Mountain region.[18]

These same avenues of travel and communication also functioned as channels for the diffusion of killer diseases, as arteries for the introduction of alien commerce, and as natural highways for invasion and retreat. The Hudson River–Lake Champlain–

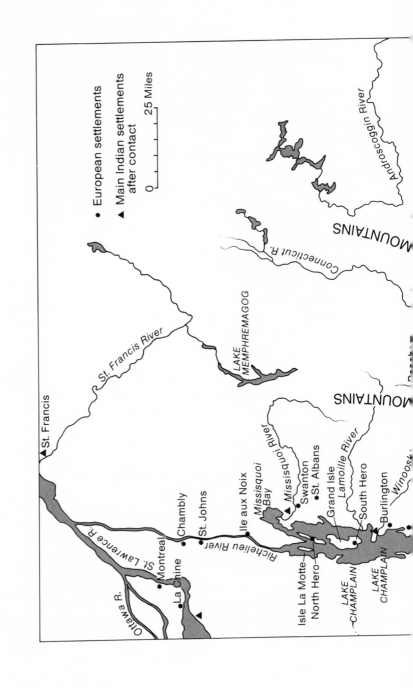

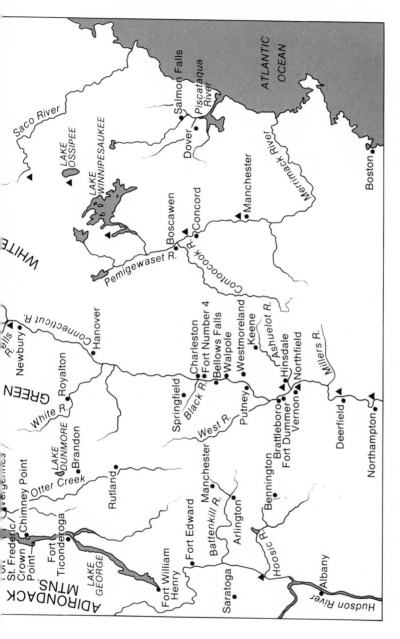

The Green Mountain frontier

Richelieu River chain—which Francis Jennings calls "the Mahican Channel" after the Indians who controlled so much of it for so long—has been aptly described as "the warpath of nations." Lake Champlain served as a trade route between Albany and Montreal, and eighteenth-century Englishmen deemed it "by far the most important Inland water in North America Because it is the key of the Enemy's Country, a Canal leading from New England and New York to the very Bowels of Canada."[19]

Long before the first invaders arrived, trade goods and diseases traveled along the trails and waterways that linked *Ndakinna* to Iroquoia, Canada, southern New England, and the Atlantic coast. Disease produced famine and worked alongside increasing intertribal warfare to shatter the Indian potential for resistance. Colonists frequently settled on lands that had been cleared and cultivated by previous occupants, although the Indians themselves were not to be seen. Unlike the decimation in southern New England, however, losses in Vermont were significantly offset by the influx of refugees, which enabled the western Abenakis to resist English invasion for some eighty years.

Escalating interethnic conflict and Puritan New England's strategy of armed conquest meant that war assumed a disproportionate importance in Indian societies and produced a distorted image of the Abenakis as warlike. The written records compound the distortion: Englishmen who wrote about the western Abenakis regarded them as primarily a military threat; the French reported on them as allies against the English. In reality, western Abenakis fought because they had to, if they were to survive in a dangerous new world.

As happened throughout North America, intertribal warfare altered and intensified under the impact of the European fur trade and firearms. The fur trade produced far-reaching changes in Indian material culture, economic activity, and society; but most dramatically, it gave the Indians firearms. Caught up in a vicious economic and military cycle which revolved around furs and guns, Indians now devoted their utmost energies to maintaining a tenable strategic position in a world thrown into dangerous upheaval by the intrusion of European men, microbes, and manufactures. The Sokokis and their neighbors, for example, were seriously weakened by intertribal conflict a decade before King Philip's War.

As long as war plagued America's northern frontiers, Indian and non-Indian Vermonters found themselves embroiled in clashes of global importance. Vermont's geographical position meant that western Abenakis inhabited a world of escalating international tension and interethnic competition. Across North America the superior numbers, resources, organization, military power, and purposefulness of the invaders inevitably took their toll. Euro-American armies pursued the Indians to their villages, destroyed their families, homes, and crops; and wore down resistance in sustained campaigns and wars of attrition. The Puritan massacre of the Pequots at their village on the Mystic River in Connecticut in 1637, the French invasions of Iroquoia late in the seventeenth century, General John Sullivan's devastation of Iroquois crops and villages in 1779, and George Armstrong Custer's winter campaign against the Cheyennes in 1868, all contained the same elements of a continentwide search-and-destroy campaign to defeat the Indians. These tactics were employed against the western Abenakis, but rarely with much success, although Rogers' Rangers managed to achieve some kind of victory by their raid on St. Francis in 1759. The process was bloody and brutal, and Indian resistance only slowed the inexorable northward march of conquest while the people sought refuge from the invaders.

Western Abenakis regularly shifted location for seasonal, social, and subsistence purposes, but the European invasion unleashed forces that drastically increased Indian movements. Lethal epidemics, escalating intertribal and interracial warfare, competition for European trade goods, and growing pressure upon diminishing resources dislocated traditional patterns of life and made migration a necessity for many individuals, families, and bands. Seasonal relocations and periodic visits gave way to pressured withdrawals to escape war, famine, and disease. Some formerly autonomous communities disintegrated, and refugees dispersed and regrouped in safer locations to create new social orders. As Laurence Hauptman observes in discussing eighteenth century Iroquois villages as havens for displaced Indian peoples, "Only in a refugee context can the Indian side of the New World drama of colonization and expansion be fully understood."[20]

Many western Abenakis withdrew to the northern reaches of their territory or removed to Canada. Others clung tenaciously to their traditional lands, going "underground" or returning seasonally to areas that they had left but not abandoned. At the same time, Indians from outside Vermont sought asylum and often amalgamated with indigenous Abenaki communities. Grey Lock, the most prominent Indian war leader in Vermont's history, was a refugee from dislocated communities in Massachusetts. But Indian refugees who fled to Vermont in search of a haven from the devastating forces that engulfed their world found no more than a temporary refuge.

No records survive, if they ever existed, to detail the internal upheavals that western Abenaki communities experienced as a result of such migrations. Migration interrupted regular cycles of subsistence and deprived people of cleared fields and intimately familiar hunting territories. Social and political relationships strained and broke as village members went their separate ways. Leaving ancestral and sacred sites that linked the people to place and past took an immeasurable emotional and spiritual toll. Families left behind memories and loved ones as well as belongings when they gathered what they could carry and departed for new locations. Years of contact, trade, and intermarriage undoubtedly eased the process of amalgamation when refugees arrived in other villages or regrouped with other migrants to form new communities, but there are few documentary records of the internal dynamics by which communities like Missisquoi and Cowass absorbed newcomers, or by which Schaghticoke and St. Francis emerged out of gatherings of disparate peoples. Shared experiences, common concerns, individual and group adjustments, intermarriage, and external threats all worked to give the people a single collective identity.[21]

A book that pays so much attention to warfare may seem to perpetuate outmoded stereotypes of the Indian as warrior, especially when new scholarship is examining other important and long-neglected aspects of Indian history—family life, tribal structures, political dynamics, economic activity. Peaceful interaction was certainly a significant part of the story. Abenakis and Mohawks traded, negotiated, and intermarried. Europeans and Indians intermarried, traded, and sometimes pursued joint diplomatic and political goals. Trade was a means of exchange, a social and symbolic activity, and a way of avoiding conflict with a potentially threatening group.

Even with the English, Abenakis interacted, cooperated, and coexisted as often as they fought. Indian and English economies overlapped and often were interdependent. Indians living close to white settlements peddled pelts, baskets, and tools, hired on as farm laborers, and shared their knowledge and skills with the newcomers. In turn, they became increasingly dependent on the trade relationships they established with the colonists. Looking back over fifty years to her first visit to Charlestown, New Hampshire, in 1744 at age fourteen, Susanna Johnson recalled that relations between the Indians and the settlers were friendly. There was such a mixture of Indians and settlers on the frontier, she said, "that the state of society cannot easily be described." Her husband, James Johnson, worked as a trader near Fort Number Four up to the eve of the French and Indian War. The Indians came in regularly to barter their furs, and "he frequently credited them for blankets and other necessaries, and in most instances they were punctual in payment." Robert Rogers, who led the attack on the Abenaki mission village at St. Francis in 1759, grew up in a frontier town in New Hampshire, "where I could hardly avoid obtaining some knowledge of the manners, customs, and language of the Indians, as many of them resided in the neighborhood, and daily conversed and dealt with the English."[22] Abenakis and settlers of Dutch descent mixed in a similar fashion around Missisquoi at the end of the century.

Even in times of recurrent warfare, Indians returned to their old haunts to hunt, fish, plant, and harvest on the periphery of new settlements, and this kind of marginal subsistence came to characterize the western Abenaki life-style by the late eighteenth and nineteenth centuries. Indians and English settlers lived alongside each other around Squakheag in the 1650s; two hundred years later, Abenaki families were still returning annually to Bellows Falls for the spring fishing.

Interaction declined dramatically when war broke out, but English soldiers and Abenaki warriors sometimes recognized each other in battle. In their fight against the Pigwackets in 1725, Captain John Lovewell's men exchanged greetings and taunts with Indians whom they knew personally from peacetime contacts. Thirty years later, John Kilburn and his neighbors likewise called back and forth to Indians they recognized as they fought off a war party at the mouth of the Cold River near Walpole, New Hampshire. During the Seven Years War, Indians served with Rogers' Rangers and the English as well as with Montcalm and the French.[23]

Fort Dummer, the first permanent English settlement in Vermont, nicely illustrates the nature of interaction on the Green Mountain frontier. Initially constructed in 1724 as a military defense against Grey Lock's raids, Fort Dummer also functioned as a trading post and as the location for a Protestant minister to cater to the needs of the Indians who frequented the place. In addition, a substantial portion of the fort's original garrison were Indians, mainly recruited from the Hudson River tribes.[24]

Fort St. Frédéric, built on Lake Champlain by the French in 1731 as a forward defence, likewise became a lively community where French soldiers rubbed shoulders with Abenakis from Vermont and St. Francis. Marriages, baptisms, and burials were held for French and Indians alike, and even an occasional Sioux Indian turned up. The fort's first recorded interpreter, Pierre Hertel de Beaubassin, had himself grown up among the Abenakis at St. Francis, where his father operated as a trader and interpreter.[25]

Cooperation and coexistence tended to be individual and local, however. Where the English population was small and the fur trade was a common endeavor, western Abenakis and isolated settlers shared a vested interest in accommodation and maintaining peace.[26] At the same time, the immediate context of competition for resources and the larger context of imperial and interethnic rivalries produced recurrent tensions, conflict,

Model of an Abenaki village. (Robert Hull Fleming Museum, University of Vermont, Burlington)

and forced migration. Life's daily and seasonal concerns continued, but war, and the threat of war, increasingly defined the context in which individuals lived their lives.

Even in times of open conflict, Indian and European cultures intermingled as well as collided. Abenaki families adopted English captives as they had traditionally adopted captives from other tribes. For a hundred years or so following King Philip's War, Abenaki warriors traveled south along familiar trails, raided places they had recently evacuated, and carried off captives from infant settlements they had watched grow up. The route that ran from Lake Champlain up the Winooski River, across the Green Mountains, and down the Black River to the Connecticut River and the English settlements was traveled so frequently by Indian war parties—and in reverse by their captives—that it became known simply as "the Indian Road"; and it was only one of many such routes.[27] Over 1,600 captives were taken from New England during the French and Indian Wars; hundreds of these followed the "captives' trails" through Vermont, and scores disappeared without a trace, many into Abenaki villages.[28]

Puritan chroniclers and later New England historians depicted Indian raiders as bloodthirsty savages intent on butchery, but the reality of Indian-white interaction, even in captivity, was far more complex. For instance, the Indians who raided Deerfield in 1704 carried a bag of mail from captives to anxious relatives and hung it from a tree branch where it would be found and distributed in the settlements. The periods of peaceful interaction, or at least cautious coexistence, meant that English captives sometimes knew their captors. When Nehemiah How was captured and taken to Crown Point in 1745, he was relieved to see an Indian called Pealtomy, and the two men shook hands. Pealtomy introduced him to the Caughnawaga husband of captive Eunice Williams: "He was glad to see me, and I to see him. He asked me about his wife's relations, and showed a great deal of respect to me." Nathaniel Segar, taken captive in Tomhegan's raid on the Androscoggin Valley in 1781, knew the Indian leader by name "for he had been at my house."[29]

Taking captives was a long-established practice in native warfare, but as warfare increased the adoption of captives became necessary to help maintain population levels. Caughnawaga métis Charles Cook met an Abenaki war party on Lake Champlain in 1754 that was returning home with five captives to "replace" five Abenakis killed by the English that year.[30]

Education in Indian ways began as soon as the captives fell into Indian hands, and continued as they became accustomed to Indian moccasins, diet, pace of travel, and techniques of wilderness survival. Some captives were wearing Indian clothing, paint, and hairstyles by the time they reached the Abenaki villages. Some prisoners were sold immediately to the French, but many others were adopted into Indian society. Kind treatment helped win captives over. Even the dreaded ordeal of "running the gauntlet," which captives faced when they reached Indian villages, seems to have been largely a symbolic event among the Abenakis. Mrs. Johnson and her family, seized by Missisquoi and St. Francis Abenakis in 1754, walked unhindered through the gauntlet at St. Francis while the Indians tapped them lightly on the shoulder as they passed by. Jesuit Pierre de Charlevoix, who lived with the St. Francis Abenakis, said they took care never to strike where a blow might prove fatal. Like many other female captives, Mrs. Johnson enjoyed considerable kindness from her Abenaki captors. Seeing she was in the advanced stages of pregnancy, the Indians caught a stray horse for her to ride and untied her husband so that he could help with the children. When she went into labor, they halted near Reading, Vermont, and constructed a brush shelter for her to lie in. They even presented the newborn child, Elizabeth Captive Johnson, with gifts of clothing, albeit clothing plundered from the Johnson home. General John Stark, captured by the Abenakis in 1752, remembered "that he had experienced more genuine kindness from the savages of St. Francis, than he ever knew prisoners of war to receive from any civilized nation."[31]

Some captives chose to remain with their adopted families even when offered the chance to return home. Eunice Williams, daughter of the Reverend John Williams of Deerfield, was captured at age seven, gradually forgot her native tongue, and married a Caughnawaga Indian when she was sixteen. Governor Joseph Dudley of Massachusetts offered to exchange two Canadian Indian sachems held prisoner in Boston for her release, but Eunice rejected all inducements to return and, apart from a few fleeting visits to New England, spent over eighty years living among the Indians. A short letter from the Reverend Williams to his son Stephen in 1716—written on part of an old letter because the minister had no paper—ends with the poignant request: "If you hear from your sister, send me word."[32]

Children proved particularly susceptible to successful adoption. Twelve-year-old Solomon Metcalf refused to return home after only a year with the Indians. Titus King reckoned it took only about six months for captive children to be wholly absorbed in Abenaki society. Mrs. Johnson, reunited with her eleven-year-old son, Sylvanus, after a separation of four years, found that the boy had forgotten the English language, spoke a little broken French, but spoke Abenaki perfectly. Sylvanus never forgot the Indian ways and values he learned at Missisquoi.[33] That an estimated 20 percent of the adult women captured from northern New England were either pregnant or carried new-born babies indicates the potential for a substantial influx of young white blood into Abenaki communities like St. Francis and Missisquoi.[34]

Abenakis were reluctant to return captives once they had adopted them. Phineas Stevens, who had himself been captured by Grey Lock's raiders at age sixteen, traveled to Crown Point and Montreal in 1749 in an effort to redeem captives from the French and Indians. One he met had no desire to return home, and he was unable to learn the whereabouts of others. On a similar mission in 1752, Stevens tried to obtain three captives from the St. Francis Indians, but the Abenakis were "obstinately set upon keeping them . . . having adopted them." Nathaniel Wheelwright encountered similar reluctance in 1754. He redeemed one child from Bécancour, but the St. Francis Abenakis refused to release two other children, assuring Wheelwright "they would by no means part with them, neither for money or in exchange for slaves." [35]

Many captives and their mixed-blood offspring lived easily in Indian societies, where they joined a growing number of marginal or bicultural individuals. Joseph Louis Gill, who rose to leadership as "the White Chief of the St. Francis Abenakis," was the son of white parents who had been abducted as children from New England, baptized in the Roman Catholic faith, brought up as Indians, and remained with the Abenakis for the rest of their lives. Gill adopted Susanna Johnson into his family when she arrived at St. Francis. By that time he ran a supply store and "lived in a style far above the majority of his tribe." He spoke Abenaki and French, wrote Abenaki, read English, and often told Mrs. Johnson that he had pure English blood and an English heart. When Gill's son, Antoine, was captured by Rogers' Rangers and taken to Charlestown, Mrs. Johnson welcomed "Sabatis," as she called him, like a brother. Henry Masta who was himself descended from the Gill family, said in 1929 that there were over 1,000 descendants from the family among the St. Francis Abenakis. [36] Oral tradition at Missisquoi states that a captive from Deerfield, named Wells, gave his name to an Abenaki family line. [37] After the Reverend Eleazar Wheelock moved his "Indian school" to Hanover, New Hampshire, he preferred to draw upon St. Francis, Caughnawaga, and other Indian reserves in Canada for students who were descended from English captives. He hoped to have more success in educating these "white Indians" in English ways.[38]

French Canada offered an alternative for individuals unable to adapt to Indian life and unwilling to face readjustment to New England society. The French regularly bought prisoners from their Indian allies, hoping to bolster their colony or to exchange them for French prisoners held by the English. New Englanders recoiled in horror at the thought of good Puritans falling into Jesuit hands, but captives usually received good treatment from the French, and many underwent conversion to Catholicism. More captives remained with the French than with the Indians.[39]

Western Abenakis fought the English as invading enemies; they also saw them as potential Abenakis. For a variety of reasons, some English captives lived out their lives among the Indians, adding another strand to the cultural and ethnic fabric of Abenaki communities in northern Vermont and Canada. Of those who returned, some functioned as cultural intermediaries, moving between English and Abenaki society; others put their Indian lives behind them; still others never fully made the transition and lived in a kind of twilight zone between Indian and European cultures. As across North America, the Indian-white frontier in Vermont was a multifaceted phenomenon, not a sharply defined racial battle line.[40]

How the Abenakis responded to new pressures, and how they fared in the debilitating new wars of the period, reveals much about the nature and resilience of their societies. By the seventeenth century Vermont was part of a Native American world thrown into chaos by devastating new forces. Time-honored patterns of life were disrupted virtually overnight, and Indian communities by the score disintegrated under the impact of war and disease. But many western Abenaki communities survived, in modified form, by adapting and extending traditional patterns of movement. Bands who were accustomed to dispersing and reassembling in seasons of scarcity and plenty responded to new dangers with similar strategies. Villages broke up into family bands who withdrew from the central community until the threat

passed. Movement from extended family bands to village communities and back became a persistent theme of western Abenaki
life. This strategy of dispersal served the Abenakis well when
the threats were military and temporary, but by the late eighteenth century the western Abenakis confronted a more permanent threat as the settlers flooded into their homelands and came
to stay. Family bands who had formerly occupied the richest and
most productive lands moved deeper into marginal lands, which
were sometimes unable to support the influx of population. Some
bands returned less often, if at all to the central community. Some
joined other communities. Those who stayed retained a tena-
cious, if tenuous, hold on their land.

The western Abenaki diaspora scattered individuals across
northern New England, New York, Quebec, and even to the
Maritime Provinces. Descendants of Mahicans, Sokokis, and
Pennacooks are to be found among the modern tribes of Maine
and the Maritimes as well as among the Abenakis of Quebec.[41]
The movement was not a single mass exodus; it was a gradual
and hesitating withdrawal, with periodic reversals in direction
and seasonal visitation of many former habitations. New social
orders emerged as the remnants of previously autonomous bands
coalesced in new or expanded communities at Schaghticoke on
the Hudson River, at Cowass, Missisquoi, and St. Francis. These
communities also afforded refuge to Indians from other regions.
Peoples who had been driven from their homelands on the south
and east filtered northward through the Connecticut Valley and
Green Mountains. A Sioux girl of sixteen or seventeen, who had
been captured in war, found her way to St. Francis as a slave in
1752. In 1753 two Abenakis visited Fort Number Four. One spoke
good English, having been a prisoner in Massachusetts in the
previous war; the other was a Cape Cod Indian "now incorporated with the St. Fransoways." In 1757 the Jesuit missionary at
St. Francis referred in passing to a Moraigan, or Mahican, Indian
"naturalized and adopted by the Abnakis Tribe."[42]

Focusing on villages to the exclusion of family bands obscures
the full picture of western Abenaki life, movement, and survival.
Abenakis endured centuries of conflict, coercion, and dispersal,
in which they saw their numbers thinned, their communities

splintered, and their spiritual certainties questioned. Yet, even as some bands withdrew to more hospitable locations in Canada, and individuals scattered throughout northeastern North America, enclaves of western Abenakis survived in Vermont and preserved their cultural and political identity. Village dispersals and band migrations were probably far less traumatic and final to Abenakis than they seemed to European observers accustomed to settled towns and permanent residence. The family band, the basic unit of subsistence and community, became the basic unit of survival. Accustomed to accommodating newcomers, adapting to new pressures, and surviving through dispersal, western Abenaki bands continued to accommodate, adapt, and survive through two centuries of conflict and disruption.[43]

Chapter 2

Contagion and Competition

In time, the invasion of English farmers from the south forced the western Abenakis into an unequal struggle to preserve their land and culture against an alien people and an alien way of life. But the conquest of Indian Vermont was the product of many invasions. In the seventeenth century the greatest threats to the native inhabitants came not from armies of soldiers and settlers but from invisible forces of change in the surrounding world. Biological, commercial, and spiritual invasions predated the encroachments of European settlers, just as significant ecological changes followed in the wake of those settlers. Epidemics of Old World diseases ushered in a new era in which the contest for furs and firearms, souls and allegiance, created zones of turmoil, competition, and ultimately confrontation.

Eastern Abenakis living on the Maine coast were in contact with European explorers and fishermen by the early sixteenth century. These first contacts initiated the beginnings of the fur trade, and the Indians distributed some of the goods they received through local trade networks that doubtless reached Vermont. With French, English, and Dutch traders edging along the St. Lawrence, the Atlantic coast, and up the Hudson River, the western Abenaki world was circumscribed by the hesitant tentacles of European invasion well before the Pilgrim landfall at Plymouth Rock. In 1609, when Henry Hudson sailed up the river that bears his name and Champlain ventured south to the Ticonderoga region, each came within seventy-five miles of the other's

farthest point of penetration. As early as 1638, the demand for
farmlands in the Massachusetts Bay Colony prompted the authorities to cast covetous eyes up the Merrimack River toward
Lake Winnipesaukee and Abenaki country.[1]

These first invaders seemed to pose no threat to the Abenakis.
They were interlopers in a land where the Indians called the
tune and they knew it. Unfortunately, they brought with them
seeds of destruction to thousands of Indians throughout northeastern North America. The introduction of Old World diseases
among New World populations constituted an invasion more
deadly than any carried out with fire and sword. From the beginning of the sixteenth century, epidemics of killer diseases scythed
through American Indian populations who lacked immunity to
the new viruses and germs. These lethal pathogens were truly the
shock troops of the European invasion of America, and the result
was one of the world's greatest biological cataclysms. Reports of
scarce Indian populations, in northern New England and across
the continent, usually described a situation that existed after epidemic disease had obliterated major concentrations of population. European newcomers did not find a virgin land; they inherited Francis Jennings' "widowed land."[2]

Direct documentary evidence about the impact of disease on
the western Abenakis is lacking because no Europeans were present to record them. Epidemics frequently spread like wildfire, ra-
diating to tribes far distant from the point where Europeans first
contaminated Indians. Some of the diseases that hit New England
were local episodes in widespread pandemics that ravaged large
areas of the continent. A survey of epidemics recorded in areas
immediately surrounding Vermont indicates the forces of destruction that hammered western Abenaki civilization in the valleys of the Green Mountains long before English settlers arrived.

An unidentified epidemic coursed the St. Lawrence in 1535, another caused great mortality as far south as New England between 1564 and 1570, and there was typhus in New England in
1586. A catastrophic epidemic struck coastal New England tribes
between 1616 and 1619, creating a power vacuum into which
moved the Pilgrims of Massachusetts Bay. Reports described
populations swept away "by heaps," tribes "almost totally de-

stroyed by the great sickness," and wigwams filled with corpses while survivors fled from the pestilence, leaving their fields and villages deserted and ripe for occupation by the English. The disease hit the eastern Abenakis in 1617 and spread along the Maine coast. Estimates of mortality rates among the afflicted tribes frequently exceeded 75 percent.[3]

Shortened Atlantic crossings and the arrival of Puritan immigrant children, who were susceptible to and possibly infected with smallpox, brought devastation to the Indians of New England. A disease that may have been smallpox raged south of the Merrimack River in 1631, but it was slight compared to the massive epidemic that broke out in 1633. Smallpox swept along the St. Lawrence, down the Connecticut River, where it disrupted the developing fur trade, through New England and westward to Huron country, affecting almost all Indian groups in the Northeast. The death rate was appalling. Governor William Bradford of Plymouth Colony reported that one Indian village up the Connecticut River had suffered "such a mortalitie that of a 1000. above 900. and a half of them dyed, and many of them did rott above ground for want of buriall." Dean Snow's researches into the epidemic provide confirmation of a 95 percent depopulation.[4] This contagion was the first in a series of epidemics that affected the area between eastern Canada and the Great Lakes in the next decade. In the summer of 1639 smallpox spread along the St. Lawrence, killing many Indians who went to trade at Quebec and Three Rivers. The epidemic seems to have broken out in New England and been carried north by Kikhesipirini Indians returning from a visit to the Abenakis. Soon, the Algonquins of eastern Canada were dying in such numbers that the survivors were unable to bury the dead and dogs were eating the corpses.[5]

In June 1646 a group of Abenakis told the French that a large part of their nation had been destroyed by a disease that caused vomiting of blood, and Abenakis on the Kennebec River were struck by a sickness against which their shamans were powerless.[6] Influenza hit the Indians of New England in 1647. In 1649–50 smallpox was again prevalent from eastern Canada to Huron country, and in 1659 New England Indians suffered from diphtheria. Smallpox struck the Iroquois and other northern tribes in

1662–63, while Indians at the Jesuit mission at Sillery, near Quebec, fell victim to the scourge in 1670. A bout of influenza hit the Iroquois and New England Algonquians in 1675.[7] Smallpox returned to the tribes of the Northeast between 1677 and 1679 and again between 1687 and 1691. The Mahicans were hit three times by smallpox in the course of the seventeenth century. At Sillery 130 people died from measles in 1687, by which time Sokokis and other western Abenakis had made their way to the French mission village.[8]

Such epidemics continued during the eighteenth century. Smallpox, plague, measles and yellow fever were the mass killers: outbreaks of smallpox hit the Abenakis hard between 1729 and 1733, and again between 1755 and 1758. Chronic diseases such as tuberculosis, diphtheria, pneumonia, influenza, dysentery, and syphilis also caused attrition of northern New England's Indian populations. The experience of the Indians on the upper Hudson River was not unusual. In 1656, Indians there affirmed "that before the arrival of the Christians, and before the small pox broke out amongst them, they were ten times as numerous as they now are, and that their population had been melted down by this disease, whereof nine-tenths of them have died."[9]

The frequency and intensity of lethal epidemics and chronic illnesses in the seventeenth century would have rendered it improbable that the western Abenakis escaped catastrophic losses, but the well-established trade routes and patterns of communication rendered it impossible. When English settlers pushed up the Connecticut River, the Green Mountains were lightly inhabited and many of Vermont's valleys appeared to be deserted. That scarcity of population is attributable at least in part to the prior invasions of killer diseases.

Long-accepted estimates that North American Indian populations totalled little more than 1 million at the time of early contacts have been effectively discredited. Upward revisions of precontact population estimates, and recognition of the impact of diseases on the aboriginal populations, have radical implications for the study of Indian history in Vermont and New England as a whole.[10] The heavier concentrations of population required far more sophisticated social, economic, and political organizations

Abenakis from one of the French mission villages on the St. Lawrence, tentatively identified as Bécancour. (Bibliothèque Municipale de la Ville de Montréal, Collection Gagnon)

than have traditionally been attributed to Indian civilizations. Population estimates for pre-epidemic New England now suggest numbers in excess of 90,000. These figures may not appear large to modern eyes, but the total English population of New England was only about 93,000 as late as 1700, while Europeans in New France numbered a mere 2,000 in 1650 and only reached 60,000 by 1763.[11]

Population estimates for the western Abenakis are necessarily rough, but "reasonable guesses" for the preplague western Abenaki of Vermont and New Hampshire suggest a figure of at least 10,000 people. Dean Snow has estimated that some 2,000 western Abenaki inhabited the upper Merrimack drainage, that perhaps 3,800 more lived on the upper Connecticut River, and that 4,200 more were in the Champlain Valley. He suggests that repeated epidemics had reduced these numbers by a staggering 98 percent to as few as 250 by the midseventeenth century.[12] The accuracy of the estimates can never be ascertained for certain, and the figure of 250 western Abenaki survivors seems low when one takes into account the number who sought refuge in French mission villages, as well as those who remained in New England. The Abenaki pattern of withdrawal to safer locations probably safeguarded them against such drastic reductions and at the same time gave writers an exaggerated impression of devastation. Nevertheless, mortality rates of 90 percent and more are consistent with figures from other regions, and there is little doubt that the invasion of Old World germs and viruses caused extensive depopulation in the Green Mountains.

The devastating impact of disease cannot be measured only in numerical losses. Epidemics left social and economic chaos in their wake and caused immeasurable spiritual and psychological damage. Killer diseases tore holes in the fabric of Indian societies held together by extensive networks of kinship and reciprocity, disrupted time-honored cycles of hunting, planting, and fishing, discouraged social and ceremonial gatherings, and drained confidence in the old certainties of life and the shamans who mediated with the spirit world.

While European viruses wrought demographic havoc, European fur traders brought further turmoil to Indian societies.

Since late Archaic times Indians in Vermont had participated in native trade networks that brought goods from as far away as Long Island and the Great Lakes.[13] The western Abenakis readily tapped into the new trade networks initiated by Europeans. In doing so, they opened their world to dramatic and deadly changes. European traders and trade goods introduced and accelerated the spread of disease, increased and intensified intertribal communication and competition, and generated disruptive chain reactions in Indian society.

The Indians of coastal Maine knew how to trade with Europeans as early as 1524, greeting Giovanni da Verrazzano with hostile suspicion. European voyagers to the Gulf of Maine in the first decade of the seventeenth century found that European manufactured goods were already abundant among the native peoples, most probably having arrived via existing native trade networks.[14] Only in the seventeenth century did European traders begin to penetrate the territories of the western Abenakis, advancing along arteries of commerce which the Indians had used for centuries. Trading posts leapfrogged up the Merrimack, Connecticut, and Hudson rivers as English traders hastened to attract business they feared would go north to the French or to the Dutch at Albany. European fur-trading rivalry continued through the seventeenth and eighteenth centuries. Indians often succeeded in playing this competition to their advantage, but the fur trade for which Europeans contested also threw the tribes into deadly rivalry.

Between 1607 and 1615 Micmacs and eastern Abenakis fought for the position of middlemen trading European goods from the coast of Nova Scotia to the tribes of New England.[15] In 1609 Henry Hudson found profits to be made trading for furs in the Albany region, and within a year Dutch trading vessels were visiting the upper Hudson River, introducing a new factor into Mahican-Mohawk relations. The Mahicans were no strangers to trade and appear to have operated as middlemen in the diffusion of shell beads from the Atlantic coast to the St. Lawrence Valley, but the European trade sent shock waves through their world. When the Dutch built trading posts at Fort Nassau in 1614, and then at Fort Orange (Albany), the Mahicans shifted their villages

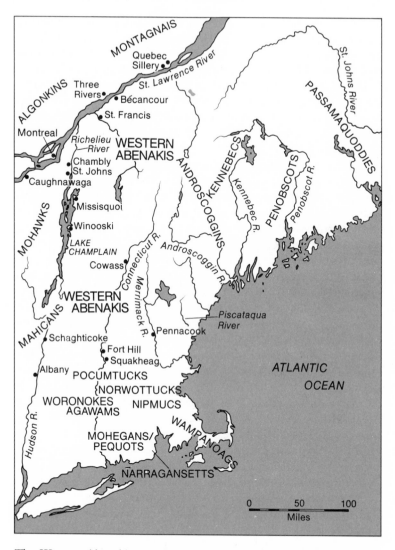

The Western Abenakis and their neighbors. (Base map adapted from Gordon Day, *The Identity of the St. Francis Indians*)

to take advantage of the situation. From the river shore opposite Fort Orange, they were able to control trade, levying tribute on Mohawks and other Indians who came there to trade. Mohawk resentment of the Mahican monopoly led to open war in 1624.[16]

In 1636 John Pynchon opened the fur trade in the Connecticut Valley when he built his trading post at Agawam (Springfield), Massachusetts, and began to tap the productive regions on the north and west.[17] Even though the Sokokis had little direct contact with the Pynchons, they were well placed to participate in the developing trade on the Connecticut River. They probably acquired manufactured goods from the French and, via Indian middlemen operating along native trade networks, from the English. Sokoki hunters ranged as far north as the banks of the St. Lawrence, and Sokokis were hunting with confidence near the Richelieu River in 1651. English colonies prohibited the sale or loan of firearms to Indians, but archaeological evidence from Fort Hill indicates that the Sokokis were able to obtain muskets and flints from the French.[18]

The Pigwackets probably served as middlemen between northern and western neighbors and coastal bands who enjoyed access to English traders. But the English had a trading post on the upper Merrimack River by 1668, when Captain Richard Waldron established his truck house at Pennacook. Fort Dummer, built on the Connecticut River as a defense against Indian raiders, also did a flourishing trade with Indian customers who brought in deer and moose skins and tallow.[19] Soon the western Abenakis were sandwiched between Dutch and English traders on the Hudson, English merchants on the Merrimack and Connecticut, and French traders on Lake Champlain and the St. Lawrence.

That situation seems to have concerned the English and French more than the Abenakis, who had few qualms about where they traded or with whom. English and French records are replete with worried statements that the Abenakis might be taking their custom to a rival, because the western Abenakis traded where it suited them. Abenakis and Iroquois alike used Lake Champlain as a trading corridor, and Chambly was a thriving port of trade on the Richelieu River. Baron de Lahontan said that Sokokis,

Mahicans, and Pennacooks used to go there "in shoals" to trade their pelts before 1685.[20]

Indians traded for social and political reasons rather than simply to make a profit or obtain technologically superior goods. In the Connecticut Valley fur trade in the seventeenth century, cloth and wampum were the items in heaviest demand among Indian customers, and both items were significant as marks of status and for cementing social and political relations. Indians incorporated European manufactured goods, metal, and firearms into their technology and in so doing lost some of their traditional craft skills and became more dependent on European merchants to satisfy their material needs. But the evidence from Squakheag shows that their dependency was limited and that the fur trade produced a blending of cultural items and values. The Sokokis looked to their traders not only for manufactured goods but also for raw materials such as brass that could be reworked into traditional ornaments and utensils. The people at Squakheag continued to use traditional artifacts made from stone, shell, and bone, and retained their traditional ceramic technology at the same time as they acquired industrially manufactured goods.[21] The fur trade in general was a relationship of interdependence rather than dependence. Individual Indian trappers and traders often played the field to advantage, and bands who functioned as middlemen occupied a valuable strategic and economic position.

Nevertheless, the new commercial situation was at best a mixed blessing. The fur trade proved to be a Trojan horse in Indian North America, unleashing catastrophic forces at the same time as it delivered desired gifts. The trade tied its Indian patrons into the expanding world of European capitalism and threw neighboring customers into desperate competition. Access to hunting grounds and to European traders became major considerations governing the movement and location of Indian bands and the decisions of band chiefs. Tribes clashed in escalating conflicts for pelts, trade, and survival. More and more time was devoted to hunting, and the diversion of economic energies disrupted traditional and balanced patterns of food procurement based on sacred symbiotic relationships with the animal world.

The fur trade introduced firearms into Indian society at the same time as European diseases disrupted native balances of power and opened up new avenues for aggression. The new weapons added a deadly and often decisive element in combat, and Indian people began to compete for them as the key to survival and supremacy. Despite the efforts of colonial authorities to prevent it, French, Dutch, and English traders all funneled firearms into the Indian world. For example, in 1637 a party of Abenakis arrived at Quebec armed with arquebuses. The Mohawks obtained firearms from the Dutch and purchased their first guns from English traders on the Connecticut River in 1639. According to the French, the Iroquois's early acquisition of firearms enabled them to spread terror throughout the continent. Indians at Sillery had a good number of muskets by 1645. At the time of King Philip's War the Indians of New England were accustomed to fighting with guns, and those in the New Hampshire region were reputed to be "excellent firemen."[22]

Indian bands became caught up in a deadly cycle of competition for furs and firearms that aggravated the worst effects of the fur trade and subjected Indian societies to tremendous strains as manpower and energy became sapped by economically motivated warfare and militarily motivated hunting. Populations weakened and reduced by disease had little chance to recover at a time when the threats to their lands and culture were mounting ominously.

Along with contagion and the competition for furs and firearms came a more subtle invasion in the form of missionaries preaching alien religious beliefs. In an age when bitter conflict between Catholics and Protestants was tearing Europe apart, European initiatives in North America embraced competition for Indian souls as well as contests for their patronage and allegiance. French missionaries labored to reap a harvest of souls equal to the harvest of pelts gathered by their fur-trading countrymen.

Abenakis traded with Europeans for a variety of reasons. This Pennacook ornament in the shape of a bird was fashioned from a copper utensil obtained from European traders. (Peabody Museum, Harvard University; photograph by Hillel Burger)

Black robed Jesuit missionaries traveled the length of New France and ventured into northern New England to carry their faith to the Indians.

French missionary activity was most prominent in Maine: Jesuits had a mission on the Kennebec River by 1646, Capuchins established another on the Penobscot in 1648, and by 1699 half a dozen Jesuits were administering sacraments in Abenaki villages on the Saco, Androscoggin, and Kennebec rivers.[23] According to a nineteenth-century tradition in St. Regis, the first French priest had visited Indians on the east shore of Lake Champlain as early as 1615. An aged Indian informant related that a missionary of the Recollect Order, with an escort of Indians in birchbark canoes, landed on Isle La Motte that summer and visited Indian villages and hunting bands along the entire eastern shore of the lake during the next three months. The excavation at Fort Hill of seven brass Jesuit rings of the kind handed out after catechism classes shows that the black robes' message had reached the Sokokis before 1664. When the French built Fort St. Anne on Isle La Motte in 1666 as a defense against the Mohawks, the Jesuits established a mission on the island, although both were abandoned within five years.[24]

Some Sokokis and about 150 Abenakis who fled north to Three Rivers and Sillery during King Philip's War received immediate instruction from the missionaries. Many were soon attending mass morning and night and reciting the catechism to the satisfaction of the Jesuit fathers, who spoke to them in Algonquin through an interpreter. Father Jean Enjalran reported, "I have stripped myself of almost everything that I could give them, and I do not account it ill employed." He requested additional small crosses, brass rings, and wooden rosaries to help him win more converts.[25] There seems also to have been a short-lived mission on the east shore of Lake Champlain, possibly near Missisquoi, around 1680, even though the Mohawks and Sokokis were fighting on the edge of the lake at the time. The mission's existence is a sure sign of substantial Indian population in the area, and French records describe the Indians there in 1682 as Abenakis and Loups.[26]

French maps show that there was a mission village at Cowass

Monument to the first Catholic church in Vermont, dedicated in 1909. The monument stands near the site of the church, overlooking the Missisquoi River outside Highgate. (Photograph by Colin G. Calloway)

sometime before 1713,[27] and western Abenakis regularly traveled to French mission villages on the St. Lawrence. Jesuit energy and dedication, the appeal of the Catholic religion, and the reputation of the Puritan English for treachery and cruelty gave the French substantial advantages in binding Abenakis to allegiance with religious ties. In September 1699, Father Vincent Bigot sent to Chartres cathedral a six-foot wampum belt made by the Abenakis. In return, Sir Vaillant Demihardouin sent the Abenakis a solid silver statue of Notre-Dame de Sous-Terre, which was housed in the church built at St. Francis in 1700 until it was stolen by Rogers' Rangers in 1759 and lost. The first church in Vermont, overlooking the Missisquoi River, was built by the French in 1700, and the Abenakis are said to have transported blocks of stone for the church in their birch-bark canoes.[28]

But the English did not give up the good fight. While their northern relatives were under the influence of French Roman Catholic priests, the Pennacooks in New Hampshire came under English influence. For three successive years in the late 1640s, Puritan missionary John Eliot traveled to the Pennacooks' spring fishing camps at the falls of the Merrimack River in the hope of converting the Pennacook sachem Passaconaway. He met with little success at first, although Passaconaway's son Wanalancet accepted baptism in the 1670s. The influence of French priests was still predominant among the Pennacooks in 1700. A group of Indians on their way to join the Pennacooks told the English "that the religion of the Penikook Indians was more beautiful than ours, for the French gave them silver crosses to wear on their necks." By 1700 the English too were sending missionaries to live among the eastern Abenakis and the Indians of the Merrimack River, and in 1735 the government of Massachusetts placed a minister at Fort Dummer to instruct the Indians who came there to trade.[29]

The killing, scalping, and mutilation of Father Sebastien Rasles during the English attack on Norridgewock in August 1724 graphically illustrated English concern over the political and military influence exerted by the Jesuits among the Abenakis. Caughnawaga Indians reminded the English that Jesuit influence among the tribes was just as strong thirty years later. Rejecting English requests that they remain neutral in the brewing conflict, the Caughnawagas said simply, "the French Priests by throwing Water upon our Heads, subject us to the Will of the Governor of Canada." New Englanders dismissed French missionary activity as subversion and displayed little understanding of the complex decisions and dynamics that surrounded Indian conversions and attracted the Abenakis to the missions. The French saw the Abenakis as their best source of converts and employed the mission to a dual religious and political purpose, but they also realized that the prospect of favorable trade with the English could strain the religious bonds that linked the mission Indians to New France.[30]

While French and English competed for Indian allegiance and conversion, missionaries and shamans competed for spiritual leadership in Indian communities. Shamans fulfilled vital roles in Abenaki society, curing the sick, predicting and supposedly controlling the weather, and exercising special power derived from their close association with the spirit world. The arrival of Jesuit missionaries threatened to undermine the position of traditional shamans, especially where simultaneous outbreaks of European disease revealed the limits of their curative powers and their inability to protect the people from new catastrophes. French priests at Sillery encouraged the Abenaki and Sokoki newcomers to reject what they termed their "jugglers" as obstacles to salvation, and they rejoiced when some of the Abenakis publicly renounced "jugglers and superstitions." At a time when their world seemed to be falling apart, some Abenakis no doubt questioned traditional certainties and looked to the French missionaries for additional sources of power and guidance in time of crisis. The missionaries' access to trade goods and military support and their ability to function as brokers between Abenaki and French society further increased their prestige and helped them usurp the traditional role of the shamans.[31]

In the mythical realities of northeastern Woodland Indians, human beings shared the social world with personages of nonhuman form. Among the Abenakis and their neighbors, humans talked with animals, addressing them as their grandmother, grandfather, uncle, brother or sister, and exchanging wisdom. They maintained harmonious relationships with these non-humans through carefully observed rituals. To Jesuit priests such behavior was primitive superstition. At a time when the European fur trade threatened the Indians' harmonious relations with their animal relatives and eroded traditional sanctions against slaughter, missionaries further undermined the Abenaki world by attacking their ritual relationships with the animal world as a peril to their souls.[32]

The missionaries not only had to compete against native shamans and the power of traditional beliefs, but they also confronted new difficulties generated by the effects of European contact on the communities they hoped to save. Inevitably, some Indians blamed the missionaries for the introduction of new diseases. Moreover, many Indians turned from trauma to the alcohol that traders made available. There were drunken Indians at Pennacook soon after Waldron opened his trading house there. French colonial authorities, like their Anglo-American successors, deplored the evil effects of the liquor trade yet recognized that it played an important role in retaining Indian allegiance and patronage.[33] The Abenakis and Sokokis who took refuge at Sillery in 1676 were commended for abstaining from drunkenness, but as early as 1683–84 Father Jacques Bigot hesitated to admit Sokokis to his mission on the Chaudière River because of what he called their "inconstance" and their propensity for drunkenness. Bigot feared that to admit "this sort of mixture" might contaminate the rest. His subsequent efforts to instill temperance made great headway, although he had to imprison one Sokoki woman for drunkenness and fine the Frenchman who made her drunk. The Marquis Jacques René Brisay de Denonville, witnessing the effects of alcohol on the Abenakis and their neighbors said simply: "It is the horror of horrors."[34]

The contest for Indian souls inevitably became a contest of lifestyles as well, since missionaries expected total acceptance of their brand of Christianity and abandonment of traditional practices that might interfere with conversion. Denonville reported in 1690 that, "Of all the Indian nations, the Abenaqui is the most inclined to christianity"; and Father Rasles declared that "The whole Abenakis Nation is Christian and is very zealous in preserving its Religion." French baptismal, marriage, and burial records testify to the incidence of conversion among the western Abenakis. Father Enjalran was moved to see Abenaki and Sokoki migrants at Sillery "receive their instructions with admirable docility," but he acknowledged there were always "some who are still rebellious to the light." Characteristically, many Indian individuals and communities survived the spiritual crisis by selective accommodation rather than by total acceptance or outright rejection of the new beliefs. Christianity as adopted by Indians ceased to be just a European religion; adapted and incorporated by Indians, it assumed some different forms and served some different purposes. Incorporation of Christian elements into their world view and acceptance of the outward forms of Christianity did not necessitate throwing out traditional belief systems. Indeed, western Abenakis living in Christian mission villages proved willing to adopt new non-Christian elements into their religious beliefs, as evidenced by their adoption of the calumet ceremony from the Fox Indians early in the eighteenth century.[35]

The degree of Indian acceptance of French religious beliefs and practices, beyond adaptation of some external trappings, and the extent to which they maintained their own in the face of change, are difficult to gauge and varied from region to region. According to John Webster Grant, conversion to Christianity was essentially "a phenomenon of the moon of wintertime, when ancestral spirits had ceased to perform their expected functions satisfactorily and angel choirs promised to fill a spiritual vacuum." But Indians seem more often to have sought to add to spiritual arsenals than to fill spiritual vacuums. Abenaki responses to the missionaries tended toward syncretism, and the Indians initially seem to have taken on Christianity as another weapon for assuring their well-being, without abandoning traditional ways of life. Indians undoubtedly looked to traditional rites to ensure successful hunting, but there was no reason why Catholic saints might not also be expected to assist a hunting party. Jesuit missionaries attempted to concentrate Abenaki populations into mission settlements like Sillery and St. Francis where the Indians could be supervised as coherent and sedentary societies. But the Abenakis and Sokokis who congregated at Sillery in the spring of 1676 followed traditional practice and left the following November to disperse to their winter quarters.[36] The mixture of Indian and Christian elements in the Catholic church at Odanak today shows that the strength and resilience of Abenaki communities, in the spiritual as in the physical world, lay in their ability to adjust and accommodate, to bend rather than to break.

These biological, economic, and spiritual forces continued to wear away at Abenaki culture and powers of resistance throughout the seventeenth and eighteenth centuries, eroding Indian strength before English settlers began to edge north in the eighteenth century and English soldiers and Abenaki warriors skirmished in the Green Mountains. But the later encroachment of English farmers was itself accompanied by an invasion that was less dramatic and visible but equally far-reaching.

Western Abenaki social and subsistence patterns allowed optimum exploitation of Vermont's bountiful natural resources with minimal disruption to the natural order. The mobility of Abenaki family bands allowed them to take advantage of the land's diversity and kept human demands on the ecosystem low. The annual cycle of life revolved around "seasons of want and plenty." Families congregated for spring fishing in one of the major social events of the year; gathered to plant corn, squash, and beans in the fertile lowlands of the Connecticut and Champlain valleys; dispersed for fall hunting; and reassembled in midwinter for shelter, festivals, and storytelling. The rest of the year the Abenaki family bands spent in their hunting territories, which the French described thus: "chaque chef de famille a une rivière où il va la faire et où un homme d'une autre famille n'oseroit aller chasse."[37]

This diversified subsistence pattern served the western Abenakis well before European invasion. Then the demands of the fur trade knocked time-honored cycles out of balance, and the encroachments of English farmers eroded the extensive and diverse land base on which Western Abenaki communities depended to support their annual cycle of subsistence. The Sokokis who built Fort Hill in 1663 selected an area rich in resources and located their village within easy access of good fishing, game-filled forests, and rich valley bottomlands for planting.[38] Cowass and Missisquoi nestled in regions of similar natural bounty. The European invasion naturally led to conflict as the newcomers competed for the more-productive areas that Indians had already utilized and cultivated. In the middle Connecticut Valley, English towns sprang up immediately adjacent to fields cleared by Indian villagers, and Anglo-Indian competition stretched the productive capacities of the land to the maximum and introduced inevitable conflict.[39]

This conflict was heightened by the very mobility of Indian life that allowed the Abenakis to subsist so effectively in the Green Mountains. The movement of family bands varied with the rhythm of the seasons and represented a sophisticated response to climate, geography, natural resources, and seasonal change. But Anglo-American colonists, who struggled to master the environment with back-breaking labor, could perceive no useful purpose behind Indian mobility and refused to recognize that Indians occupied the land in any meaningful sense. By Abenaki standards the land was both inhabited and effectively utilized; by Euro-American standards Vermont appeared to be barely inhabited. The invaders thus armed themselves with a convenient ideology for conquest and dispossession.[40]

Moreover, as William Cronon has shown, the European invasion and settlement of New England "was as much an ecological as a cultural invasion." As English farmers and Indians competed for the same choice lands, so the colonists' grazing animals began to compete with the native wild-animal population for food resources. English farmers aimed to reduce the forest to a land of cultivated farms and fences, and while the Green Mountains did not suffer the deforestation that marked English conquest of southern New England, settlers nonetheless made serious inroads, which by the 1760s had caused the king's ministers concern about preserving the forests on the west side of the Connecticut River. Indians found themselves forced increasingly into marginal areas where their ability to exploit the land base in the traditional cycle of subsistence was greatly reduced. The ecological transformation that changed the face of New England between 1600 and 1800 may have been less marked in Vermont than in the south, but it was another weapon in the invaders' arsenal of forces destructive of Indian life in the region. In the first decade of the nineteenth century traveler Edward Augustus Kendall noted that the Indians from Cowass, "the place of the pines," who then lived at St. Francis, still called themselves Cowasucks, but that the pine trees that gave their homeland its name had been removed and replaced by meadows.[41] The conquest of Indian Vermont was achieved against a background of biological catastrophe, economic dislocation, spiritual questioning, and ecological adjustment for the western Abenakis.

Chapter 3

Relations with Algonquins and Iroquois, 1603–1669

Indian societies, reeling under the devastating impact of new diseases, the disruptive effects of new technology, and the disturbing influence of new religions, experienced further turmoil during the seventeenth century as a result of escalating intertribal warfare. The western Abenakis' relations with their Indian neighbors had always fluctuated between war and peace. Coexistence seems to have been more common than conflict in the first half of the seventeenth century, and recurrent peace councils between Mohawks, Mahicans, and vaguely identified "North Indians" punctuated hostilities later in the century. But European invasion unleashed pressures that upset existing intertribal relations and that increased, intensified, and radically transformed existing patterns of Indian warfare. For seventy years before English settlers penetrated western Abenaki territory, rival groups of Europeans, Algonquians, and Iroquoians sought to assert control over sources of military, economic, and political power. Wars waged in surrounding regions brought dramatic and often deadly changes to the Indian communities living in the hills and valleys of Vermont. Western Abenakis fought for supremacy and survival in a world of flux, creating a distorted impression of Abenaki society as inherently warlike.

The Iroquois Confederacy, with the Mohawks as the keepers of their eastern door, emerged as a dominant power in northeastern North America, but the western Abenakis were not simply victims in this era of upheaval. Sokoki delegates held their own

in councils with the Iroquois; Sokoki warriors fought Algonquins on the north and Iroquois on the west, and frequently gave
as good as they got. Bacqueville de La Potèrie reported that the
Iroquois came to regard the Sokokis with healthy respect as "des
gens intrépides dans le combat."[1] But recurrent warfare took its
toll on the western Abenakis, and Sokoki survivors were driven
to seek refuge in safer locations.

The defensive locations of many Indian village sites on riverbanks and hills indicate that war and survival were familiar concerns for western Abenakis before Europeans arrived.[2] After white
contact, however, competition for furs and dominion quickly de-
stabilized existing harmonies and balances of power, and placed
the western Abenakis in the mainstream of conflicting tensions.
Mahican, Abenaki, Iroquois, French, Dutch, and English traders,
warriors, and statesmen traveled on errands of commerce, conflict, and diplomacy. Mohawk warriors passed down Lake Champlain to raid French settlements, attack Indian villages, and disrupt the northern fur trade. French armies braved harsh winters
to invade Iroquoia via the ice-bound lake. Mohawk and Algonquian war parties filtered back and forth across the Berkshires.
Sokoki warriors raided as far north as the St. Lawrence and
joined anti-Iroquois campaigns. Meanwhile, on the south, English colonists and New England Indians began to clash in bloody
racial conflicts that augured ill for the Indian communities in the
foothills of the Green Mountains.

Indian societies waged traditional war as much to satisfy internal needs as in response to external demands. Warriors contested
for prestige, revenge, and captives and as a means of ritually as-
suaging the grief of bereaved relatives. As a result, Indian battles
tended to be ritualistic, seasonal encounters that were smaller in
scale and, as Roger Williams said, "farre lesse bloudy, and de-
vouring then the cruell Warres of *Europe*."[3] But intertribal conflicts altered and intensified under the triple impact of disease,
trade, and firearms. Epidemics carried off tribal members, oblig-
ing the survivors to seek captives as replacements. Competition
for trade goods and guns transformed native warfare into an
unrelenting struggle for supremacy and survival. Caught in a
vicious economic and military cycle that revolved around furs and

firearms, Indian bands now devoted their utmost energies to maintaining a tenable strategic position in a world thrown into dangerous upheaval.

In 1535 the French explorer Jacques Cartier traveled up the St. Lawrence River, passing cultivated fields and visiting thriving Iroquoian communities at Stadacona (Quebec) and Hochelaga (Montreal). At Hochelaga he climbed Mount Royal, where the Indian chief Donnaconna pointed out the Green Mountains on the south.[4] Less than seventy years later, Samuel de Champlain found the St. Lawrence Valley much changed. By 1603 the Iroquoian inhabitants had disappeared, and the area had been transformed into a no-man's-land as a result of warfare between the Algonquins and Montagnais on the north and the Iroquois on the south. Iroquois raids down the St. Lawrence, diseases that swept the valley, and recurrent warfare had destroyed and dispersed the communities visited by Cartier. Champlain guessed that the warfare had begun around 1570. By 1603 the Algonquins and Montagnais were united against the Iroquois for control of the empty St. Lawrence Valley and were winning victories as far south as Lake Champlain.[5]

On an August evening in 1642, some Indians took a group of French missionaries to the summit of the mountain at Montreal. The Indians stretched out their hands towards the hills lying on the south and east: "'There,' said they, 'are the places where stood Villages filled with great numbers of Savages. The Hurons, who then were our enemies, drove our Forefathers from this country. Some went towards the country of the Abnaquiois, others towards the country of the Hiroquois, some to the Hurons themselves, and joined them. And that is how this Island became deserted.'" Since Missisquoi was the closest known Abenaki village to Montreal, and since fragments of St. Lawrence Iroquoian pottery have been found there, it seems likely that western Abenaki bands absorbed some of the refugees. Vermont Abenakis felt the reverberations of what had happened along the St. Lawrence in other ways. Champlain's Indian allies told him in 1609 that the Richelieu River and the "four beautiful islands" in Lake Champlain—Isle La Motte, Grand Isle, North Hero, and Valcour—had recently been abandoned. As his party paddled across the

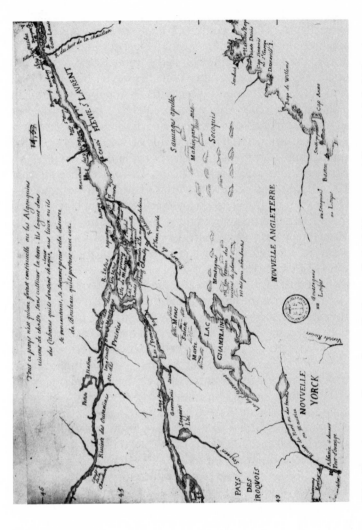

This French map of 1680 shows Indians called Mahingans and Socoquis inhabiting large areas of northern New England. (Public Archives of Canada NMC 10333/902/1680)

lake, Champlain noted, "This region although pleasant is not inhabited by Indians, on account of their wars; for they withdraw from the rivers as far as they can into the interior, in order not to be easily surprised."[6] Western Abenakis were to adhere to the same strategy of withdrawal in time of war for the next two centuries.

Champlain's guides also reported that the country east of the lake was a land of beautiful valleys and rich cornfields, and that it was inhabited by the Iroquois. The Mohawks may have attempted to extend their sway as far east as the Connecticut River, and they appear to have established a number of temporary outposts in western Abenaki territory between about 1540 and 1640, although this could indicate overlapping utilization of resources rather than hostile occupation. Henry R. Schoolcraft described the upper Connecticut Valley as a kind of "debateable ground" between the Mohawks and the Pennacooks. He said Indian parties were to be found at Bellows Falls and farther downriver, but none dared make permanent settlements there. This may explain otherwise enigmatic statements made by eastern Abenakis in the 1720s that the Connecticut River "was formerly the boundary which separated the lands of the Iroquois from those of the Abenakis."[7]

Linguistic, archaeological, and historical evidence, however, points to Lake Champlain as the boundary between Iroquois and Abenaki territory, and Champlain may have had problems with his interpreters. One of the earliest maps of Lake Champlain, made by the Jesuit Pierre Raffeix, gives distinctly western Abenaki place-names on the eastern shore and clearly indicates western Abenaki occupation there in the second half of the seventeenth century. Sir William Johnson, the British Indian agent who lived among the Mohawks in the eighteenth century, and Lewis Henry Morgan, the pioneer ethnologist who conducted firsthand research among the Iroquois in the nineteenth century, each recognized Lake Champlain as the western border of Iroquoia. The Abenakis viewed subsequent Iroquois claims to western Vermont as based on temporary incursions, not on permanent occupation or original rights.[8]

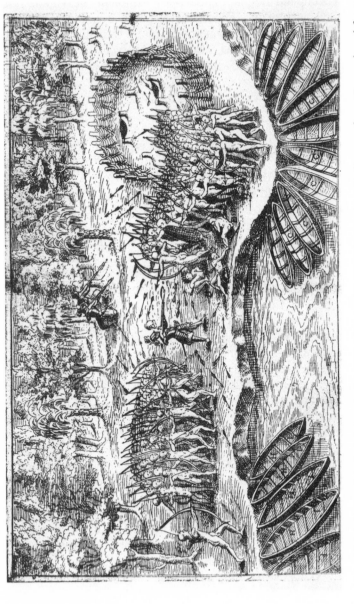

Champlain's fight with the Mohawks introduced a deadly new element into Indian warfare. (Reproduced from *The Works of Samuel de Champlain*, edited by H. P. Biggar [Toronto: Champlain Society, 1922–36])

In the first half of the seventeenth century relations between the Mohawks and Algonquian peoples in southern New England were characterized as much by cooperation as by conflict, with reciprocal exchanges based on distribution of the supplies of wampum that were crucial in Iroquois war and diplomacy. Mohawk–western Abenaki relations at this time involved similar peaceful interchanges of trade, tribute, and kinship ties in the Champlain Valley. But Mohawk encroachments and French allegiance with the Abenakis in the seventeenth century soon gave the Champlain lowland the character of a frontier region and gave rise to traditions of Vermont as a no-man's-land and the scene of bloody interethnic conflicts.[9]

When Champlain joined his Montagnais and Algonquin allies in the famous battle against the Mohawks in 1609 on the lake that bears his name, he was carrying on French policy that had been formulated several years previously. The French realized that it was essential that they ally themselves with the Montagnais and the Algonquins and drive the Mohawk raiders from the St. Lawrence for the protection of their fur trade. The skirmish was no chance incident; as Champlain declared, "I had no other intention than to make war."[10]

The Indian war parties that met on the lake fought and behaved according to time-honored patterns. There was much ritual, threatening behavior, and preparation for combat, but in the actual battle—which took place on the shore, probably near Ticonderoga—both sides adopted essentially defensive positions and engaged in a long-range exchange of arrows and insults. Champlain's decisive interference, gunning down a number of Mohawk warriors and putting the rest to flight, initiated the Iroquois hostility to the French and set in motion radical changes in the style and purposes of intertribal conflict. Within a generation, woven shields and defensive tactics disappeared, replaced by deadly guerilla warfare governed by the possession of firearms. Ranks of warriors, wielding stone-age weapons and often wearing cumbersome wooden, woven, and leather body armor, gave place to mobile and lethal war parties armed with firearms. Champlain expressed abhorrence at his allies' torture of their Mohawk prisoners (an incident that may have occurred at the mouth of Otter Creek), even as he and his kind fueled the ferocity of intertribal conflict.[11]

Nowhere did firearms, and the European fur trade that peddled them, exert more far-reaching consequences than among the Iroquois. The exact role of economic motivation in the Iroquois wars of the seventeenth century has been the subject of some controversy, but the fur trade produced circumstances in which the Iroquois embarked on a program of military activity that sent shock waves through eastern North America. For most of the century, Mohawk warriors from the west posed a greater threat to both the French in Canada and the western Abenakis than did English soldiers and settlers from the south.[12]

For a long time, however, the Iroquois suffered as much as they inflicted, and they barely deserved the reputation for militarism and ferocity accorded them by later historians. Rival groups pressed them back on several fronts, and the Mahicans evidently considered them fair game for both raiding and levying tribute. When Dutch merchants on the Hudson River established Fort Nassau near Albany around 1614, they turned to the neighboring Mahicans, not the more-distant Mohawks, for cooperation in use of the Mahican Channel and for help in securing furs from the north. The Mahicans exploited their position to monopolize trade with the Dutch and deprive the Mohawks of direct access to the traders. Mohawk resentment of the Mahican monopoly finally led to open war in 1624.

The Mohawk-Mahican War swung back and forth, and the Pocumtucks and perhaps the Sokokis seem to have been involved on the side of the Mahicans. But in 1628 the Mohawks "beat and captured the Maikans and drove off the remainder who have settled towards the north by the Fresh [Connecticut] River, so called; where they begin again to cultivate the soil; and thus the war has come to an end." Some Mahicans may have settled in Indian communities in the Connecticut Valley; many, however, remained in or returned to the Hudson Valley, and the Mahicans retained three of the five villages near Fort Orange at Albany until the end of the century. Others established a new village on the north at Schaghticoke, from which they could exploit remote trapping grounds in Vermont and continue a lucrative commerce with the Dutch, and Mahicans continued to drift away from the Hudson throughout the 1630s. The Mohawk victory produced a new set of relations with the Dutch and with other tribes. They now had access to Dutch traders at Albany, which allowed them in turn to exploit their position at the expense of their western relatives.[13]

Soon equally momentous struggles were taking place in the south. By the mid-1630s Puritans had begun to migrate into the lower Connecticut Valley, and in 1636 the Massachusetts Bay Colony enlisted aid from the Mohegans and the Narragansetts and launched what was supposed to be a preemptive strike against the powerful Pequot tribe. The Pequot War ended with the English destruction of the main Pequot village on the Mystic River. The Puritans surrounded the village, put it to the torch, and slaughtered several hundred men, women, and children. This "First Puritan Conquest" introduced the appalled Indians to the Europeans' concept of total war, increased English power over the tribes of southern New England, and cleared the way for English expansion up the Connecticut Valley. In Governor-General William Kieft's war against the Indians of New Netherland in 1643–44, Dutch and English troops inflicted similar devastation among the tribes on the lower Hudson River.[14]

After the Mohawk-Mahican War a new set of relations seems to have been established between the two tribes. The Mahicans now paid tribute in wampum to the Mohawks, which may have indicated allegiance and cooperation, with the Mahicans sharing their wampum income, rather than domination.[15] The Mohawks stepped up their raids on the north. In 1629 they destroyed an Algonquin and Montagnais village at Three Rivers. As they began to penetrate Algonquin and Montagnais territory in order to hunt and raid for furs, the Mohawks made peace with the Mahicans and Sokokis to secure their eastern frontier and focus their energies in one area. By the late 1630s Algonquins and Montagnais were seeking refuge from Mohawk attacks at French missions. The Mohawks struck out in every direction from the Mohawk Valley, intercepting fur-laden canoes en route to Albany and Mon-

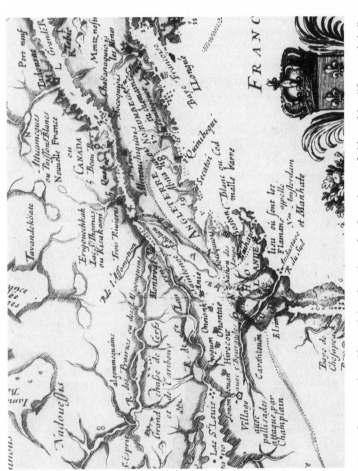

Part of a map by Champlain showing the locations of Abenakis, "Socoquiois,"
Loups, and "Hirocois." (Public Archives of Canada, NMC 14080, H3/900/1677)

treal. Francis Jennings compares them to "medieval banditti on heights overlooking caravan routes." The Mahicans too began to exert new pressures on neighboring groups as their own supplies of beaver became seriously depleted. They compelled groups east of the Hudson to acknowledge their supremacy, levied tribute from smaller groups, and sent raiding parties as far afield as western Long Island.[16]

Competition for fur resources also brought the Sokokis into conflict with neighboring tribes. In fact, the first recorded encounter of the French with the Sokokis stemmed from Sokoki-Algonquin hostilities. In November 1642 a band of northern Algonquins arrived at Sillery with a "Socoquiois" prisoner, named Messabitout, who had been severely tortured. The French interceded to secure his release, treated his wounds, and sent him back to his own country. The following spring Messabitout, "seeing that the French had saved his life," sent a gift of wampum to the Mohawks to try to secure the release of their Jesuit captive, Father Isaac Jogues. The attempt failed, but the incident marked the beginning of amicable Franco-Sokoki relations.[17]

The Sokokis were said to be allies of the Iroquois at this time, and like them posed a threat to Indians settled around Sillery and other French missions. Mahicans and Sokokis joined Mohawk war parties in commercially motivated raids. In the fall of 1645 a war party killed three Montagnais hunters near Sillery and left a woman scalped and for dead. At first the French feared the killers might be Mohawks, but they later discovered they were Sokokis exacting revenge for losses sustained several years previously and for the torture of Messabitout by the Algonquins.[18]

The *Jesuit Relations* for 1646 reported that: "besides these Iroquois there are other Nations, more to the North, who seem disposed to undertake war with our Savages,—as the Sokoquiois, whom our Savages call Assokwekik; and the Mahingans, or Mahinganak, with whom the Algonquins formerly had extensive alliances,—but the Annierronon [Mohawks] Iroquois having subdued them, they have ranged them upon their side." That same year, however, the Iroquois considered

Iroquois allant a la Decouverte

This engraving of an Iroquois warrior, by J. Larocque after Jacques Grasset St. Saveur, conveys the French view of the Iroquois threat. (National Archives of Canada C-3165)

making peace with the Algonquins. The Sokokis did everything in their power to prevent such a diplomatic reversal and sent ambassadors to the Mohawks to break the peace with the Algonquins. The Sokoki spokesman harangued and taunted the Mohawks, saying: "For a long time I have heard you say that the Algonquins were your irreconcilable enemies, and that you hated them even beyond the grave,—so that, if you could meet them in the other life, your war would be eternal. As we are your allies, we enter into your passions and into your interests." Whereupon the Sokokis presented them with a wampum belt and the scalps of the three Montagnais killed in the fall. The Mohawks were taken aback and indignantly refused the Sokokis' bold offer as likely to embroil them in renewed warfare.[19]

Mohawk war parties continued to spill out across New England, traveling up the Champlain Valley to harass Indians and whites on the St. Lawrence, raiding traffic on the Connecticut, and striking farther east against the Abenakis in Maine. Tensions inevitably increased among the western Abenakis, Sokokis, and Mahicans, escalating into open war by midcentury. In 1647 an Iroquois war party raided into Maine and returned after a six-month absence with twenty Abenaki captives.[20] Before 1650 the Sokokis and other communities in the Connecticut Valley paid tribute in wampum to the Mohawks, but in 1650 the Mohawks asked the Dutch at Fort Orange for permission to cross their territory, and they evidently launched a campaign that struck both the Sokokis and the Abenakis.[21]

However, in a period when the Iroquois were winning spectacular victories on the west against the Hurons, Neutrals, and Eries, the Sokokis, Mahicans, and their neighbors successfully held their own on the east, bolstered by firearms and access to the Pynchon trading post in Springfield. Mahicans continued to limit Mohawk access to the Hudson, and in 1650–51 the Sokokis emerged as a driving force in a projected alliance of New England tribes united under French auspices against the Iroquois threat.

By the early 1650s the Iroquois had defeated and dispersed their most populous Indian neighbors and had reduced to a shambles the trading network on which the economy of New France depended. The European population of New France at the time comprised a mere two thousand people scattered along the banks of the St. Lawrence; a dozen years later it totaled "no more people than constituted a small Iroquois tribe." Small wonder that the French sought allies against the Iroquois.[22] In 1650 the Jesuit missionary Father Gabriel Druillettes—accompanied by Noel Tekouerimat (or Negabamat), a Montagnais chief of the Christian Indians at Sillery, and a small group of Indians—traveled south to New England to enlist the aid of New England's colonies and tribes against the Iroquois. The Council of Quebec urged the Commissioners of New England to make common cause "to check the insolence of these Iroquois Indians, who massacre the Sokokinois and the Abenaquinois." Druillettes said that all the Indian nations in New England hated and feared the Iroquois and that the Sokokis in particular had good reason to join the proposed alliance. The Sokokis were, he reported,

> very glad to deliver themselves from the annual tribute of porcelain [wampum] which the Irocquois exact,—nay, even, to revenge themselves for the death of many of their fellow-countrymen, killed by the Irocquois. Besides that, they hope for the beaver hunt about quebecq, after the destruction of the Irocquois.

Druillettes proposed his offensive alliance to the Abenakis and a Sokoki delegate on the Kennebec River that fall. The Abenakis sent wampum belts to the Sokokis, and the Sokokis held council with the Mahicans, Pocumtucks, and Pennacooks during the winter. In the spring a Sokoki messenger brought word to Druillettes that the four tribes had agreed to join the French and their allies whether or not the English supported the venture. The English, however, had no desire to embark on a war against the Iroquois. Noel Tekouerimat declared: "The Englishman replies not; he has no good thoughts for us. This grieves me much; we see ourselves dying and being exterminated every day." No united action resulted from the negotiations, but the new Sokoki-Abenaki-French alliance challenged Iroquois power for a generation.[23]

Relations were not stabilized, however, and Sokoki-Algonquin hostilities continued. Three Sokokis paddled their canoe into Sillery one evening in September 1651. One of them had been there in the spring as an ambassador. They said that they had come in company with one hundred other Sokokis, whom they had left hunting near the Richelieu River. But, reported the *Jesuit Relations*, "they contradicted themselves in their story, so that there was every reason to suspect that there might be some trickery in the behavior of these *sokoquinois*, and that they came *animo potius hostili, quam amico*." A report that there were 200 Iroquois near Sillery sent two of the Sokokis hurrying away, although the third remained, to sneak away a month later in a stolen canoe.[24]

A year later nine Algonquins arrived with five Sokokis whom they had captured in the south. Their lives were spared so that two of them could be sent back to give warning of what was going on and secure the release of some Algonquin women held by the Sokokis, but the prisoners were so badly wounded and beaten by the Algonquins that the journey had to be postponed. The Sokokis were fighting on two fronts: an Algonquin who had been captured by the Mohawks brought news in 1652 that "the Annie'ronnons and *sokoquinois* are killing one another." Finally, in 1653, under French auspices, the Sokokis and the Algonquins released their prisoners and made peace.[25]

The Iroquois kept their enemies on the defensive. Mohawk fur raiders harassed the Mahicans, the Sokokis, and the Abenakis throughout the 1650s, and remained a threat on the St. Lawrence through the end of the decade.[26] This pressure contributed to the movement of Indians northward in search of a refuge among the French. In 1653 there was already "a gathering from different Nations" at Sillery. When some captives from the south were brought to the village, the inhabitants fell on them and beat and tortured them, thinking they were Iroquois, until Noel Tekouerimat identified them as Abenakis or friends and neighbors of the Abenakis. Indian tradition maintains that there were twenty families living at St. Francis as early as 1660, and the contention is rendered probable by the record of a Sokoki baptism at Three Rivers in 1658.[27] English power by contrast remained relatively limited. In 1658–59, at a time when Indian leaders in the middle Connecticut Valley were going out of their way to avoid offending the Mohawks, a Pocumtuck war chief named

Onapequin raided the Mohegans in open defiance of the English authorities in Connecticut.[28]

The 1660s were years of turmoil in both the Old and the New World. In 1660 the English restored the Stuart monarchy after Oliver Cromwell's Protectorate and brought the son of their beheaded king back to the throne as Charles II. The next year, Louis XIV assumed full powers as absolute monarch of France after years under the tutelage of Cardinal Mazarin. English, French, and Dutch rivalries collided in the commercial, military, and diplomatic arenas. In northeastern North America the early 1660s witnessed radical shifts in the balance of power among competing groups of Indians and Europeans alike. New Netherland surrendered to the English, and the Sokokis and the Pocumtucks declined in power and were forced to abandon their villages as the Iroquois stepped up their activities on the west. Meanwhile, in an effort to stem the Iroquois menace, the French built Fort St. Anne on Isle La Motte, an established port of call for Indian war parties crossing Lake Champlain.

In 1660 the Iroquois turned their attention against the Abenakis of Maine. They accused these "Northern Indians" of having assisted Canadian Indians in battles that cost the Mohawks 100 men. In November they planned a raid on the Kennebec River Abenakis, and in April 1662 a war party of 200 set out to attack the Etchemins, or Abenakis of the Penobscot River.[29] Hostilities between the Mohawks and the Mahicans also continued through the early 1660s, sometimes with heavy losses on both sides.[30]

Warfare and increasing competition for diminishing resources disrupted village life and altered basic subsistence strategies at Squakheag. Sometime in the early 1660s most of the families in the area congregated into a single village and constructed Fort Hill for their protection on a steep promontory overlooking the Connecticut River at Hinsdale, New Hampshire.[31] Mohawk attacks appear to have been responsible for both the occupation of the fort in September 1663 and its evacuation early the next year.

Sporadic clashes between Sokokis and Mohawks culminated in 1663. Early that year Sokokis from Squakheag and their allies attacked the Mohawks. Floods and an outbreak of smallpox brought a brief respite, but Indians lower down the Connecticut River feared that escalating hostilities would embroil them in the war. In July, through trader John Pynchon, the Pocumtucks, the Agawams, and others petitioned the Dutch to intercede on their behalf. They deplored the recent killings of some Mohawks, saying the deed was the work of the "Sowquackicks" who lived at the head of the Connecticut River. They "swore" at the Sokokis and declared their resolution to remain on good terms with the Mohawks. The Mohawk chief Adogodquo, or Big Spoon, replied that it was good that these tribes should have nothing to do with the Sokokis, and suggested that they send presents to strengthen the peace between them.[32]

In September the Dutch met with the Mohawks in council at Fort Orange and urged them to make peace. Saheda, the Mohawk chief, replied haughtily that they should leave him and his people alone and not worry about their war with the northern Indians or the Sokokis. He announced that the Mohawks did not consider themselves at war with the Abenakis, but requested that they "be allowed to make war against the Onejagese, also called Soquachjk, and their adherents."[33]

In November a large war party of Mohawks, Senecas, and Onondagas left for the Connecticut Valley, and in December they laid seige to Fort Hill. They emptied the Sokokis' corn storage pits outside the fort walls and stormed the village, but without success. Both sides lost heavily in the fighting before the Iroquois withdrew. The Dutch, who saw Iroquois detachments filtering home, heard rumors that they had lost between 200 and 300 men, and they certainly sustained at least 100 losses. Pennacooks and Cowasucks came to the aid of the Sokokis, who remained at their fort during the winter, but by the spring the Sokokis had abandoned their stronghold and dispersed.[34]

The Iroquois attack saw the beginning of a gradual Sokoki exodus from Squakheag. Sokokis began to appear in increasing numbers along the St. Lawrence. In 1662 and 1663, Sokoki names began to appear in the register of Notre-Dame de Montréal, and there were Sokokis at St. Francis and near Sorel as early as 1669, when three Sokokis were involved in a violent altercation with a

French officer of the Carignan regiment. Others went south and took up residence with the Pocumtucks.[35] Within a year these Sokokis were refugees once again.

War and smallpox took its toll on the Mohawks and northern Indians alike, and in May 1664 the Mohawks sent a delegation to Pocumtuck, accompanied by two Dutchmen, who were anxious to see peace restored for commercial reasons, and three Mahicans, who probably went along as interpreters. They crossed the Berkshires, arrived at the Pocumtuck "castle," and then crossed over steep hills to another castle. The Pocumtucks said: "We have had no war for 36 years and have not troubled ourselves about our neighbors, the Socquackicks, when the Maquas were at war with them last year." The Mohawks and the Pocumtucks reached an agreement and exchanged presents. Then, they said, "we sent for the Soquackick chiefs, who had taken refuge in the aforesaid Castle, to the number of 35 or 36." The Sokoki refugees were urged to make peace, as they were now too weak to have a chance against the Mohawks. The Mohawk delegates told them, "You have acted like fools, the *Onoganges* [Abenakis], our real enemies, have instigated you."[36]

The following month, Saheda and the Mohawk ambassadors were murdered as they traveled to Pocumtuck to confirm the agreements. Suspicion fell on the Mahicans, the Pocumtucks, and the English, and, as Gordon Day points out, "The Sokwakis and Abenakis also had reason not to want the Mohawks to make a separate peace with the Pocumtucks." The Mohawks were in no doubt about who was responsible and made preparations for retaliation. In September the Iroquois made an agreement with the English "That the English do not assist the three nations of the Ondeakes [Sokokis], Pennekooks, and Pacamtekookes, who murdered one of the Princes of the Macques, when he brought ransomes & Presents to them upon a treaty of peace." The Mohawks also made provision that, in the event of being defeated, "they may receive accomodacêon from ye English."[37]

In July 1664, Mahicans, Sokokis, and others raided the Mohawks, and John Pynchon reported that all the Indians in the region were "at deadly feud" with the Mohawks. Then the Iroquois launched a devastating campaign against the Pocumtucks.

They destroyed their villages and scattered the survivors, and it seems that Pocumtuck was never rebuilt. The invaders then swung north against the Sokokis and east against the Penna-cooks. Tradition recounts a Mohawk assault on the Pennacook village on the east bank of the Merrimack about this time, and the Pennacooks may have taken a beating.[38]

The evacuation of Fort Hill and the destruction of Pocumtuck in such a short space of time produced dramatic dislocations among the Indian populations of the middle and upper Connecti-cut Valley. Refugees from the abandoned villages fled south to Norwottuck and Agawam, sought asylum with the Pennacooks and other groups on the east, or began to migrate northward to Cowass, Lake Champlain, and Canada. In Peter Thomas's words, "the valley towns took on the look of a war zone," and the Indian population of the middle Connecticut Valley may have dropped from about 2,300 to 1,700 between 1660 and 1665. In any case, the power of the Sokokis and Pocumtucks was broken a decade be-fore King Philip's War.[39]

In the summer of 1665 Mohawks raided as far east as Boston.[40] 1665 Their attacks were said to have driven many Indians to the English settlements to seek protection and a livelihood. Daniel Gookin painted an exaggerated picture of Mohawk military prowess and the terror they inspired among New England Indians, but his protrayal of the effects of years of warfare on the Massachusetts, Pennacooks, Abenakis, Pocumtucks, Quaboags, Nipmucks, and Nashaways (or Nashuas) conveys a sense of the disruption of nor-mal patterns of life. The Mohawk threat produced hunger and poverty: "For they were driven from their planting fields through fear, and from their fishing and hunting places; yea they durst not go into the woods, to seek roots and nuts to sustain their lives . . . necessity forced them to labour with the English in hoeing, reaping, picking hops, cutting wood, making hay, and making stone fenses, and like necessary employments, whereby they got victuals and clothes."[41]

The Iroquois were not immune from attack themselves, how-ever. The 1,200-strong Carignan-Salières regiment was sent to New France, and in 1665 and 1666, French expeditions led by Courcelles and Tracy marched "over the frozen Lake of Canada" into Iroquoia and burned the Mohawks' fortified villages. The Mohawks felt the blow severely, and in April 1666 they asked the English for help. Governor Richard Nicolls of New York promised to ask the French for terms if the Mohawks would make peace with the Mahicans and the Sokokis and other northern Indians. Mahican, Sokoki, and Pocumtuck chiefs assembled at Hartford to talk peace, but news of a Mohawk raiding party near Norwottuck aborted the proposed negotiations. The Mohawks and Mahicans made peace, but, urged on by a delegation of Pennacooks and Pascataways, the New England chiefs voted against peace, and raiding parties went out against the Mohawks. During the summer it was rumored that a huge Iroquois army was moving east, and Gordon Day suspects it may have struck Pennacook. A year later, in 1667, Indians from the Connecticut Valley joined Abenakis from the Kennebec River to resume raids on the Mohawk villages.[42]

Hard pressed by their many enemies, the Iroquois in 1667 made a peace with the French that lasted for more than a decade.[43] But raids from Indian New England continued. In the summer of 1669 the Massachusetts sachem Wampatuck (or Chickataubut) and 600 or 700 warriors invaded Iroquoia and laid siege to Gandouagué, the easternmost Mohawk village. Unable to take the village, the Algonquians withdrew. Whereupon they fell into a Mohawk ambush. A bitter struggle ensued in which both sides suffered heavy losses.[44] Sporadic hostilities between the Mohawks and the Mahicans continued throughout the late 1660s, although a peace was made in 1670 between the Mohawks, the Mahicans, and northern Indians.[45]

In December 1671 the Mohawks and some Connecticut Valley chiefs agreed to try and make a peace under Anglo-Dutch auspices, but there is no record of a real peace being concluded, nor of further significant conflict before 1675.[46] In that year, under pressure from Albany, the Mohawks and the Mahicans made peace again,[47] but neither tribe had a chance to enjoy the respite, as each soon became embroiled in King Philip's War. The Sokokis of Squakheag evidently saw the arrival of whites from the south as some protection against the Mohawks, and many returned to their old lands and reset their wigwams near to the English settlers. But this situation too was short-lived, and the Indians disappeared again when King Philip's War erupted.[48]

The western Abenakis felt the reverberations of wars raging around their homelands in the first seventy years of the seventeenth century. They fought against Algonquins and Mohawks, ventured north and west to raid enemy territory, and dispersed and sought refuge from Iroquois attacks. The Iroquois were the major threat to the French and the other Indians. The governor of New France feared that the Iroquois intended to destroy all the Indian nations allied to France, wipe out the mission villages, disrupt the fur trade, and ruin the colony. He urged that "the utmost efforts must be made to prevent them from ruining the nations, as they have heretofore ruined the Algonquins, Andastaz, Loups, Abenaquis, and others, whose remnants we have at the settlements of Sillery, Laurette, Lake Champlain, and others, scattered among us."[49]

Despite recurrent truces between Mohawks and "North Indians," the Iroquois threat remained strong through the end of the century. Sokokis and Abenakis accompanied Lefevbfre de La Barre's expedition against the Senecas in 1684. Jacques Paquin, curé of St. Francis du Lac and missionary to the Abenakis from 1815 to 1821, recounted the tradition that the Iroquois scattered a village of Sokokis and Loups as late as 1690 and sent the survivors fleeing to St. Francis for refuge, and Iroquois raiders struck St. Francis itself that year.[50] But the destruction of the Pequots in 1637 had given warning of a dangerous and growing power in the south. By the late seventeenth century the English threat had replaced the Mohawk threat as the major factor governing the location, composition, and survival of Indian groups in Vermont. Before long the western Abenakis were caught in a new era of imperial warfare in which European rivals on the north and south competed in the North American phase of a struggle for global supremacy. The Sokokis who took refuge in French mission villages along the St. Lawrence would be joined by repeated influxes of neighboring peoples in the ensuing century of conflict.

Chapter 4

King Philip's War and the Great Dispersals, 1675–1677

King Philip's War initiated a new era in which the western Abenakis confronted the direct effects of the English invasion. The war scattered the tribes of southern New England and sent shock waves reverberating up the Connecticut Valley and across the Green Mountains. The fighting touched the edges of the western Abenaki territory, some western Abenaki warriors took an active part in the conflict, and western Abenakis continued to feel the effects of the war long after it was over. The defeat and death of King Philip, or Metacom, initiated what André Sévigny calls "le grand dérangement abénaquis." The hegiras and social fragmentation generated by the war dwarfed the disruptions caused by the Mohawk campaigns in the previous decade, and it is impossible to reconstruct the mosaic of Abenaki dispersal without proper appreciation of the conflict and its consequences.[1]

By 1670 the Indian communities that had nestled in the middle Connecticut Valley were scattered and broken. The Sokokis' military power had disintegrated, and the once-flourishing communities of Squakheag and Pocumtuck never revived.[2] When the first English settlers pushed upriver to Northfield around 1670, they found only a core community of twenty or thirty Indians living there, on both sides of the river. But, in what was to become a common pattern among the western Abenakis in the aftermath of catastrophe, some Sokokis quietly moved back to their old lands, reset their wigwams, and resumed their lives alongside the newcomers. In July 1673 a woman, identified as "the daughter of Sowanett who was the true and Proper owner of that Parsell of Land," and three other Indians sold a tract of land at Squak-heag to Joseph Parsons and William Clark of Northampton for 200 fathoms of wampum. When King Philip's War erupted in 1675, the remaining Indians disappeared as quickly and quietly as they had come, withdrawing before the approaching storm. Many joined Metacom's forces and returned with them to Squak-heag after the settlers had evacuated the area.[3]

King Philip's War broke out in the south as the Wampanoags struck back against English expansion. It spread as the Nipmucks of central Massachusetts and Indians from farther up the Con-necticut River joined in the war effort. Squakheag and its vicinity became a center of Indian operations during the war and at-tracted Indians from throughout New England. In the autumn of 1675 a body of "River Indians" were encamped in the pine-woods at South Vernon. Following the Puritan army's destruc-tion of their stronghold in December, Narragansetts from Rhode Island arrived at Squakheag to join the gathering forces. Accord-ing to nineteenth-century historian George Sheldon, the Indians also established winter quarters in the valleys of southwestern Vermont near Manchester and Sunderland, where warriors from various tribes congregated in preparation for the spring offensive.[4]

The Wampanoag chief, King Philip, or Metacom, spent the winter of 1675 at Schaghticoke, but, according to an English cap-tive released by the Indians, another "mighty Sachem" held a ren-dezvous near the Hoosic River. Although hundreds of well-armed young warriors attended, including "about 500 of those with Straws about their Noses, commonly called French Indi-ans," Metacom and his men were not there. In fact, Metacom was said to have little authority among these warriors. The North Indians behaved contemptuously at the rendezvous and, "in a va-pouring Manner, declared, that their Intent was, first to destroy Connecticut this spring, then Boston in the Harvest, and after-wards the Dutch." Gordon Day suggests warriors from Mis-sisquoi may well have been among these northern visitors. The North Indians later gave the English captive to the Mahicans, or River Indians, "who have been always suspected to be too kinde to those bloody Ones of the North."[5]

At this point, however, Governor Edmund Andros of New York, instigated and armed the Mohawks to strike a decisive blow against Metacom and his allies. The Mohawks were said to be "the only Persons likely to put an End to the War, by hindering the Enemy from Planting; and forcing them down upon us." The Mohawks needed little prompting to fall upon their old enemies, and in a surprise attack they scattered the army Metacom had assembled. They "marched out very strong, in a warlike Posture upon them, putting them to Flight, and pursuing them as far as Hossicke River . . . killing divers, and bringing away some Prisoners with great Pride and Triumph." This sudden and unexpected catastrophe "did very much daunt and discourage the said Northern Indians; so that some hundreds came in and submitted themselves to the English . . . and Philip himself is run skulking away into some Swamp, with not above ten Men attending him." In fact, Metacom fled across the Green Mountains with a few followers, reaching Squakheag late in February 1676.[6]

By early spring almost 3,000 warriors had gathered in the Squakheag region, around Vernon, Vermont. The assembly of Wampanoags, Pocumtucks, Nonotucks, Agawams, Quaboags, Nashaways, Naticks, Hassanamesetts, and Sokokis, under the leadership of Metacom, Cononchet, and Pessacus, made this the most important Indian gathering in southern Vermont on record. Captive Mary Rowlandson was awed by the "numerous crew of pagans" that she saw preparing for the final onslaught against the English settlements. Reminded, like many others in similar situations, of Psalm 137, Mary too broke down and wept "by the waters of Babylon." Despite the Indians' efforts to comfort her, Mary remained unconsolable and resolute, even refusing Metacom's invitation to smoke. Although formerly a pipe smoker herself, Mary now regarded tobacco as the Devil's bait. Her reflective comment on the Wampanoag chief's considerate treatment was, "Surely there are many who may be better employed than to sit sucking a stinking tobacco pipe."[7]

Metacom soon moved his headquarters to Mount Wachusett, and, at the beginning of May, the Indians who had assembled in the Squakheag country dispersed. One group, which probably comprised mainly Sokokis, gathered at the Pasquamscut falls for the spring fishing. In a battle that gave the town of Turners Falls, Massachusetts, its name, Captain William Turner's command from Hadley attacked them in mid-May. Turner's men surprised the sleeping Indians before dawn, "so that our Souldiers came and put their Guns into their Wigwams . . . and made a great and notable slaughter among them." Nathaniel Saltonstall reported that several hundred Indians perished, "they being out of any Posture or Order to make any formidable Resistance," and the English destroyed their ammunition and provisions. Many of the Indians were shot down as they attempted to escape across the river. A month later, the English received word "that the greatest number of the enemy are gone towards the head of Connecticut River, where they have planted much corn on the interval lands and seated three forts very advantageously in respect of the difficulty of coming against them."[8]

Benjamin Church's rangers and Indian allies hunted down and killed Metacom in August 1676, but the English created a second war on the northern frontier that persisted long after hostilities had ended in the south and kept Indian bands continually on the move. The same month that Metacom died, the English sent soldiers "to cut down the Indians' corn at Squakheag, etc., which is accordingly done and not any Indians seen thereabouts."[9] The war constituted an ecological disaster for the Abenakis. It disrupted their agricultural, trapping, and trading activities and curtailed the seasonal mobility which was vital to their effective utilization of resources. Faced with the threat of starvation and of continued Mohawk attacks, many Abenakis fled to Canada, where they tried to rebuild their communities around the Jesuit mission villages. Some bands withdrew northward as soon as the war broke out, and the first group of Sokokis arrived at Three Rivers in the spring of 1676 after an arduous winter journey during which famine took its toll on their numbers. From the French point of view, the Indian exodus was a fortunate, even a divinely ordained, event:

> At the very beginning of the war that the abnakis have waged with the English, many Of them, dreading Its consequences, Resolved to take Refuge in the country inhabited by the french. They thus

advanced, without realizing it, toward their own blessedness, in coming to the missionaries, who could not have gone to them in their country. Two tribes especially—namely that called the Sokokis, and that of the Abnakis—carried out that design, and set out upon their Journey about the beginning of The summer of The year 1675.

Most of the Indians who headed for Three Rivers were Sokokis, and the Abenakis found shelter at Sillery. No sooner had they arrived than the Jesuits "talked with them about their salvation and about the mysteries of our Religion." Other Sokokis moved to the west and, along with many Pocumtucks, took up residence at the village of Schaghticoke on the Hudson.[10]

Dislodged from their homelands, other Indians found their way farther afield. Mahicans and other "Loups" had been visiting the Midwest since about 1669 and seem to have obtained permission from the Miamis and the Ottawas to hunt on their lands. A number of Abenakis, Sokokis, and "Loups" accompanied the French explorer René-Robert Cavalier de La Salle on his expedition to the Great Lakes and down the Mississippi in the early 1680s, and some remained in the Midwest. Some Sokokis and Mahicans were adopted by the Sacs and Foxes in the seventeenth century; others were living in Miami and Potawatomi villages near southern Lake Michigan in 1700. When the Sieur de Courtemanche arrived at the St. Joseph's River in December of that year to negotiate with France's Great Lakes allies, he found Sokokis and Mahicans there alongside the Miamis, the Potawatomis, the Foxes, and the Hurons. These people probably blended into the melting pot of Great Lakes tribes, but they established contacts that facilitated the Abenaki acquisition of the calumet ceremony from the Foxes in the mideighteenth century.[11]

The war by no means produced a complete exodus. Some displaced Sokokis returned to their Squakheag homes. Many lingered in southern Vermont long after the dispersal of their community, quietly frequenting the Connecticut Valley and maintaining contacts with their relatives who had moved north and gravitated toward Missisquoi and other centers.[12]

The Sokokis' eastern neighbors, the Pennacooks, suffered a

similar displacement as a result of King Philip's War, even though they tried to avoid entanglement in that conflict. The Pennacook chief, Wanalancet, tried to continue the course of neutrality that his father, Passaconaway, had embarked upon some forty years before. When the war broke out, Wanalancet led part of his people to more remote places in the woods around Pennacook where they would be less vulnerable to attack, and he refused English entreaties to return. An English expedition marched up the Merrimack, and, finding no Indians at Pennacook, they burned the wigwams and destroyed the stores of cured fish that the Pennacooks had prepared for the winter. Wanalancet and his people retreated deeper into the woods. Messengers searching for Wanalancet that fall were told he had gone to Winnipesaukee. It is possible that the Pennacooks spent the winter of 1675–76 in Canada and returned to their village the following summer, but they probably retreated no farther north than the upper reaches of the Merrimack or Connecticut rivers, and they may have regrouped at a seasonal camping ground near Lake Winnipesaukee. The Pennacooks remained neutral, and Wanalancet himself returned to the Merrimack at the end of the war and made a treaty of friendship with the English in the summer of 1676. But many of Metacom's defeated followers also went into hiding in the upper Merrimack Valley. Some concealed themselves among the Pennacooks; others sought refuge among the Ossipees and Pigwackets, who had already made peace. English efforts to hunt the refugees down generated further dislocation. Some Pennacooks made for Schaghticoke, following Major Waldron's infamous seizure, during peace talks at Dover, of some 200 Indians "who had fled hither for protection." In November 1676, in a pattern to be repeated many times during the next hundred years, an English expedition marched four days through difficult terrain to Ossipee only to find the Indian "fort" there deserted, although it was reported that about 100 Indians had been there a few days before. In 1677, Wanalancet and many of his people resumed their migration northward, probably following the route from the Connecticut River to Lake Memphremagog and then to the St. Francis River, although they were to return to the Merrimack in later years.[13]

The Pennacook refugees came under French influence, and they were among the first Abenakis to arrive at Sillery, but that did not mean that they were tied down in their new locations or that they had completely abandoned their old haunts. Father Henri Nouvel, the Jesuit superior of the Ottawa missions, encountered some Pennacooks near Lake Huron in the winter of 1675–76. They had married Algonquin and Nipissing women from the missions and followed the fur trade west. When Wanalancet withdrew in 1677, the "warlike portion" of the tribe remained around Pennacook. Kancamagus, nephew of Wanalancet and grandson of Passaconnaway, emerged as their leader as an influx of refugees from the tribes of southern New England increased Pennacook numbers. In 1685, Pennacooks who had been living at Chambly returned south to visit relatives who were still living around Pennacook. About this time Governor Edward Cranfield of New Hampshire planned to employ the Mohawks to disperse this concentration of Indian population. Despite Kancamagus's entreaties, Cranfield did little to alleviate Pennacook fears of renewed Mohawk raids. The Pennacooks harvested their corn and retreated to safety, probably to Lake Winnipesaukee and Lake Ossipee. Kancamagus and his band withdrew east to the Androscoggin and could not be induced to return until the English signed a treaty assuring them of protection from Mohawk attacks. Only a handful of Pennacooks remained at Pennacook, and there is evidence to suggest that a group of Pennacooks had settled on Lake Champlain by 1687.[14]

King Philip's War resulted in the creation of a new multitribal community in the upper Hudson Valley that acted as a magnet for Indians throughout Vermont and northern New England and as a feeder for other Indian villages farther north. In an effort to strengthen his colony and to halt the exodus of Indians to New France at the end of the war, Governor Andros of New York encouraged settlement at Schaghticoke near the mouth of the Hoosic River and offered asylum to any Indians who wished to place themselves under his protection. He was urged on by reports that "the ffrench do receive North Indyans under their Protection, and its said, that five hundred of them are already there." In the first year, over 200 survivors of tribes scattered during the war took refuge at Schaghticoke, and the results encouraged Andros's successors to accelerate recruitment. Located in Mahican territory, the village probably had a Mahican substratum, but a new social order emerged as Sokokis, Pocumtucks, Nonotucks, Woronokes, Agawams, Pennacooks, Narragansetts, Nipmucks, and Wampanoags congregated on the east bank of the Hudson. Tribal identities became confused, and the English referred to all Indians at Schaghticoke as "River Indians," although the neighboring Mohawks distinguished between the original Mahican inhabitants and the newcomers. The Schaghticoke Indians retained close connections with their Abenaki relatives throughout the eighty years of the Schaghticoke community's existence.[15]

Schaghticoke played a pivotal role in the Anglo-French contest for western Abenaki allegiance. The French hoped to attract Indians from Vermont, Maine, and New Hampshire; and "Loups" and Abenakis already living in Canada tried to convince their relatives at Schaghticoke to move north and join them. The English meanwhile tried to draw more Indians to Schaghticoke, and successive governors of New York asked the Indians living there to encourage their relatives on the north and east to settle on the Hudson. In 1685, 156 men, women, and children, under a sachem named Sadochquis, returned from Canada to take up residence at Schaghticoke. Schaghticoke Indians repeatedly assured the English of their gratitude and their determination to stay where they were, pointing out that those who left for Canada comprised no more than a handful of malcontents. But growing English pressure, combined with unfair dealings by Albany traders, prompted increasing numbers to leave Schaghticoke. Many drifted north to Lake Champlain and the St. Lawrence Valley; some later migrated west to Pennsylvania.[16]

Schaghticoke was not the only community that functioned as a melting pot for various refugee bands but eventually became a departure point for Indians moving on into Canada or northern Vermont. The Great Oxbow of the Connecticut River near Newbury was a center of Indian habitation, activity, and movement. When English captives passed through the area in the early 1700s, the meadows on both sides of the river were cleared and cultivated, and early settlers found the remains of an Indian village.

Cowass may have been the site of more than one village or the location of a "central headquarters" for various bands throughout the area. The Cowasuck tribe itself probably numbered at least 300, but that figure would have fluctuated as different groups passed in and out of the vicinity. Cowass was a pivotal region halfway between Canada and the Atlantic coast and the junction of several Indian trails, and various bands utilized the area for its good fishing and fertile soil.[17]

It is not clear whether Cowass was an ancient community, but refugees from villages farther south which had been dispersed by King Philip's War certainly added to its population and altered its composition. Cowass was a logical stopping place for Indians migrating up the Connecticut. From there, they could ascend the Wells River and cross the Green Mountains to the Champlain Valley, or continue up the Connecticut and make their way to the St. Francis and St. Lawrence rivers. Mahican refugees may have spent some time at Cowass after their defeat by the Mohawks, but there is no reason to assume that the Cowasucks were displaced Mahicans. Some writers feel that Cowass was a Pennacook village, and Pennacooks certainly passed through the area during King Philip's War. Gordon Day believes that Cowass was occupied at least as early as 1663, that the community was established before refugees from King Philip's War arrived, and that the Cowasucks were closely related to the Sokokis. Cowass certainly offered a logical destination to Sokokis withdrawing from Squakheag in 1669. Whatever its original cultural composition, after 1675 Cowass became a refugee village and the nerve center of a region infiltrated by the remnants of various tribes. An area that the English regarded as a "forboding wilderness" afforded a fruitful haven to displaced refugees and transient Indian bands en route to Canada.[18]

In the fall of 1677 a party of twenty Indians led by an Indian war chief named Ashpelon fell upon the town of Hatfield. They were "this Country Indians belonging to Nalvotogy, [Norwottuck]" except for one Narragansett. They had come down from Canada three months before, with half a dozen women, and had been hunting in the area. They took seventeen captives from Hatfield and three more from Deerfield, and then, worried that there might be Mohawks around, they took to their canoes and criss-crossed the Connecticut River northwards until they were about two days' journey above Squakheag, well into Vermont. At that point about half of the group split off and went to Nashaway (Nashua) "to call of[f] some Indians yt have bin there all this time of ye war." The Indians, probably Pennacooks, who had been living at Nashaway promptly "Pluckt up their Stakes having Plenty of fish especially Eeles, & many dryed huckleberrys but noe Corne," and joined the retreating raiders on their way north. Progress was slowed by the women and children, but, traveling in bark canoes and on foot through terrain that the English regarded as impassable, the band made their escape. One of the Indian leaders who had been at Nashaway resolved to head for Canada "yet talkt of making a fort a greate way up the River & abiding there this winter."[19] This fort may have been located at Cowass or higher upriver.

Historians have tended to interpret lack of sightings and confusion of movements as indications that the Indians who were displaced in King Philip's War and subsequent conflicts fled directly to the Jesuit mission villages in New France. But Abenaki exiles who set out for Canada often stopped short when they reached a suitable refuge, namely the remote areas of northern Vermont and New Hampshire. The country around the headwaters of the Connecticut River, which seemed so inhospitable to the English, offered the Indians an advantageous strategic location with easy access to their French allies. The Androscoggin, Saco, Merrimack, and Connecticut rivers all originate in the White Mountains and provided the Indians with great mobility, while across the Green Mountains the Otter, Winooski, and Lamoille rivers connect with the Hudson–Lake Champlain–Richelieu river system. Moreover, the region afforded the Indians a better living than they were to find around mission villages like Sillery. Many Indians who moved north in search of safety found their refuge among the rivers and lakes of northern Vermont and New Hampshire and had little need to go directly to the French mission villages.[20]

On the western side of Vermont, Missisquoi was a nerve center for Indian peoples seeking refuge in the northern Champlain

Valley in the same way that Cowass functioned in the upper Connecticut Valley. The lower Missisquoi Valley was an advantageous location within reach of Lake Champlain, the St. Lawrence River, and Lake Memphremagog. It was rich in resources and yet less exposed to attack than were Otter Creek and the Lamoille and Winooski rivers. The area received a substantial influx of population as a result of King Philip's War, and as Indians from central New England filtered north via Schaghticoke. For Mahicans and Schaghticokes, Lake Champlain represented a natural route of retreat. John C. Huden maintained that Mahicans congregated at the mouths of Winooski River and Otter Creek, and the Winooski Valley seems to have been an area of significant Indian settlement and a favorite resort for hunting and planting. Indians from various Abenaki and Algonquian bands who had been driven west and north by the English began to reach Otter Creek, the Winooski River, and Missisquoi Bay by about 1680. French Governor Frontenac referred to Sokokis on the shore of Lake Champlain in that year, and Sokokis came to be located at Grand Isle and Missisquoi.[21]

By 1682, the French seem to have established a short-lived mission on Lake Champlain.[22] The "Loups" to whom the mission catered were probably Sokokis, Pennacooks, and Mahicans, since the Baron de Lahontan wrote that, prior to his residence at Chambly in 1685, "Soccokis," "Openangos," and "Mahingans" used to visit that place, "in shoals," to trade. These people most likely had retreated to Lake Champlain from their homelands on the Connecticut, Merrimack, and Hudson rivers after King Philip's War, but their presence on the lake did not necessarily indicate a one-way stream of refugees seeking permanent asylum and abandoning their lands in the south. By 1685, the Indians who had been trading at Chambly had returned south to escape Mohawk attacks or persecution by French traders and had taken up residence nearer to the English.[23]

The Abenaki presence around Lake Champlain continued to grow in the eighteenth century, and Missisquoi became the major fortified village and nerve center for numerous small satellite communities. Refugees gradually were assimilated into the original band, and writers began to refer to all Champlain Valley

Abenakis as members of the Missisquoi tribe, while many of the "St. Francis Indians" mentioned by historians came from Missisquoi rather than the Canadian village.[24]

Most of the Indians who made their way north through Vermont in the wake of King Philip's War arrived eventually at the French mission villages in Canada or developed family ties with those who settled there. Migration to these villages was slow and halting, and residence there was often temporary, but for generations population displacements in New England furnished migrants north of the border. The mission villages served as crucibles in which Abenakis and others built new social orders on the ruins of their old tribal communities.[25] The Jesuit mission at Sillery, originally established in 1630 as an experimental community of Christianized Indians, failed because of war, disease, alcoholism, lack of funds, and cultural resistance from the Montagnais and Algonquin neophytes. More and more Abenakis began to settle at the village, and then the 1670s brought a new influx of population, including some Sokokis fleeing the northern front of King Philip's War. The newcomers found the country around Sillery barren compared with the fertile and game filled lands they had left, and many endured hunger and misery in their new homes. Yet large numbers of Abenakis migrated to Sillery between 1681 and 1684. In June 1684 the Baron de Lahontan reported that the villages of Sillery and Sault de la Chaudière sheltered 300 families of Abenakis, and Sillery soon had more inhabitants than it could handle.[26]

Eventually the village of St. Francis, Quebec, emerged as a community of immigrants, but probably not before 1660. The mission of Saint François-de-Sales was established in 1683 on the Chaudière River. In 1700 Father Jacques Bigot moved the mission to the banks of the St. Francis River, where Sokokis and some other Abenakis had already settled. The village has been regarded most commonly as a refuge for Abenakis from Maine, but Charland pointed out that Sokokis preceded the Abenakis at St. Francis. He found only Sokoki names in the registers at Sorel before 1687 and in the St. Francis registers before 1690. Gordon Day has shown that Indians from as many as twenty tribes found their way to St. Francis and that surviving linguistic and cultural traits indicate a predominance of Sokoki, Pennacook, and Cowasuck influences. St. Francis lay in direct reach of the headwaters of the Connecticut and represented a logical place of retreat for Indians traveling through or residing in the northern part of Vermont. The original Sokoki village was strengthened by the migration of more Sokokis and the addition of Pennacooks and other Merrimack River peoples. Eastern Abenakis arrived from the Chaudière mission in 1700, and by the turn of the century, the St. Francis mission was reported to comprise "abnaquis, loups, and sokokis," to whom two priests ministered. Perhaps the single most important source of migrants to St. Francis was Schaghticoke on the Hudson, itself a community of refugees.[27]

With some exceptions, the western Abenakis were spared direct involvement in King Philip's War, but they could not be shielded from the repercussions of that conflict. The neighboring Mohawks and Mahicans were embroiled in the war, warriors from Vermont joined the southern tribes in some of the fighting, and refugees from the war made their weary way into and across Vermont as the war came to its bloody close. The war destroyed forever the power of the Indian tribes of southern New England. The Narragansetts were a remnant of their former strength— "God hath consumed them by the Sword & by Famine and by Sickness," gloated Increase Mather—and other tribes were similarly decimated and scattered like leaves in a gale.[28] The English colonists were on their knees, but they had served grim warning of what the Indians farther north might expect at their hands. Western Abenakis, some already in new homes, looked south to face the English expansion that threatened to engulf their world.

By 1676 Indians in southern New England had fought two major wars against the English and their allies. Directly and indirectly, by deliberate tactics and as an inevitable by-product of new kinds of conflict, the European invaders raised Indian warfare to new levels of ferocity. The Indians found themselves engaged in wars that resembled the bloody campaigns of contemporary Europe more than the traditional combats of native North America. French commanders who invaded Iroquoia in the late seventeenth century tried to bring the Indians to their knees by destroying villages and food supplies. The English created new militia systems and learned from experience that forest combat demanded tactical changes.[29] The lessons of the Pequot and Narragansett experiences were not lost on the western Abenakis. A palisaded village could become a deathtrap when surrounded by English muskets and put to the torch. The English were far less deadly when their mobile Indian enemies used the forest to their advantage. When English expeditions plunged clumsily into the Green Mountains in subsequent wars, the Indians responded not by congregating in assailable villages but by dispersing into the surrounding countryside.

Along the northern front of King Philip's War, refugees from once-autonomous communities dispersed and regrouped in safer locations. Many western Abenakis fled to Canada or withdrew to locations in the northern reaches of their territory. Indians from other areas sought asylum in Vermont. Indian bands and villages in the Green Mountains ceased to be exclusive ethnic or even linguistic units as they accommodated and amalgamated migrants from other regions who brought with them their various cultural and linguistic traits and their particular experiences of contact with the English. Displaced warriors waged wars of reprisal from their new residences. Despite considerable disruption and relocations, the Abenakis retained their hold on Vermont, presenting a formidable barrier to English expansion in the era after King Philip's War had devastated the tribes of southern New England.

Chapter 5

Echoes of Distant Storms, 1688–1715

King Philip's War destroyed Indian power in southern New England, sent shock waves through Indian country, and alerted northern tribes to the English threat. The Mohawks played a decisive role in the defeat of Metacom's forces, but they ceased to outweigh all others as the force to be reckoned with by the western Abenakis. Instead, English power continued to grow and a new era emerged in which European wars cast their deadly pall over Indian America. European colonists tried to bolster their strength with a network of Indian allies while simultaneously trying to undermine the alliances of their adversaries. Colonial authorities in Boston, Albany, Montreal, and Quebec expected the various Indian tribes to perform predetermined roles in wars generated by distant monarchs and ministers. But the western Abenakis, like their eastern Abenaki relatives and their Iroquois neighbors, pursued their own strategies in this cauldron of conflict. Limited alignment with the French in Canada was but one of several policies they adopted as the Champlain and Connecticut valleys echoed to the sound of storms conjured up in the courts of Europe.

Whenever Anglo-French conflict spilled over into North America, Vermont became a thoroughfare for Indian raiding parties and European campaigns. New England colonists lived in fear of Franco-Indian raids and complained bitterly against the use of "savage" allies. Meanwhile, New England's own efforts to secure Indian allies proved relatively fruitless, and colonial efforts at defensive cooperation were inadequate. Every colonial government employed Indian auxiliaries at one time or another. Recruitment of local Indians offered a solution both to pressing manpower problems and the difficulties Europeans faced in waging war in the forests. Indians were easily mobilized and disbanded, could move quickly and live off the land, and were indispensable as scouts and guerilla fighters. The New England colonies persistently tried to enlist the assistance of the Iroquois in their Indian wars, and their efforts increased as they found themselves confronted with elusive northern bands who proved less vulnerable to the search-and-destroy tactics that had stunned the Indians in southern New England. Colonists confronting Abenaki warriors in their own territory found it "very necessary to maintain a number of southern Indians for soldiers, who are best acquainted with the manner of these Indians' skulking fight."[1]

The French in Canada felt similarly threatened by incursions from the south and complained that the English in New York instigated Iroquois raids on their settlements.[2] French policy makers aimed to attract the Sokokis and Loups, "by nature arrant and declared enemies of the Iroquois," toward Quebec, hoping they would carry their peltry trade with them and provide a protective barrier against Iroquois attacks. Abenaki communities that disintegrated in the south reintegrated around Abenaki villages and Catholic missions in the north. In 1690 Governor de Denonville reported that as many as 600 Abenakis from the vicinity of Boston had arrived in a short time at the recently established mission of St. François-de-Sales. On the other hand, the Indians were reluctant to come to the missions unless they could expect to receive protection themselves.[3]

The Abenakis looked to New France for assistance in stemming English advances, but they were not subservient tools of the French. As Kenneth Morrison has shown, the religious dimension helped to win the allegiance of the Maine Abenakis, but the Indians maintained a significant degree of independence from French and English alike. Jesuit missionary Sebastien Rasles said, in reference to the Abenakis, "there is not one savage Tribe that will patiently endure to be regarded as under subjection to any Power whatsoever; it will perhaps call itself an ally, but nothing more." The Abenakis gave their French allies ample evidence that they intended to follow their own course.[4]

The religious and dynastic struggles that bloodied the battle-fields of Europe in the War of the League of Augsburg and the War of the Spanish Succession would have seemed as incomprehensible as they were remote to the western Abenakis. But the North American counterparts of these continental clashes—King William's War, 1689 to 1697, and Queen Anne's War, 1702 to 1713—initiated a new phase of conflict as Indians and Europeans waged raids of attrition that affected the future of North America.

KWW

Even before King William's War broke out, there were ominous signs of conflict in the upper Connecticut Valley. An Indian war party from the north killed five "friendly" Indians near Springfield and six Christians at Northfield, the northernmost English settlement, located at Squakheag. The killers had fled north from New England during King Philip's War. One version presumed them to be Sokokis from New York; New York's Governor Andros felt sure that they had been sent from Canada by Governor Denonville. News of the killings alarmed the English, many of whom assumed that a massive Indian war was brewing. In fact, an Indian, named Magsigpen or Graypoole, provided the fullest information on the killers. Magsigpen had been fighting in Canada with a Mohawk war party, but on their return he left the Iroquois on Lake Champlain and joined a hunting party of Schaghticokes.

As the Schaghticokes traveled home, eleven Indians began to trail them. On reaching the Connecticut River, the strange Indians confronted the Schaghticokes, just as they were about to launch their canoes, and demanded to know who they were. The Schaghticokes identified themselves and asked the northern Indians the same question: "The North Indians said, wee live in Canada, we are goeing to fight by order of the Governour of Canida who told us the Maquaes have done great mischiefe in Canada, therefore goe yow revenge the same, either on Christians or Indians; . . ." The war party and the hunting party traveled down the Connecticut together in uneasy company until they reached "Soquagkeeke, where some Indians live," and Deerfield. Three of the North Indians stayed there with the Schaghticokes, but what became of the others they did not know. The Schaghticokes spread the alarm among the upper Connecticut River towns that there were strange Indians in the region. The leader of the party was a Pennacook, called Wampolack, and his followers had formerly lived in several villages in New England. Some of the group returned to Canada, but the party that had committed the murders apparently lingered in the area. In July 1689 "a parcel of Indians come from the French at Canada" were rumored to be "stalking" around Northfield. Such events made the Squakheag region a hazardous place for Indians and whites alike.[5]

There were still Sokokis at Squakheag at this time. King Philip's War may have resulted in some previously displaced Sokokis being driven back to their home territory, and the reemergence of the old community saw an increase in Squakheag's population in the 1670s and early 1680s. However, four land sales to the English, between 1671 and 1678, reduced the resources available to support this population, and Indians sold tracts of land around Squakheag again in 1686 and 1687. The outbreak of King William's War placed the Squakheag community in the direct path of war parties like that led by Wampolack and slowed trade to a standstill. In the face of such pressures and perils, most Sokokis pulled out, resettling in Canada or northern Vermont along with other refugees and throwing in their lot with the French.[6] A French map, originally published in 1686, placed "nations errantes de Abenaquis Socoquis" as far to the northeast as present-day New Brunswick, Maine, where many individuals stayed and mingled with the local natives. Other individuals took up residence with the Penobscots. Mananset, recorded as a "Sockoquis Commandant" in 1669, was acting as a Penobscot sagamore by 1702.[7]

Indians did not move all in one direction, however. A group of "River Indians" returned south from Canada late in the summer of 1687 and were reported to have received good treatment from the Abenakis, who gave them enough provisions to carry them to the Pennacooks, "where they wanted for nothing." Despite rumors that armed Frenchmen had built a fort at Pennacook, many Pennacooks wanted no part in the conflict. They assured the English that they would remain neutral, and even offered to leave their regular villages and resettle near the English to avoid being caught up in the fighting. Other Pennacooks, however, followed the lead of their resolute war chief, Kancamagus, and joined Saco River Abenakis in attacking Dover, New Hampshire, in 1689. The English pursued them as far as Lake Winnipesaukee, where, according to Cotton Mather, "They kill'd One or Two of the Monsters they Hunted for, and cut down their Corn." Kancamagus and his followers quit the Merrimack Valley and joined bands at the sources of the Saco and Androscoggin rivers. After Benjamin Church attacked a village on the Androscoggin in September 1690, capturing Kancamagus's wife and children, the war chief made peace at Sagadahoc. Other Pennacooks, adherents of Wanalancet and "ever peaceably disposed," were scattered up and down the Merrimack Valley, "few in numbers, dragging out a precarious existence in hunting and fishing and scanty tillage."[8]

The Champlain and St. Lawrence valleys proved to be as dangerous as the Connecticut and Merrimack war zones. Iroquois, Abenaki, and French warriors traveled along old war routes. In August 1689 a massive war party of 1500 Iroquois in 250 canoes fell upon the French settlement at La Chine just seven miles from Montreal, burnt houses and crops, and killed or captured over 100 of the inhabitants. Governor Frontenac badly needed to restore morale and revive French prestige among the tribes as the Iroquois continued to harass his colony. Earlier expeditions into Iroquoia had proved costly and had yielded few dramatic results; so, instead of mounting a punitive expediton against the Iroquois, Frontenac organized a three-pronged offensive against the English colonies on the south.

In the winter and spring of 1690 a party of French and Indians (mainly from Caughnawaga, but including some western Abenakis) went up Lake Champlain, crossed the Hudson River, and sacked the town of Schenectady. Another expedition of twenty-four French, twenty to twenty-four Sokokis, and five Algonquins—led by François, Sieur d'Hertel—left Three Rivers, crossed Lake Memphremagog to the Connecticut River, and, after three months of hard traveling, attacked Salmon Falls on the New Hampshire frontier. One Sokoki and Hertel's nephew died in the raid. A third war party of Canadians and Abenakis struck Casco Bay on the Maine coast. The expeditions marked the beginning of systematic French-directed Indian attacks on the New England settlements, in which Abenakis served as the shock troops of the French war effort.[9]

A Sokoki, who had been held captive in the area, brought news to the French that an Anglo-Iroquois retaliatory campaign had petered out on the shores of Lake Champlain in the summer of 1690. The Iroquois had planned to send hundreds of warriors to rendezvous with the English on Isle La Motte, but, the Iroquois said, "the Great God has stopt their way." Smallpox had swept through the Iroquois tribes, carrying off hundreds of victims. But English and Indian war parties continued to travel the Lake Champlain–Richelieu River route and fight skirmishes against the French and their Indian allies.[10] Such hostilities soon took their toll on Indian communities. Iroquois war parties raided as far as St. Francis in 1690 and in the summer of 1692, and a year later the Indian grapevine even carried a rumor that St. Francis had been destroyed and all its inhabitants killed by Indians from New England. Christian Iroquois living in New France complained in 1692 that they had lost nearly half their number defending the French against their Iroquois relatives and the English.[11]

Delegates from the eastern Indians—the Penobscots, the Kennebecs, the Androscoggins, and the Saco Abenakis—made peace with the English in 1693.[12] But Abenakis from Vermont and Canada continued to fight. Sokokis from Three Rivers and Abenakis from the Falls of the Chaudière participated in the expedition against the Mohawks led that year by Lieutenants Manteth, Courtemanche and Lanoue, and in Frontenac's campaign against the Onondagas in 1696.[13] While Frontenac launched such counterstrokes against Iroquoia, Abenakis from Acadia and the missions along the St. Lawrence kept New England at bay, striking close to Boston and carrying off captives.[14] The English responded with the offer of scalp bounties, ranging from fifty pounds for the scalp of an Indian adult to ten pounds for that of a child, and contemplated employing the Iroquois to fall upon the Abenakis.[15]

Migratory Indians were a source of concern to French and English colonial authorities laboring to keep their defenses intact. In 1691, Governor Henry Sloughter of New York resettled the Schaghticoke Indians at the Half Moon at the mouth of the Mohawk River to strengthen Albany's defenses and, no doubt, keep an eye on Indians who might be wavering in their loyalties.[16] But war and disease took their toll on the Schaghticokes, and a steady trickle of migration northwards drained the village of its military value. Governor Benjamin Fletcher expressed his concern in council, admonishing the River Indians that by becoming dispersed "you become weak and a prey to your Enemies."[17] The "River Indians" were suspected of keeping up constant communication and even joining forces with the hostile eastern Indians under the pretense of hunting on the east, and the Schaghticoke-Abenaki connection caused the New Yorkers continued concern. John Pynchon and others felt that the English had "nourished vipers" by providing refuge to the Schaghticokes, who, they said, were thieves and murderers: "Sometimes they live at Skachkook, sometimes to eastward, intermingling with the Eastern Indians, sometimes in Canada; and they live like beasts of prey upon the destruction of others."[18] In the summer of 1695 a skirmish occurred when Indians from the north fell on a party of Albany Indians hunting on the east bank of the Connecticut River in southern Vermont.[19]

About 800 River Indians still lived in their old homeland in 1689, not counting those mixed with other Indians at Schaghticoke. But the River Indians around Albany dwindled from 250 to 90 men between 1689 and 1698, and the Schaghticokes told the governor of New York that they had not seen the sun during those nine years of bloody warfare, which had reduced them from a strong people to a weak remnant.[20] Migration away from the Hudson continued. Indians from Schaghticoke were reported to have a village two days from Montreal in the direction of Albany (possibly near Missisquoi) in 1696. A group of "Amalingan" Indians, who settled near Norridgewock in the Kennebec Valley and then moved to Acadia in 1696 or 1697, may have been Mahicans from Schaghticoke (or even Mohegans from Connecticut), although Gordon Day thinks it more likely that they were Pennacooks.[21]

The War of the League of Augsburg came to an end with the inconclusive Treaty of Ryswick in 1697, and Europe and North America enjoyed a brief lull in hostilities. For many of the Indian tribes, the five years before the beginning of Queen Anne's War in 1702 were a time of reassessment and readjustment. Movement and temporary relocations continued among some bands, while the tribes took stock of their situation in the light of recent bitter experience.

After their sufferings in King William's War, many Schaghticokes sought less perilous locations. In June 1698, the Earl of Bellomont was instructed "to take some Orders with ye Maquas to call or draw of any of the Scatecooke or other Indians under their Command from Winepesocket the White Hills or the places thereabouts."[22] The English clearly believed that Mohawk influence still extended so far as to reach itinerant bands in White Mountains.

The following winter a band of Schaghticokes settled at "Winooskeek," where the Winooski (Onion) River enters Lake Champlain. The New York authorities immediately took alarm that this defection would place the Indians in the French orbit and mean more enemies in time of war, and they sent messengers to request that the Indians return. The band that had settled at Winooski sent their reply by an Indian named Callolet, who told the New Yorkers that the reason the Schaghticokes had left was that they had had a poor hunt and were hard pressed by Albany traders. Floods had ruined much of the last year's corn harvest and the English had taken most of what was left. The Indians were afraid to return to Schaghticoke:

Our people having caught soe few beaver last winter which will not answer their debts, so that they are afraid to come home, but lye in the lake at a place called Winooksek, where they formerly have dwelt, Doe desire when they doe come that no hurt be done to them.

Callolet urged the New Yorkers not to think ill of the band nor to think they intended to defect to Canada: "They only intend to stay at the said Winooskeek for one yeare to hunt thereabout for beaver to pay our debts when we come home. . . ." The English promptly assured them they would not be mistreated, and urged them "not to creep so neare your late Enemy for a settlement, but return to our own habitation with all speed." As it happened, the Schaghticokes were "warned off" by a party of "Boston Indians" who encountered them on the lake. These Boston Indians may have been Sokokis or fugitive Pennacooks living near Missisquoi. Or they may have been refugees from communities further south. At any rate, they considered Lake Champlain their hunting territory and effectively warned off the intruders.[23]

In 1699 eastern Abenakis agreed to remain neutral in future Anglo-French conflicts. The opening of the new century also saw the Iroquois adopt new policies. Years of intertribal and imperial warfare had brought starvation and suffering to their longhouses. French armies, transported from the mother country, had attempted to bring the Iroquois to their knees by striking at the heart of their homeland. In most cases the Indians withdrew before the invaders and sustained minimal direct casualties, but the destruction of shelter and crops hit hard in Iroquoia. The English failure to provide protection against French incursions caused the Iroquois to seriously reassess their alignment. The mourning war complex which maintained population levels by the adoption of captives was crumbling. At the end of the seventeenth century Iroquois populations in general, and Mohawk numbers in particular, were falling at an alarming rate.[24] The Iroquois war effort in the west, which half a century earlier had smashed the Hurons and scattered the Neutrals and Eries, ground to a halt in defeats at the hands of Ojibwas, Ottawas, and Wyandots.[25] By 1700 Iroquois power had reached nadir.

In the next year, Iroquois statesmen at Onondaga, Montreal, and Albany charted a new course for the confederacy which allowed the Five Nations to recover from twenty years of warfare while accommodating the deep divisions that had developed within the confederacy. In 1701 the Iroquois and Governor Louis Hector Callière met with headmen of the Abenakis, the Algonquins and western tribes to make peace and establish rough boundaries. They agreed to accept French arbitration instead of armed conflict, and the Iroquois undertook to remain neutral in the event of an Anglo-French war. This "Grand Settlement" marked the beginning of a policy of official neutrality that served the Iroquois well until they were dragged into the Seven Years War and then torn apart in civil war during the American Revolution.[26] French missionaries and Mohawk converts at Caughnawaga may have played critical roles in arranging the treaty. Abenakis and Iroquois alike interpreted and remembered the agreement as "submission" by the other party, but the treaty established the basis for future peaceful relations and even laid the groundwork for the creation of the Seven Nations confederacy in later years. After 1700, Caughnawagas became active allies of the Abenakis, and war parties composed of warriors from both tribes became more common.[27]

The turn of the century saw ominous stirrings in the Pennacook country in preparation for renewed war, and growing English concern at that tribe's connections to Canada. Wanalancet, the friend of the English, had died around 1696. In the winter of 1699 a general rendezvous of sachems and principal councillors assembled at Winnipesaukee apparently to form plans for a general confederacy against the English. A Pennacook sachem declared "he had the longest bow that ever was in New England it reached from Penobscot into the Mohawk country," meaning that it embraced all the Indians within that arc and that even the Mohawks might be induced to fight. He said that, when a breach occurred with the English, the French would invite the Indians to join them and would protect them. In the spring of 1700 fifteen Natick Indians were reported to have gone to Pennacook to stir up the Indians, and the Pennacooks sent emissaries to the Kennebec Abenakis to incite them to war. The Kennebecs refused, and the

Pennacooks were too weak to act alone, but an anonymous letter that spring warned the English that "Mischief will be done before these Moonlight nights do pass."[28]

The English feared that, even if the Mohawks were not involved in the planned insurrection, there was good reason to suspect the River Indians at Schaghticoke, although Suckquans, a Schaghticoke sachem, assured them that "if there were windows in his breast and we could see his heart we should find nothing amiss in it."[29] War seemed certain, and Indians from other regions congregated at Pennacook in search of refuge or to join the warriors in preparation for war. Mohawks were reported to be at Pennacook weekly, as well as Indians from Canada and the east, and the Pennacooks appeared to be the prime movers in gearing the tribes for war. While some Pennacooks plotted, others found themselves caught up in the turmoil: "Sabin Menequabben with tears in his Eyes said he was in a great Streight his Family was gone to Pennecook to the other side, and he thought he must go too, And if he did he must fight against the English and that lookt hard." Other Pennacooks declared their continued friendship for the English.[30]

The movement of Indians to Pennacook alarmed the English who feared that the Jesuits had seduced them.[31] In addition, by 1700, a village of refugee Pennacooks and Sokokis, probably together with some Mahicans and Pocumtucks, had grown up near Fort Chambly on the Richelieu River in northern Vermont. From there they traded their pelts to the French. With so many Pennacooks settled around Lake Champlain and carrying their furs to the French, the English became concerned about the "great Indian trade at Canada."[32]

A tug-of-war developed as the English and French vied for the Pennacooks' allegiance. The English encouraged the settlement of various Indian groups at Schaghticoke, just as the French tried to attract them to Sillery and St. Francis, and the resulting contest added to the pressures on Indians in and around Vermont to move west and north. Indian messengers from the Earl of Bellomont carried wampum belts to the Pennacooks and other Abenakis, inviting them to settle at Schaghticoke. The earl hoped to combine the Abenakis, Pennacooks, Schaghticokes, and Iroquois in one league, "by which means I will strengthen our Indians and disappoint the French of those Eastern Indians who were so many swords in their hands against us."[33]

When the English met the "Eastern Indians" (including the Pigwackets under Atecuando) at Casco Bay in June 1701, they voiced their concern at the Indians' connections with the French. The Indians' response reaffirmed the tribes' determination to remain independent and pursue their own interest: "In case we should stop up our roads to Canada many of our Brethren would be hindered from coming over to us, besides many amongst us care not to be deprived of the liberty of going whither they please." The Indians thanked the English for alerting them to the likelihood of war with France; said that they anticipated little need to go to the French, since they would be so well supplied by the English; and promised to use their influence among the Indians in Canada. But they emphasized that "we desire to keep ourselves free, and not to be under the command of any party."[34]

The Pennacooks displayed similar independence. In 1702 the governor of Canada sent a message inviting the Pennacooks to relocate and settle in the French colony. Governor Edward Cornbury in Albany immediately countered with an invitation to the Pennacooks to settle at Schaghticoke. The Pennacooks rejected the French offer, and some moved west to Schaghticoke, but many continued to move back and forth between New England and New France.[35] Promises of protection carried little weight with Indians who saw that "protection" required them to sacrifice their freedom of action and place themselves in a perilous position as a buffer between colliding forces.

In May 1702, England, the Netherlands, and the Hapsburg emperor declared war on Louis XIV of France, who had put his grandson, and the Bourbon dynasty, on the throne of Spain. As the dispute over the Spanish succession flared into open war in Europe and produced Queen Anne's War in North America, New England colonists geared themselves for a revival of border warfare against French and Indian enemies from the north.[36] As in 1690, however, the fragile defenses on New England's northern and western frontiers proved inadequate to the task of protect-

Hertel de Rouville's French and Indian raiders left their supplies at the West River near Brattleboro before making their final onslaught on Deerfield. (National Life Insurance Company, Montpelier)

ing her infant settlements. Indians living on well-worn invasion routes took steps to avoid the coming storm. In the summer of 1703 a group of Indians left Schaghticoke to join the Mohawks. When Major Peter Schuyler intercepted them at Schenectady and advised them against it, they refused to listen to his objections. Declaring that they had suffered enough in the last war and were not about to lose what little they had left, they stalked off "in a Passion" to continue their journey to the Mohawks.[37]

In the winter of 1703 and 1704, Hertel de Rouville led 200 French and 142 Caughnawagas and Abenakis up Lake Champlain, along the Winooski River, and across the Green Mountains to the Connecticut River. Traveling south, they left their supplies at the mouth of the West River near Brattleboro, then completed the final stretch to Deerfield on snowshoes. Two miles from the town they halted, discarded their snowshoes, because the snow had formed a strong crust, and waited for the opportune moment to strike. The raiders were exhausted after an arduous trek of 200 to 300 miles in the dead of winter, but, when they attacked the sleeping town before dawn on the morning of February 29, they took Deerfield completely by surprise. According to Deerfield's minister, John Williams, "the enemy came like a flood upon us." The attackers killed between 40 and 50 people, carried off 109 captives, and left the town smoldering behind them. Retreating up the frozen Connecticut, the party reached the mouth of the West River on the fourth day, where they collected or constructed light sledges to carry their wounded and the captive children. Anxious to escape pursuit and to avoid an impending thaw of the river, the raiders hurried north, and, tomahawking those unable to keep up, set a killing pace that carried them to the mouth of the White River by the ninth day. There they separated. One group crossed the mountains to Lake Champlain, spent two or three days with a band of Indians on Missisquoi Bay, and then continued on to Chambly and St. Francis. Another party headed up the Wells River. When he was redeemed after two and a half years in captivity, the Reverend John Williams produced a graphic account of the event and the march northwards up the frozen Connecticut River. A score of captives died on the twenty-five-day trek to Montreal. The survivors faced an even more severe test at the hands of black-robed Jesuit priests eager for converts. When he preached to his fellow captives at the mouth of the river that bears his name, near Rockingham, Williams chose Lamentations as the text for the first Protestant sermon delivered in Vermont: "The Lord is righteous, for I have rebelled against his commandments; hear I pray you, all people, and behold my sorrow; my virgins and my young men are gone into captivity." As the danger of pursuit abated, the Indians displayed increasing care for their captives. They had killed Williams' wife in the early stages of the flight, but they carried his seven year-old daughter, Eunice, the whole length of the journey and looked after her with "a great deal of tenderness." The other children were drawn along on sleighs, to be ransomed or, like Eunice Williams, adopted into northern Indian communities. In Quebec, Governor Philippe de Rigaud, Marquis de Vaudreuil, voted the raid a complete success and a boost to the Abenakis' confidence in their French allies.[38]

Some of the Indians from the Deerfield raid took their captives to Cowass. There, at a tract of pines near the mouth of the Wells River, with many acres of cleared meadows nearby, they built a camp and planted the meadows with corn.[39] As usual, however, the western Abenakis responded to the outbreak of war by moving to safer locations. The Cowasucks seem to have withdrawn from their village in 1704 and not to have returned for some time. Queen Anne's War disrupted Abenaki subsistence activities, and some bands appealed to the French for help in staving off hunger. The French were eager to have the Abenakis settle among them, "tant pour leur seureté que pour le notre," and to employ them as a barrier protecting the colony against the Iroquois and the English. Some Abenakis accepted French invitations to settle in Canada.[40]

In June 1704 a delegation of Cowasucks visited Governor Vaudreuil in Quebec. Vaudreuil invited them to move north and settle on the St. Lawrence, where they could be better protected against the English. The Cowasucks declined the offer, pointing out that Cowass afforded them a better location for launching attacks against their enemies.[41]

Even as the Cowasuck delegates were turning down Vaudreuil's offer, however, an expedition with five Mohegan Indians, led by Caleb Lyman, was marching north from Northampton against their village. The soldiers had gone "nine Days journey into the Wilderness" when they surprised a party of nine Indians about twenty miles south of Cowass and killed eight of them. News of the attack alarmed the community at Cowass, and, according to Samuel Penhallow, they "immediately forsook their Fort and Corn at Cowassuck, and never return'd to this Day, that we cou'd hear of, to renew their Settlement in that place." Stephen Williams, one of the Deerfield captives, saw Indians coming away from Cowass carrying news of Lyman's attack. The Cowasucks may have fled to Canada and settled at St. Francis for a time. But there was smallpox at St. Francis in the winter of 1704–1705, and it is more likely that they simply retreated to the upper reaches of the Connecticut or to less-accessible interior locations around Lake Memphremagog.[42]

The tribes engaged in the war tended to break up into smaller bands and to move frequently so that the English did not know their whereabouts. Among the lakes and mountains of northern Vermont and New Hampshire the Indians were able to play cat and mouse with the English, quietly slipping away as the enemy approached. The Pigwackets occupied a vast territory on both sides of the Maine–New Hampshire border, but the English knew of only one permanent village. In 1704 Major Winthrop Hilton led a punitive expedition against Pigwacket only to find that the "fort" of about one hundred wigwams had been deserted in haste about six weeks previously. The Indians' corn barns were abandoned, and there was corn scattered around the open doors. When Hilton made a second attempt four years later he again found the village deserted and the Indians "gone clear off." The majority of the Pigwackets had moved to St. Francis, where they remained until Queen Anne's War ended in 1713.[43]

In the spring of 1707, Captain Stoddard and a dozen men from Deerfield tracked some Indians up the French, or Winooski, river. On the shore of Lake Champlain three of Stoddard's men discovered a group of Indians and shot an Indian woman in the back. But when a soldier ran over to cut off her head with his hatchet, he found that he had killed a white captive, "which very much startled him." The party returned home in short order.[44]

In contrast, Abenaki raids met with considerable success. In the fall of 1706, Abenakis boasted to Iroquois and Mahican (Loup) delegates at Albany, "Nos cabanes sont remplis de cheveleures angloises qui flottent au gré du vent" ("Our wigwams are full of English scalps blowing in the wind").[45] War parties of Abenakis from St. Francis and Bécancour, accompanied by French officers, gathered at Missisquoi Bay before descending on the New England frontier. Abenakis joined French and Indian raiders who rendezvoused on the shores of Lake Winnipesaukee in the summer of 1708 and fell on the town of Haverhill some thirty miles north of Boston.[46] Abenakis from St. Francis, Three Rivers, and the northern end of Lake Champlain continued to perform a vital function in defending Montreal against enemy thrusts, and Governor Vaudreuil exploited the close association between the western Abenakis and the Mahicans to secure information on English military preparations from St. Francis Abenakis who visited the Schaghticokes.[47]

Massachusetts and New Hampshire colonists bore the brunt of the Indians' "bloody incursions" and complained that New York not only remained unsupportive but even traded with the "French Indians" while the Iroquois kept their neutrality. The Abenakis themselves drew a distinction between New York and New England. A group of Adgekantekokes (Abenakis) passed through Albany in the summer of 1707 on their way to renew the friendship of the Owenagungas (Abenakis) with the Mohawks. They gave a wampum belt as a token of their friendship to New York, but, when asked about their intentions towards New England, they answered ambiguously and refused to accept a belt that was offered to engage them to make peace with those colonies. In the following winter the Adgekantekokes who hunted near Wood Creek came to Albany and "declar'd that tho' they had another father (meaning the French) yet they desir'd to live in & peace & friendsp. wt ys Govt."[48]

With the English and the French probing each other's defenses in the Champlain Valley, skirmishing on the lake was inevitable. In May 1709, Vaudreuil sent out several small parties of Indians from Montreal in search of prisoners and information. A party of twelve to fifteen Englishmen from Northampton, with two Natick or Mohegan Indians under Captain Benjamin Wright, were on the lake for the same purpose. Forty miles from Fort La Motte they clashed with a party of French and Caughnawagas, and killed and scalped two of them. Making their way home via the Winooski River, the English ran into another group of French and Indians returning home with captives. After a sharp skirmish and an abortive attempt to rescue one of the captives, Wright's men, "considering they were so far in the *Indian* Country, and like to be encompas'd, were forced to make a running Fight." They scattered in the woods, abandoning their packs, and one man who became lost was thought to have starved to death. Wright and his men claimed their foray was a success, and the Massachusetts House of Representatives voted them bounties in recognition of their services in killing, "as they suppose," seven or eight Indians. The French and Indians likewise considered the skirmish a success and followed it up with a raid against Deerfield. The town was alarmed, however, and repulsed the raiders.[49]

Such events were a cause of concern to the River and Schaghticoke Indians around Albany, who feared that the enemy would harass them since they were now few in number and "bare and uncovered" at Schaghticoke. They asked New York Governor Robert Hunter to build them a stockade, both as a defense and to draw back those who had left. Hunter assured them that the enemy would not threaten them at Schaghticoke, promised them a stockade, and urged them not to allow their people to straggle away but to make every effort to persuade those who had already left to return.[50]

The Abenakis who had settled on the St. Lawrence were equally uneasy. In 1711 the threat of Admiral Sir Hovenden Walker's attack on Quebec and General Francis Nicholson's campaign via Lake Champlain caused the Abenakis at St. Francis and Bécancour to evacuate their villages. The warriors sent their women and children to Montreal and Three Rivers, then went to Quebec to help defend the city. An English spy reported that the "indian fort called st franswa" held 260 warriors at the time.[51] When the English fleet met disaster in the St. Lawrence, the two-pronged campaign came to an end, and Vaudreuil dispatched 100 Indians to Lake Champlain to burn the canoes that the enemy had abandoned. Despite the avowed neutrality of the Iroquois, their warriors continued to join English expeditions, and the French were acutely aware of the need to prevent "les Sauvages d'en haut" from going to Albany to trade, since, if those Indians ever made an alliance with the Iroquois, Canada would be lost.[52] The allegiance of the Abenakis along Lake Champlain and the St. Lawrence loomed ever larger in the siege mentality of the French.

Sporadic raids and counter raids continued in the Green and White mountains. The frontier of New England consisted of open villages scattered over 200 miles, and English companies were hard pressed to prevent the Indians' incursions and to destroy their corn, harass their fishing places, and "put them to destress." In the spring of 1711, Colonel Shadrach Walton and two companies of men marched to Lakes Winnipesaukee and Ossipee, well known as favorite Indian resorts for hunting and fishing. But Walton's men saw no Indians and found only a few deserted wigwams, "for being so closely pursued from one place to another, they removed to other Nations, leaving only a few Cut-throats behind which kept the Country in a constant Alarm."[53]

In the spring of 1712, Captain Thomas Baker led a party of men from Deerfield up the Connecticut River, "Designing for Cowass on purpose to Destroy a family or two of Indians that we heard was there." But either Cowass was still deserted or the Indians slipped away, because Baker's men found no sign of them there, although they did kill nine Indians on the upper Merrimack. French maps of 1713 and 1715 show a village at Cowass, marked with the symbol for a mission and labeled as "Koēs, ancien village des loups," which implies that the village was still empty at that time. Gordon Day suspects, however, that Indians reoccupied it as soon as peace was restored. Such filtering back to former habitations was typical of western Abenaki strategy.[54]

In 1713 the Abenakis of St. Francis, "harassés par les guerres continuelles," decided at a council of war to ask their missionary to write to the king and explain the misery that they were suffering. Father Joseph Aubrey agreed with the conditions that the letter be written in both French and Abenaki and that it be addressed to "His Majesty Louis XIV, King of France."[55] But the restoration of peace that same year did not end the Abenakis' suffering.

At the Treaty of Utrecht, Louis XIV kept a Bourbon on the Spanish throne at the expense of surrendering Hudson's Bay, Newfoundland, and Acadia to the English. News of the treaty created considerable alarm among the eastern Abenakis, who immediately sent delegates to Governor Vaudreuil to learn if it was true that the French king had ceded their lands to the English. Henry Masta declared that the Treaty of Utrecht presented the Abenakis with the choice between extermination or expatriation, and André Sévigny saw it as the beginning of a second major stage in the migration of the Abenakis. Confronted with the loss of their lands and the threat of English occcupation, many Abenakis decided to emigrate to the Abenaki villages already in place along the St. Lawrence. Others, however, opted to return to their homelands, and the Abenakis, the Micmacs, and the Malecites retained effective control over Acadia and held off English occupation until the conquest of 1763.[56]

Elsewhere the return of peace saw Abenakis returning home rather than opting for expatriation. Missisquoi remained essentially undisturbed; Cowass was probably reoccupied. The Pennacooks seemed to disappear in the forests of northern New England after 1713. One estimate of Indian populations in New England in 1726 said the Pennacooks were reduced to five men; another ignored them altogether, although Pennacooks around Concord saved the English settlers from starving that winter. Sévigny suggests that after evacuating Pennacook others withdrew up the Merrimack and reassembled at Winnipesaukee, probably a seasonal encampment, where some may have remained well into the middle of the eighteenth century.[57] The low English counts reflected Pennacook invisibility, not Pennacook extinction.

Many Pigwackets also returned to their homes. Father Aubrey's map of 1713 also marks Pigwacket as a "village de Sauvages Chrestiens." In 1715, Atecuando (also known as Athurnando or Squando) and his sixty "Pegouakis" warriors were reported to have been living at St. Francis for the past eight years, but they had returned to their old village to hunt in the winter and plant

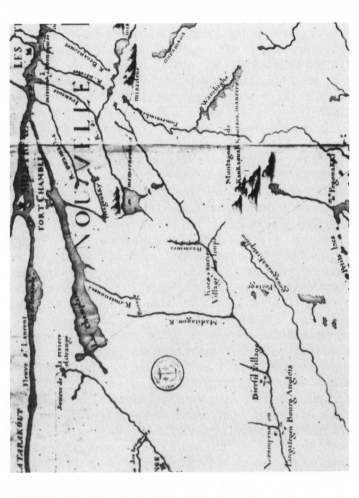

This French map of 1713 shows Koes (Cowass) as a former mission village. (Public Archives of Canada NMC 6359 H3/900/1713)

corn in the spring, before returning to St. Francis in August. Clearly, the Pigwackets withdrew north to avoid entanglement in Queen Anne's War—which explains why Hilton found their village deserted in 1704 and 1708—and began a seasonal return to the village when the fighting ended. The French attempted to discourage Atecuando and warned him that his old village lay only a couple of days' march from the English. Moreover, they said, it would be impossible for him to make his village as large as it had been before, "because many of the people of his former village are scattered in various missions, and a great number of them have died." But the return of peace opened up the possibility of trade with the English and gave the Pigwackets a chance to reoccupy their homeland and village. In October 1716 the Pigwacket chief left St. Francis with twenty-five men, promising to return in the event of renewed war.[58] The composite community at St. Francis was already accustomed to bands arriving and leaving.

The English had only a vague sense of the location, movements, identity, and objectives of western Abenaki bands in the closing years of Queen Anne's War. Abenaki raids were assumed to emanate from Canada under French direction, and Indians in the Green Mountains and on Lake Champlain were lumped together with their northern relatives as "French Indians." A report on the Province of Massachusetts Bay, sent to the Lords of Trade in 1719, identified the Pennacooks, the Androscoggins, the Penobscots, and the Pigwackets, but could say little about the Indians in Vermont: "Northwest and toward Canada there are some Tribes of Indians, but there Situation is so near the French Settlements that we call them the French Indians and they are perfectly under their Governments and at three or four hundred Miles distance from us; their Numbers not very great."[59]

Closer to the Indians, and conscious of their vulnerability, the French took more note of Abenaki movements and motivations and dared not take Abenaki allegiance for granted. Indeed, around 1719, Abenakis at St. Francis seem to have accepted an offer of alliance from the Fox Indians in Wisconsin and joined the Foxes in their calumet ceremony, a ritual cementing of alliance. Since the Foxes were at war with the French, acceptance of the alliance implied Abenaki willingness to support the Fox tribe in that war. The Mahicans may have received a similar request, since in 1721 some Mahicans and Abenakis wanted to move to the Midwest. The Mahicans made their way to Indiana, where they settled among the Miamis on the Kankakee River, but the French, alarmed at the prospect of an Abenaki-Fox alliance, tried to prohibit the Abenakis from going. As usual, the Abenakis could be expected to pursue their own interests.[60]

The English too would soon be compelled to take more notice of western Abenaki motives and movements. In the final years of Queen Anne's War, Grey Lock and his warriors from Missisquoi began to carry the conflict to the Connecticut Valley towns on the Massachusetts frontier.[61] During the next decade Grey Lock focused English attention on Missisquoi and Lake Champlain, and served notice that the western Abenakis were not about to stop fighting just because the French and English had temporarily patched up their differences.

Chapter 6

Grey Lock's War, 1723–1727

Rivalry between England and France dominated northeastern North America in the first half of the eighteenth century, shaping the destinies of Indians and Europeans alike, and New Englanders invariably saw a French impetus behind Indian raids on their northern frontier. However, the border skirmishes that occurred in and around Vermont in the years between 1723 and 1727 dispel the notion that the Indian raiders were merely tools of the French. Sandwiched in time and dwarfed in magnitude by Queen Anne's War (1702–1713) and King George's War (1744–1748), this conflict has received little attention. Known elsewhere as Lovewell's War, Father Rasles' War, and Dummer's War, the Vermont and western phase of the fighting should properly be referred to as Grey Lock's War, after the warrior chief who dictated its pace and character. Grey Lock's War occurred at a time of formal peace between England and France, and Grey Lock's followers operated independently of French allies and of neighboring tribes. They fought for their own reasons, waged their own style of guerilla warfare, and held out for peace on their terms.

Grey Lock's War also illustrated the complexities of Indian-white conflict and the variety of motivations and situations involved. Colonial governments and Indian tribes not directly involved in the war pursued diplomatic goals while avoiding actual conflict. Warriors from the north raided English settlements while other Indians served as scouts and emissaries for the English and even helped to garrison frontier outposts.

The Treaty of Utrecht in 1713 brought peace but did not resolve fundamental issues of Anglo-French or Anglo-Abenaki conflict. Substantial population growth in the English colonies in subsequent years pushed the frontier steadily eastward along the coast of Maine, northward up the Connecticut Valley, and westward into the Berkshires and northwestern Connecticut. The Indians became increasingly alarmed by the advance of the pioneer farmers and the building of English forts, and outraged by the sharp practices of frontier traders. Anglo-Abenaki conferences in 1717 and 1719 did little to reassure them.[1] After years of increasing tensions and eventual hostilities, Governor Samuel Shulte of Massachusetts declared war on the Maine Abenakis in 1722, proclaiming "the said *Eastern Indians*, with their Confederates, to be Robbers, Traitors and Enemies to his Majesty King George."[2] The Abenakis, of course, saw things very differently: in their eyes the war was the inevitable result of repeated English breaches of faith and sustained encroachment on their lands.[3]

Unlike other wars of that era and area, Grey Lock's War never developed into a full-scale conflict involving the English colonies, the French, and their respective Indian allies. Massachusetts and New Hampshire fought the war, and, although New York and other colonies sympathized with their neighbors' plight, they remained on the sidelines. Lack of unity dogged the English colonial war effort for years and gave encouragement to the Indians.[4] The French, for their part, shared the Abenaki view of the war and recognized that their support was crucial to the future of Franco-Abenaki relations, but they were determined not to get involved in the actual fighting. Acting on direct instructions from Louis XV, Governor Vaudreuil secretly encouraged the Abenaki war effort, prompted other tribes to support them, and helped keep the Iroquois neutral, all the time reminding the Indians "that the design of the English is to make themselves masters of the entire continent." The French king established a fund to support Abenaki families who had been forced to retreat to St. Francis and Bécancour, as long as their warriors were actively engaged against the English, and the French carefully monitored war parties emanating from the mission villages.[5]

If English neighbors and French ministers refused to become entangled in the war, so too did the tribes of the Iroquois Confederacy. Commissioners from Massachusetts met with the Five Nations in Albany in the spring and summer of 1723 in an effort to enlist their help in the war, and they reminded the Iroquois that their delegates to Boston had promised to endeavor "to prevent the Merrimack and Meseeskeek Indns Confederating or Acting with the Eastern Indns against us." The commissioners clearly wanted the Iroquois to use their influence to call off the Pennacook and Missisquoi warriors located on the Merrimack River and on the northern parts of Lake Champlain. Moreover, if the Iroquois could be induced to take up the hatchet, other tribes would follow their lead. The Massachusetts government offered presents, arms, and ammunition, as well as substantial scalp bounties "for the further Encouragement of your Warlike people"—one hundred pounds in New England currency for the scalps of males aged twelve and over, fifty pounds for all others. The warriors were also to receive fifty pounds for each prisoner and to be allowed to keep all plunder and all female captives and prisoners under age twelve, in clear recognition of the Iroquois custom of adopting captives to sustain population levels. The Iroquois were certainly in contact with Indians on Lake Champlain, and they sent emissaries northward to inform them of their displeasure that they had taken up the hatchet against the people of New England and to urge them in turn to dissuade the eastern tribes from waging war. They also sent messengers three times to the eastern Indians to counsel peace. They offered to act as mediators in the conflict, but the commissioners had no instructions how to respond to such an offer; it was, they said, "forraign to our Business." Massachusetts wanted war and wanted the Iroquois to serve as scalp-hunting auxiliaries. Yet the Iroquois refused to be bought. Like the Albany government, they would mediate in negotiations, but they were not prepared to be drawn into a war that was not of their making and not in their interests. Similarly reluctant to send their young men against the eastern Indians, the Iroquois explained that to take up the hatchet would bring the Indian allies of Canada's governor down upon them, "and That would Set all the World on Fire."[6]

Grey Lock, Massachusetts's arch enemy in the western theater of the war, became known as the leader of the Missisquoi Indians at the northern end of Lake Champlain, but, in fact, he seems to have been a Woronoke Indian from the Westfield River in Massachusetts. Massachusetts historian George Sheldon described him as "a chieftain of one of the Pocumtuck confederate clans" and a refugee from King Philip's War. A contemporary account called him "Sachem of the Warenokes." In the great dispersal of New England tribes that King Philip's War produced, Grey Lock probably relocated first to Schaghticoke and then to Missisquoi. During Queen Anne's War he was known as a "French Indian" who led small war parties against the settlements on the Connecticut River, and in 1712 he apparently led one of the last raids of the war against the town of Northampton.[7] By 1723, Grey Lock had attracted a following of refugee warriors including discontented Schaghticokes, who were determined to resist English expansion. The warriors frequently operated from Otter Creek, but Grey Lock established his "headquarters" on a small creek some distance from the main village and fields at Missisquoi. Grey Lock's "castle" thus seems to have been a separate composite community of warriors which drew on the main village for manpower.[8]

In the years that followed, Grey Lock left his lair time and again to strike his enemies in the south, and Massachusetts levies proved no match for the war chief. He harried the frontier, depleting Massachusetts's resources, tying up its manpower, and eroding the morale of its citizens. Small war parties of mobile and seemingly invisible warriors filtered silently south through the Green Mountains, waited patiently until the time was right, then struck without warning and retreated from whence they had come before a defense could be organized or a pursuit mounted. Grey Lock acquired the name Wawanolewat, meaning "he who fools the others or puts someone off the track," and the ease with which he eluded pursuit frustrated and demoralized his enemies. Small wonder that Massachusetts tried to enlist Indian help to fight fire with fire. During the war Missisquoi became "a truly legendary place" in the eyes of Grey Lock's enemies. It came to be identified as the major fortified village of the Lake Champlain Abenakis, and it was the target for English expeditions that sought to cripple the enemy by destroying his home base. This English strategy had succeeded in the Pequot War and in King Philip's War, and it succeeded at Norridgewock in 1724 and was to succeed at St. Francis in 1759; but Grey Lock and Missisquoi remained ever elusive.[9]

Early in the spring of 1723, Lieutenant Governor William Dummer of Massachusetts, in conjunction with the military commanders of Hampshire County, attempted to conciliate Grey Lock and other chiefs living near Lake Champlain. Employing Colonel John Schuyler of Albany as an intermediary, Dummer sent gifts, a wampum belt, and the offer of favorable trade terms to Grey Lock; but the chief could not be reached, and in the following months he made his first raids on the northern settlements, keeping the small garrison at Northfield on almost constant alert. On August 13, Grey Lock and four warriors killed two citizens near Northfield. The next day they attacked Joseph Stevens and his four sons as they were haymaking in a meadow near Rutland, Massachusetts. Stevens Senior escaped, but two of the boys were killed, and the other two were captured. The Indians killed another man, the Reverend Joseph Willard, and then hurried north. Grey Lock gave the younger of his captives, Isaac Stevens, to the Caughnawaga Indians, thereby tying them to his interest. The other prisoner, Phineas, was later redeemed and played a prominent role in the French and Indian wars in New Hampshire. When news of the raids reached Boston, Lieutenant Governor Dummer issued orders to Colonel Samuel Partridge to impress eighteen able-bodied and well-armed men to serve as scouts at Northfield, Brookfield, Deerfield, and Sunderland.[10]

In September 1723, Grey Lock was ready to resume the offensive. Initial successes had boosted his following, and it seems that some warriors from Caughnawaga had joined him. At 5:00 P.M. on the evening of September 8 the Albany commissioners sent an express to Massachusetts with

Erected as a defense against Grey Lock's raids, Fort Dummer was garrisoned by Indians and English. (National Life Insurance Company, Montpelier)

the Surprising news that fifty Indians from Canada were about 8
days ago in the Lake at the Otter Creek with a design to fall on
Some of your settlement we think it our Duty to acquaint you
with this Intelligence without any Loss of Time, hoping that you
may be on your Guard at the fronteers to frustrate the Barbarous
and Bloody Designs of these Inhumane Brutes whose mercy is
nothing but Cruelty we shall be glad to hear that this Indian War
may soon cease that Christians may not be murthered and fall as
a prey to those Savages.[11]

While the governor put troops on alert throughout the Connecticut Valley, Grey Lock bided his time and then, on the morning
of October 9, struck two small forts near Northfield, inflicting
casualties and carrying off one captive. Hopes that a force of Indian auxiliaries might intercept the raiders at Otter Creek proved
empty: Grey Lock was long gone before such a force could be
raised and despatched. Warriors from St. Francis and Bécancour
also raided the Massachusetts frontier, killing settlers, burning
buildings, and carrying off captives, while sustaining little or
no injury to themselves.[12] The raids sparked a series of defensive measures. Colonel Partridge moved troops to Deerfield and
Northfield, and Lieutenant Governor Dummer sent a request for
help to Connecticut. In November, Joseph Kellogg, a former captive of the Indians and French, was granted a captain's commission with orders to raise a company of soldiers, forty of whom
were to be stationed at Northfield and the rest to scout the Connecticut River.[13]

In December 1723, Benjamin Wright submitted a request to
assemble a command of 35 to 40 men to pursue the enemy as far
as Otter Creek, cross to the White River, and return home down
the Connecticut; but nothing seems to have come of the pro-
posal.[14] Two days after Christmas the Massachusetts legislature
voted to build a blockhouse above Northfield "and to post in it
40 able men, English and Western Indians, to be employed in
scouting a good distance up Connecticut River, West River, Otter Creek, and sometimes eastwardly above Great Monadnock for
the discovery of the enemy coming toward any frontier towns."
The blockhouse was constructed near Brattleboro and named

Fort Dummer. Efforts to enlist the Mohawks as soldiers for the fort's defense proved fruitless, but the original muster roll of 1724 showed that, of the 55 men who garrisoned the fort under Captain Timothy Dwight, a dozen were Indians. Some were Mohawks; others, probably Mahicans, came from the Hudson River; and another was from Schaghticoke. The two Indian sachems were paid two shillings a day.[15]

Grey Lock's War developed into a contest waged between two fortresses at opposite ends of Vermont. On the north Missisquoi and Otter Creek served as bases for Abenaki forays against the English settlements. On the south Fort Dummer protected the settlements. The English found that the only means of defense against skilled and mobile enemies was to take the offensive and adopt a strategy of scouting out and destroying Indian villages and crops. Fort Dummer became the major base of operations for scouting and punitive expeditions into Abenaki country, but the strategy proved inadequate to the task of defeating the Indians, especially so long as the colonial war effort remained plagued by disunity. The best Captain Dwight could do was to try and intercept the enemy, and he despatched scouting parties "up ye West River Mountain and there to Lodge on ye top and view Evening and Morning for smoak, and from thence up to ye mountain at ye Great Falls [Fall Mountain, across the river from Bellows Falls] and there also to Lodge on ye top and view morning and evening for smoaks." Joseph Kellogg likewise despatched scouting parties from Northfield up the Connecticut and West rivers looking for signs of enemy activity.[16]

In June 1724, Samuel Dickinson, who had been taken captive from Northfield in October, arrived in Albany from Canada with two companions. They reported that Grey Lock and eleven warriors were heading south to raid New England's frontiers. Another war party of thirty Abenakis had set out immediately after Grey Lock's. Dickinson and his companion had eluded this second war party at the north end of Lake Champlain, but warned that about forty more "have sung their War Songs, and are preparing to goe out." Dickinson also reported that about ten Caughnawagas were in favor of the war, despite the opposition of their sachems. The authorities in Albany also sent word to the

Massachusetts frontier that "a party of seven Caughnawaga Indns were 13 days hence at the Otter Creek in the Lake wt an Intent to go Skulking to N England" and were out with several parties of eastern Indians.[17]

On June 18, Grey Lock attacked a group of men working in a meadow near Hatfield. A hastily organized party of seventeen men from the town pursued the raiders as far as Otter Creek, but returned empty-handed and emaciated. Instead of fleeing northward as expected, Grey Lock had retired a short distance to the west, and he spent the summer prowling around the settlements, killing men at Deerfield, Northfield, and Westfield. A company of men under Captain Thomas Wells went in search of the raiders up the Connecticut River but, finding no trace of them, headed home to Deerfield. When only a few miles from home, three of the men, "Supposing themselves out of Danger," rode ahead of the main body and promptly fell into an ambush near a swamp. Their companions arrived at the scene in time to catch sight of the Indians lifting the scalps of their victims. There was a brief skirmish and the Abenakis fled into the swamp. The English "trackt them a considerable way by the Blood of the wounded," but, though they believed they had killed two of the raiders and maimed a third, the men from Deerfield saw no more of the enemy.[18]

The war with the Abenakis was taking its toll on Massachusetts. In July 1724, Lieutenant Governor Dummer wrote again to Governor Gurdon Saltonstall of Connecticut to repeat his request for military assistance on the western frontiers. Summer was the Indians' preferred season for raiding, and reports "that there is not now an Indian Man to be seen in such places as they use to frequent gives us strong grounds to conclude they are preparing to make a Violent effort on some place or other." Connecticut had not declared war on the Indians, but, Dummer reminded Saltonstall, the king's subjects were all in the same boat when it came to defending themselves, "especially inasmuch as our Western Towns are the immediate Barrier & Cover to yours & that if ours should be broken up or drawn off, yours would be exposed to the Fury & Ravages of the Enemy in the same manner as ours now are." The reinforcements that Dummer had sent to the town garrisons were insufficient "to give the Enemy a warm Repulse," and he requested 100 men from Connecticut, to be posted at Northfield, Deerfield, and Westfield until the danger had passed. He asked in particular that some of the men be "trusty Indians" familiar with the woods. Connecticut had 200 men ready to march, but Dummer knew from grim experience that that kind of strategy was worthless,

> for you are sensible that the Indians alwaies make a Sudden onset & then retire forthwith so that if your forces remain as they now are before they can be got together & march to the places attackt the enemy will probably be got out of reach & so it will be too late to follow them.

This time Saltonstall responded, sending a total of 105 men and 42 Mohegan scouts. Employing Indians caused problems of identification, and some Indian scouts wore emblems to ensure that they would be distinguished from the enemy.[19]

Despite the reinforcements from Connecticut, the frontier settlers lived in fear that summer, knowing that the enemy was "lurking about, waiting to shed blood." Men went to work on the harvest in groups of thirty or forty, accompanied by armed guards. In July, Dummer appointed Edmund Goffe commander of the western frontiers with orders to perform the dual functions of "Guarding the Inhabitants in their Husbandry & Scouting on the Borders of the sevl Towns in order to Discover & Repel any approaching Enemy." Goffe was to send scouting parties to scour the countryside between the Merrimack and the Connecticut and engage any war parties that they encountered, while at the same time leaving enough soldiers to protect the towns.[20] Even with reinforcements, the colonists clearly were hard pressed to be on the defensive and the offensive against an enemy who seemed capable of striking at will.

Grey Lock, meanwhile, continued to attract recruits. Indians from Schaghticoke and adjoining areas moved north to Missisquoi, where, according to the Albany commissioners, they fell under the influence of "some base Indians" who turned them against the people of New England. The Schaghticokes who remained asserted that those Indians who had gone to Canada were "an Evil Sort of people" who wanted to avoid paying their debts to merchants in Albany. Nevertheless, the defection of the Schaghticokes was particularly worrying, because those Indians knew the valley and the disposition of the settlements so well "that they would be able to take great advantage against our people." The commissioners despatched Indian emissaries with a wampum belt to invite the deserters to return to Schaghticoke, where they could be kept under observation and out of the way of creating mischief on the frontiers. But Schaghticokes took an active part in the war, and an Indian named Schaschanaemp, who figured prominently in raids on New England's frontier, was believed to be one of the deserters from Schaghticoke.[21]

In August the colonists inflicted a telling defeat on the eastern Abenakis when they destroyed the village of Norridgewock and killed the influential French priest, Father Rasles. One hundred and fifty refugees from the smoldering village arrived in Canada "in a deplorable condition." The French received them and helped them to settle at St. Francis and Bécancour, adding their manpower to the ongoing war effort of the two mission villages. The Norridgewock refugees represented a new influx of Abenakis to the community of St. Francis, although this was not the first time Norridgewocks had relocated to St. Francis and some of them returned to their village and rebuilt their cabins in 1725.[22]

The western frontiers enjoyed no respite, however. Lieutenant Governor Benning Wentworth of New Hampshire reported that, despite the victory at Norridgewock, the Indian war was taking a heavy toll on his province. Ten percent of the population were constantly on guard duty, yet someone was killed or taken captive every week. Writing to the Massachusetts agents in London, Captain Kellogg of Northfield reported that Governor Vaudreuil of Canada had drawn distant western tribes into the Indian confederacy and that the colony's western frontier had suffered almost continual annoyance, "and although we have had great advantage over ye eastern Indians by such a slaughter of them at Norridgewock as has not been known in any of ye late wars, yet by this junction of the western tribes the enemy is become more formidable than before." The demands of the war had impoverished the whole province, and many inhabitants sought refuge in neighboring colonies, which, with the exception of New Hampshire and Connecticut, "being in perfect peace and prosperity themselves sit still and see us languishing under all the calamities of war without affording us the succor of either men or money." Meanwhile, the Iroquois continued to find pretenses for not entering the war. The day after Kellogg penned his report, Fort Dummer fended off an attack by a large Indian war party.[23]

Early in November, Grey Lock retired to Missisquoi. No longer preoccupied with having to guard farmers, Kellogg was able to send his scouting parties farther afield, up to Mount Monadnock and deeper into southern Vermont. But the respite was temporary, and the governor ordered every town to organize snowshoe companies to be ready for renewed raids in January and February, when the Indian raiders would be able to travel on snowshoes.[24]

The victory at Norridgewock stood as a reminder to the colonists of what they could accomplish if they could strike the Indians at their home base. Captain John Lovewell's ambush and annihilation of an Indian war party of ten men east of Lake Winnipesaukee in the winter and his pyrrhic victory over the Pigwackets in the spring of 1725 gave further hope for success if the Indians could be pinned down in battle. As 1725 opened, military expeditions were proposed against Indian villages at St. Francis, at the head of the Connecticut River, on the Ammonoosuc River, and at Grey Lock's fort. Meanwhile, however, Massachusetts and New Hampshire had sent a three-man diplomatic mission to Montreal to negotiate for the return of captives, and Colonel John Stoddard feared that any military operations would jeopardize the chances of that mission: "if our people had gone to Gray Lock's fort . . . and had made spoil upon the Indians, those that escaped would in their rage meditate revenge upon our commissioners, either in going to or returning from Canada." The springtime, when the commissioners were safely returned and the Indians were planting their corn, would be the best time for the projected expeditions.[25]

Accordingly, a series of expeditions ventured north in the

spring of 1725. The Pennacook River was known as a region "where some Indians live who have ever been the Worst Enemies to our People," and scouting parties probed the upper Merrimack River past the Pennacook fortress and into the region around Lake Winnipesaukee. Setting out on snowshoes in March, Captain Thomas Wells led a party of men from Deerfield, Hatfield, and Northampton on what proved to be an abortive mission in search of Grey Lock. After about a month in the wilderness the expedition ended in tragedy: returning home down the Connecticut, three men drowned when their canoe capsized at the falls just below the mouth of Miller's River. As soon as Wells withdrew, Grey Lock's warriors left their winter quarters and traveled south to harry the settlements.[26]

Frustrated by an enemy who seemed to be able to strike at will, Captain Benjamin Wright recruited a company of fifty-nine men and, on July 27, left Northfield determined to carry the war to Missisquoi. They mended their canoes at Fort Dummer, carried them around the Great Falls at Bellows Falls, and were at the White River by August 2. From there they journeyed upriver to Cowass and the mouth of the Wells River and, following the path of Indian raiding parties, headed west by northwest through "very bad woods." Men became sick and lame before the party came in sight of Lake Champlain. Delayed by rain and with virtually no provisions, the party got no farther than the Winooski River. The prospect of further hard traveling to the northern end of the lake proved daunting, and, on August 23, the men turned toward home without seeing an enemy. Two days later, as they approached the mouth of the Wells River, they saw three Indians in the distance, but mistook them for their own Indian scouts who had gone out hunting that morning. By the time they realized their mistake, the enemy had slipped back into the woods. Wright made it back to Northfield at the end of the month, but his retreat had not gone unwatched. Late in August, Grey Lock and some 150 warriors left Missisquoi to monitor Wright's movements and to harass the Connecticut River towns. Another expedition up the Merrimack River that fall likewise failed to locate any Indians.[27]

Again, the authorities in Albany tried to keep the Massachusetts frontier alerted to dangers even while they refrained from taking an active role in the war. On September 6, Albany sent word that the 150-person war party was on its way to Massachusetts with "Barbarous & Bloody designs" and warned that the Indians "probably are yet Skulking or hovering abt to comitt barbarities." A few days later, however, Albany reported that the war party seemed to have moved to the east. Another large war party, reported to be assembling at Chambly, also apparently dispersed to their homes. Nevertheless, the Albany authorities warned the justices of the peace at Westfield, "we are told that one party of nine and another of 14 Indians are out w/th design to be Skulking about your Western fronteers, of the last grey Lock is Leader." [28]

Grey Lock's growing reputation had clearly increased his ability to attract warriors for his raids from the various groups around Lake Champlain. After their defeat by Lovewell, most of the Pigwackets fled to Canada, to the source of the Connecticut, or over towards Lake Champlain, where some no doubt joined Grey Lock and continued their war against the English. The Sokokis and other bands continued to filter toward St. Francis. The Cowasucks may have retreated further north at the same time. Some may have withdrawn to Canada and eventually mingled with relatives at St. Francis, although, contrary to certain traditions, Lovewell's fight did not make the tribe relinquish their hold on Cowass. [29]

Grey Lock was no doubt drawing recruits from Caughnawaga and St. Francis as well as from the Lake Champlain region. But he wisely adhered to his tried and tested guerilla tactics, harrying the frontier in mobile raiding parties of a dozen or so warriors who were able to use the terrain to their advantage, rather than presenting the colonists with an Indian "army" that they could confront in pitched battle. With a handful of warriors, Grey Lock kept the frontier on edge for yet another summer.

In September 1725, Captain Timothy Dwight sent a scouting party of six men out from Fort Dummer. As often happened, they saw no sign of the enemy and headed for home. And, as so often happened, Grey Lock was watching and caught them off guard. A party of fourteen Indians ambushed them just west of the Connecticut River, killing two and wounding and capturing three others. The only man to escape back to the fort said that he had seen only two Indians fall in the fighting.[30]

English morale received a boost the next month, however, when Governor Vaudreuil died. The hard-pressed colonists took heart in the belief that the Abenaki war effort would falter now that the French governor's guiding hand was removed. Reports from Albany and from the Penobscots indicated that the Abenakis were indeed tiring of the war and were inclined to make peace, even though they complained that the English had taken away their lands "contrary to the rights of men." In December 1725, the eastern Indians made peace at Boston, and the agreement was ratified at Falmouth the following August. From then on the Penobscots urged the other tribes to make peace. But Grey Lock did not attend the peace negotiations, and the western Abenakis were not bound by the treaty. In the spring of 1726 the intransigent chief was reported to be assembling yet another war party on Otter Creek, and the Connecticut Valley towns could not rest easy so long as Grey Lock remained at war.[31] Governor Wentworth of New Hampshire reported to the Council of Trade and Plantations in England that "The Indian war cramps us extremely, driving the people into garrison that they cant work half their time etc." Lt Governor Dummer feared that the war was so expensive "that Unless it shall please God to put a speedy End to it, it will inevitably ruine us. . . ."[32]

In the fall of 1726 instructions were sent to the commissioners at Albany to try and encourage Grey Lock to come in and parley by sending him presents and messages of good faith.[33] But nothing came of these efforts, and the New York authorities continued to try and stem the steady trickle of Indians who left Schaghticoke and the Hudson and headed north, some of whom no doubt amalgamated with the community at Missisquoi.[34]

As hostilities abated, the frontier communities in the Connecticut Valley began to reduce their military preparedness. The military company at Northfield was dismissed in the fall of 1726, and during the winter Dwight's company at Fort Dummer was discharged. Captain Kellogg was ordered to recruit a small company for garrison duty at the fort, where he remained in command until 1740.[35] In January 1727 the Albany authorities sent Grey

Lock's brother, Malalemet, to invite the war chief to come to Albany and negotiate. Malalemet, however, reported that his brother could not be found.[36] In March, Dummer asked the Penobscots to try and bring the Vermont Abenakis to the peace table. Writing to the Penobscot sachem Wenungennet, Dummer called upon his "good friend" to render the assistance that he had undertaken to supply under the treaty. Informing Wenungennet "That an Indian call'd Grey Lock has enticed a Party of Indians about Otter Creek & that they are preparing to come upon our Frontiers with mischievous Designs," Dummer urged the Penobscot to inquire into the matter and prevent the Abenakis "from Acting their Ill Purposes & to oblige them to come in & ratify the Treaty as you have done."[37]

Dummer believed that the best way to prevent Grey Lock from carrying out his planned raids was "to draw him by good Usage," and he instructed Colonels John Stoddard and Samuel Partridge "to get some private Intimations to him" that would encourage the war chief to come in and ratify the treaty. The chief was to be guaranteed safe conduct, and any northern Indians who came in were to receive gifts.[38] Partridge forwarded Dummer's instructions to the commissioners at Albany, adding his own request that the commissioners send Indian emissaries to invite Grey Lock and other intransigent chiefs to come in and treat. In addition, the Norridgewock and other eastern tribes promised to do their best "to Flatter or Force Any Ill Minded Indians In or about Canada to Joyne with ym in ye Ratification of Peace."[39]

The Albany commissioners were ready to do all they could to mediate a peace, although they feared the French would do everything they could to prevent it. The commissioners had already sent a wampum belt to St. Francis, and they said they would send a message to Grey Lock as soon as the opportunity arose, although they did not have an appropriate wampum belt. The message would be sent in their name so that the Abenakis would not think it came from Massachusetts. New York would guarantee the Indians safe conduct and good treatment, but the commissioners doubted that Grey Lock could be persuaded to come to Massachusetts, "for ye Latter has done Much Mischief on ye fronteers & has doubtless a Guilty Conscience."[40]

Whether or not the message ever reached Grey Lock, there was some confusion between Massachusetts and New Hampshire about the policy to be pursued with regard to the chief. In April, Josiah Willard, secretary of Massachusetts Bay province, wrote to inform the Albany commissioners that Colonel Partridge had mistaken the lieutenant governor's orders and that there never was any intention of sending a message to Grey Lock and the other Indians, "But the good People of the County of Hampshire being more apprehensive perhaps than was Needfull of the bad faith of Greylock they had direction privately to discourse & notifie Him to Come to them to confirme them in his good intents."[41]

The war was gradually dying out, however. The French had accurately predicted the way the conflict would go, recognizing that, unless they assisted the Indians, "the Abenaquis, tired of the War, will abandon their country, or what is more probable, will, without quitting it, make the best terms they can with the English."[42] The Abenakis of Norridgewock and St. Francis had been "made to feal the frowns of Heaven" more severely than any other tribes engaged in the war, but proved dilatory in making peace. The English attributed the reluctance of the holdouts to inherent stubbornness and insolence, fueled by French influence.[43] The intransigents from St. Francis and elsewhere were also under pressure to make peace from their eastern Abenaki relatives, who lived closer to the English and who complained that raids by the Canadian warriors exposed all Abenakis to "la boucherie des Anglois." The Canadian Abenakis finally joined the Penobscots in making peace with Massachusetts in July 1727, but neither Grey Lock nor any of his warriors participated.[44]

An English estimate of Indian population drawn up in 1726 showed the Norridgewocks reduced from 250 warriors in 1690 to 25; the Androscoggins down from 160 to 10, and the Pigwackets from 100 to just 7. These numers were surely inaccurate: John Gyles, an interpreter on the Maine frontier, reckoned the Pigwackets at 24 warriors, and the Norridgewocks at 40 the same year, and they were about to increase. By the spring of 1727 Indians from Norridgewock, Androscoggin, and Pigwacket who had fled with their families to Canada during the war, were on their way back to their homes and expressed concern lest the English fall upon them while they were hunting near the Connecticut and Kennebec rivers.[45]

Grey Lock remained as shadowy a figure at the end of the war as he had been at the beginning. In April 1727 the Penobscot, Wenungennet, replying via John Gyles to Dummer's inquiry said, "As to what you mention to me Concerning Gray Lock I nor my old men haue no knowledg of him for we ar not aquainted wth ye Olbeni Indians."[46] In the years of peace that followed, the warrior chief of Missisquoi virtually disappeared from view. In 1744 several Schaghticoke Indians returned from a journey to the north where they had seen "Gray Lock a Massesqueek Sachem."[47] Grey Lock had a daughter in 1737 and a son in 1740, and the chief and his wife were both apparently baptized. It is thought that Grey Lock died sometime between 1744 and 1753, but the exact circumstances and date of his death, like the place of his burial, are unknown. The descendants of Grey Lock's enemies paid belated tribute to the elusive warrior chief by giving his name to the highest peak in the Berkshire Mountains.[48]

Traditional New England histories that attribute all their Indian wars to French intrigue ignore the reality and complexity of interethnic conflict in colonial North America. Grey Lock maintained connections with the French and with the eastern Abenaki tribes, but, while the French remained officially neutral and the eastern bands gradually came to terms with the English, Grey Lock carried on his own war, raiding the frontier settlements of Massachusetts and New Hampshire but assiduously avoiding hostilities against New York. While some other Indians pursued their own strategies of survival by acting as scouts, emissaries, or auxiliaries, Grey Lock diplomatically avoided giving any offense to the Iroquois that might have prompted that powerful confederacy to abandon its neutrality in the conflict. Grey Lock's reputation grew, and with it his ability to assemble strong war parties, but he never abandoned his successful strategy of draining the colonists' resources by small-scale guerilla warfare and the threat of lightning-fast raids. Employing the Green Mountain forests to his advantage, he successfully eluded reprisals and often turned back to inflict further damage on pursuers who struggled to cope in Indian country. While other Indian "fortresses" succumbed to English search-and-destroy missions, Grey Lock's "castle" remained intact and undetected. If Grey Lock did not win his war, neither did he lose it. He remained defiant and undefeated as the Connecticut Valley lapsed gratefully into long years of peace. His war may have been little more than a holding action to stem the tide of settlement on Abenaki lands, but when war broke out again in 1744 in Grey Lock's twilight years, Missisquoi and Otter Creek served the same function in King George's War as they had in Grey Lock's War: supplying warriors for raids on the frontier settlements of northern New England.[49] And long after the struggle for the Champlain Valley was over, the Missisquoi community survived behind the frontier, proving as elusive in peacetime as it had during Grey Lock's War.[50]

Chapter 7

Peace in the Valleys, 1727–1744

Issues of war and empire have dominated the traditional histories of eighteenth-century North America, and the threat and reality of war were recurrent concerns for Indians and Europeans alike in northern New England. The image of the beleaguered settler, musket at the ready behind barred shutters while Indian foes lurked in the forest looms vivid across the pages of the region's frontier history. Franco-Indian raids were a real terror for English settlers, and French and Abenakis feared military strikes from the south, even though, in fact, long periods of peace and coexistence characterized Indian-white relations in northern New England.

Even during the half-century and more of Anglo-French rivalry for imperial hegemony in North America, peace was more common than war. With the exceptions of Grey Lock's War in Vermont and Lovewell's War in Maine, the thirty years between the Treaty of Utrecht in 1713 and the outbreak of King George's War in 1744 constituted a generation of peace in the Champlain and Connecticut valleys, and Dummer's Treaty, negotiated in a series of conferences between Massachusetts and the eastern Abenakis between 1725 and 1727, initiated seventeen years of relative harmony in Anglo-Abenaki relations. French, Abenakis, and English resumed prewar pastimes and attended to matters of commerce, religion, and diplomacy. Yet all operated in a context where a renewal of war in Europe would disrupt their lives, and all lived with an eye on that possibility. Theirs was the bittersweet peace of cold war.

Drained by global war and concerned with economic and dynastic problems at home, Britain and France welcomed the post-Utrecht years as an era of recuperation. Tensions and basic enmities remained, but, for the time, there was peace. For northern New England also, the period was an opportunity for rebuilding and resettlement after the devastation of King William's War and Queen Anne's War. Peace offered hopes of better times for Abenakis too: Pigwackets and Norridgewocks who had fled north in 1724 and 1725 were anxious to return home once the fighting was over.[1]

This generation of calm saw significant developments, numerous interactions, and life-affecting events that were just as important to contemporaries and to history as the dramatic conflicts that overshadow the area and the era. The period was not unique, but as the longest continuous stretch of peace in the seventeenth and eighteenth centuries it offers insights into the lives and relations of Indians and Europeans on the frontier of northern New England and Canada in the absence of open conflict.

Western Abenakis in the 1730s found themselves operating between English and French powers making competitive maneuvers and bidding for Indian support. The Abenakis responded to English and French initiatives and frequently shifted location for better access to trade and church, as well as for reasons of safety and strategy. According to Ira Allen, a "mortal sickness" struck Missisquoi in 1730 and the inhabitants abandoned "their beautiful fields which extended for four miles along the river," and fled to their relatives at St. Francis, returning only during the hunting season for several years. Three years later some Abenakis from St. Francis and Bécancour fled to Acadia to escape "la petite vérole" (smallpox), returning after the disease had run its course. It is doubtful that the Abenakis totally evacuated Missisquoi at this time, or that those who left went all the way to St. Francis. Indeed, Thomas Charland describes this period as one of exodus *from* St. Francis towards the Missisquoi River. Attracted by better hunting grounds and the prospect of trade with the English, beginning in 1731, about forty Abenaki families left St. Francis and moved to Missisquoi, adding to the population of the core village. A report of 1738 counted "more than 20 Abenaki cabins" (at least 100 and perhaps more than 300 people) at Missisquoi, and others may have been located in secluded spots in the surrounding countryside.[2]

Movement between Missisquoi and St. Francis was common, and the French were not always able to distinguish precisely between the inhabitants of the two villages. In his list of the number of warriors in each of the several Abenaki villages in 1736, Michel Maray de La Chauvinière estimated 180 for St. Francis, but included in that total "ceux de Michioukoui et les errants."[3] The "errants" were probably those who moved regularly from site to site or those who were out hunting, rather than actual "wanderers." European observers had only a vague understanding of the pattern and purpose of movement between and around Abenaki villages.

Other Abenaki movements and activities are directly traceable to French or English initiatives in the Champlain and Connecticut valleys. Perhaps the most significant of these was the building of Fort St. Frédéric by the French in 1731 at Crown Point on the Lake Champlain–Lake George waterway. It seems that French and Indians were already accustomed to trading in the area. In 1730 Governor Charles de Beauharnois despatched a force of thirty French soldiers to Lake Champlain to drive away English traders, who he had heard were coming to deal with the Indians. That fall, Beauharnois recommended to Louis XV that a fortified post be constructed at Crown Point. The king approved the plan in 1731, and a detachment of twenty soldiers and workmen were sent to build a stockaded fort. Across the narrows of the lake, a small French settlement grew up at Chimney Point, present-day Addison, Vermont. The fort's garrison was steadily increased until its peacetime population included sixty soldiers, an interpreter, a blacksmith, a baker, and a laundrywoman. A windmill was built in 1739, and by the early 1740s Fort St. Frédéric had become a stronghold of major strategic value as the advance post of New France controlling access via Lake Champlain.[4]

In 1728 Louis XV ordered that the funds intended for support of warriors' families at St. Francis and Bécancour be continued and extended to all Abenakis who had missionaries among them. French priests catered to Abenaki spiritual needs along the St. Lawrence, but with the building of Fort St. Frédéric came a priest in residence at the southern end of Lake Champlain. Abenakis from Missisquoi, St. Francis, and elsewhere, as well as Christianized Iroquois, began to gravitate to Fort St. Frédéric for services. Six Abenakis from Missisquoi received baptisms at the fort between 1737 and 1741. Grey Lock, the terror of the Massachusetts frontier for twenty years, was there with his family in the spring 1737 and again three years later. The register recorded the baptism of a daughter, Marie-Charlotte, in April 1737, and a son, Jean Baptiste, in April 1740. The parents were entered as "Pierre-Jean dit la Tête Blanche et Hélène, Sauvages abenaquis de Missisquoi," and a French officer acted as "parrain," or godfather, at each baptism.[5] The fort's registers also offer testimony to tragedy in the lives of individuals. For example, in the fall of 1738, Thomas Cadenait and his wife, Abenakis from Missisquoi, buried their five-year-old daughter, Madeline Monique, in the fort's cemetery. Other Abenaki infants were buried there in later years.[6] That the registers show men like Grey Lock and Cadenait indicates that such prominent individuals were in the forefront of contact between the western Abenakis and the French.

The interpreter at the fort at this time was Pierre Hertel de Beaubassin. Born in 1715, he had grown up among the Abenakis at St. Francis, where his father was both an interpreter and trader. Hertel grew up speaking Abenaki as well as his native French, and at age twenty he became interpreter at Fort St. Frédéric. Occasionally, he acted as godparent at the baptism of Abenaki children at the fort.[7] Clearly, this advance post of New France, at the very edges of New York and New England, was more than just an armed camp. It was a vital community where soldiers, traders, and chaplain interacted with Abenakis who visited the fort regularly to trade or to receive religious instruction, baptism, and the last rites.

At the same time, the French authorities began to issue royal patents to Crown officials and officers for seigneuries along both shores of Lake Champlain. These seigneuries were designed to bring French settlers to the Champlain Valley and provide a buffer against English encroachments from the south. By 1737 there were a score of these grants. That of Philippe-Réné Le Gardeur de Beauvais, granted in July 1734, encompassed the region around Missisquoi. The Abenakis seem to have displayed little anxiety about this activity, although the Mohawks protested French claims to territory on the east side of the lake. In fact, the Indians had little to worry about. The recipients of the grants were soldiers not farmers, and in 1741 a royal decree revoked most of the grants because the owners had failed to promote settlement. A new series of seigneuries was initiated two years later, and settlement grew in the seigneury of Hocquart near Fort St. Frédéric during the 1740s and 1750s, but the French vision of colonization of the Champlain Valley was never realized.[8]

In 1743 the French decided to build a mission for the Abenakis at Missisquoi. Father Étienne Lauverjat was dispatched to establish the mission, and a chapel was built, probably in the present town of Alburg, just across the bay in the Seigneury of Foucault. Besides providing the Abenakis with spiritual guidance, the mission was intended as a measure to strengthen the Indians' allegiance to France, enlarge their village as a barrier against the English, and help curb the contraband trade between Indians in Canada and New England. In 1744 the king gave orders that Father Lauverjat should receive every assistance in his efforts to detach the Loups and Abenakis of the region from the English. Clearly, the Abenakis and English were not inveterate enemies in these years and their contacts were commercial rather than hostile. In the fall Governor Beauharnois and Intendant Gilles Hocquart were able to report that so far the mission had occasioned no other expenses than the building of a stone house and the purchase of some furniture and utensils of little value for the missionary's use, a total of 1,500 livres.[9]

As the French sought to strengthen their position and expand their influence among the Indians in the north, the English took similar steps in the south. Tensions with white neighbors, disputes over land, harassment and abuse by traders and settlers,

continued to drive many Schaghticokes north to Canada throughout the 1730s and early 1740s. The New York authorities dismissed their motives for migration as "ffrivolous pretences and
wrong Notions," but nevertheless promised to look into their
complaints and take care of them if they remained, and they
urged those who stayed to prevail on the deserters to return.[10]

Meanwhile, in 1731, Dutch trader John Henry Lydius built a
post at "the Great Carrying Place" between the Hudson River
and Wood Creek, halfway between Albany and Fort St. Frédéric.
Lydius had been expelled from Montreal the previous year, probably on charges of espionage or illegal trading activities. He selected the portage location for his new post to tap the largely
illegal trade between Montreal and Albany. Abenakis from St.
Francis and Bécancour became involved in the flourishing illicit
trade. The post was destroyed in 1744 but rebuilt by 1751, and
Lydius operated among the Indians for some thirty years. His
influence was apparent in the summer of 1732 when, with Joseph
Kellogg interpreting, two Caughnawagas at Northampton delivered a speech for Governor Jonathan Belcher of Massachusetts,
saying, "We of the Caknawage are Desirous that Mr Lydius may
dwell at the Otter Creek that we may resort to him, inasmuch as
he may not be allowed to Live in Canady: Many of our People
are Indebted to him & will be able at the Otter Creek to Dis-
charge their Debts." That same year, Lydius made a dubious
claim that, in consideration of his teaching them to read, translat-
ing the Psalms, and other services, the Mohawks had granted him
two tracts of land, one on Wood Creek, the other on Otter Creek.
The Indians apparently asked why, when the French had built a
fort at Crown Point, the English could not just as easily build
a fort at Otter Creek. Lydius made no attempt to settle his "Otter
Creek purchase," however, and the New York authorities refused
to recognize his title to it. But Lydius's post at Fort Edward became the English defense pitted against Fort St. Frédéric.[11] The
almost-simultaneous establishment of the French and English
forts opened a new era of competition for the Champlain Valley
and intensified interest in the Indians and their trade.

The English also took official steps to strengthen the attraction
of existing posts for the Indians of the region. A trading house

was established at Fort Dummer in 1728, and Indians visited the post in great numbers to trade. The captain and truckmaster at the fort was Joseph Kellogg. Kellogg had been captured at age twelve during the Deerfield raid, along with his brother and two sisters, and had lived the life of an Indian in Canada, where he learned French and several Indian languages. In December 1740, Kellogg was appointed "Interpreter in the Indian Language and for Indian Affairs." In 1754, two years before his death, he served as interpreter at the historic Fort Albany Treaty. Kellogg's brother, Martin, taught Mohawk children at the school at Stockbridge, and another former Indian captive, the Reverend Stephen Williams, visited the Indians at Housatonic in 1734 and was instrumental in sending them a minister.[12]

Recognizing that French priests had long wielded great influence among the Abenakis, the government of the Massachusetts Bay Colony appointed a minister to Fort Dummer the next year. The Reverend Ebenezer Hinsdale was to cater to the Indians who came down the Connecticut River or across the mountains to trade, as well as those who lived in the neighborhood. In late August 1735, Governor Belcher held a series of Indian councils at Deerfield to proclaim and explain the appointment. Present were chiefs and delegates from the Caughnawaga, Housatonic, and Schaghticoke Indians, along with some "St. Francis Abenakis," "who at their own desire were included in the treaty with the Cagnauwagas." Many of the Indians had brought their wives along with them.[13]

After the usual ceremonial presentation of wampum, and with Joseph Kellogg interpreting, Governor Belcher told the Schaghticokes that the government had set up a trading house at Fort Dummer under Captain Kellogg so that the Indians could get the best trade with no fear of being cheated. They had also sent a minister to Fort Dummer, as well as to Housatonic, to instruct the Indians in Christianity. All the government asked in return, said Belcher, was that the Indians lead "better lives than ever yet you have done, and that you yourselves as well as your wives will make it your business to attend on the ministers, and observe their instructions, especially on God's holy day, and that you will command your children also, that they may be taught to read and write, and that they may be instructed in the true religion of Jesus Christ." The Schaghticokes thanked Belcher for his words, presented him with a belt of wampum, and drank to the health of King George II before leaving.[14]

In council with Caughnawagas, some of whom he knew frequented Fort Dummer, Belcher assured the Indians that they need have no fear in receiving knowledge of the true religion and that it would cost them nothing to have their children instructed by the minister at Fort Dummer. Ountaussogoe, an old Caughnawaga chief, promised he would carry Belcher's words home to his people who "are now upon their knees waiting for our return." The latest news from England was that King George and the French king were still at peace, but if war broke out, said Belcher, he had no doubt that the Indians would see it in their best interests to maintain faith and remain at peace. He assured them: "You will be always honestly dealt with by Capt. Kellogg at the Truck House, where you may have such things as you need, at a cheaper rate than any others can or will let you have them." The governor drank to the health of the Caughnawagas, and Ountaussogoe drank to King George.[15]

Speaking for the Housatonics, Captain Cuncaupot (otherwise known as Konkapot, Cockapotami, or Captain John) said that they were eager to receive the gospel "and hope that our hearts are in what we say, and that we don't speak only out of our lips." But, clearly thinking about past unfortunate experiences with Albany traders, he voiced the Indians' concern about the consequences of trade with the English:

"Our children are afraid of strict laws, and of being brought into trouble and put in prison for debt, &c., and we pray that care may be taken by your Excellency as our father, and by the General Assembly, that we be not hurt by the severity of the laws, seeing we don't understand how to manage in such affairs, so that there may not be any danger at any time that our children be taken away from us for debt, &c."[16]

On the final day of the councils, Belcher assured the Schaghticokes that as long as they remained faithful subjects of King

George, they would receive equal treatment and protection from the government of Massachusetts. He expressed his pleasure that they had come near to the fort to live and urged them to attend diligently to the instructions of the Reverend Hinsdale. Reminding the Indians that the morrow was the Lord's day, Belcher declared: "I expect you to keep yourselves sober, and attend on the public worship of God at the meeting house." On Sunday, September 1, 1735, the Housatonic Indians sat by themselves in one of the galleries of the Deerfield meetinghouse. Many Caughnawagas and Schaghticokes also attended the service, and "the whole affair was carried on with great decency and solemnity."[17]

Behind Belcher's council-fire rhetoric lay the very real purpose of strengthening the Indians' political ties with Boston, confirming their economic attachment to Fort Dummer, and reducing the magnetism of the French missions for the Caughnawagas, the Abenakis, and others by placing a minister at the fort. Nor were the English efforts merely verbal: in May 1736 an account rendered by Captain Joseph Kellogg for miscellaneous disbursements at Fort Dummer included an item "for Improving Land for ye Indns." Even so, the Abenakis were not induced to sever their diplomatic ties with France: in 1737, St. Francis Abenakis expressed their desire to visit Paris.[18]

Caughnawagas regularly passed through western Vermont in the 1730s and 1740s en route to Fort Dummer to trade and to parley. Ountaussogoe and other delegates returned in the fall of 1737, expressed their determination not to break the covenant with the English, and drank to the king's health. Even so, the Caughnawaga visits did not always pass off without incident: in the spring of 1730, on the West River, twelve Caughnawagas who had been drinking heavily at Fort Dummer slew a Schaghticoke Indian who had come to smoke with them.[19] Moreover, the Caughnawagas continued to operate as middlemen in a lucrative trade between Canada and Albany. The Indians' unrestricted movement, "passing & repassing our frontiers into heart of country," caused the English growing concern as the threat of renewed war mounted.[20]

In this period, as the French attempted to establish their claim to the Champlain Valley with land grants and settlement, English settlement edged northward. English land speculators secured title to lands in the Connecticut Valley that were formerly occupied by Sokokis and to which displaced Sokokis still held claim, while settlers ventured into territory where Abenakis still held sway. In August 1735 at Fort Dummer, John Stoddard and Captain Israel Williams bought two tracts of land on the Connecticut and upper Deerfield rivers from Indians who were then living at Schaghticoke. On August 6 an Indian woman named Nechehoosqua, the wife of Massequnt, sold them a tract of land on the Connecticut north of Fort Dummer for one hundred pounds, "Which parcel of land aforedescribed Descended to me the said Nechehoosequa from my Mother Conkesemah Wife of Auma Sancooaneh Indians of the Scautecook Tribe." Nechehoosequa's husband and two children affixed their marks to the deed, which was confirmed by seventeen other "Subscribers of the Scauhtecook Tribe whose Ancestors habitation was by or near unto Connecticutt River." On August 29, with Joseph Kellogg as witness and interpreter, four Indians—"Ompontinnuwas, Penawanse, Cockiyouwah and Wallenas Sons to Woolauootaumasqu"—sold another tract of land for fifty pounds, which was similarly confirmed by other Schaghticokes. Pinawans, who also confirmed the first deed, was probably a Sokoki who had retreated to Schaghticoke. Twelve years later he would be back in the Connecticut Valley waging bitter war against the invaders of his ancestral lands. As English pressure mounted, his descendants would move again, leaving Schaghticoke and migrating north to St. Francis.[21]

Six river towns were laid out in 1736: Westminster and Rockingham on the west bank of the Connecticut; Westmoreland, Walpole, Chesterfield, and Charlestown on the east side. English settlements were still very much in their infancy in 1744 in Vermont's Connecticut Valley, but small communities of settlers grew up protected by little forts and blockhouses. In 1742 or 1743, Nehemiah How of Grafton, Massachusetts, settled at the Great Meadow at Putney and, in company with several other Massachusetts settlers, built a small fort there. Around 1740, three families named Fainsworth moved from Lunenberg, Massachusetts and began a settlement at Charlestown. They were joined by others, including Phineas Stevens in 1743, and in 1744 they built a fort (Fort Number Four) and a corn mill. Later, they added a sawmill. By 1744, Charlestown was a town of nine or ten families, out on a limb in Indian country, standing at the intersection of Indian trails running from Canada, the Atlantic, and the west. But, as Susanna Johnson recalled, relations were predominantly harmonious. Indians and settlers mixed freely, and, although the Indians in the neighborhood were numerous, they "associated in a friendly manner with the whites." Indians peddled baskets, occasionally hired on as laborers, and gave guidance in hunting, fishing, planting, and maple sugaring.[22]

For a time, when individual relations and the character of the communities on the New England frontier were not dictated by war and turmoil, settlers and Indians managed to coexist without conflict. At small, exposed communities like Fort Dummer and Charlestown, English settlers and traders rubbed shoulders with Abenaki hunters and trappers, and cautious coexistence rather than armed vigilance typified relations. As the 1730s came to an end, there were hopes that a nonaggression pact might be signed between New York and "Grey Locks Tribe" in the event of war between France and England, and the Missisquois participated in neutrality negotiations, along with St. Francis Abenakis, Schaghticokes, and eastern Abenakis, as late as July 1744.[23]

But competition and concern over land tempered peaceful relations and cooperative inclinations. When Walter Bryant's survey party met two Indians near Pigwacket in March 1741, the Abenakis furnished them with information and the material to mend their snowshoes and offered to trade for a gun. But they were disturbed by the presence of Englishmen so deep into their territory, thinking it must mean war, and they warned Bryant "that there were sundry Companies of Indians a hunting and they believed that none of said Companies woud let me proceed if they shou'd meet with me."[24] Moreover, isolated communities were affected by decisions made half a world away, and western Abenakis and European settlers soon responded once again to drumbeats sounded in Paris and London.

Chapter 8

King George's War, 1744–1748

During the 1730s the English had strengthened their ties with the Indians trading in the Connecticut and Champlain valleys, and English settlers in small frontier communities had come to know many of their Abenaki neighbors. Hopes that the Indians would remain friendly in the event of renewed war proved groundless, however, for "no sooner was it known to them that war had been resolved upon, than all these Indians withdrew to Canada, and at all times acted as guides to the French soldiers."[1] The Indians may not have rallied to the French with the immediate unanimity that Samuel Drake suggested, but certainly the old battle lines reformed. The French were counting on the Abenakis as a major arm of their war effort.[2] Abenakis looked to the French as their tried help against English invaders of their lands. According to a statement prepared by Governor George Clinton of New York, the French had almost 600 Indian warriors directly in league with them when war began. Of those, 230 Caughnawagas, 90 St. Francis Abenakis, and 40 Missisquois were within easy striking range of the western New England frontier.[3] The English colonists lacked the unity, the resources, and the expertise to match this array of Indian power, and within five years after 1744 every English settler was driven out of Vermont. Only Fort Dummer and Fort Number Four remained as English toeholds on the upper Connecticut.

The War of the Austrian Succession saw massed armies clash on the battlefields of Europe. In America the conflict brought a renewal of the guerilla warfare that had come to typify conflicts between the western Abenakis and the English. The outbreak of war in 1744 generated a flurry of movement and military activity in English, French, and Abenaki towns and villages. New Hampshire Governor Benning Wentworth proposed building a blockhouse and using whale boats on Lake Winnipesaukee, which had been "the Asylum & safe retreat of the Indians in former wars." Governor William Shirley of Massachusetts raised five hundred men, who were to be stationed at the points most likely to be attacked, two hundred of whom were intended for the Connecticut Valley. Forts Dummer, Number Four, and Massachusetts were the key defensive outposts, with Northfield serving as a depot and rallying point behind the front lines. When war broke out, Fort Dummer was garrisoned by Captain Josiah Willard and twenty men; Colonel Ebenezer Hinsdale had his own small garrison at his blockhouse, and Captain Phineas Stevens was at Fort Number Four without men. In September 1744 the king ordered that Fort Dummer be properly garrisoned and maintained, but six months later this still had not been done. Lack of cooperation and jurisdictional disputes between Massachusetts and New Hampshire, and New Hampshire's reluctance to finance the fort, hindered the garrisoning of Fort Dummer in particular and the war effort in general.[4]

The Indians adopted their own defensive measures. Several hundred Indians from the Atlantic coast headed for Canada and the St. Lawrence.[5] The Cowasucks, remembering that English expeditions had come within striking range of Cowass in Queen Anne's War, withdrew northward. Some headed for the French missions, but most regrouped in locations within their homelands that were less well known to the English.[6] Some groups sought safety in neutrality. When the war broke out, the majority of the Indians still living at Pigwacket probably headed for St. Francis. The remnants of the Pigwackets—men, women, and children—"came to a fort near where they lived; and desired that they might live among the English; for that they desired they might not be concerned in the war." They were granted a refuge about fifty miles from Boston. In his declaration of war against the Indians of Cape Sable, Nova Scotia, and St. Johns, Governor Shirley numbered the Pigwackets among "Our Friend Indians." Nine Pigwackets volunteered to fight with the English "& prov'd themselves good soldiers" at the siege of Louisburg and elsewhere in Nova Scotia. In return, the English provided them with clothing and protection at the end of the war, and Spencer Phips assured the governor of Quebec that the Pigwackets remained in the English settlements voluntarily. These Pigwackets were still in Boston in 1750, after which they seem to have disappeared from the records. William Douglass, writing at midcentury, described the Pigwackets as formerly a considerable tribe of Indians, with a French missionary, who were then almost extinct with no more than a dozen fighting men.[7]

The English knew, after Grey Lock's raids, that Missisquoi would be at the core of western Abenaki resistance, and they sent Indian scouts to gather evidence of the warlike preparations being made by the Abenakis at the north end of Lake Champlain. In the fall of 1744 an Abenaki from Missisquoi intercepted and warned off three Loups in the Great Marsh north of Whitehall, near Ticonderoga, who had been sent from Albany to discover whether any Indians were out hunting or whether they were under arms and ready to wage war. The French likewise sent out Indian scouts, despatching one party, for example, to the head of Otter Creek to see if the English were fortifying the place.[8]

The French had great hopes that Missisquoi would be both a magnet that would draw Indians from the English orbit and a launching point for Indian war parties. In October 1744, Beauharnois and Hocquart reported that the village had grown considerably since the previous year and now numbered about sixty warriors, "all young men." William Douglass likewise reported that the "Masiassuck Indians, on the East or *Dutch* Side of Lake *Champlain*; in the *French* Interest, do not exceed 60 fighting Men." Louis XV noted the progress made at the Missisquoi mission village and made it clear that Beauharnois was to exploit the Missisquois' good disposition to engage them in raids against the English. Beauharnois had despatched an officer to Missisquoi

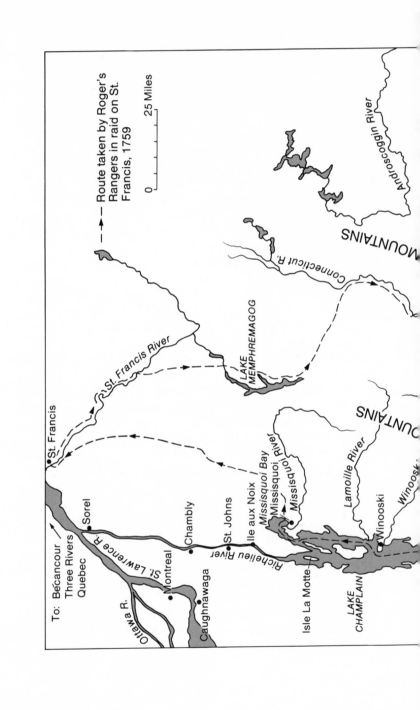

To: Bécancour
Three Rivers
Quebec

St. Lawrence R.

Ottawa R.

Montreal

Caughnawaga

Sorel

Chambly

St. Johns

Richelieu River

Ile aux Noix

Missisquoi Bay

Missisquoi River

St. Francis

St. Francis River

LAKE MEMPHREMAGOG

Connecticut R.

MOUNTAINS

MOUNTAINS

Androscoggin River

Isle La Motte

LAKE CHAMPLAIN

Lamoille River

Winooski

Winooski

– – ▶ Route taken by Roger's Rangers in raid on St. Francis, 1759

0   25 Miles

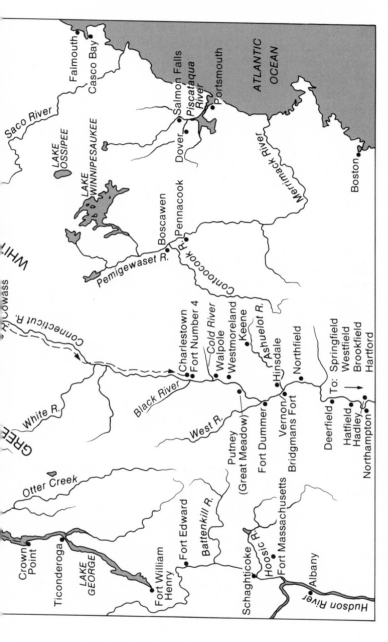

Western Abenaki country during the French and English wars

in the summer to "chanter la guerre," and the Indians had accepted the war belt and hatchet with enthusiasm. The French hoped that the newly established mission would attract other Indians—namely, "Loups d'Orange," or Schaghticokes—to the village and terminate their links with the English, especially since the construction of Fort St. Frédéric at the southern end of the lake meant that Missisquoi was no longer in the front line.[9]

Missisquoi exerted a crucial pull in the Anglo-French tug-of-war for Schaghticoke allegiance. Late in the spring of 1744 a delegation of Schaghticoke Indians traveled north to the Missisquoi and "Asschicantecook" Abenakis. Among others, they met the old chief Grey Lock. The Abenakis were glad to see them, and they renewed their treaties with the Schaghticokes "to keep open the road" and renew the covenant between them.[10] Reports from Lydius's trading house, which the "French Indians" frequented daily, and from Schaghticoke, said that many young Schaghticoke warriors had been with the governor of Canada, "owing him to be their father and praying him to assign them a place where they should go well and he apointed them to dwell at Massicksqueaq at Grey Locks fort where they Have a french Priest among them." The war increased the exodus from Schaghticoke, despite New York's usual efforts to stem the tide and recall the defectors. Some Schaghticokes joined "our Uncles the Six Nations"; others journeyed to St. Francis or Missisquoi as a refuge and center of resistance to the English.[11]

The English received reports of war parties emanating from Missisquoi as early as the fall of 1744. A Caughnawaga Indian, who assured the New York authorities that his own nation had no warlike intentions, brought secondhand news, obtained from an Abenaki woman whom he had met on Lake Champlain, that a war party of "20 Asschincantecook Indians went from the Missitqueck Castle alighting to some part of new England" and traveling up Otter Creek to strike somewhere in the east.[12] This may have been the same group (or a party of Caughnawagas) of which Joseph Kellogg heard: "I am informed that Secunnundook with Seven Cunnews is Come from Cannaday and is come over the Lake and is gone up otter Kreek in Expectation of many more

A reconstruction of Fort Number Four on the banks of the Connecticut River near Charlestown, New Hampshire (Photograph by Colin G. Calloway)

cumming and joyning with them in their winter hunt all Expecting to get their Corn at number four above the greate falls for their hunt."[13] Missisquoi and Isle La Motte served as rendezvous points for French and Indians as they made military preparations.[14]

The pattern of the war was soon established. On July 5, 1745, an Indian war party raided the Great Meadow at Putney, about sixteen miles upriver from Fort Dummer, and captured William Phipps as he was hoeing corn. Phipps tried to escape, wounded one of the Indians with his hoe, and was promptly killed. Five days later the Indians killed and scalped Deacon Josiah Fisher at Upper Ashuelot (Keene, New Hampshire).[15] The killings spread alarm among the colonists, who heard that the men killed near the Connecticut River had been "most Barbarously murdered haveing their Eyes plucked out their heart taken out the Crown of their head taken off and most Inhumanely mangled an butchered." The Indians left a war hatchet next to one of the bodies, daring the English to take it up and return it.[16] A company of fifty-six men were sent to guard the Connecticut River towns from mid-July to early September.[17]

On October 11, a force of about eighty French and Indians attacked the Great Meadow fort again. They slaughtered the cattle, killed David Rugg, and captured Nehemiah How, the original settler of the place. Soldiers from Northfield and Fort Dummer pursued the raiders beyond Fort Number Four, but gave up when the Indians' tracks split in different directions. How was taken to Crown Point, and finally to Quebec. A fellow prisoner in Quebec recorded in his journal on May 24, 1747: "This Day Cloudy high winds and Cold, Died Nehemiah how of ye Fever, a Good Pious old Gentleman aged Near 60 Years has been In prison Near 18 months and ye most Contented and Easy of any man in my Prison."[18]

The garrisons of the little river forts were strengthened as winter approached. The new year brought a resumption of the raids. French records show thirty-five different war parties despatched against the English frontier in the spring of 1746.[19] In March, with the Indians "doing mischief" around Fort Dummer, Josiah Willard reported that the settlers were "much Disheartened by being left so Naked" at a time of such danger. That same month Ensign Boucher de Niverville went with fifty-three Iroquois to Lake Champlain. By April 19 they were at Fort Number Four, where they surprised and captured Captain John Spafford, Isaac Parker, and Stephen Fainsworth.[20] Four days later the Indians, probably the same party, attempted to surprise the garrison of Upper Ashuelot, burnt some buildings, killed some cattle, and carried off Nathan Blake to Canada. Samuel Drake recorded the event as "a furious attack" launched by about one hundred Indians.[21]

St. Francis provided greater numbers of warriors, and the English often assumed that Abenaki raiders from the north came from St. Francis; but the French records show that Missisquoi played its part in keeping the New England frontier on the defensive. On April 26, 1746, a party of twenty Abenakis from Missisquoi set out towards Boston and returned with prisoners and scalps.[22] A month later a war party of eight Missisquoi Abenakis, who had been equipped by the French and sent out against the New York frontier, returned with more prisoners and scalps. Four days later twenty Missisquois returned with prisoners and scalps taken in the region of Albany. Most of the farmers on the east side of the Hudson River north of Albany soon abandoned their farms and moved with their families to Albany for protection.[23] In June a war party of ten Abenakis raided "the River Kakecoute" (probably Boscawen, New Hampshire, where the Contoocook falls into the Merrimack). Although they returned with scalps, "their chief Cadenaret, a famous warrior, has been killed." The dead chief was undoubtedly Cadenait, who had buried his daughter at Fort St. Frédéric in 1738.[24]

May 1746 opened with a string of Indian raids and skirmishes at Fort Number Four, Lower Ashuelot (Swanzey, New Hampshire), and Fall-Town (Bernardston, Massachusetts). After a two-week lull, a large force of French and Indians ambushed a troop of soldiers at Fort Number Four on May 24. Captain Stevens led a relief squad from the fort, and, after a sharp skirmish in which five Indians and five English died, the raiders were repulsed, taking captive Obadiah Sartle (Sartwell) with them. Lying in the path of war parties coming down the Black River from Lake Champlain and down the Connecticut from Lake Memphremagog, Fort Number Four soon became "a backwoods Castle Dangerous" on the cutting edge of the English frontier.[25]

At the beginning of June, Massachusetts voted to raise an additional 207 men to be posted on the western frontier,[26] but Indian raids continued unabated. On June 19 a large war party was repulsed at Fort Number Four after a sharp fight with Stevens and fifty men. Five days later, Indians attacked a group of men working in the meadow below Bridgman's Fort at Vernon, inflicting casualties and taking captive Daniel How and John Beaman. The same day, Indians surprised a scouting party as they rested at Cold Spring, a little below Fort Dummer, and captured some guns. On July 3, a small war party skirmished with Colonel Josiah Willard's men at Hinsdale, New Hampshire. A month later, dogs gave the alarm of another attack on Fort Number Four. One man was killed as he went from the fort. The Indians ran off, but when the men from the fort later went to fetch the body, "the ambush arose and fired about a Hundred Guns at them." The English retreated to the fort, and sporadic firing continued until the next day, when the Indians withdrew after burning some buildings and killing cattle. The next month an Indian war party killed and scalped five men near Pennacook and carried off two captives.[27]

Then, on August 20, 1746, the French and Indians delivered a stunning blow when Rigaud de Vaudreuil, brother of the future governor of New France, with a force of 700 Indians and Canadians, captured Fort Massachusetts on the Hoosic River, between present-day North Adams and Williamstown. Most of the captured garrison were returned the next year, but the loss of the fort was a tough blow to English morale, driving home the message that the enemy was capable of carrying a major military objective.[28]

By mid-1746, things looked grim on the New England frontier. English settlers abandoned the fields they had settled in the last twenty years. Joseph Ashley, chaplain at Fort Dummer, wrote to the Reverend Jonathan Ashley at Deerfield in June, saying that he expected the "new plantations" to break up directly and that he had no desire to continue as chaplain there, whether the war continued or not.[29] A plan to use dog patrols on the western frontier failed, and that winter the General Court of Massachusetts resolved to resume paying scalp bounties as a boost to the flagging war effort and in the hope of securing Indian aid. Indians who went out on service to Canada were to be paid five pounds and receive forty pounds for every male prisoner above twelve years of age, or thirty-eight pounds for his scalp. For female and young male prisoners, the fee was twenty pounds or nineteen pounds for their scalps. New Hampshire offered bounties on Abenaki scalps throughout the war. Just before Christmas, Massachusetts Governor Shirley wrote to Governor Wentworth of New Hampshire urging an attack on St. Francis by a force of at least 500 men. His was not the only plan "for breaking up the Indians at St. Francois," but not until thirteen years later was a such a strike executed.[30]

In early March 1747, Abenakis from Missisquoi attended a council of Indian nations held at the Château in Montreal. In

addition to Abenakis from Missisquoi, St. Francis, and Bécancour, and Iroquois from the Lake of the Two Mountains, there
were Algonquins, Nipissings, Ottawas, Potawatomis, Winn'eba-
goes, Illinois, Menominees, Hurons, Sauks, and Malecites. All
the nations agreed to declare war on the Mohawks and, after
singing the war song, dispersed into war parties into the Connecticut Valley and New York. In May, responding to Mohawk
raids south of Montreal, eight Missisquois accompanied a Lieutenant Saint-Pierre against a party of Mohawks believed to be
encamped above Chateaugay in New York.[31]

Iroquois distractions aside, the Abenakis seemed to increase in
confidence as the English became more distressed. At the end of
March 1747, thirty or forty Indians attempted to burn Shattock's
Fort between Northfield and Hinsdale. Captain Eleazar Melvin's
men pursued them as far as the Great Meadow. Shooting across
the river, they killed one of the Indians, who burnt the fort that
the English had deserted there.[32] On the next day, April 1, these
Indians dictated a defiant and haughty message to the General
Assembly from Fort Number Two (Westmoreland) on the Connecticut River. Knowing that there had been great complaints in
the province about the cost of defending the frontiers, they declared they had taken it upon themselves to reduce the necessity
for such expense. While peace lasted, the Indians were happy to
be allies of the English and accept their presents,

> but now as we allways are in a time of war subjects to the King of
> France, have undertaken to free you from such an extraordinary
> charge by killing & taking Captive the people & driving them off
> & firing their fortification. and so Successful have we been in this
> affair that we have broke up almost all the new Settlements in your
> western frontiers: so yt you need not be one half of charge you
> were in past in Maintaining a war in these parts: for now there
> are but little else besides the old towns, and if they will not fortifie
> & defend themselves; we think they ought to be left to our mercy.

The Indians suggested they even deserved a small reward for their
services and declared their willingness "to bring your frontiers to
a Narrower Compass Still & Make your charges Still Smaller."
They inquired:

whether it be more acceptable to you that we man your Deserted
Garrisons our Selves and Eat up the provisions which your poor
Distrest Neighbours Leave in ym when they flee in their Hurry &
confusion or whether we Burn up the forts with the provisions;
for we assure you we find much more in them than we want for
our own Support whilst Carrying on this Business.

Describing themselves as "your very humble and obsequious Ser-
vants," four Indians signed the "petition" on behalf of themselves
and others. One of the four was Pinawans, the Sokoki warrior
from the Connecticut Valley who had relocated at Schaghticoke
and sold lands on the upper Deerfield River in 1735.[33]

While the English river towns bore the brunt of the fighting,
and the Abenakis were able to launch repeated incursions from
the Canadian mission villages with apparently no danger of reprisal, the war nevertheless took its toll on both sides. The French
inhabitants of Fort St. Frédéric abandoned their lands, and the
"inhabitants of Lake Champlain" evacuated their lands completely out of fear of enemy attacks.[34] Probably the Abenakis of
Missisquoi thought it prudent to withdraw northward from a
village so clearly marked as a target for enemy operations, and the
small size of war parties from Missisquoi even at the height of
the war raises the possibility that many Missisquoi Abenakis dispersed into surrounding neighborhood sites away from English
soldiers and French recruiting officers.

Charlestown, New Hampshire, was abandoned, but Captain
Phineas Stevens and thirty men regarrisoned Fort Number Four
and ranged the forests to intercept enemy war parties filtering
down out of the Green Mountains. In early April 1747 a war party
of about 60 French and Indians (some English accounts spoke of
an "army" of 500, and the French general, Debeline, bluffed that
he had 700) laid siege to the fort for two days. Using fire arrows
to try and dislodge the defenders, they threatened the garrison
with total destruction if they continued to resist. When that
failed, two Indians "formerly acquainted with Captain Stevens"
came forward with a flag of truce to parley and asked to exchange
some furs for corn. The attackers clearly were in worse straits
than the defenders, and, when the offer to trade was refused, the

French and Indians withdrew on the night of the third day. "By the above account," reported Stevens,

> you may form some Idea of the Distressed Circumstances we were under, to have such an army of starved Creatures around us whose necessity obliged them to be more ernest. They seemed every Minute as though they were going to swallow us up, using all the threatening Language they could possibly invent, with shouting & firing as if the heavens & earth were coming together; but notwithstanding all this our Courage held out to the last.

Before the siege ended, one of the French lieutenants had told the garrison "that they had some thousands of *French* & *Indians* out and coming out against our Frontiers."[35]

Increasingly, the English tried to forestall such attacks by sending out scouting parties into the country above the Connecticut River, up the Black River and as far as Otter Creek. The Massachusetts General Court voted to increase the frontier garrisons and earmarked a portion of these forces "to intercept the French and Indian enemy in their marches from Wood Creek to Otter Creek."[36] But the colonists were competing with warriors operating in familiar territory, and Indian war parties regularly slipped past English scouts with ease.

In late October, Indians burnt Bridgman's Fort and took Jonathan Sartwell captive. The next month a war party from the Lake of the Two Mountains ambushed and killed some men at Fort Number Four.[37] In March of 1748 ten Indians on snowshoes ambushed a party of men in deep snow near Number Four. They killed one man, wounded another, and took a captive, retreating at their leisure since the English had no snowshoes with which to pursue them. "Thus poorly have our Garrisons been stored," lamented the contemporary chroniclers, "while many hundred pair of Snow Shoes have lain spoiling somewhere or other which the Province have paid for." Two weeks later three men died in an Indian ambush about a mile below Fort Dummer.[38]

"Melvin's Disaster" in May 1748 illustrated the advantages the Abenakis held over an enemy who ventured to confront them in their own country. Captain Eleazar Melvin and eighteen men left

Fort Dummer on a scouting expedition on May 13. At Fort Number Four they were joined by sixty men under Phineas Stevens and Humphrey Hobbs. The combined force marched up the Black River, crossed the Green Mountains through Mount Holly pass, and descended to Otter Creek. Here Melvin crossed the stream and went on toward Crown Point while Stevens and Hobbs continued along the east bank. Melvin's party reached Lake Champlain on May 24 and, within sight of Crown Point, fired on two canoes of Indians. As the alarm sounded at the fort, Melvin's men retreated, traveling along the south branch of Otter Creek and over the height of land to the headwaters of West River. Weary and hungry, they stopped to rest and fish. The pursuing Indians, who knew the country, had gotten ahead of them, however, and were lying in ambush when Melvin arrived at the West River. Somewhere near Londonderry, the Indians sprang from their ambush, killing six men and scattering the rest. Melvin and the survivors straggled into Fort Dummer the next day. The town of Northfield proclaimed a fast to mark the defeat, and the Reverend Benjamin Doolittle noted its effect on English morale: "This was a surprising Stroke and struck a great Damp into the Spirits of our Men who had thoughts of going into their Country when they found how far the Indians would pursue to get an Advantage upon them." Stevens and Hobbs returned after a fruitless two-week expedition.[39] As if to drive home the point, the Indians ambushed thirteen or fourteen men between Hinsdale and Fort Dummer, just one day after Stevens returned, taking three scalps and seven captives.[40]

In the last week of June, Captain Hobbs and forty men left Fort Number Four en route to Fort Shirley, Massachusetts. An Indian war party pursued them and ambushed them about twelve miles west of Fort Dummer. The Indian leader was said to be a chief named Sackett, reputedly the descendant of a white captive. In fact, Sackett was probably Jacques Sacket of Missisquoi. After a four hour battle, in which Sackett was supposedly killed or wounded, the Indians withdrew, carrying their dead and wounded with them. Hobbs's party limped back to Fort Dummer under cover of darkness with three dead and wounded, but after the Melvin fiasco this was a welcome opportunity to claim a measure of victory. The Reverend Doolittle commented: "The Enemy doubtless lost many; they went off without Shouting, and when some Captives saw them about a Week after, they looked very sorrowful. This was a very manly Fight; and all will grant our Men quitted themselves like Men who Need not be ashamed."[41]

Any celebrations were short-lived. Some of the war party that had fought Hobbs caught Sergeant Thomas Taylor and sixteen men in ambush less than a mile below Fort Dummer on July 14. Two men died in the first rush; the Indians killed two wounded later. Only four men escaped as the Indians retreated with nine captives up the Connecticut and West rivers, and down Otter Creek to Lake Champlain and Canada. Soldiers and militia from Hatfield, Deerfield, Northfield, and other Connecticut River-towns went in pursuit, but they were unable to overtake the enemy and could do no more than bury the dead.[42]

Fort Dummer remained a crucial outpost as the war ground to a halt, and its garrison was strengthened in the summer of 1748 and again the following winter.[43] Sporadic skirmishing and small-scale raids continued around Fort Number Four, and in the spring of 1749 the English urged the Penobscot and Norridgewock Abenakis to send word to St. Francis to call in their war parties. The Norridgewocks indicated that their relatives would come around to making peace but "they say the St. Francies Indians has Lost a Grat Number of their young men and seems yett to be Revengefull." St. Francis's warriors were reduced to about two hundred by the end of the war. But by June the St. Francis Abenakis were ready to make peace, and, when Phineas Stevens traveled to Canada that year in search of English captives, the St. Francis Indians he met "appeared friendly, and one of my old acquaintance presented me with two wild geese."[44]

The Reverend Doolittle summarized the English frustrations at fighting a purely defensive war: "Not a Man of ours has seen a French Settlement all this War, except such as were carried Captive or went with a Flagg of Truce." The English rarely obtained an Indian scalp, even at Fort Number Four, where the fighting was fiercest, because the men would not venture out after the enemy. The English were plagued by vacillating policies, expired enlistment terms, inadequate supplies, inequitable pay for soldiers on service, and inexperienced officers. The French and Indians on the other hand clearly recognized the strategic importance of the river forts and concentrated their efforts on trying to destroy them. The English failure to keep out scouting parties allowed the enemy to approach with ease and to be gone before the English could muster an effective pursuit. "So they come Securely Week after Week upon us; yea we have since found that the Enemy have camp'd several Months within thirty or forty Miles of Fort Dummer." The war left the inhabitants of New England's western frontier distressed and demoralized. The longer it went on, the bolder the enemy grew—a warning, said Doolittle, of what the English could expect if war broke out anew.[45]

The war had also been disruptive for the Indians and took some Abenakis far from home. Joseph Louis Gill, "the white chief" of the St. Francis Abenakis, served with the French in Beauharnois's campaign against the Miamis in 1747, and Abenakis were living in an Ottawa village on the southern shore of Lake Erie in the 1740s.[46] Yet, while the English were pushed back in the Champlain and Connecticut valleys, and settlers abandoned their fields in Vermont, Missisquoi never was in immediate danger during the war, and the Abenakis soon resumed their lives there. Those who withdrew from the village were back by the end of 1749. Peter Kalm, who traveled on Lake Champlain near Missisquoi in 1749, did not see the village, but he saw Indians in birchbark canoes fishing for sturgeon and three women wearing conical caps and clothing characteristic of the Abenakis. Clearly there was a village close by.[47]

In October 1749 the French governor, Jacques-Pierre Taffanel, Marquis de La Jonquière, reported that the village at Missisquoi was "entièrement rétabli" and that the Abenakis had displayed great zeal in putting their houses in good order. The Indians were out hunting that fall and had not yet resumed planting corn, but La Jonquière hoped the mission would grow in strength. Some twenty Abenaki families lived on Missisquoi Bay. In 1748, Nicolas Réné Lavasseur, seigneur of St. Armand and the French naval constructor, was issued a tract of land "of six leagues in front along the Missiskuoy, in Lake Champlain, by three leagues in depth on both sides of same," including the right to hunt, fish, and trade with the Indians. The grant was confirmed in 1749 and, after consulting the Abenakis, a sawmill was erected at the Taquahunga Falls, a few miles from the mouth of the Missisquoi River. Lumbering operations began to supply pine masts for French vessels, and the Abenaki village developed into "a busy French and Indian settlement of 50 huts, with a church that boasted a bell." Grey Lock's fort may no longer have existed, but with the mission and sawmill, Missisquoi was a community of two or three villages by the end of the decade. An English map of 1749, prepared for Governor Shirley, showed the Missisquoi village intact and in alliance with the French.⁴⁸ The French hoped that Missisquoi would develop into a mission community like those at St. Francis, Caughnawaga, Lorette, and the Lake of the Two Mountains, as well as provide a barrier against English encroachment.⁴⁹

In five years of sporadic fighting, the Abenakis of Missisquoi and St. Francis had carried the war to western New England's frontier, besieged and destroyed English forts, and pushed the invading settlers out of Vermont. Indian war parties filtered through the Green Mountains, evading the small garrisons to strike almost at will. As in Grey Lock's War, the Abenakis called the shots and dictated the nature of the conflict, while hastily assembled and poorly equipped English militia companies struggled to respond when and where they could. There was much truth in Vaudreuil's war's end assessment that, of all the Indians, the English feared the Abenakis most and they had never been able to gain the advantage over them except by perfidy.⁵⁰

Chapter 9

The English, French, and Indian War, 1754–1760

The 1750s constituted a watershed decade for the western Abenakis. In the first half of the eighteenth century, despite devastating losses, cultural disruption, and expulsion from their lands on the south, they had remained a major force to be reckoned with in northern New England. Supported by their French allies in Canada, they had carried the war to the English in the 1740s, stemming the tide of encroachment and virtually clearing Vermont of English settlers. Before 1750 the warriors had kept the majority of the western Abenaki homeland clear of invaders. By 1760, however, the western Abenakis found themselves treated as a defeated people, the troublesome but impotent allies of a vanquished foe.

The opening of the decade saw Indians and whites coexisting in the foothills of the Green Mountains, resuming a pattern of relationships that had been disrupted by war. Mohawks and Abenakis returned to trade at Colonel Lydius's truck house on the Hudson River, and that post became again a conduit by which northern Indians filtered news and information to the English. Phineas Stevens met many Indians there in the winter of 1749–50 and found the ones from St. Francis and Caughnawaga peaceably inclined. Several told him that they would be at Fort Number Four in the spring. Another Indian, named Pinnewanie (who may have been Pinawans), said he would be coming to the fort before long to pick up the traps he had left there before the war.[1]

In 1752, Stevens met large numbers of St. Francis Indians on their way to Albany to trade beaver, and English traders also pushed north into territory claimed by France to distribute low-priced goods in the Indian villages. As late as November 1753, when Abenaki blood had already been spilled, a chief from St. Francis, named Pau'perwasomit, who was hunting on the head-waters of the Connecticut River, sent word to Stevens that he and his companions intended to come down to Charlestown at Christmas or when the ice on the river was strong enough to travel on. In February Stevens recorded in his account book trading "Sundrys artickles" to an Abenaki called Paupuwaremet, presumably the same Indian. Stevens himself was sending goods up-river for the Indians in the winter of 1754. A number of Abenakis came to trade at the fort that spring. Stevens' account book records regular visits by an Indian, named Philip, whom he clearly knew well and trusted. Philip brought in otter, beaver, marten, and raccoon skins, and bought meat, bread, powder and shot, and even a silver cross. On one visit he billeted at the fort for four days; another time, when war was brewing, Stevens sold him powder, shot, bullet molds, and even vermilion, presumably to be used for war paint. Little over a year later, an Indian called Philip was leading a war party against the settlers at Walpole, downriver from Fort Number Four. One of the Walpole settlers was John Kilburn, who was also a customer of Stevens.[2]

Stevens also acted as an intermediary between the English and the Abenakis. In 1752 he was despatched by Massachusetts to get news of prisoners, "whether English or Indian," who had been taken from that province. Stevens paid 300 livres for two captives whom the Abenakis brought to Montreal from St. Francis, but he was unsuccessful in his efforts to redeem several others. While Stevens, himself a former Indian captive, was in Montreal, he met his "old Indian father," who had come down from St. Francis. His Abenaki father gave him a hat and, when the time came for Stevens to leave, accompanied him in the canoe as far as Crown Point.[3]

While such interactions continued, English settlers resumed their slow and halting encroachment up the Connecticut Valley. Colonel Benjamin Bellows began a settlement at Walpole in 1751.

Rockingham was settled briefly in 1753, until the first few settlers withdrew in fear of Indian attack. According to tradition, a band of Abenakis lived on the "French meadows" near Springfield in 1750; two years later they were joined by the first white settlers of Springfield, John Nolte and his mixed-blood wife.[4]

But the dynamics of English-Indian contact, and the global forces that affected life and lives in northern New England, ensured that the peaceful years around 1750 were no more than an interlude. Tension between Abenakis and English persisted and increased as France and England moved closer to a final showdown in North America. The rumblings of a conflict that erupted into a world war in 1756 had begun in North America in 1754. Western Abenakis occupied precarious positions on the war routes and in the war zones of a key region in the North American part of this global conflict. Quickly enlisted as soldiers and scouts, they also became the targets of English counterstrokes that grew more threatening as the redcoats pushed back the French. The outbreak of hostilities generated a new series of movements and migrations among the Indians of Vermont and produced widespread repetition of the strategy of withdrawal in time of military activity.

From the early 1750s, the English worried about the threat from the "Canadian" Indians. Phineas Stevens was convinced "that were it not for ye French it would be Easy to Live at peace with ye Indians," and others viewed the St. Francis Abenakis as a constant menace and a bad influence on the eastern Abenakis who would otherwise be willing to live in peace.[5]

The Abenakis were equally alert to the English threat. Rumors that the English intended to cut a road from Fort Number Four and build a fort at the Cowass Intervales alarmed them. At a conference with Phineas Stevens in Montreal in the summer of 1752, in the presence of the French governor and delegates from Caughnawaga and Lake of the Two Mountains, the Abenakis reasserted their ownership of the region, even though it was empty at the time. They drew a clear boundary line, refused to cede "one single inch" of land above Fort Number Four, and forbade the English to kill a single beaver or cut one stick of timber on Abenaki lands. They asked only to be left alone, but threatened to go to war if the English occupied their land. Their chief spokesman, Ateawanto, or Jerome Atecuando, denounced the English as aggressors and liars: "Your mouth is of sugar but your heart of gall; in truth, the moment you begin we are on our guard." At the same time the Abenakis affirmed that they spoke "of our own accord" and that their attachment to the French in no way deprived them of their rights or independence: "We are entirely free; we are allies of the king of France, from whom we have received the Faith and all sorts of assistance in our necessities; we love that Monarch, and we are strongly attached to his interests."[6]

The following January 1753 six Abenakis came to Fort Number Four under a flag of truce and asked to speak with Captain Phineas Stevens. They displayed great uneasiness at the English intentions to occupy Cowass and reminded Stevens of what their chief men had said at Montreal, "and what they Say is always Strong." Finally, as they were about to depart the next morning they told Stevens in no uncertain terms that

> for the English to Settle Cowass was what they could not agree to, as the English had no need of that Land, but had eno' without it, They must think the English had a mind for War, if they Should go there, and Said, if you do we will endeavour, that you shall have a Strong War, that they should have the Mohawks and Ottawas to help them—That there was four hundred Indians now a hunting on this Side St. Francis River, and that the owners of the Land at Cowass would be all there this Spring, and that they at No. 4 might expect that if the affair of settling Cowass went forward, to have all their houses burnt.

They emphasized that they had no desire for war, urged Stevens to use his influence to prevent the English from going to Cowass, and repeated that, if war occurred, it would be brought about by the English. The Abenakis were not about to tolerate English trespass on their ancestral Cowass lands. Nor was their talk of assistance from the Ottawas and the Mohawks an idle threat. The Ottawas were senior allies of the confederacy of tribes that had developed as the Seven Nations of Canada. The mission communities on the St. Lawrence formed the core of the confederacy;

membership fluctuated but included the Iroquois, the Algonquins, and the Nipissings at Lake of Two Mountains; the Caughnawagas, the Abenakis of St. Francis and Bécancour; the Hurons of Lorette; and the Cayugas and the Onondagas of Oswegatchie, who later moved to St. Regis. The English shelved their plans in the face of the determined Abenaki resistance. Massachusetts directed Stevens to assure the Indians that their government had no intention of settling at Cowass and warned Governor Wentworth of the grave danger of igniting an Indian war if New Hampshire went ahead and tried to make a settlement without first satisfying the Abenaki owners. In March 1753, Robert Rogers was one of twenty men who started to blaze a trail to the fertile meadows at Cowass under authorization of the New Hampshire Assembly. They followed the Merrimack, Pemigewasset, and Baker rivers to the Connecticut Valley and then turned back. The Abenaki threat of retaliation for any penetration of the region proved strong: the axe marks on the trees were almost effaced before any settlers dared follow the trail blazed by Rogers and his companions.[7]

Even as the English backed away from confrontation with the Abenakis over the Cowass lands, they became increasingly concerned by reports that the French intended to build a fort there, as well as at the head of the Kennebec River, where the tribes had rendezvoused for war against the English thirty years before. English fears that the French intended to stifle their colonies with a barrier of forts in the west were already acute; the new reports were particularly worrying because Cowass was a key location and afforded easy access both to the St. Francis Abenakis and to English settlements down the Connecticut and Merrimack rivers.[8] In 1754 Governor Wentworth despatched Captain Peter Powers and a detachment of soldiers to locate and dislodge the French. Powers penetrated farther into the woods than any English expedition had done before, but found no sign of French activity. In fact, the Abenakis curtailed French as well as English ambitions in their territory. French plans to build a trading post at the north end of Lake Memphremagog had to be shelved when the Abenakis asserted it would spoil their hunting territory and refused to give their consent.[9]

Wentworth believed that only the concentration of French efforts on the Ohio that summer had prevented them from occupying Cowass, and he repeatedly pressed the New Hampshire Assembly to seize the chance and fortify the area. The Indians had already captured fifteen people and scalped two more on New Hampshire's frontiers that summer. A fort at Cowass would cut off communication by the Indians between the New Hampshire frontier and the French fort at Crown Point; it would also curb the incursions of Indians from St. Francis and Montreal by shutting off the short and easy water passes they utilized. It would give the English an advance post from which to invade the enemy's country in the event of a general war, and "it must Be Considered that a Fortification at Coos will be an infinitely greater Security to all His Majesties Colonies, Exposed to the Hostilities of the Indians, than a Fort Erected in any other Place whatsoever." The members of the assembly appreciated the need for a fort at Cowass, but doubted their capacity to maintain it, and, despite Wentworth's efforts over three years, it seems doubtful that "Fort Wentworth" was ever built.[10]

In the spring of 1753 two St. Francis Indians—Sabattis and Plausawa—left Charlestown to go hunting in New Hampshire. They never returned. In an affair in which they may have stolen two negroes, the Abenakis were killed near Contoocook, New Hampshire. Two men were indicted for their murder, but a mob freed them from jail. Governor Shirley suggested giving presents to the Indians' relatives "for wiping off the Blood" according to Indian custom, but the Abenakis believed that the English had poisoned the Indians with rum and the chiefs were unable to restrain their young men, who were determined to seek revenge. The chiefs notified the French governor that they intended "to do mischief" on the English frontiers come summer, and Abenakis sent a warning to the English "to take care of themselves." Charles Cook, a Caughnawaga of French and Indian descent, met an Abenaki war party from Bécancour with five English prisoners on Lake Champlain in the summer of 1754. He asked them why they had been out fighting when the kings of England and France were at peace: "[T]hey answered that that was nothing, for the English at the Fort No. 4 had some time past, poisoned two Indians (when at the same they were sitting and discussing together and seemed to be good Friends) by giving them a Dram at Night, and in the Morning they were both dead." Continued encroachments on the Connecticut River further incited the Abenakis, who complained to the governor of Canada that "the English have abused us, in driving us from our Lands, and taking them from us."[11]

Three Missisquois, including a sachem named Otasagquenape, were among the St. Francis Abenakis who attended the Albany conference in August 1754. The commissioners, hearing that the Abenakis were at Schaghticoke, sent wampum and invited them to come and smoke. They urged them to give up their hostile designs against the New York settlements and to follow the lead of the Caughnawagas in renewing the covenant chain and keeping the road open between them. The Indians from the "Missisque Castle" agreed to do their part to keep the road open:

> Brethren be assured that we Massiesque Indians, open the Road to this our House, and since this Road has been a good Road to our Forefathers we therefore clear the same that it may be as good as ever it has been—Don't mind Brethren, if may be bad wind or Tydings should blow in your Ears, for that proceeds from the Devil.

The Missisquois also affirmed that they had authorized the Caughnawagas to represent them and that whatever they did would have to "be approved of by both our whole Nations." St. Francis Abenakis had empowered the Caughnawagas to act on their behalf in treaty negotiations as early as 1724, and the Caughnawagas enjoyed considerable influence among the Abenakis. That did not mean, however, that the Abenakis could not act independently of Caughnawaga. Bad winds were already beginning to blow, and within a year the Abenakis "closed the road," going to war against the English despite Caughnawaga warnings and their own agreement at the Albany treaty not to do so. The St. Francis Abenakis who took James Johnson captive in 1754 told him that they already had war parties out. One had gone to the Merrimack to revenge the deaths of the two Abenakis killed in

New Hampshire; another had gone against Fort Number Four "because the English had set down upon lands there which they had not purchas'd." The Abenakis declared that next spring they intended to drive the English on the Connecticut River as far south as Deerfield. Abenakis from Bécancour took the lead in a raid on Hoosick, New York, early in September, despite French efforts to prevent it. Indeed, the Caughnawagas themselves rejected Mohawk and English requests to remain neutral and joined the Franco-Abenaki war effort.[12]

The exodus of Indians from Schaghticoke north to St. Francis, which had been going on throughout the century, culminated in 1754 as the war clouds gathered. Schaghticoke delegates at the Albany Court House in July declared: "Your Honour may see that we are but young and unexperienced, our Antient people being almost all Dead, so that we have no Body to give us any advice but we will do as our fathers have done before us." They asked the governor once again to put a stop to sales of rum at Schaghticoke and pointed out that they lost more and more of their land as the English grew more numerous. Caughnawaga visitors to Albany reported that the Schaghticokes had requested help from the St. Francis Abenakis in taking revenge for an Indian who had been murdered in Albany by Negroes, who had flung his body in the river. In September 1754 a raiding party of twenty-one Abenakis from Bécancour swung by Schaghticoke on their way home from Deerfield and took the last inhabitants—about sixty men, women, and children—with them back to Canada. The French at Crown Point supplied a vessel to carry the migrants down Lake Champlain, where Charles Cook, the Caughnawaga métis, saw them. Captain James Johnson, who was at Crown Point at the time and was later at St. Francis, reported that the French vessel took about seventy-five Schaghticokes to the fort at St. Johns, and that from there they went to St. Francis, "where they had an interview with those Indians and were by them received as part of their nation." Other members of the Schaghticoke community dispersed into surrounding areas, and Abenakis survived around Lake George throughout the eighteenth century.[13]

Abenakis congregated near the headwaters of the Connecticut

River. There they enjoyed an incomparable strategic location, close to French support in Canada and with easy travel down the Androscoggin, Saco, Merrimack, and Connecticut rivers. However, the Indians seem to have kept clear of the Connecticut Valley itself during the war. Captain Powers saw no Indian villages on his expedition to the upper Connecticut in 1754, and Rogers' Rangers saw none on their retreat downriver five years later.[14] One group of Cowasucks, who may have been pro-English or, more likely, simply wished to remain neutral, withdrew to the Clyde River in northern Vermont, where they stayed until the end of the war, when they probably moved on to St. Francis.[15] Another tradition records that in 1755 several hundred Indians were living on the upper Androscoggin in the eastern foothills of the White Mountains, but they caught smallpox from the French and were decimated. The survivors fled the area, and many joined their relatives in Canada, although a few returned in later years. Molly Occutt (or Ockett), Metallak, and Oozalluc, who featured in later town histories and traditions, were survivors of these upriver groups.[16]

By 1754 it seems that there were two good-sized communities of Indians and some French settlers living near Missisquoi. In addition to at least twenty Abenaki families at Missisquoi Bay, some Schaghticokes appear to have been living at or around Missisquoi. The French were operating their sawmill on land leased from the Abenakis at Swanton. There were also small temporary villages at Thompson's Point, Sand Bar, Charlotte, Mallett's Bay, and the mouth of the Winooski River. Missisquoi served as a core village for refugee bands and for the families scattered around the surrounding countryside.[17]

As the French forces under François Charles Bourlamaque and the English under Jeffrey Amherst stepped up their activities on and around Lake Champlain, the Missisquoi Abenakis pulled back from their central village to safer locations in the hinterland. With war threatening in the southern Champlain Valley, Missisquoi Abenakis stopped traveling to the chaplain at Fort St. Frédéric in favor of safer locations at Fort St. John and Chambly.[18] According to an anonymous French memoir, the inhabitants of Missisquoi withdrew to St. Francis and Bécancour at the beginning of the war. The warriors apparently lived around Ile aux Noix and took part in scouting operations for the French army.[19] If the Missisquois did evacuate their village, most did not go far and did not stay away. Later French warrior counts indicated that Abenakis frequented the region during the war, and many Abenakis returned to Missisquoi as the war came to an end.

The population of St. Francis at the turn of the decade seems to have hovered around one thousand. Migrants from the south continued to arrive before the outbreak of war, and the village served as a rallying point during the conflict. Not all movement was into the village, however. In 1755, the Jesuit fathers suggested building a new mission among displaced Loups living on the Ohio River and relocating some of the more fervent Abenakis to the new site. Jerome Atecuando, "un des cinq grands chefs de Saint François et orateur attiré de la nation," complained forcefully to Governor Vaudreuil against any attempt to make the Abenakis leave the bones of their ancestors in their native land and relocate their council fire. The Jesuits apparently threatened to refuse the sacraments to Abenakis who opposed the venture. Despite Vaudreuil's disapproval, a dozen Abenakis were living with the Loups on the Ohio River by May 1757, and in July Father Virot led a deputation of about twenty Abenakis to the Ohio. The Ohio Loups—who were probably Delawares—and their Shawnee neighbors proved unresponsive to these evangelizing efforts, however, complaining that the French sent them no troops or goods but only a black robe and some apostles. The Abenakis returned home to St. Francis three years later.[20]

While the English failed to achieve intercolonial cooperation or to enlist the aid of the Iroquois at the beginning of the war, the French and their Indian allies scored impressive victories in the west, most notably the rout of General Edward Braddock's army on the Monongahela in 1755. An Indian from Cowass—Captain John Soosap—was at Braddock's defeat, where he boasted he killed a British officer.[21] In northern New England, it seemed that the fighting might follow the pattern of King George's War, with the Abenakis striking their foes with impunity and the English rarely able to mount effective counteroffensives. The English rebuilt the fort on Great Meadow near Putney and reoccupied it in 1755, but in July an Indian war party traveled down the West River and ambushed seven men close to Hinsdale's fort across the Connecticut. Colonel Ebenezer Hinsdale immediately wrote to Wentworth, advising the governor of the settlers' distress and warning that they could not stay where they were without support: "We are loath to tarry here merely to be killed." The inhabitants of Fort Number Four felt similarly exposed as Abenaki warriors slipped by them. In August, Colonel Benjamin Bellows and his neighbors clashed with an Indian war party at the mouth of the Cold River near Walpole. John Kilburn recognized the leader of the war party as Philip, an Indian who had frequented the Connecticut Valley settlements during the spring, and presumably the same Indian who had been trading at Fort Number Four the previous year.[22]

Years of frustrating warfare had taught the English that new measures were necessary to confront the western Abenakis. One way was to increase the use of Indians against Indians. In 1756 Governor Shirley of Massachusetts raised a company of forty-five Stockbridge, or Mahican, Indians, commanded by Indian officers, for service between Lake George and Montreal, and he planned to raise another company among the Indians living on the east side of the Hudson River. Stockbridge, Mohegan, and Mohawk Indians all served with Rogers' Rangers in their campaigns against the French and Abenakis.[23] But the English recognized that for the most part the Indians were apt to "lie by, and let us fight our own Battles ourselves" and see which way the wind blew.[24]

Increasingly, the English placed their main hopes of containing the western Abenakis in the construction of strategically located posts and the services of companies of rangers specially trained in Indian fighting. They recognized the need to acquire thorough knowledge of the country between Fort Number Four and Crown Point if they were to prevent Abenaki war parties descending at will, and one plan proposed building a fort on the high lands between the sources of the Black River and Otter Creek, both well known as Abenaki war routes.[25]

While Amherst, Wolfe, and Montcalm fought the epic clashes that helped decide the fate of the continent, their less-famous counterparts—Benjamin Bellows at Walpole, Phineas Stevens at Fort Number Four, and their largely unidentified Abenaki adversaries—waged the Green Mountain phase of the struggle for continental supremacy as the English battled to establish a toehold on the upper Connecticut. As usual, western Abenaki warriors carried the war to the small English settlements down the valley, but they also found that this war hit closer to their homes in northern Vermont and Quebec as the French and the English and their respective Indian allies fought the length of the Champlain Valley and skirmished through the Green Mountains.

Abenakis joined Pierre Marin, the French commander in the Ohio Valley, as early as the summer of 1753. When Governor Vaudreuil passed through Three Rivers in July 1754, Jerome Atecuando told him that the St. Francis Abenakis were ready to set out by canoe or on foot to "beat all your enemies, who are our enemies, and drive them as the wind scatters the dust." The Abenakis kept their promise: about 100 warriors took the field the next month and helped repel a projected English attack on Fort St. Frédéric. Missisquoi Abenakis also served with the French throughout the war. Missisquoi, St. Francis, and Bécancour were crucial sources of manpower for the French war effort. According to captive James Johnson, St. Francis contained about 120 fighting men—both Schaghticokes and St. Francis Indians—in 1754, and the French supplied them liberally with arms, powder, coats, and food. French officers traveled to the Abenaki villages "to sing the war song," and one French estimate credited the Missisquoi Abenakis with between 100 and 150 men in 1757. Missisquoi warriors were among 110 Indians with Lieutenant Chaussegros de Léry at the capture of Fort Bull in the spring of 1756, and Abenaki scouts and raiding parties operated around Fort Carillon (Ticonderoga) throughout that summer. Five Missisquois, together with 21 warriors from St. Francis and 33 from Bécancour, joined a multitribal force of 260 warriors with Montcalm's army at the siege and capture of Fort Oswego on the south side of Lake Ontario the following August. In 1757, 112 Abenakis from St. Francis, 26 from Bécancour, and 18 from Missisquoi served with Niverville. Twenty-five Abenakis from Missisquoi served with Montcalm's army that year, along with 180 more from St. Francis and Bécancour; and 245 Abenakis from Missisquoi, St. Francis, Bécancour, and Panaouamaské (Penobscot) were among the 1,800 Indian allies with the French at the capture of Fort William Henry. Abenaki warriors also fought with the French at the Monongahela, Lake George, and Quebec and were in the French and Indian force that inflicted heavy casualties on Rogers' Rangers in the Battle on Snowshoes in March 1758. Western Abenakis fought alongside as many as thirty-three different Indian nations during the war, and the French selected chiefs from St. Francis to carry the news of their victory at Fort William Henry to the Oneidas.[26]

But Abenakis were not pliant auxiliaries. The French complained that they could not be relied upon to serve for an entire campaign and that they were prone to stealing. They blamed the Abenakis of Penobscot for starting the massacre of the English garrison at Fort William Henry and then justifying the act as retaliation for past English treachery. The French also found it galling that, "Of all the Indian tribes, the Abenaki is that in which the young men have the least submission to the old men and the chiefs, either in peace or in war." French complaints at the inability of Abenaki chiefs to control their warriors were not new. At the beginning of the war the Marquis de Vaudreuil, governor of Canada, defended himself against English charges that he had incited the Abenakis. He had actually restrained the Abenakis from taking revenge for English murders of their chiefs, "But as all the Tribes of Indians are free and value themselves much upon this Freedom, in the beginning of May the Abenakis let me know, that they should be very Sorry to displease me but they could not prevent their young men, who had determined to go & revenge the Death of the Chiefs." In fact, St. Francis Abenakis informed the governor that they intended to go to war with or without his support and that they were fighting "not for him . . . but for themselves." Vaudreuil's attempts to dissuade them produced an angry exchange. The governor admitted that he could do nothing to stop them, even when the Penobscots complained that the actions of the St. Francis Abenakis threatened to disturb *their* peace with the English.[27]

Western Abenakis fought their own war, and, their war parties conducted their own raids against the English colonists, continually harassing the little forts on the Connecticut River. Abenaki raiders attacked Charlestown, New Hampshire, in 1754, carrying the Johnson family into captivity and subsequently adopting Mrs. Johnson into the St. Francis community. They attacked Vernon, Hinsdale, and Walpole in 1755. The Indians killed and scalped the husband of Jemina Howe at Bridgman's Fort and carried Mrs. Howe into captivity. Despite considerable kindness on the part of her captives, Mrs. Howe endured a harrowing experience. The Abenakis took her child to Missisquoi, while Mrs. Howe spent the winter hunting season moving from place to place with her captors around the Lake Champlain islands, and she passed the spring tapping maple trees and making sugar in the woods before she was finally sold to the French at St. Johns.[28]

In 1757 Indians from Canada again attacked Fort Number Four, where they burned a mill and killed or carried off about seven people. In March 1758 Indians attacked the house of Captain Fairbank Moore on the West River near Brattleboro, and in September a small war party of Abenakis and Iroquois took a scalp and two more prisoners near Number Four.[29] Indians also slipped past the forts to raid settlements further south. In March, seven Abenakis from Missisquoi, "always hunting through the woods," penetrated to within twenty leagues of Boston, where they looted and burned a lavish country house, killed three men, and carried off a woman and her two children. In July twenty-three Abenakis returned to Canada, carrying scalps from their raid between Albany and Fort Edward.[30]

The tide of the war was beginning to turn, however. Following his election as prime minister in 1757, William Pitt directed the English war effort with energy and genius. By paying German armies to fight the war in Europe, he was able to commit unprecedented military forces to the North American theater. By 1758 the redcoats were winning victories and winning over the Iroquois. Meanwhile, the English colonies achieved an unusual amount of mutual support and agreement on the most effective tactics. Massachusetts, Connecticut, New Hampshire, and

Rhode Island agreed "That 800 men be employed to range [in small parties] from some convenient Lodgments at or near Connecticut River towards Lake Champlain & St. Lawrence River, from Kennebeck River by the Chaudiere toward Quebec, and also from Connecticut River to Hudsons River." They also agreed it was vital to build forts in the Penobscot country and on the upper Connecticut.[31]

Things remained perilous, however, for the small settlements on the Connecticut River. In the winter of 1759, Benjamin Bellows sent Major General Amherst a petition on behalf of the inhabitants of Walpole, Great Meadow, Canoe Meadow, and Winchester, describing the settlers' distressed situation since the troops assigned for their protection had returned home in November "without so much as leaving One Man for their Security and defence." Amherst despatched 100 men to be divided among the several garrisons "to quiet the minds of those poor People and prevent their quitting their Settlements," as well as "to keep a Watchful Eye over the motions of the Enemy, and by frequent Scouts, endeavor to intercept any small Parties of them, that might be lurking thereabouts, with a design of getting Scalps." A subaltern officer and twenty rangers were stationed at Number Four.[32]

Governor Wentworth continued to press for a fort at Cowass, without which "All our Old Settled Towns are open to the St. Francis and other Indians in Confederacy with the French." Plans to build a fort on Otter Creek foundered when a survey revealed the river to be unnavigable, with eight falls instead of three as reported. Amherst commented on "what an Ignorance many people have been in about this River." The Indian war route along Otter Creek remained open.[33]

The English turned with more success to the use of search-and-destroy tactics against their mobile foes. As early as October 1757 five English soldiers from northern Massachusetts traveled the "old Indian path" along the foothills east of St. Albans and burned the French mill at Swanton Falls.[34] With the organization of Rogers' Rangers, trained in forest warfare, the western Abenakis confronted for the first time in their wars against the English an enemy who was capable of pursuing them to their home base, threatening noncombatants and food supplies and placing them on the defensive. In the fall of 1759, Robert Rogers led his famous expedition against St. Francis. For decades New Englanders had loathed the St. Francis Abenakis as the scourge of the frontier, and Rogers' raid was designed to put a stop to the Indians' incursions once and for all.

In August 1759, as his army began to edge up Lake Champlain and Rogers' Rangers probed the northern end of the lake, Amherst sent Captain Kinton Kennedy and Lieutenant Archibald Hamilton to the Saint Francis Abenakis with a flag of truce and a message purportedly seeking their neutrality in the coming British campaign against New France, although in fact carrying letters to General Wolfe. Led by seven "Wolves" (Stockbridge Mahicans), the officers slipped by Missisquoi Bay and headed for the Yamaska River. Bourlamaque said Abenakis from the bay were there everyday but complained that the Indians either did not see or did not *want* to see anything. An Abenaki hunting party intercepted the English officers near St. Francis, refused their offer of money and neutrality, and handed them over to the French at Three Rivers. Having learned that one of the officers had been tortured, and exasperated by "the enemy's Indian scoundrels," Amherst ordered Rogers to destroy the Abenaki village at St. Francis.[35]

With a force of 200 Rangers, Iroquois, and Stockbridge Indians, Rogers eluded the French vessels on Lake Champlain, left his seventeen whale boats at Missisquoi Bay, then proceeded on foot to the St. Francis River. On the twenty-second day after leaving Crown Point, the Rangers arrived at the Abenaki village. According to the official report that Rogers sent to Amherst, he attacked the village at six o'clock the next morning—October 6—before sunrise, when the inhabitants were sleeping, killed two hundred and took twenty captives, fifteen of whom he later released. He redeemed five English prisoners and counted six hundred scalps hanging on poles in the village. Some of the Indians were shot down and drowned as they tried to escape in their canoes. Five years earlier, James Johnson had counted about forty buildings in the village, including some stone houses under construction. Rogers burned the church and all the houses, engulfing

LE MAJOR ROBERT · ROGER
Commandant en Chef les Troupes Indiennes au service des
Américains

Robert Rogers, the "White Devil." (National Archives of Canada, C-6875)

the French priest and others who had taken refuge there. By seven in the morning the attack was over. Rogers reported an officer and six men slightly wounded and one Stockbridge Indian killed (although, as will be seen, this Indian may well have been missing rather than dead).

At the time of the expedition, the French had scouting parties around Missisquoi Bay and Isle La Motte, and Missisquoi Abenakis who had temporarily evacuated their village kept an eye on the area around the bay. The Abenakis had heard the sound of boats on the lake as Rogers' men went by them at night, and, soon after, the French and Indians discovered and burned the boats that Rogers had left at Missisquoi Bay. Learning that the enemy was already in pursuit, Rogers decided to return by way of Lake Memphremagog and the Connecticut River to Fort Number Four. After marching for eight days, he split his company into small parties. Pursued by Abenaki warriors and French troops, the Rangers "suffered every hardship which men could endure" and sustained over 30 percent casualties on their 230-mile odyssey through Vermont. Nevertheless, the English celebrated Rogers' victory in destroying the "nest of Barbarians" that had so often furnished scalping parties for raids in New England.[36]

French and Indian accounts provide a rather different picture of the raid from that reported by Rogers, repeated by Amherst, and fictionalized by Kenneth Roberts in the novel *Northwest Passage*. Rogers wrote his account of the campaign to impress the British authorities with a view to furthering his own career, and he exaggerated both his own achievements and the impact of the expedition.

When news of the attack came to Ile aux Noix, Bourlamaque immediately sent couriers to Governor Vaudreuil and to St. Francis and despatched troops in pursuit of the raiders, together with about one hundred Indians. One of Rogers' three bands, thirty-five men, was caught and exterminated. Indian hunters brought word that they had seen and heard Englishmen at their deserted village at Missisquoi. Bourlamaque sent a party to the village and the Abenakis returned with five prisoners. The prisoners said they had left ten of their companions dying of hunger and exposure up the Missisquoi River. The Abenakis set out to scour the country and found five Englishmen coming back from St. Francis with an Indian woman prisoner. Two of the rangers were found to be carrying pieces of human flesh from an Indian child whom they had killed for food. The Abenakis strangled and scalped them on the spot and returned with the other three prisoners. Emaciated and exhausted, the survivors of Rogers' expedition straggled back to the English settlements. By the French reckoning, Rogers' raid killed about 30 Indians, not the 200 of which he boasted. The Abenakis killed about 40 rangers and carried 10 prisoners back to their village, "where some of them fell victim to the fury of the Indian women, notwithstanding the efforts the Canadians could make to save them."[37]

Abenaki oral tradition, as recorded by Gordon Day, offers an explanation for the discrepancy between Rogers' estimate of 200 Indians killed and the French report of 30 dead. According to Day's informants, a stranger came into the village the night before the raid and gave warning so that the women, children, and old people could be moved to a safe refuge. The warning was probably brought by one of the Stockbridge Indians serving with Rogers, possibly the one he reported killed. At any rate, many of the Abenakis had time to go into hiding before the attack. In addition, many of the men may have been away hunting.[38]

Contrary to Rogers' assertions and New England's hopes, St. Francis was not obliterated and the western Abenakis were not destroyed. A war party from St. Francis executed a successful retaliatory raid against Charlestown, New Hampshire, the following year and carried off another batch of captives to Canada.[39] Moreover, a major concentration of Abenaki warriors—some 200 in all—remained untouched around Ile aux Noix with Bourlamaque's army. Warriors from Missisquoi had withdrawn to this place at the beginning of the war, and Abenakis from St. Francis and Bécancour had joined them there. The English referred to this conglomeration of Abenakis as Wigwam Martinique. The encampment was probably located at some point north of Missisquoi Bay near the present-day town of Sorel in Quebec. In June 1760 Rogers and 300 rangers again made their way down Lake Champlain to attack

Plaque commemorating Rogers' raid at Odanak (St. Francis). (Photograph by Colin G. Calloway)

St. Johns and Chambly. Fifty rangers went ashore at Missisquoi Bay with orders to locate and destroy Wigwam Martinique, but they failed to locate their objective. Rogers' command was intercepted by over 300 French and Indians, and after a sharp skirmish the English withdrew to Isle La Motte. Oral tradition at Missisquoi, however, recalls a raid on the village about this time when a chief was killed and "the river ran red with blood."[40]

Despite its limited success, the raid on St. Francis constituted a disaster for the western Abenakis, who were accustomed to sustaining minimal casualties in battle and eluding pursuit by their enemies. After Rogers' Raid some Abenakis from St. Francis returned to Missisquoi, and there is evidence to suggest that for a time there were more Indians there than at St. Francis.[41] Other

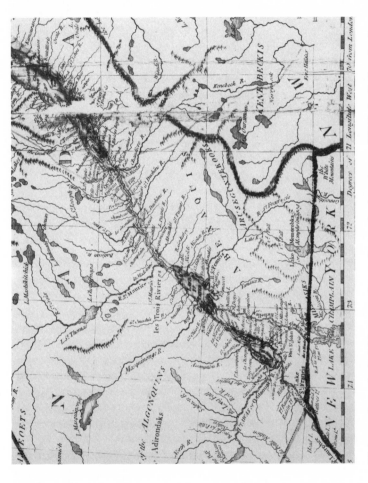

This portion of a British map of 1776 shows the locations of "Missiasiks" and other Abenakis. (Public Archives of Canada, NMC H2/300/1776)

refugees from St. Francis passed through Missisquoi on their way to seek asylum at the Iroquois mission village at St. Regis.[42]

In the summer of 1760 some 800 New Hampshire militiamen began cutting a road through the Green Mountains that opened the western Abenaki homeland to direct assault. Starting near the mouth of the Black River opposite Fort Number Four, the Crown Point military road crossed the mountains to Otter Creek, then to Brandon where it divided, with one branch going to Chimney Point and the other to Lake Champlain.

The Missisquoi Abenakis' participation in the later stages of the war was slight. But the Missisquoi village reemerged and seems to have become a core community for all the Lake Champlain Abenakis. Besides the three major groups of western Abenakis—the Missisquoi and St. Francis bands and the group that settled at St. Regis—an unknown number of Abenakis, Sokokis, Pennacooks, Schaghticokes, and refugees from St. Francis were living in small family bands throughout the Champlain Valley. Missisquoi served as a physical, military, cultural, and spiritual focus for these Indians as the war drew to its close. When Joseph Powers of Ferrisburg, Vermont, returned home after the capture of Quebec via the Missisquoi River, he found a flourishing settlement "and a large body of Indians" living on the riverbanks; and later a British map based on French surveys conducted after the war showed *"MISSIASIKS"* prominently occupying the area between the Missisquoi River and the north end of Missisquoi Bay as far east as the height of the Green Mountains.[43]

Such was the complex interplay of forces operating on Vermont that continental and global events played as great a part as local harassment by colonial troops in bringing western Abenaki raids to a halt. The year 1759, which was highlighted by Roger's pyrrhic campaign against St. Francis, was also Great Britain's "annus mirabilis," when English arms won victories on the ocean and in India, Africa, and the West Indies, as well as in North America. The British successes at Crown Point and Ticonderoga, and the capture of Quebec, represented the North American phase of a world war which ended with France defeated and humiliated on every front. The fall of New France to the English left the western Abenakis and other tribes without allies to face their victorious enemies. Fort Dummer, for so long the English bastion against western Abenaki raids, was abandoned in 1760.

After the end of the war, some Missisquoi Abenakis filtered to St. Francis. Other Indians returned as usual to reoccupy lands they had evacuated during the conflict. Some families returned to Cowass and were living in the meadows alongside the river when the English first settled Lower Cowass in 1761. They remained there for many years, and from their number Captain Joe and other individuals made their way into town histories and local memory as the last Indians in the area.[44] Many other western Abenakis who were living in small family bands in and around Vermont when the war ended simply remained where they were. The pattern of small bands living a dispersed life-style continued and may even have intensified as a result of the war in which western Abenaki core villages in the north suffered direct attack for the first time.

The English conquest of New France demonstrated that the western Abenakis' fate had been taken out of their hands. No longer could they look to the French for support and asylum. In the hard years ahead they would have to adopt new strategies and accommodate to the new situation created by England's hard-won hegemony.

Chapter 10

Adjustment to Conquest, 1760–1775

Missisquoi emerged relatively unscathed from the Seven Years War. Western Abenakis from St. Francis dispersed after their village was burnt, but despite sporadic skirmishing on and around Lake Champlain, which may have reached the village, the Missisquoi community survived intact. At the end of the war the Abenakis returned as usual to reoccupy their lands. Missisquoi was neither so well known nor so notorious to the British as was St. Francis, and the community attracted less attention from the victorious redcoats in the postwar years. Nevertheless, the British conquest of New France subjected the western Abenakis who remained in northern Vermont, as well as those who had removed to other locations, to a new era of intensified pressure and change.

The Abenakis had been the allies, not the subjects, of France. They had maintained an independent status under French sovereignty and were not bound by French treaties nor the French surrender. The British victory not only robbed the western Abenakis of their strongest ally; it also removed fears English settlers had harbored for generations about the "French and Indian menace." Before 1760, English encroachments on western Abenaki territory had been tentative and hesitant. Now victory over the French broke the dike, initiating the fifteen-year period of migration, land speculation, and settlement in northern New England that historian Charles E. Clark has described as "the great swarming time." Soldiers returning from the north told of rich lands

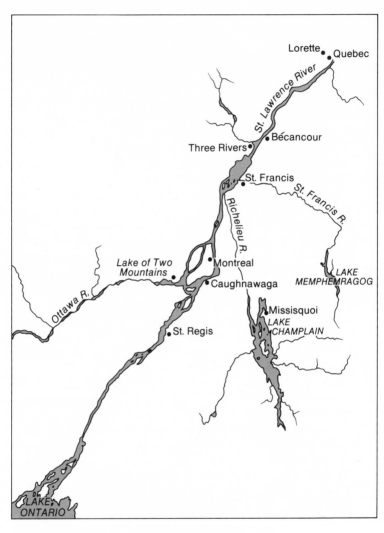

Abenaki and neighboring villages after the conquest

and game-filled forests, stimulating a flood of immigration from western Massachusetts and Connecticut, where the population had increased by 500 percent in thirty years. In 1761 alone, seventy-eight new townships were granted in the Connecticut Valley, sixty of them on the west bank of the river. Settlements were begun in six Vermont towns that year. Bennington was the first town on the west side of the Green Mountains. Six more Vermont towns were settled in 1763, another seven in 1764. Between 1760 and 1774, seventy new towns were settled in Vermont, one hundred in New Hampshire, and ninety-four in Maine, "many of them peopled by restless migrants making their second or third move toward the frontier." Some 20,000 migrants moved north across the Massachusetts border, up the Connecticut Valley, and west from coastal New Hampshire. By 1776 all but the northeastern corner of New Hampshire had been staked out and much of it thinly settled. The non-Indian population of northern New England increased from perhaps 60,000 to 150,000 in just fifteen years, and the number of settlers in the Connecticut Valley jumped from a few hundred to several thousand.[1]

An anonymous English observer described the pace and character of this unprecedented invasion of western Abenaki lands in the years between the conquest of New France and the American Revolution:

> Farms on the river Connecticut are every day extending beyond the old fort Dummer, for nearly thirty miles; and will in a few years reach to Kohasser [Cowass] which is two hundred miles; not that such an extent will be one-tenth settled, but the newcomers do not fix near their neighbors, and go on regularly, but take spots that please them best, though twenty or thirty miles beyond any others. This to people of a sociable disposition in Europe would appear very strange, but the Americans do not regard the near neighborhood of other farmers; twenty or thirty miles by water they esteem no distance in matters of this sort; besides in a country that promises well the intermediate space is not long in filling up. Between Connecticut river and Lake Champlain upon Otter Creek, and all along Lake Sacrament [George] and the rivers that fall into it, and the whole length of Wood Creek are numerous settlements made since the peace.

After the conquest Abenakis had to become accustomed to the presence of increasing numbers of English settlers. This drawing, *Indian Neighbors*, depicts the "last Abenaki family at Bellows Falls," in the nineteenth century. (National Life Insurance Company, Montpelier)

Another petitioner asserted that the fertile lands between Lake Champlain and the upper Connecticut, which had for so long been closed to the British by the French and Indians, were "now filling very fast with Industrious People and likely to become very Populous." Vermont's fertile valleys attracted settlers not only from Massachusetts and Connecticut but also from Britain. The Scots American Company of Farmers purchased lands at Ryegate in the early 1770s as a refuge for troubled farmers and artisans from the west lowlands of Scotland who were seeking to start a new life. Another company from Perthshire and Stirlingshire bought lands in Barnet in 1774. About the same time, a number of Irish immigrants settled in southern Vermont near the Battenkill River. One group, which settled near Camden, comprised Irish Methodists of German descent.[2]

As Abenakis filtered back to their homelands after the war, they encountered newcomers in their old territories. Northern town histories and local traditions record numerous instances in which Abenakis returning to their homes and English settlers advancing from the south "mingled in frontier communities from Lake Champlain to the upper Androscoggin River."[3] Western Abenakis confronted a new situation in which they had to adjust to the close proximity of English settlers backed by the power of the British military. The western Abenaki strategy of dispersing in time of danger and returning when the coast was clear had worked well as long as the threat was military and temporary. Now the threat was permanent and tended to increase rather than diminish as more and more settlers came to stay.

While English settlers benefitted from Abenaki knowledge, adopted Abenaki practices in their hunting, fishing, and planting, and utilized native herbal remedies, Abenakis had to come to terms with European notions about ownership and utilization of the land. Moreover, as William Cronon has explained, English settlements produced changes in the land that presented the Indian inhabitants with a new set of ecological challenges. By the late 1760s, the British colonial authorities were concerned about the impact of these changes on lands formerly occupied by the western Abenakis. Settlers thronged the Champlain Valley, cutting its oak and pine forests, and marketing their lumber, potash, and agricultural produce in Quebec. In 1768 Governor Guy Carleton of Quebec was ordered to take measures to protect the rich timber around Lake Champlain from destruction. In June 1769 the Earl of Hillsborough, secretary of state for the colonies, warned that the "waste and destruction" caused by unrestricted settlement of the "King's Woods" on the west bank of the Connecticut River posed a threat to timber supplies for the masts of the Royal Navy.[4]

Western Abenakis inhabited a changing world in which the immediate presence of British settlers governed their options and their actions. "Quite a number" of Abenakis had returned to Cowass by 1761, but, as the Reverend Grant Powers exalted, "The loss of their strong ally the French, and the chastisement which Rogers inflicted upon their brethren at St. Francis, had cooled their ardor, and rendered the idea of our men taking possession of those meadows far more acceptable to them than it was in 1752." By 1764 there were eighteen white families in Newbury and five more across the river in Haverhill. At least thirty Indians continued to live in the area, some with their families, although for the most part they came to the settlements only to trade.[5]

As they had in the past, western Abenakis adjusted to new situations on the family level. The limited authority of Abenaki chiefs, which had so troubled their French allies during the war, seems to have declined further after the defeat. The prestige of past war chiefs like Grey Lock never revived, although new leaders were appointed when the people needed spokesmen to negotiate with the British. A "great chief" of the St. Francis Abenakis died in 1762; they lost others in the years that followed. When the St. Francis Abenakis appointed two new chiefs in 1768 "according to ancient Custom," they brought them to Sir William Johnson, superintendent of the British Indian Department, for approval.[6] Family bands reverted to patterns of subsistence and the decentralized political organization that had served them well for generations and which allowed them to cope with new conditions without traumatic disruption of traditional social, political, and economic practices. But the bands found they had to withdraw further from their homelands and that it was more difficult to return. Some opted to seek a new life with relatives at St. Francis, although the St. Francis Abenakis faced problems of their own at the war's end.

Before 1760 the French had provided Abenakis from the St. Lawrence villages with powder and shot, clothing, and other supplies. The British victory terminated that source of supply. In addition, the fur trade that had flourished along the St. Lawrence was now considerably reduced. Those Abenakis who remained at St. Francis after Rogers' raid found that they often had to hunt far and wide in search of sustenance. During the next decade or so, western Abenakis moved freely and widely, sometimes mingling with other communities and hunting on distant lands, sometimes encroaching on neighbors' territories.[7]

Some St. Francis Abenakis relocated to the Missisquoi region after Rogers' raid. Another group of Abenakis and Schaghticokes from St. Francis settled at the Iroquois mission village at Oswegatchie in 1760; when that mission closed, they moved to St. Regis (Akwesasne).[8] While some St. Francis Abenakis returned to familiar hunting territories on the upper Kennebec and Androscoggin rivers, others hunted as far afield as the Ottawa River in the winter of 1761–62 and in Acadia in 1763.[9] At least one Abenaki from St. Francis traveled as far west as the Mississippi River, where he spent four years, and then he returned east via the Great Lakes, bringing news of Indian, French, and Spanish activities in the west to the Mohawks on the eve of the Treaty of Fort Stanwix in 1768.[10] The British Indian Department's "Enumeration of Indians within the Northern Department" in 1763 recorded only 100 Abenaki warriors and reported that since the burning of St. Francis "they have lived scattered except a few," but noted that "if they were all collected they would amount to more than is represented."[11]

The distressed situation of the St. Francis Abenakis complicated the conduct of their intertribal relations. In August 1759 the Abenakis had put to death one of the Stockbridge Indians accompanying Captain Kennedy. The Stockbridges subsequently complained to Sir William Johnson, who insisted the Abenakis give satisfaction for the killing. The Abenaki chiefs met in council and

decided to send wampum belts and a young Indian slave to replace the one they had killed, but they were unable to take action
until after they dispersed for their winter hunting. Meanwhile,
Johnson advised his deputy, Daniel Claus, to sound out the
Stockbridge chief, Captain Jacobs, who was said to be opposed
to any settlement. In June 1761, delegates from St. Francis came
to Claus pleading extenuating circumstances for the killing and
requesting the British to intercede and arrange a peace settlement. They had wampum to send and had purchased a Panis
slave to replace the murdered Stockbridge. But the affair dragged
on and the Abenakis had not heard from Johnson by the time
they dispersed for their next winter hunt. The next February, an
Abenaki who had returned from hunting near Crown Point reported that the Stockbridges were losing patience and planned to
exact revenge in the spring. Immediately, five Abenaki chiefs
made the arduous trek to Fort Johnson, where, in the presence of
Mohawk and Onondaga delegates, they presented Sir William
with two wampum belts and the Panis slave to be delivered to the
Stockbridges in atonement for the man whom they had killed
and to settle all differences between the two nations. The Abenakis apologized for their delay. They had suffered great distress
since the destruction of their village, had sustained additional
losses in a fire, and "have been hitherto scattered and dispersed
so that we could not have a proper Meeting upon your Messages
concerning *Capt* Jacobs, and his Nation." In April Johnson delivered the wampum and the slave to two Stockbridge sachems
from the Housatonic River and the affair came to an amicable
conclusion.[12]

Sir William Johnson commended the Abenakis on their efforts
to live in peace with the other Indian nations, assuring them it
was the only way to get along with "your New Friends the English." He further urged the Abenakis "to collect your people
together in one Village, apply yourselves to your hunting, planting and Trade, and leave off Rambling about through the Country." In this way, said Johnson, the Abenakis would become
"more respectable than you are at present." The British Indian
Department clearly wanted to see the western Abenakis concen-

trated in one or two villages for easy supervision. Moreover, Johnson informed the Abenakis:

> As You are now come into the Indian Confederacy of which I have Superintendency I must desire you will not enter into, or hold any private or publick Meetings with any Nations of Indians whatsoever, without my knowledge and approbation, as such meetings must raise in us suspicions of the sincerity of your Intentions & tend to overset the happy state, you are now Entering into.

Shortly afterwards, Johnson thanked the Caughnawagas for having "admonished your Cousins the Abenaquis to act a proper part, . . . and I hope you will take care to see that they act up to the promises they have made."[13] The British expected the Caughnawagas to exert their influence to keep other members of the Seven Nations in line, and Johnson apparently and erroneously assumed that the alliance embraced all the "rambling" Abenaki bands, as well as the communities at St. Francis and Bécancour.

Johnson had reason for his admonition. The Abenakis' distressed situation, coupled with General Amherst's parsimonious refusal to afford them more than "some small trifles out of Charity," rendered them susceptible to the stirrings of anti-English sentiment prevalent among many tribes at the end of the war. In October 1761, the Jesuit priest Pierre Roubaud warned Sir William that the Abenakis had hardly shown themselves at St. Francis that summer. They had been attending councils at Caughnawaga, debating messages sent by Ottawas from the Ohio country and even by Cherokees from Carolina urging all tribes to unite. Indeed, said Roubaud, most of the Abenakis had gone hunting on the Ottawa River, "to be the readier in the Spring to decide what is to be done." The Jesuit reminded Johnson: ". . . nothing is more prejudicial to the Service as such Journeys of Indns. to strange Nations. That wch. would make the Abinaquis a faithful People is to draw them to their native Country, some to Acadia & others to Albany where they come from." Roubaud had been a missionary at St. Francis for many years, had accompanied the

Abenakis on their campaigns at Fort William Henry and Quebec, and knew his charges well. But Amherst dismissed Roubaud as unreliable and wrong in the head, and even Daniel Claus acknowledged that the priest had the reputation of being "a little flighty" and "a little cracked brain." Nevertheless, Johnson was taking no chances.[14]

Even though the St. Francis Abenakis survived Rogers' raid and rebuilt their village, it would take the community many years to recover from the blow and the distress of defeat. And they would spend those years under the watchful eyes of the British, who were determined to control their relations with other Indian groups. After the conquest, a contingent of British soldiers occupied St. Francis. With Pontiac's war rumbling in the west, Joseph Louis Gill assured General Frederick Haldimand that the St. Francis Abenakis had no communication with the tribes in the upper country who were aligned with the Ottawa war chief, and had nothing but peaceful intentions. Indeed, the St. Francis Indians and other nations of Canada sent a wampum belt to the western tribes, condemning their rash and foolish actions in taking up the hatchet and urging them to hold fast the chain of friendship with the English king who was now sovereign over all lands as far as the Mississippi. Nevertheless, the British remained suspicious and on guard.[15]

Western Abenakis who remained in their Lake Champlain homelands and reoccupied Missisquoi also soon felt the presence of British soldiers and settlers. With the forts at St. Johns and St. Frédéric now in British hands, many Missisquoi Abenakis turned to Catholic churches in Lower Canada for religious guidance.[16] Contact with the redcoat garrisons proved unavoidable, however, and it was not always friendly. In July 1765 an altercation occurred at St. Johns between the commanding officer and a "St. Francis or Misisqui Indian." A dispute over ownership of a dog ended with the soldiers seizing the Abenaki, administering 300 lashes, and threatening to hang him, after the Indian had killed the coveted canine.[17]

More serious than the Missisquois' occasional relations with nearby garrisons was the steadily growing threat to their homelands. When the British marched to Montreal in 1760, they had given the St. Francis Abenakis "solemn assurances that if we did not assist the French, but permitted you to descend the River without interruption, we should be placed among the number of your friends, and enjoy our rights and possessions and the free exercise of our Religion forever." The Abenakis complied, Montreal fell, and the Articles of Capitulation included a clause protecting the lands, rights, and religion of France's Indian allies. In addition, in an effort to stabilize Indian relations and regulate the frontier, the Royal Proclamation of October 1763 established the Appalachian watershed as the western boundary of settlement in the colonies. The proclamation limited settlement past "any Lands beyond the Heads or Sources of any of the Rivers which fall into the Atlantic Ocean from the West and North West," thereby ostensibly safeguarding Abenaki lands west of the Green Mountains. The proclamation reaffirmed British policy that Indian lands were to be obtained only by purchase by the proper authorities in open council. Sir William Johnson's contention that the proclamation line in the north did not apply to the Caughnawagas and Abenakis, because they were not original occupants and had been invited to Canada only to serve as a barrier for the French settlements "and a Nursery of Warriors for distressing our Frontiers," ignored the fact that the Abenakis were the original owners of the lands they continued to inhabit around Lake Champlain. British assurances soon proved to be empty promises. In a letter later destroyed by fire, Daniel Claus informed Sir William that the Missisquoi Abenakis were becoming increasingly anxious about their lands.[18] The Missisquois had ample reason for anxiety: individual encroachments posed a greater threat to the community than did military occupation in the postwar years.

Despite the Royal Proclamation, in 1763 Governor Benning Wentworth of New Hampshire granted some Abenaki lands around the present-day townships of Swanton and Highgate to Samuel Hunt and Isaiah Goodrich. However, repeated royal instructions prohibited colonial governors from making grants of land where Indians still held occupancy rights, and New York at that time also claimed the lands between Lake Champlain and the Connecticut River (in 1764 the Privy Council established the

Connecticut River as New York's eastern border). Wentworth's grant was thus of dubious legal validity. In March 1765, Lieutenant Moses Hazen of the Forty-fourth Regiment of Foot requested a land grant of two thousand acres on the Missisquoi River. Governor James Murray of Lower Canada ordered an investigation of the claim and a survey of the land, found it to be Indian land, and rejected Hazen's request.[19]

Later that spring, however, a group of Abenakis leased an area of timberland about 4.5 miles long by 1.5 miles wide near the Missisquoi River to James Robertson, a merchant from St. Johns. The document does not, as it has sometimes been interpreted, indicate that the Missisquoi Abenakis were selling out and preparing to move off and join their relatives at St. Francis. The lease contained clear provision for continued Abenaki occupation of the area and expressly reserved twelve farms on both sides of the Missisquoi River for the use of several named Abenakis. It also included a provision that the fields of the Abenaki farms should be plowed annually "as shall be sufficient for them to plant their Indian corn every year." Among the Indian signatories was one "Charlotte widow of the late chief of the Abenackque Nation at Missique." Robertson evidently observed the terms of the agreement, since for the next five years he ran a successful sawmill and trading business at Swanton Falls and he and his workers appear to have lived in harmony with their Abenaki landlords.[20]

In early September 1766, Sir Guy Carleton of Quebec and Henry Moore of New York met on Isle La Motte at the north end of Lake Champlain to settle the joint boundary between their provinces. Caughnawaga Mohawks and Missisquoi Abenakis also attended the council. Against the backdrop of the first fall colors in the foliage around the lake, the Caughnawagas addressed the assemblage. They asserted their claim to hunting and fishing rights over much of the Champlain Valley, maintaining that the Six Nations were the original owners of the lands and lake in question and that the country was "chiefly occupied in the hunting Seasons by the Antient Mohawks whose Descendants we are." The Caughnawagas made no objection to the settlements that had been made in this country since the British takeover, but they did insist that they should continue to enjoy hunting rights there. The Caughnawaga claim to the lands they ceded was flimsy, but, as Francis Jennings has shown, British agents regularly exaggerated the extent of Iroquois claims so that they could then secure desired lands by agreement with compliant Iroquois rather than with the Indians in actual possession.[21]

Isle La Motte had long been a favored location for Abenaki occupation. The Missisquoi Abenakis at the council were standing on land they considered their home ground. The Missisquois were still closely associated with the St. Francis Abenakis, who in turn were members of the confederacy known as the Seven Nations of Canada; and the Caughnawagas were the recognized speakers for the confederacy. Yet, while they chose not to confront the Caughnawagas directly, the Missisquoi delegates made it clear they had no intention of abandoning their lands and were concerned with more than just hunting and fishing rights:

> We the Missiskoui Indians of the St. Francis or Abenakis Tribe have inhabited that part of Lake Champlain known by the Name of Missiskoui [since] Time unknown to any of us here present, without being Molested or any one's claiming Right to it, to our knowledge.

The only grants they had made in the area had been about eighteen years earlier when the French had surveyed a suitable location for constructing their sawmill and had "convened our People to ask approbation." After the French had abandoned the sawmill at the beginning of the last war and buried their ironworks, the Abenakis expected that "everything of the kind would Subside." But soon after the end of the war, a group of English people had arrived to rebuild the mill "and now claim three Leagues in Breadth & Six in Depth, which takes in our Village and Plantations by far." Proffering a wampum belt, the Missisquoi delegates requested that the governor look into the affair and obtain justice for them, "as it is of great Concern to us." They also asked that measures be taken to prevent traders from bringing liquor among them; if the Abenakis wanted to trade, they could go to Montreal rather than have traders peddling liquor in their village.[22]

The immediate cause of concern to the Missisquoi Abenakis

was Simon Metcalfe of Albany. Metcalfe, a veteran officer of the Seven Years War, was surveyor for the province of New York. He carried out surveys around Missisquoi and requested grants of land from the governors of New York and Quebec. In July 1771 he was granted 2,000 acres between East Bay and Missisquoi Bay, which included Abenaki farm lands and the site of their village as well as a substantial portion of Robertson's lease. The same month, the governor of New York granted additional lands on the east side of Lake Champlain to be included in the township of Prattsburgh, which covered parts of present-day Swanton and Highgate, Vermont. Metcalfe also established a trading post at the mouth of the Missisquoi River, where he exchanged goods with the Abenakis for their furs.[23]

In late June 1773 the Abenakis sent a delegation to complain to deputy Daniel Claus, who duly reported the conference to Sir William Johnson:

> The Abinaquis of Misisqui sent me a Deputation since my Arrival abt. Mr. Metcafes taking Possession of their Lands at Misisqui wch. was contrary to our promise in 1760 of letting them keep their Lands unmolested I told them as Mr. Matcaff was not here I could not say anything abt. this Matter but all I could tell them now was that the Govrs. of NYork & Canada had settled it with the Caughnaws. when in Lake Champlain in 1766 abt. setting the 45 Dege. that the Indians should have free hunting & fishing in Lake Champlain but that the Ground belongd. to the king & his Subjects to wch. the Caughnaws. in behalf of the rest agreed.

In other words, British Indian agents chose to accept the Caughnawaga position expressed at the Isle La Motte council—that the Indians claimed only hunting and fishing rights—as binding on the Lake Champlain Abenakis as well. The land belonged to the king to dispose of as he saw fit. Claus added that he thought the Missisquois had been put up to making the complaint by some individuals who claimed that land themselves by purchase from the French.[24]

The western Abenakis had fought for generations without seeing their Missisquoi homelands come under immediate threat. They had made no concessions to the British and they had not suffered defeat in the long wars against the redcoats. Yet they were on notice that their lands now belonged to King George and his subjects. Moreover, in an effort to bring order to their relations with an array of Indian peoples, the British Indian Department endeavored to employ the Seven Nations of Canada as a conduit for Indian affairs, as they used the Six Nations for dealing with tribes in the Ohio Valley. In practice, this meant that British agents looked to Caughnawaga and St. Francis to control member and associate tribes. Thus Missisquoi was circumvented, and the sovereignty of the Lake Champlain Abenakis was ignored. The Missisquoi Abenakis were about to become strangers in their own land.

Conflicting Iroquois-Abenaki claims to the Champlain Valley and the encroachment of settlers on the Missisquoi homeland-land complicated the position of the Abenaki band who had taken up residence at the Iroquois mission village at St. Regis and were uncertain whether they would be able to move to Missisquoi. This band included those Indians who had taken refuge at Oswegatchie until that mission closed, and Gordon Day has suggested that many of these "Abenakis" may have been displaced Schaghticokes from St. Francis or Missisquoi whose long association with the Iroquois made it logical for them to join an Iroquois mission community.[25]

In the years after the conquest, the inhabitants of St. Francis reassembled and rebuilt their village. They erected a wooden church to replace the one burned by Rogers, reignited their council fire, and attempted to reconstruct their war-torn lives. In July 1768, a party of St. Francis Abenakis reminded Sir William Johnson that, "On the reduction of Canada eight years ago, You desired us to collect our selves, and to light our fire again at our Village, since which you have recommended the same to us four times, the last of which was last year." They had now complied with Sir William's wishes, had reestablished their mission, and needed help to support their priest. The following spring, Sir Guy Carleton issued a proclamation forbidding white people to settle on the land of the St. Francis Indians.[26]

Not all of the scattered bands returned so promptly, however. The Abenakis who had received asylum at St. Regis were reluctant to leave their new homes, and by 1769 they had overstayed their welcome. The sachems and principal men of the St. Regis Mohawks met with Daniel Claus at Caughnawaga in August and aired their grievances. The refugees had fled to St. Regis after their village was attacked, "desiring our Protection for one Night as their Expression was, or untill their Village was reestablished." The Mohawks had granted the Abenakis' request and taken them in, but, when the St. Francis mission was reestablished, the chiefs had asked the Abenakis to collect their people and go home. The Abenakis, however, refused to leave. The St. Regis sachems attributed this reluctance to the machinations of the Abenakis' trader, John Jacob Hertel. Hertel had obtained a letter from Sir Guy Carleton granting the Abenakis permission to reside at St. Regis. Now, said the sachems, the Abenakis were becoming arrogant, destroying their hosts' beaver traps and taking over their hunting grounds. The St. Regis mission had existed since 1755, but the sachems declared, "We never would have settled here, had we known that Strangers might mix & settle amongst us whenever they pleased." They warned that unless the situation was resolved "the Peace & Tranquility of our Town is at an End."[27]

The issue arose at the German Flats council in New York's Mohawk Valley in July 1770 when the Six Nations, the Indians of Canada, and a delegation of Cherokees met with Sir William Johnson and the English. The Canadian Indian delegation was dominated by seventy-eight Mohawks from Caughnawaga and St. Regis; only two St. Francis Abenakis attended—probably Joseph Louis Gill and Toksus. The spokesman for the Canadian Indians reminded the English of the promise they had made ten years earlier to preserve Indian rights and possessions. Now, they said, evil-intentioned individuals were causing problems and "our Brothers at St. Regis have been distressed for sometime past by Intruders imposed on them from another Nation, who have no pretensions to live in their Village." They requested that Johnson do something; Sir William replied he understood the affair had been recently settled.[28]

As the chiefs of the Seven Nations returned from the German Flats conference, they learned that a delegation of Abenakis from St. Regis were on their way to Johnson Hall to present their own version of the quarrel. The chiefs warned Daniel Claus that Hertel and the Abenakis intended to take advantage of their absence to misrepresent the case, and that Hertel would put words in the Abenakis' mouths for his own ends.[29]

In the event, when the Abenakis met with Johnson between August 6 and 11, they received short shrift from the Indian superintendent. Speaking to Daniel Claus, they asserted they had been at St. Regis eleven years: "Our Brethn. the Iroquois received us then well, but after we had cleared our fields, we heard bad News from our Brethern wch. was that we could not remain there." They said they thought Governor Carleton had settled things to their satisfaction and begged the English to take pity on them and instruct the Iroquois to let them live in peace at St. Regis. They attributed their reluctance to leave to the "Drunkenness wch. so much prevails in the other Indn. Town in Canada [St. Francis]." In addition, they knew the St. Francis Abenakis at this time were threatened with loss of their lands, despite British assurances that they would be left in "the quiet & peaceful Possession" of those lands. They also asked that Hertel be appointed as their official interpreter.[30]

Sir William Johnson pointed out that the Abenakis had been "rambling" between Oswegatchie and St. Regis ten years before, and that the St. Regis chiefs had afforded them temporary residence and no more. The Caughnawaga and St. Regis Mohawks had both complained more than once, and the Six Nations were also displeased at the Abenakis' behavior. St. Regis was not the only place free from drunkenness and, if the Abenakis wanted to avoid that vice, Johnson advised, they should cultivate self-restraint. Smaller tribes than they did not have their own interpreter, and Johnson said the Indian Department could not afford to provide them with one. He advised them to leave and return to their homes, and the sooner the better.[31]

Jean Baptist Portneuf replied for the Abenakis. They agreed to do as Johnson recommended, but begged that they be allowed to remain two more years until they could find a suitable place to move to, "as we have land of our own but it is now Cut into pieces by the English, except a Small piece." Johnson replied that, if Englishmen had taken their land, it was with the king's permission, as a reward for their services in the war. A fragmented document in Sir William Johnson's papers makes it clear that Portneuf was referring to Missisquoi. The Abenakis at St. Regis still looked to Missisquoi as "land of our own," but their willingness to move back there was tempered by the English encroachments and the uncertain claims stemming from the Isle La Motte council of 1766.[32]

In council at Caughnawaga in October 1770 the chiefs declared that Hertel and the Abenakis had from the very beginning been the cause of disputes and factions at St. Regis and were disturbing the peace. They reached the unanimous conclusion "that the Abenaquis and consequently Mr. Hertel should quit the village without delay." Daniel Claus feared bloodshed if measures were not taken, and blamed Hertel for prolonging the crisis. In his view, Hertel had insinuated himself at St. Regis by "prevailing upon a few of the most weak & debauched Inds." to let him trade at their houses and then set himself up in opposition to the original inhabitants of the village. Hertel had not only kept the whole town "in hot water" but also attracted and encouraged "a parcell of vagrant Abinaquis who formerly lived at Misisqui & who have been warned off by the 6 Nations of whose hunting ground they yearly encroach." In fact, said Claus, things had come "within an ace" of hostilities when an Iroquois encountered an Abenaki who had robbed his hunting ground and taken away both the game and an iron beaver trap. Had the Iroquois been killed, the tribe would have exacted revenge on the whole Abenaki nation at St. Francis, "for any Indn committing hostilities within an other Nation that Nation makes reprisals upon the Aggressors Nation indiscriminately be they ever so innocent or ignorant of what happend." Fortunately, Hertel told Claus that he intended to leave St. Regis. In addition, he had "a Message to deliver from the Abinaquis of St. Francis to those of St. Regis desiring them to settle at Misisqui wch if he effects I shall be happy of." Hertel and the Abenakis were ready to leave St. Regis in the fall. Hertel was to winter on the Ottawa River; the Abenakis below St. Regis on Cornwall Island.[33]

Some of the refugee Abenakis may have returned to St. Francis, but Gordon Day found no record that the whole band returned either to St. Francis or to Missisquoi. The persistence of certain Abenaki surnames at St. Regis indicates that some families remained, and there were Abenakis in the village at the outbreak of the War of 1812. The Abenaki band on Cornwall Island remained there until they were absorbed into the Mohawk community in the nineteenth century. John Moody's analysis of Abenaki names in church registers indicates a three-way movement of population between the communities at St. Regis, St. Francis, and Missisquoi through the nineteenth century.[34]

Other western Abenakis remained dispersed across northern New England, from the Champlain Valley to the eastern foothills of the White Mountains. The lakes and mountains of this remote territory continued to provide Abenaki bands with a haven in the wake of English conquest, just as they had earlier in the century. Henry Tufts, an adventurer, thief, counterfeiter, army deserter, bigamist, and ethnographic observer of some merit, spent three years living with the Abenakis between Lake Memphremagog and Lake Umbagog on the eve of the American Revolution. Tufts took an Indian wife, marrying a niece of the chief Tomhegan, whose band lived in the upper Androscoggin Valley; and he was treated by Molly Occutt, who became renowned among Indians and whites alike for her doctoring skills. In the summer of 1772, prompted by curiosity and a desire to become intimately acquainted with the Abenakis' customs and way of life, Tufts followed the daily practice of moving from place to place until he had visited the whole band.

He estimated that perhaps 300 Indians inhabited that particular area, while "The entire tribe, of which these people made a part, was in number about seven hundred of both sexes, and extended their settlements in a scattering desultory manner, from lake Memphremagog to lake Umbagog, covering an extent of some eighty miles."[35]

Though the Abenakis depended on hunting for their sustenance, their skill and the faunal wealth of the region meant that they were in no danger of starving. Each spring, the Indians who lived around Bethel, Maine, traveled to Quebec to trade their winter catch of furs for blankets, guns, and ammunition, but they obtained the rest of their goods from New England. A band of about 150 Indians who lived on the upper Connecticut were trading in Newbury, Vermont, on the eve of the American Revolution.[36] The Abenakis with whom Tufts resided were clearly a mobile and independent people, supporting themselves through hunting and trading, in regular communication with trading centers in Canada and New England, and no doubt in contact with western Abenakis at St. Francis and Missisquoi as well as with Penobscots in Maine.

The years between the conquest of New France and the outbreak of the American Revolution saw western Abenaki bands adjusting to the new reality of British dominance. For many, the British takeover initiated a new era of distress. St. Francis Abenakis who had dispersed following Rogers' raid slowly rebuilt their community, although some may never have resumed residence at the village. Missisquoi Abenakis expressed grave misgivings about encroachments on their lands even as they coexisted with the newcomers. Some resettling occurred in the postwar years as western Abenaki bands reoccupied familiar territories and returned to their villages, but the influx of English settlers presented them with new challenges and pressures. Confronted with permanent settlements on their lands, Abenaki bands found it more difficult to return and resume their normal life-style after the war. Many found themselves edged into marginal lands on the peripheries of their traditional territories. Some moved off to new regions. With bands moving between key communities, western Abenaki society increasingly came to resemble a mobile mosaic of family bands scattered through northern New England and Quebec, as well as New York. At the same time, however, the dispute over Abenaki residence at St. Regis, British Indian Department insistence on concentrating all western Abenakis at St. Francis and Bécancour, and British attempts to conduct their Indian relations through Caughnawaga and St. Francis, all contributed to a growing rift between the western Abenaki bands focused around Missisquoi and those in Quebec or with ties to New York. In British Indian agents' eyes, St. Francis represented the last vestige of western Abenaki political power; any bands not living there were regarded as "wanderers."[37] Even as they adjusted to new conditions and remained in their traditional homelands, the western Abenakis at Missisquoi and Lake Champlain suffered an implicit loss of political status and a denial of their continued existence as an independent community—which boded ill for the future.

Chapter 11

Western Abenakis and the American Revolution, 1775–1783

Traditionally, the final quarter of the eighteenth century stands as the time when the last western Abenakis disappeared from Vermont and New Hampshire, when the few survivors finally pulled up their roots and followed their relatives to Canada. The period constitutes another phase in the dispersal and dispossession of the western Abenakis, but it did not terminate their presence in Vermont. Indeed, some Abenakis who had taken up residence at St. Francis returned to the upper Connecticut River during these dangerous times. For Indians and non-Indians alike, the Revolutionary era constituted a complex and divisive time necessitating painful decisions and eliciting a variety of responses. Western Abenakis suffered further relocation and loss of land, but their role in the conflict often was ambiguous, and their movements were more varied and complex than the traditional notion of a final migration into Canada conveys.

Vermont occupied a critical position in the Revolutionary War. Its strategic importance guaranteed that it would be the focus of British and American military efforts. Yet the British hopes that there was substantial loyalist sentiment in the region, the protracted Haldimand negotiations between 1779 and 1781, and the uncertain destiny of the Green Mountain Republic combined to temper the impact of the war and complicated the picture. In times of uncertainty, the disposition of settlers in the Green Mountains, of French-Canadians chafing under British rule in Quebec, and of Indian bands throughout the region assumed additional significance. Would the Indians align themselves with the Crown as a means of checking American encroachment on their lands, or would they side with the rebels and hope for a return of French power in Canada? From the beginning of the conflict, rebels and redcoats kept a sharp eye on the western Abenakis, tried to gauge their attitude, and endeavored to enlist them as allies.

When Briton fell to fighting Briton in the American Revolution, the western Abenakis confronted an unprecedented situation. Like other Indian peoples in eastern North America, they faced confusing and sometimes conflicting choices as they sought to safeguard their interests in a world turned upside down. In the spring of 1775 an Abenaki woman on the Androscoggin River "expressed much concern about the Times; said their men could not hunt, Eat, nor Sleep; keep calling together Every night; courting, courting, courting, courting. Every night, all night. O, straing *Englishmen* kill one another. I think the world is coming to an end." Settlers in the area were alarmed to see Indians wearing paint for the first time.[1] In many cases, Abenakis responded to the new uncertainty with uncertainty, and the Revolution produced both confusion and division in western Abenaki communities. Most tried to remain neutral; although some became involved on each side of the conflict, others evidently played both sides of the fence. If western Abenakis were bewildered by the Revolution, British and Americans were equally confused by the western Abenakis' responses and regarded their movements and behavior with suspicion. On the whole, however, like other Indian peoples in this period, western Abenakis were doing pretty much what the American rebels were doing: struggling to preserve their freedom in a time of turmoil.

From the first shots of the conflict, settlers in Vermont looked nervously northwards in anticipation of Indian attacks from Canada. The new inhabitants of the Connecticut and Champlain valleys were aware of their vulnerability, sensitive to Indian movements and whereabouts, and petitioned throughout the war for protection and assistance against Indian raids, real or imagined.[2]

General Philip Schuyler at Albany feared that the Indians would prove hostile and attack via Lake Champlain, and in the

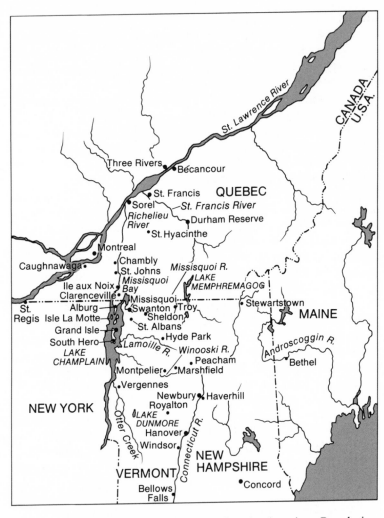

Western Abenaki Country during and after the American Revolution

summer of 1775 he warned General Washington against the danger of an impending attack by "the Misisque Indians." An undated document from the same period illustrates the anxiety that was prevalent among Green Mountain settlers in the first year of fighting. A scouting party brought news "that there is a body of Indians now lying on the west side of the Lake Champlain near opposite the mouth of Onion River what the particular number of them is, we cannot certainly determine, but by the best Information not less than four or five hundred." This may well have been a large Abenaki village on South Hero Island. The scouts saw ten canoes of Indians from Canada join this encampment and also reported that Governor Carleton was busy enlisting the support of the same tribes that had terrorized the frontier under Montcalm in the French and Indian War.[3] General Jacob Bayley at Newbury emphasized "the danger we might be in of a visit from Canada," and warned that his Indian informants told him they would be forced to take up arms unless the Americans helped them by sending an army to Canada, where French and Indians alike would rally to their support.[4]

The Western Abenaki commitment in the opening campaigns was ambiguous. Before his abortive attack on Montreal, Ethan Allen sent a Stockbridge ambassador in May 1775 to win the support of the Caughnawaga, St. Regis, Lake of the Two Mountains, and St. Francis Indians, promising them blankets, tomahawks, knives, and paint, and proclaiming his love of Indian people and his knowledge of their ways. The Seven Nations of Canada declared their intention not to fight the Yankees, and the Penobscots, Passamaquoddies, Micmacs, and St. Johns Indians displayed pro-American sentiments. In December 1775 the Continental Congress passed a resolution to call upon the Stockbridge, St. Johns, Penobscot, and St. Francis Indians "in case of real necessity," and took active measures to engage the St. Francis Abenakis. Caughnawaga became a major center of Indian activity in the opening months of the war as redcoats and Yankees vied for Indian support and the tribes assessed the new state of affairs. St. Francis Abenakis joined their neighbors in giving the Americans assurances of friendship, but in reality most Canadian Iroquois and Canadian Abenakis wavered between neutrality and hostility to the Americans, and gave only half-hearted support to either side.[5]

In August 1775 a St. Francis Abenaki chief, named Swashan, with several followers visited Washington's camp at Cambridge and offered their services. They told Washington that half their tribe was willing to take the rebels' side, and they remained with the army besieging Boston. Some forty Abenakis from St. Francis joined the American cause during the invasion of Quebec in 1775, and Abenakis from Penobscot and St. Francis guided Benedict Arnold through the northern New England wilderness to Canada. Timothy Bedel had both Canadians and Indians under his command near St. Johns in the fall of 1775; and thirteen men from the remnant group of Pigwackets living near Fryeburg, Maine, offered their services to the Patriot cause, as did Indians around Cowass.[6]

On the other hand, Caughnawagas and their allies fought alongside British regulars at the defeat and capture of Ethan Allen, and General Carleton despatched Abenakis from St. Francis to the unsuccessful defense of Fort St. Johns in 1775 and to the defense of Quebec the next year. "Considerable numbers" of Indians occupied Grand Isle in the early years of the war, and these and other Abenakis fought for the British in skirmishes around Lake Champlain. They helped defeat Benedict Arnold's fleet at the Battle of Valcour Island in October 1776, demonstrating the emptiness of Arnold's threat that he had it in his power to destroy the St. Francis Abenakis and Canadian Iroquois if they failed to remain neutral.[7] The question of Indian allegiance in general, and the disposition of the western Abenakis in particular, remained ambiguous throughout the war. The Caughnawagas told the Americans that Governor Carleton had threatened them and that they helped the British "only for self-preservation" and "to save themselves from being destroyed." An exasperated Guy Carleton concluded that Indians, like Canadian peasants, simply joined the strongest side and could not be relied upon; and Americans too complained of the Indians' "fickle disposition" as the tribes proceeded with caution in these turbulent times.[8]

The defeat of the American expedition to Canada sent an alarm through the Champlain and Connecticut valleys. The news that the smallpox-ridden Continental Army was in retreat, pursued by British regulars, Canadians, and Indians, prompted evacuation of the towns on the Winooski River, and the summer of 1776 saw settlers along the northern frontier packing up their possessions, ready to flee from "the ravages of the Canadians & Indians"[9] who "destroyed everything in their way." An unusual amount of Indian activity was reported down the Connecticut River, and families in the upper valley retreated to Newbury, where 300 to 400 men fortified the oxbow with breastwork and blockhouses in expectation of the Indian attack that seemed sure to come. But "the Indians that was in the habit of visiting the place all flocked in, to know if they were in Danger, for they took the alarm also." As the panic subsided and the Abenakis in the area proved friendly, settlers began to drift back to their homes, and Indians and non-Indians resumed some of their daily lives. Jonathan Elkins of Peacham said that the Indians during this time made his father's store their home as they regularly brought in furs to trade. Elkins' store was "a place of rendezvous, for scouts, Indians, and Deserters," that attracted chiefs from Caughnawaga and St. Francis. Joseph Louis Gill, the "White Chief of the St. Francis Abenakis," spent almost a week there.[10]

In fact, the Patriots looked to the western Abenakis to provide a protective barrier for the settlements on the upper Connecticut. From the beginning of the war, Colonel Timothy Bedel, who was said to possess "the greatest influence over the Indians of any man," kept open communication with the tribes who might threaten New England's frontiers, and sent Indian scouting parties out to keep him apprised of developments at St. Francis and Missisquoi Bay. He worked "to cultivate a friendship with the Indians and engage them if possible in the service of the United Colonies," even on one occasion meeting in council with Caughnawaga chiefs when he was ill with smallpox. In an effort to counteract the economic leverage of the British among the Abenakis at St. Francis and to attract Indians to relocate near the settlements, Bedel and General Jacob Bayley sent Indian messengers to the Abenakis' hunting grounds, promising them trading terms at Cowass comparable to those they received in Canada, for "if the Indians trade with us we need no Soldiers." From the

American viewpoint, Indians who could be induced to settle on the upper Connecticut represented a useful line of defense against enemies coming down the old war road.[11]

Elsewhere, the Vermont frontier remained vulnerable. In June 1777 a war party of 500 Tories and Indians was reported heading up Otter Creek. In July, General John Stark was ordered to march with reinforcements from Fort Number Four to Vermont "to oppose the savages and coming forward of the enemy."[12] After the British attempt to sweep the Champlain Valley clear of rebels in 1777 faltered at the Battle of Bennington and ended in disaster with Burgoyne's surrender at Saratoga, military activities quieted in the northern theater. Continental troops withdrew to fight the war in the south, and Governor Clinton of New York reported that "Since the affair at Bennington not an Indian has been heard of to the northward, and the scalping business seems to have ceased." Indeed, by the end of the year, Bedel's scouts reported widespread unrest in Canada and that the Caughnawagas were "ready almost to a man to rise if call'd upon even in their sleep to fight against the Red Coats."[13] But Lake Champlain remained a war road, exposing Abenaki and white occupants of the valley to attack. Moreover, Burgoyne's employment of Indian allies as a psychological weapon, and the Patriots' propagandizing of the Indian murder of Jane McCrea, hardly encouraged the Americans to look favorably on the Abenakis in and around the Champlain Valley, especially since Abenakis from St. Francis had joined Burgoyne's army.[14]

In the fall of 1778 General Sir Frederick Haldimand stepped up efforts to destroy rebel harvests and settlements in the Champlain Valley. In October Major Christopher Carleton (who had lived for a time among the Indians) led an armed fleet of 354 officers and men and about 100 Indians in canoes south from Isle aux Noix in a campaign designed to destroy rebel provisions and capture rebel settlers. He netted 39 prisoners in three weeks.[15] Continued British control of Lake Champlain after the Battle of Valcour Island made it easy for them to strike the Vermont frontier. The colonists built a string of blockhouses stretching from the lake to the Connecticut Valley, but the frontier guard was unable to prevent small parties of Indians and Tories slipping through the forests and raiding the settlements. Most settlers pulled back from Lake Champlain and Otter Creek to safer locations farther south. Those who stayed on the northern frontier begged for protection "against the fury and Rage of Savages and Diabolical Tories" and lived with their muskets within easy reach until the war's end.[16]

The Reverend Eleazar Wheelock's policy of enrolling the sons of sachems in his Indian Charity School, which had moved from Lebanon, Connecticut, to Hanover, New Hampshire, in 1769, and the influence of Mohawk alumnus Joseph Brant may well have spared the infant settlements on the upper Connecticut from the worst Indian attacks. Joseph Louis Gill's sons and nephews attended the college at Dartmouth, albeit with mixed results, and after Eleazar Wheelock's death the new president, John Whee-lock, urged the Continental Congress to recognize that the expense required to keep the sons of principal Caughnawaga and St. Francis families at Dartmouth was a small price to pay for strengthening the tribes' attachment to the United States.[17]

Nevertheless, Indian raids in Vermont during the Revolution climaxed at the valley town of Royalton in October 1780. Lieutenant Richard Houghton of the British Indian Department and "330 Men & Devils," mainly Caughnawagas, crossed Lake Champlain and headed along the Winooski River toward Newbury, where they hoped to capture Major Benjamin Whitcomb. Learning that the militia had rallied to Newbury's defense, the raiders changed course and hit Royalton. Taking the town by surprise, they burned houses and barns, destroyed livestock, killed two people, and carried off twenty-six prisoners and some horses. Leaving "the Horrid Sceen of Devastation," the Indians and Tories shook off a hastily organized pursuit, inflicted some additional damage at Randolph, and then retreated via Lake Champlain and Grand Isle to Isle aux Noix and St. Johns. Jonathan Carpenter, one of the militia who joined the unsuccessful pursuit, wrote in his journal: "1780. Oct. ye. 19—we returned home in peace, some moving off over Connet River, and our savage Enemy gone with flying Couleurs into Canida which is a poor story for a Whig to tell." The raiders threatened their captives with death in the event of being caught, but, once the pursuit was abandoned, they displayed considerable kindness. Zadock Steele reported that the Indians were so eager to feed their captives that a prisoner could not pause to pick a berry along the way without the Indians taking it as a sign of hunger and offering nourishment. Steele found his Indian captivity to be far less harsh than his subsequent imprisonment in a British jail.[18]

General Frederick Haldimand had declared his opinion that there was little hope of "reclaiming" the inhabitants of Vermont for the Crown, as they "are a profligate Banditti, and are now become desperate." Nevertheless, he endeavored to carry out the king's wishes and win over the Vermonters. In November 1780, in the midst of the Haldimand negotiations, the British ordered an end to Iroquois scouting activities in the Green Mountain region for fear they might drive isolationist and undecided Vermonters into the Patriot camp. Haldimand refused to send Indians into Vermont when the warriors could not be restrained, and apparently he regretted that the Royalton raid had occurred.[19] But Indian raids in surrounding areas continued. In 1781 the Abenaki chief Tomhegan, with whose band Henry Tufts had lived a decade earlier, raided Bethel, Maine, carrying off captives to St. Francis or the upper Connecticut. Tomhegan was reportedly "well known to every settler" in the town, even having eaten in some of their homes. In March of that year the news that the enemy had captured four men at Peacham threw settlers on the upper Connecticut into great alarm and three hundred men rallied to arms at Newbury.[20] Such raids and tensions strained but did not completely eradicate relations of cooperation that had developed in less troubled times. When a large Indian war party, on their way to attack Newbury, surrounded the Elkins house and took Jonathan Elkins captive, some of Elkins's Indian acquaintances had warned the family to stay indoors to avoid being killed.[21]

What effects did all this wartime activity have upon western Abenaki communities around Lake Champlain, the upper Connecticut, and St. Francis?

The Abenakis at St. Francis had reestablished and reoccupied their village by the time war broke out. The community's location made it inevitable that it would be caught up in the revolutionary turmoil on the borders of Quebec and Vermont, where individuals like Joseph Louis Gill played key roles. An "Englishman belonging to the St. Francois Tribe" assured Americans on the Penobscot River that he could engage the tribe on the colonists' behalf. Having lost a wife and children in Rogers' raid, Gill had good reason to hate the British, and he seems to have acted as an American agent in the early years of the war, passing back and forth between St. Francis and the upper Connecticut, gathering information for projected American campaigns. In November 1779 George Washington forwarded to Congress Colonel Moses Hazen's recommendation that Gill be given a commission as a major in the American army. Washington added his own endorsement of "the fidelity and good services of this Chief, and those of his Tribe," and pointed out that the Abenakis would be useful in helping to ensure the neutrality of allied tribes in Canada. (That same month, several St. Francis Abenakis attended a council where Passamaquoddy, St. Johns, and other Indians reaffirmed their loyalty to the U.S.) Gill had heard that Continental Army commissions had been granted to other northern chiefs "and therefore expects something of the same nature." Washington imagined he would be contented with the rank of major, "to which he thinks himself entitled as having been a long time a Captain." The following April, the Board of War recommended and Congress enacted:

> That a Commission of Major to be dated the 1st May 1779 be granted to Joseph Louis Gill an Indian Chief of the St. Francois Tribe & that all Indians of that Tribe who are willing to enter into the Service of the United States be collected & formed into a Company or Companies under the Command of the said Joseph Louis Gill & receive while in Service the like pay Subsistence & Rations with the officers and Soldiers of the Continental Army.[22]

Meanwhile, other St. Francis Abenakis tried to avoid becoming caught up in the conflict. Abenakis from St. Francis comprised the bulk of the Indians who settled on the upper Connecticut under Bedel's auspices. As the British increased the pressure on them to enlist in the service of the Crown, many Abenakis sought refuge in the territory between St. Francis and Cowass.

In February 1777 several families arrived near the American settlements on the upper Connecticut, complaining that the British troops were "very severe upon them to take up arms" and that General Guy Carleton refused to allow them to purchase blankets or gunpowder unless they did so. They said that few Indians in Canada would resist the Americans, but clearly they hoped to keep out of the war: they requested the Americans to build a blockhouse on the Connecticut River near the Canada line, "where they would make their abode until this dispute is Ended." Bedel's scouts encountered another band of four families out hunting not far from St. Francis the same month. The Abenakis had a pass from the British officer at the village permitting them to hunt but not to go near the Connecticut River "on pain of death." They said "that the British troops used them extremely ill" and that, if they could get supplies at Cowass, they would never go to Canada again.[23]

In July 1777 a party of Abenakis came to Cowass by way of Otter Creek. In response to British pressure to enlist and Bedel's offer of trade incentives at Cowass, forty-five families of Abenakis—a substantial part of the village—had left St. Francis and taken up residence near Lake Memphremagog by September 1777, with the expressed intention of settling on the Connecticut River somewhere above Cowass. General Schuyler ordered Bedel to remove these people out of the woods and relocate them near the American settlements, and he furnished Bedel with $800 for provisions and ammunition so that he could "supply them with every necessary they shod. want." The Abenakis would not be allowed to sit out the war, however. Even though it was too late to expect any service from them in the present campaign, Schuyler stressed that "we Expect that they hold themselves in readiness to give us their aid should it be wanted in the next," and General Horatio Gates immediately sent orders for a party of these Indians to join him at Stillwater, New York. Bedel did his best to bring the Abenakis to Cowass, and by November he had resettled a number of families and expected to have about thirty Indians at Haverhill that winter. He was using some as scouts into Canada and reported that they were ready to enlist when called upon. He requested supplies of clothing and wampum belts and believed that the Indians were "very well satisfied with their treatment." In 1778 he had about ten families, drawn from several different neighboring tribes, who had been employed in the Patriot service.[23] Bedel's "List of St. Francis Indians" that June named twenty warriors, including Swashan, who had been with Washington in 1775, five of whom had their wives and children with them. The new Abenaki community around Haverhill suffered considerable hardship while Bedel waited for orders and begged for supplies. In January 1779, Bedel informed his superiors, "We have upwards of 30 Families of Indians here, almost naked, am obliged to furnish them with Provisions, they are ready for any service when called upon cod they be furnished with Blankets &c." The next month the hungry Abenakis tired of waiting and dispersed to go hunting.[24]

Bedel estimated that there were about 200 fighting men among the St. Francis Indians, but this figure probably encompassed warriors from all the bands around Lake Memphremagog and scattered between Cowass and St. Francis, as well as at the village itself. He included the St. Francis Abenakis (but not the Caughnawagas) in a list of tribes he felt were mainly friendly to the Americans, and the Abenakis who opted to leave St. Francis told him that most Indians in Canada hoped for French intervention in the war and would be ready to assist the Americans. An Abenaki chief from the Chaudière River informed Bedel that 100 families had left their village at Sartigan because Governor Carleton threatened to burn their village if they allowed rebel scouts to infiltrate their country again. He said his people moved south to the Androscoggin River and were "Determined not to return to Canada."[25]

Other reports, however, indicated that large numbers of Indians from St. Francis and elsewhere had joined the British troops and could be expected to strike the frontiers come spring. Canadian Indians sent wampum belts to the Penobscots, warning them to have nothing more to do with the Americans because "The Indians are coming a Cross the Woods as soon as the Leaves are as big as our Nails, and are Determin'd to Destroy the White People, 300 on the River Penobscutt, 300 upon Norridgwalk, & 300 upon Cohos."[26] As might be expected, British and American

records painted a different picture of the experiences and sentiments of those Abenakis who settled on the upper Connecticut.
By February 1779, British sources said, the Abenakis who had
relocated in the colonies were discontented and very poor and
told visiting relatives from St. Francis that they would gladly return home if they could be su re of a good reception.[27]

Whatever their situation, and despite threats from the north,
Abenakis remained around Newbury and furnished warriors for
the American cause. On May 1, 1780, a company of seventeen
Indian rangers from "the St. Francis tribe" enlisted for one year's
service. They were led by Captain John Vincent, a Caughnawaga
who had fought against Washington at the rout of Braddock but
espoused the American cause from the start of the Revolution.
Vincent had served with Arnold and against Burgoyne, and had
received a commission from Washington in 1779. The following
May, General Bayley sent Washington the muster roll of the
company of St. Francis Indians at Newbury, adding that "a much
larger number has been here at times but are rambling in the
woods those inserted have been serviceable as scouts &c."
Among those who returned from St. Francis to their old hunting
grounds around Cowass and fought with the Patriots were the
families of Captain John Soosap and Captain Joe, who became
well known to settlers in the area.[28]

Abenaki movements between St. Francis and the upper Connecticut greatly concerned the British. In the fall of 1777 Captain
Hertel de Rouville was despatched to occupy St. Francis and
check the flow of Indians, French-Canadians, and deserters passing along the St. Francis River in both directions. The route to
the upper Connecticut via Lake Memphremagog was a well-
known and well-traveled Indian trail, and "in spite of de Rouville's clamp-down Indians and whites went hither and yon prac-
tically unmolested."[29]

In the summer of 1778, Lieutenant Wills Crofts of the Thirty-
fourth Regiment arrived to take up residence at St. Francis with
orders to organize the Abenakis into scouting parties, but Indians
and French-Canadians continued to penetrate the British cor-
don.[30] Crofts had a hard time even keeping control over the
Abenakis in the village. In September he reported that most of

the Indians had gone out hunting despite his efforts to prevent and regulate it. He had sent messengers to call in those who had gone farthest afield and expected some would return soon, "but I fancy with an intention to go out again soon; others I am pretty confident will not pay any attention to it." Such independence worried the British. In October, Haldimand reported the rebels were using the St. Francis River extensively "and this communication is the more dangerous to us as there is a tribe of the domiciled Indians upon that river that are lately become very ungovernable and 'tis feared attached to the rebels."[31]

Thus the Revolution split the St. Francis Abenakis. Not only did some families move away and resettle near the Americans, but by 1778 there were two opposing factions in the village: one group supported the Crown, the other followed Joseph Louis Gill. Crofts suspected that the opposition party, who formed the majority, were threatening those who favored the Crown, "for the old people who have shewn the greatest steadiness begin to be a little alarmed, and have intimated that should our affairs turn out contrary to their expectations, their only security will be in quitting this Village, and attaching themselves to some other in the upper Country." Some of the Abenakis went so far as to say they would hold the British responsible and exact revenge if anything happened to Gill.[32] Gill was in the vicinity of Cowass and Fort Number Four in the winter of 1778–79. His whereabouts were of great importance to the British that winter. Colonel Campbell of the Indian Department visited St. Francis in an attempt to win over the Gill party to the British side and tried to locate the elusive "white chief."[33]

The British employed Indians from the Seven Nations of Canada to scout the New England frontier, and Abenakis from St. Francis and the upper Connecticut seem to have passed back and forth with relative ease, scouting and carrying news and messages. Redcoats and Patriots alike suspected them of subterfuge and espionage.[34]

Late in May 1779, an Indian couple from the Connecticut River arrived at St. Francis with news that a large force of American troops were at Cowass ready to march against Missisquoi. The St. Francis Abenakis were eager to send a war party to Cowass "to put that country in confusion." Crofts was prepared to accompany them if necessary, but he confessed to misgivings about entering enemy territory on an Indian raid, which might result in a situation where it was "every man for himself." General Haldimand doubted that the Americans were heading for Missisquoi in force and thought the move might be a feint. He ordered Crofts to despatch twenty of his most faithful Indians to collect prisoners and information on the Connecticut. The Indians duly returned with two prisoners, but they provided little information other than that the rebels had abandoned their plans for an invasion that summer. In fact, the American show of force at Cowass had been only to create a diversion for General John Sullivan's campaign against the Iroquois.[35]

Meanwhile, as had happened so often in the past, war disrupted the Abenakis' normal patterns of subsistence. In the fall of 1779 the Abenakis from St. Francis, as well as some from Bécancour, assembled waiting to know if they were to be employed. If not, they wanted permission to go out hunting so that they could repay the debts they had contracted. Crofts urged them to wait a little longer, but reported that they were "really wretchedly off in point of provision." He felt they made unreasonable demands on him, but he added a few bottles of rum to their rations to encourage them to stay.[36]

Crofts' difficulties in regulating the Abenakis' movements persisted. He diligently issued passes, but "you know perfectly well," he complained, "that when Indians go out hunting there is no preventing their going where they please." He also encountered some difficulty in distinguishing who was a resident of St. Francis and who had moved to Cowass.[37] The British tendency to label all western Abenakis as "St. Francis Indians" added to the confusion, while the continuing close connections between Abenakis at St. Francis and at Cowass camouflaged movements back and forth between the groups.

The British kept up their pressure on the St. Francis Abenakis to support the loyalist cause. Haldimand offered Joseph Louis Gill a pardon and on October 9, 1780, just six months after the Continental Congress granted him a major's commission, Gill finally took an oath of allegiance to the Crown. He promptly guided a British scouting party into northeastern Vermont.[38] The following February, Lieutenant Crofts called a council and informed the Indians at St. Francis that "His Excellency" (Governor Haldimand) anticipated a rebel invasion that winter and "expected every Abenaki would distinguish himself on the occasion, and listen to nothing but the words that came from their Father['s] mouth."[39]

The same month, however, Captain Alexander fraser of the Indian Department visited St. Francis and found the plotting and politics there were worse than anywhere else, even Caughnawaga. He met with Gill to discuss "the present deplorable state" of affairs in the village, which Fraser attributed to evil councils or "a want of wisdom in their chiefs." The British offered to "make" Gill grand chief, "provided he would undertake to unite the Village and conduct them in a loyal and useful manner"; but Gill declined, suggesting that his son Antoine would be more acceptable, as he was the grandson of a grand chief. Fraser agreed, and assured Gill that his son would be appointed chief as soon as his family gave "a thorough proof of their sincerity in the Cause of Govt. by striking a blow against the Rebels." He warned Gill that any further connivance with rebel scouting parties would prompt the redcoats to burn the village and drive his family into exile. Gill admitted the error of his ways, and, as evidence of his change of heart, he volunteered to try and bring back all the Abenakis who had gone over to the rebels and to be responsible for their future good behavior. He also declared that he was ready to strike the rebels at any time. But when he and ten warriors went on a secret mission to the upper Connecticut in May and captured the American Major Benjamin Whitcomb, Whitcomb escaped when they were less than twenty-four miles from St. Francis. Britons and Indians alike accused Gill of complicity in the affair.[40]

When an Abenaki chief at St. Francis died, evidently of a lung disorder, rumors flew that Lieutenant Crofts was somehow involved in his death. The British investigated and found the reports groundless, but nevertheless removed Crofts, lest his continued presence add to the turbulence in the village. Crofts' replacement, Captain Luc Schmid, inherited a volatile situtation that was made worse by illegal trading of alcohol. Abenakis from St. Francis continued to scout the upper Connecticut, bringing back prisoners and information from the Cowass-Newbury area until the end of the war; and the British allowed them to disperse into their hunting territories when not required for service. But the village remained a channel for rebel intelligence, and the Indians chafed under the watchful eye of the British, anxious to be free "to Goe to their Different occupations." The St. Francis Abenakis in general and Gill in particular remained suspect in British eyes.[41]

The Americans received conflicting information on the Missisquoi Abenakis during the first summer of the war. Some reports said the Missisquois were supplying the British at St. Johns with scouts and "scalping parties"; others maintained that they refused to take up arms against the Americans. In fact, the Missisquois virtually disappeared from the records during the Revolution, as rebels and redcoats focused their attention on St. Francis. Lake Champlain and the Richelieu River were once again transformed into a war road, and the Missisquois witnessed fighting on their doorstep from the very beginning of hostilities, as they had not in previous wars. Abenaki communities on and around the lake found themselves vulnerable to assault. Gordon Day recorded an Abenaki oral tradition of an attack from the north on the Abenaki village located near the southern end of South Hero Island. This may have occurred around 1777. The assailants were probably Indians in the British service—an indication that the South Hero Abenakis were pro-American. The inhabitants of Missisquoi pulled back as usual from the thoroughfares of war: when Colonel Frye Bayley arrived at Swanton in February 1776, he commented that "a small tribe of Indians" had formerly resided in this place"; in December 1777 he found only "two starved Indians."[42]

The Missisquois' reluctance to get involved in the conflict caused the British some anxiety of the beginning of the war, but before the war was over warriors from Missisquoi served with the British as partisans. Abenakis remained in the Missisquoi area throughout the war years, keeping an eye on American activities. Captain Remember Baker, en route from Crown Point to Canada in July 1775, "fell in" with some Indians at Missisquoi, and there were Indians at Missisquoi Bay late in the summer of 1776. When Louis Cook and John Vincent, Bedel's Caughnawaga scouts, went from Cowass to Caughnawaga in December 1777, two armed Abenakis confronted them in the woods near Missisquoi Bay and raised the alarm at Isle aux Noix. Cook and Vincent had to travel three days and three nights without rest before they dared make a fire, and only deep snow saved them from further pursuit. After the war, Major Clement Gosselin sent a report to Ira Allen indicating that Abenakis from the Missisquoi River— "which land they still hold"—had served with both the Americans and the king's forces, and had frequently carried intelligence north to Canada.[43]

Although British maps of the time continued to display the Missisquois prominently in their original homeland, the Indians appear to have lived some distance back from the main village, and some dispersed into secluded surrounding areas. Sheltered from immediate danger, they remained in touch with their village, and they were in the area when Dutchman John Hilliker moved to Swanton in 1779 and leased from them one hundred acres of land two miles below the falls, on the south side of the Missisquoi River. An Indian encampment that was probably composed of Missisquoi Abenakis was located five miles inland from the head of Lake Champlain near present-day Clarenceville, Quebec, in June 1782; and that Abenakis were taking infants to be baptized at Chambly indicates that some families were still living near Missisquoi in the closing years of the war.[44]

As the Revolution drew to a close, some Indian groups were rewarded for backing the winners and another piece was added to the puzzle of Indian population in Vermont. A company of Indians from Stockbridge, Massachusetts, fought with the Americans at the Battle of Bennington, and in 1782 Stockbridge Indians were granted lands in Vermont in recognition of their services. Requesting a tract of land near "the Great River" and "the ponds of Dunmore," Joseph Shausesqueth, sachem of the

"Moheakunnocks," or Mahicans, of Stockbridge, reminded his "Brothers of the Great Green Mountains" that Vermont was once Indian country:

> We and our fathers were once the rightful possessor of all your Country, it was the Gift of the Great GOD to us & them; But when the belt of Friendship was interchanged with our American breth- eren, we became one people with them, and possessed and en- joyed freely our Lands, since which we have grown smaller & smaller until we are become very small, but we would have you call to mind brothers, how big we were once, and not hear us altogether as though we was Small.

Instead of the lands that Shausequeth requested, the Stock- bridges received land several miles east of Montpelier. They later sold these lands to Captain Isaac Marsh, who founded the town of Marshfield.[45]

Vermont's original, Abenaki inhabitants received no such con- sideration, either at the war's end or in its aftermath. The Peace of Paris that recognized American independence in 1783 and brought an end to the conflict was negotiated without reference to Indians, and the treaty itself contained no stipulations regard- ing Indians. Since the Missisquoi Abenakis had not been con- sulted before Britain made her concessions, they did not consider they had relinquished any claims to their lands. Bands of western Abenakis continued to live in northern Vermont after the Revo- lution, but American independence, and establishment of the forty-fifth parallel as the international boundary, further sepa- rated them from their relatives at St. Francis and even technically cut them off from some of their lands around the north shore of Missisquoi Bay. The Peace of Paris imposed an artificial boundary on western Abenaki social reality. After 1783, British in Canada and Americans in Vermont regarded the forty-fifth parallel as a crucial determinant in any dealings or responsibilities they might have with the Abenakis. But western Abenakis lived on both sides of the border and crossed it at will. Western Abenaki history has to be traced in Quebec as well as Vermont.

British and American failure to recognize western Abenaki

claims and the continuity of western Abenaki occupation of lands in Vermont would have dire consequences for the Missisquoi Abenakis. They had managed to keep their involvement in the Revolution relatively slight, yet the outcome of that conflict was of tremendous significance to their future. In the French and Indian wars, the Abenakis wholeheartedly supported the French and lost. In the American Revolution, they displayed ambivalence: most tried to remain neutral, and some even supported the Americans. They still lost. The American victory in their struggle for independence proved to be a major step in reducing the remaining western Abenakis to dependence.

Chapter 12

Exiles in Their Own Land

After the American Revolution many Abenakis withdrew from their contested homelands in Vermont to find refuge in Canada, and by the end of the century the old village at Missisquoi ceased to exist as a physical entity. But bands, not villages, had always been the core of western Abenaki community, subsistence, and survival, and many more Abenakis remained in Vermont, living in extended family bands that continued to make northern Vermont "Indian country" even into the next century. But those who stayed found themselves denied of any rights to their land and relegated to the status of unwelcome wanderers in their own country.

Perhaps as many as a dozen Abenaki families left Lake Champlain and removed to St. Francis between the Revolution and the end of the century. These Abenakis had probably sided with the British during the war and rightly assessed that Indian loyalists stood a better chance north of the new border.[1] Other Abenakis remained in various locations around Lake Champlain. "[Q]uite a numerous body" of Indians wintered on Stave Island on South Hero in 1783, and this may have been the same Abenaki settlement that was reported in that region at the beginning of the war.[2]

Residents of the Champlain Valley witnessed another period of intensive settlement and exploitation of the area's resources in the years after 1783. Abenakis who remained around Missisquoi saw a mix of ethnic groups settle on their lands in the decade after the Revolution, as Yankee settlers and loyalists of Dutch descent moved into the area alongside the French and Indians already living there. The Abenakis coexisted and even intermarried with the Dutch as they had with the French, but there was persistent tension between them and the Yankees. The Yankee invaders wanted the Abenakis' land. Many Abenakis had acculturated, practiced the Catholic faith, and spoke French as their second language, but, in Yankee eyes, they had chosen the wrong culture. The newcomers had no more intention of allowing these "French Indians" to frustrate their designs than their Puritan forebears had had of allowing "savages" to stand in the way of their mission to settle New England.[3]

The immediate postwar years saw a short-lived loyalist settlement on the east side of Missisquoi Bay, just north of the Vermont frontier of what later became the Eastern Townships. Hoping to reconcile independent Vermonters, Governor Haldimand of Quebec prohibited any loyalist settlements near the Vermont border, but a group of loyalist New Yorkers, most of whom had been stationed at St. Johns, defied orders and began a settlement at Missisquoi Bay early in 1784. They claimed the lands they settled were included in the old James Robertson lease and persistently petitioned Haldimand for permission "to proceed in settling them Indian lands, as we have begun." The government denied that any of the Abenaki lands lay in Quebec, and Haldimand threatened to use troops to move the loyalists, but the settlers remained and the government relented.[4] The Missisquoi Abenakis could expect little protection of their rights to lands north of the new border.

South of the Canadian border, Ira and Ethan Allen headed the *Allens* movement to dispossess and deny the Abenakis their sovereignty. The Allen family had migrated north from Connecticut and had figured prominently in the Revolution. Together with Vermont frontiersman Remember Baker, they had formed the Onion River Land Company in 1773, and they were determined to secure control of the fertile and potentially lucrative lands around Missisquoi for themselves. As William Haviland and Marjory Power observed, the Allens set about achieving their end by doing exactly what their Puritan ancestors had done: systematically portraying the natives as wanderers who could have no legal claim to lands they did not effectively occupy; "And here, the Abenaki tactic of strategic withdrawal from the Missisquoi village, which had served them so well in times of war, played right into the Allens' hands." Accustomed to thinking of the Abenakis as blood-thirsty raiders who had swept down from Canada, Yankee settlers found it easy to believe that the only Indians they encountered around Lake Champlain were trespassers from St. Francis who had no business being in Vermont.[5]

At the same time, the Allens cultivated the notion that the Abenakis continued to pose a threat to white settlers. On September 20, 1784, Ira Allen wrote to Governor Frederick Haldimand, asserting the Allens' claim to "the Township of Swanton which Included some old Indian fields on the River Massisque," which had been granted in 1763 by Governor Benning Wentworth of New Hampshire. When the government of New York had obtained jurisdiction over the area, Governor John Murray, Earl of Dunmore, had granted these lands to Simon Metcalf, a British officer who had served in the French and Indian War. Metcalf had made improvements on the land, but during Metcalf's prolonged absence, Ira Allen bought the original New Hampshire title. As soon as the war was over, he established several families of settlers on the lands. When Metcalf returned and attempted to resume his claim, he found it disputed. He brought suit in freeholders' court for possession of the lands, but the court found in Allen's favor. According to one account, Allen then turned Metcalf off his land "naked and destitute."[6]

Allen also discounted as invalid a claim to the land made by Captain James Hunter and Charles Grajon of St. Johns, who had purchased Robertson's lease of 1765. In Allen's opinion, land transfers conducted after 1763 were invalid. The Abenakis, he said, had "forfeited any Claims they might have had to sd Lands in the former wars Between Great Brittain and France & what Strengthened my opinion was the Indians Abandoned Sd Lands & have made no Claims by themselves or assigns till Lately." Again, a freeholders' court found in Allen's favor. The decision angered Captain Hunter, who, according to Allen, made threats that the Lands must be fought for that the Indians would Assert their Rights Insinuating that a Scalping match would ensue with the Indians since which I am informed that some of the St. Fransway Indians have Lately been on the Ground in a Hostile manner threatening the Inhabitants that if they do not Leave the Ground, they would Burn their Houses over their Heads, said Indians then took so much Corn as they Thought Proper & Retired a Small Distance for fowling.

Allen insisted he had no objection to the Abenakis having a fair trial for any rights they claimed to the land, but he entreated Haldimand to take measures to prevent the Indians from committing depredations against the settlers.[7]

Allen kept up the pressure. On September 27, he wrote Haldimand again from the Onion River, reporting that on his arrival there, "I found the minds of the People Greatly Iritated at the Treatment the Inhabitants of the Town of Swanton met with by the Indians." Other reports in September 1784 said that Indians had ordered the settlers at Swanton off their lands, threatening their persons and their property. One Abenaki "from St. Francois" apparently told settlers on the Missisquoi River to leave before the Indians burned their houses and killed their cattle. The Abenaki informed them that the Indians were coming there to live and "that was there land." The Abenaki then loaded his canoe with corn from the fields as rent. Allen blamed the troubles on "the Diabolical machinations of some Individuals residing at St. Johns" (clearly Hunter and Grajon) and urged Haldimand to intervene before "the Peasible Citizens of this Commonwealth" resorted to arms to defend themselves. Still hopeful that the independent Republic of Vermont might yet be wooed to Canada, and anxious to avoid any quarrel with its citizens, Haldimand duly responded, warning both Captain Hunter and the St. Francis Abenakis against this kind of behavior.[8]

When Thomas Butterfield, an agent in Allen's employ, arrived in Swanton in 1786, he found "a few Indians and a Dutchman" living at the falls, with the settler's house and the Indians' wigwams located side by side on the flat land on the east side of the river. Many Abenaki families had pulled back from the main village but they were still in the vicinity and coexisted with their new neighbors. John Hilliker, the Dutchman in question, leased one hundred acres of land from the Abenakis for a crown per annum. In August 1786, Major Clement Gosselin wrote to Ira Allen, telling him that the Abenakis still held their lands on the Missisquoi River and were determined to preserve them from settlement. They had given warning that "if any one took possession of their lands they would burn and destroy all Misiscouy." The Abenakis had neither abandoned the area nor relinquished their claim to it.[9]

Whatever the relations existing between settlers and Abenakis, the Allens ignored any cooperative relationships and persisted in promoting fear of the Abenakis as a threat to the settlers. In July 1788 Ira Allen sent Guy Carleton, now Lord Dorchester, the new governor of Quebec, an affidavit apparently sworn by settlers John Wagoner and William Tichout the previous month. According to this deposition, an Indian named Captain Louis "and about twenty more supposed to be of the St. Franceway Tribe" came to the town of Swanton and Highgate on the Missisquoi River in October 1787. They hoisted a [British] flag on a pole, forced the settlers to give them food at knifepoint, asserted their right to the lands, and took ten bushels of corn from Wagoner and fifteen bushels of potatoes from Tichout. They also destroyed some fences in the town. The following April, the same Indians returned and threatened to dispossess Wagoner "unless he would pay them a forth of all he raised on said lands as Rent to them." Allen reminded the new governor that a similar incident had occurred four years earlier, and he persisted in calling the Abenakis St. Francis Indians. Allen's version of events could tolerate no Abenakis still living on their original lands.[10]

Lieutenant Colonel John Campbell of the Indian Department at St. Johns was ordered to examine the dispute. On receiving the depositions of Wagoner and Tichout, he lost no time in calling the accused Abenakis before him. The Abenakis admitted that they had been at Missisquoi Bay the previous October and April "in search of their livelihood by Fishing and Fowling." They said that they always displayed the king's colors on such occasions and confessed to feelings of "mortification" when they found Wagoner and Tichout occupying "part of the lands handed down to them by their Predecessors, who were the proprietors of the same long before the French came to Canada." But they flatly denied having threatened the settlers. They said they were but nine men, a boy, eleven women, and eight children on the breast; and they appealed to John Hilliker, who served as interpreter, to testify to the truth of the affair. Determined to get to the bottom of things, Campbell summoned the Abenakis, Wagoner, Tichout, and Hilliker to meet with him at St. Johns in August 1788. The Abenakis complied, but the settlers failed to appear, which induced Campbell to think unfavorably of their complaint.[11]

The "Purport of a Declaration by Louis Outalamagouine, an Abenaqui Indian of Misiskoui," dated September 11, 1788, recounts how he and another Abenaki went to Missisquoi in August under orders from Campbell to request Wagoner and Tichout to come to the meeting. Louis confirmed that the two men delayed in responding and that the meeting did not materialize, but he added that, when pressed, Wagoner and Tichout denied ever having sent a complaint against the Abenakis: "We have never mentioned anything of the sort, and it cannot possibly be so, because we can neither read nor write, unless Colonel Allen has played us this trick and without our knowledge." That the deposition in question had been sworn before Justice of the Peace Thomas Butterfield, friend and agent of the Allens, raises further doubt as to its authenticity. With or without the connivance of Wagoner and Tichout, the Allens were determined to dispossess the Abenakis of land which, Louis Outalamagouine stressed, "had *always* belonged to them."[12]

Despite white encroachment, land leases, and denial of their presence, many Abenakis remained at Missisquoi. Daniel Portneuf, one of the signatories to Robertson's lease in 1765, died at Missisquoi, aged sixty-five, in December 1789 and was buried in Saint Joseph's cemetery at Chambly.[13] Abenaki oral tradition, as reported by Henry Masta, tells of fifty Indian cabins and extensive cornfields at Swanton in 1790.[14] A map of Lake Champlain, prepared by a captain in the Royal Engineers in June 1791, showed an Indian "castle" on the Missisquoi River, but gives no indication of the size of the village nor any date for the source of the information on its existence.[15]

As the white population increased and settlers encroached along the Missisquoi River, tensions with the Abenakis mounted. In 1790 a group of Abenakis burned a barn in Sheldon, and the presence of the Indians, who "tenaciously held claim" to their rights to use the land, remained a cause of apprehension to the new inhabitants until well into the next century. Abenakis still frequented the settlement at Highgate Springs around the turn of the decade and sometimes pitched their wigwams near the settlers' cabins. Yankee John Pratt reported seventy Indians living in Swanton in 1793 and noted growing tensions. The Abenakis "were a source of disquietude to the inhabitants, as they uniformly claimed the land as theirs, and often threatened the new comers, especially when they had been taking strong drink."[16]

When Vermont became the fourteenth state in 1791, it came under the federal Trade and Non-Intercourse Act of 1790, which stipulated that no transfers of Indian lands were valid without congressional approval. Nevertheless, as the eighteenth century entered its final decade, more and more Abenakis removed from the old village sites as it became clear that settlement would engulf their lands and that their rights would be denied and assumed by the Allens and their like. In 1788–89, Abenakis at St. Francis appealed to Governor Lord Dorchester for compensation for lands they had lost on the Missisquoi River, but their claim was denied because they could show no title or proof of ownership.[17] The Allens built another sawmill at Swanton in 1794, and, as they increased their hold, the Abenakis pulled back. John Pratt recalled that when the Indians departed they dismantled their church and transported both the stones and the bell by canoe to the village of St. Hyacinthe on the Yamaska River in Canada, where a new church was constructed. Louis Outalamagouine's eighteen-year-old son was buried at St. Hyacynthe in April 1799, and Missisquoi Abenaki names began to appear in the registers of the mission of Saint François du Lac as Abenakis moved north.[18]

Lake Memphremagog, a key area of retreat and residence for

Abenakis from Cowass and Missisquoi in time of war, also sheltered Indians from St. Francis during the Revolution. In the fall
of 1786, Pierre de Sales Laterrière met several Abenakis on the
shores of the lake and noted that the route between St. Francis
and Lake Memphremagog was still well traveled. Josiah Elkins
traded with "St. Francis Indians" on the shores of Lake Memphremagog in the 1790s.[19] But Abenakis from the Cowass-
Memphremagog region now moved further north as the pressure
of settlement increased. In June 1796 an Indian living on the upper Connecticut River, identified as "King Philip the great Warrior & Chief of the Upper Coos Indians," together with two Indian women, sold a huge tract of land to the Eastman Company,
a group of New Hampshire land speculators. The sale included
some three thousand square miles east of Lake Memphremagog
and south of the St. Francis River and spanned parts of Vermont,
New Hampshire, Maine, and Quebec.[20] Most of the Cowasuck
Abenakis seem to have been at St. Francis in 1798 when they
deeded their lands in northern New Hampshire to the Bedel
Company, but hunting and fishing parties still visited their old
lands a decade later.[21]

Cowasucks and other Abenakis lingered in northern Vermont
into the 1800s, however. White settlers who moved to the Troy
and Potton area around the headwaters of the Missisquoi River
in the winter of 1799–1800 encountered a small party of Abenakis
under Captain John Soosap. Soosap had fought for the colonists
during the Revolution, and after the war he brought his family
back to their old hunting grounds. The Indians joined the settlers, built their camps on the river, and lived near them through
the winter. The Abenakis were suffering from ecological changes
in their world as a result of white settlement, "being in a necessi-
tous and almost starving condition, which probably arose from
the moose and deer (which formerly abounded here) being destroyed by the settlers." The Indians' principal means of subsistence was making baskets, birchbark containers, and trinkets and
selling them at the settlements. They evidently left in the spring
and did not return. One of the group was Molly Occutt, well
known among Indians and settlers for her skills as a doctor.[22]

Soosap's old comrade-in-arms Captain Joe had fallen on

Wallet of Molly Occutt, a Western Abenaki well known for her skills as a doctor. (Collections of the Maine Historical Society)

equally hard times. In the fall of 1792 citizens of Hyde Park, Vermont, petitioned the state legislature for help in supporting "two Indian Natives of Cannada by Name Joe & Mol both advanced in years and the man much disordered in mind." The two had been living in the area for some years but were unable to support themselves, especially in the depths of winter. The state appointed a guardian for the two old and infirm Indians, who was to provide them with such supplies as he deemed necessary, "not to exceed the sum of three pounds." Joe continued to receive relief until the end of his life, but Mol evidently died sometime before 1801, since there was no mention of her in the grant of relief that year.[23]

Captain John Vincent, who had served the Americans throughout the Revolution, was likewise reduced to seeking relief in his old age. Petitioning the Vermont General Assembly in 1804, he declared: "Since the last war, Brothers, I have stayed on your mountains and in your forests, and I have preserved that *staying*, by means of hunting and some handicraft business, and at no time (for I appeal to the men of Rutland, and others, who know Captain John) have I departed from the path of friendship and honesty." Now, however, he was obliged to solicit assistance "to procure me meat and blankets till the *Great Alknomak* shall call me away." The state of Vermont provided Vincent with relief until his death in 1810.[24]

At St. Francis the influx of Missisquoi Abenakis from Lake Champlain and of Cowasuck Abenakis from the Cowass-Memphremagog region prompted the St. Francis Abenakis in 1797 to request a grant of additional lands in the eastern township of Lower Canada. The Abenaki chief and agent, Francis Annance, warned Lieutenant Governor Milnes of Lower Canada that his people were concerned that the day would come when they would not have sufficient lands to support themselves and their children. The Abenakis petitioned for "Some of the King's waste Lands" and acknowledged "that they shall Cultivate & improve the Same & that under penalty of forfeiting their sd. Claim." In 1805 the Crown granted them over 8,000 acres of new lands in Durham township, just south of St. Francis. Each chief received 400 acres, each head of family 200 acres, and each woman and child 50 acres. But the grant expressly stipulated that the Abenakis could never alienate, lease, transfer, or otherwise dispose of their lots; if they ceased to occupy them, the land would automatically revert to the Crown. The Durham grant became a satellite village for seventeen families at St. Francis, including several who had recently migrated from Missisquoi. The Sokoki warrior Pinawans had been one of four Indians who sent a confident and defiant message to the English from Westmoreland in the spring of 1747 when the Abenakis rolled back the tide of settlement in the Connecticut Valley. Less than sixty years later, the Pinawans or Capino family, like the Gills, found themselves in exile, petitioning the government of lower Canada for a conditional grant of land on which to live.[25]

The modern Abenaki community in Vermont asserts that the

"bulk of the Indians stayed,"[26] but western Abenakis who did not migrate to Quebec found themselves pushed into marginal areas and compelled to disperse into small family bands for hunting, fishing, and trading as settlers took over their orchards and farmlands. Small groups of Abenakis congregated around St. Albans Bay, Swanton's Back Bay, the Highgate woods, the Georgia shore, Alburg, and the Lake Champlain islands. An enclave of Missisquoi Abenakis seems to have survived around St. Johns, maintaining a long-standing Abenaki community there: one account of the council on Isle La Motte in 1766 referred to the Missisquois as members of the "Abinaquis or Saint Johns Tribe."[27] Temporary Abenaki campsites dotted the region between Missisquoi and St. Francis, and Abenakis in the area continued to use the large inland peninsula formed by the Missisquoi, Richelieu, and St. Francis rivers as their main hunting territory.[28]

Individual Abenakis and family bands who appeared in northern town histories early in the nineteenth century may have been visitors from St. Francis who had taken up residence in the Canadian village but who maintained ties with their ancestral homelands in Vermont. Others were members of western Abenaki communities that remained and survived on the edges of lands recently occupied by white settlers. St. Albans's first English settlers remembered "a tribe of St. Francis Indians" who lived just north of the village, and before 1800 the only physician available in the area was an Indian doctor known as Madam Crappo. Old inhabitants of Franklin and Grand Isle counties remembered that Missisquoi Abenakis continued to live in the region at least until 1800 and habitually drifted back in bands of eight or ten families to spend part of the year at favorite camping grounds, well into the nineteenth century.[29]

In the view of most of the white community, the western Abenakis seemed to have "disappeared" from Vermont by 1800.[30] But large numbers stayed, living in family bands and off the land as they had for centuries by hunting, fishing, and gathering. Usually poor, often intermarried and French-speaking, these people came to live a nomadic existence, and they cropped up in local records as "gypsies," wandering vagrants who appeared on the edges of white communities. Others adjusted to the new world around them by taking on work as day laborers, carpenters, tanners, and traders in or near the settlements.[31]

After almost two hundred years of disruption, dispersal, and forced migration, in which western Abenaki villages had been dismantled and rebuilt with the ebb and flow of war and peace, the Abenaki family band remained intact and continued to function as the basic unit of community and survival for hundreds of Abenakis in dozens of remote locations. Vermont remained a special place in the world of the western Abenakis, and large stretches of northern Vermont effectively remained "Indian country." But the Abenakis who inhabited that special region were now regarded as intruders, viewed with suspicion by the alien people who occupied the land and claimed it as their own.

In addition, with the Caughnawagas acting as head of the Seven Nations of Canada, Abenakis often had to sit by while Iroquois spokesmen voiced claim to lands in their Vermont homeland. The Caughnawagas were Mohawks and claimed parts of western Vermont on the basis of ancient incursions. In 1798, five chiefs from the Great Council Fire at Caughnawaga representing the Seven Nations presented the Vermont legislature in Vergennes with a petition signed by twenty chiefs of the different nations, requesting compensation for hunting grounds they had lost in Vermont. The lands they claimed were "Beginning on the east side of Ticonderoga, from thence to the great falls on the Otter Creek, and continues the same course to the height of land that divides the streams between Lake Champlain and river Connecticut; from thence along the heights of land opposite Missisquoe, and then down to the bay." A committee appointed to investigate the claim declared they could make no settlement with the Indians without the consent of the United States because they were bound by the terms of the Trade and Intercourse Act of 1790. Nevertheless, the Indians were requested to provide proof and documentation to support their claim while Governor Isaac Tichenor obtained information from New York on settlement of a similar claim brought by the Seven Nations in that state. The

General Assembly also provided the Indian delegation $100 as a "present of affection" and paid their expenses during their visit to Vergennes.[32]

Governor Tichenor learned that the state of New York had indeed paid compensation to the Indian claimants, but he dismissed this as a measure of policy rather than justice and asserted that the situation in Vermont was different because most of the lands had been granted by the king of England "without any express reservation of the Indian claim." Tichenor was unable to obtain any documentation to substantiate the Indians' ancient claim, and he felt sure their rights had been extinguished by "long and settled usage."[33]

The committee delivered its report in October 1799. After carefully examining the merits of the Indians' claims, they were "fully of opinion that their claim, if it ever did exist, has long since been done away and become extinct, in consequence of the treaty of peace in 1763 between the King of Great Britain and the French King, and the treaty of peace between the King of Great Britain and the United States, of which this State is a part, in the year 1783, and that said Indians have no real claim either in justice or equity." Governor Tichenor furnished a visiting delegation of Seven Nations chiefs with a copy of the resolution, but they "alledged" (Tichenor's word) that they were there on other business and could not officially receive it.[34]

In 1800 another delegation, accompanied by a representative of the Abenaki Nation, appeared before the legislature, now in Montpelier, with proper authorization to make a final settlement of their claims. Governor Tichenor held "repeated conferences" with the Caughnawaga and Abenaki delegates and explained to them why the legislature had rejected their claims. The details of Tichenor's conversations with the Indians have never been found, but the governor's report to the legislature gives some indication of the attitude the Indians encountered. He stated, "It would be too tedious, as well as in some measure unentertaining, to detail on paper to the General Assembly, everything that has passed at the different interviews I have had with their Chiefs." Tichenor flattered himself that the Indians were now fully satisfied that, "if ever a claim existed, it is wholly extinguished," and he assured the legislature that, "although they will not acknowledge it in their official capacity," the Indians would not trouble them again.[35]

In fact, the Indians brought their claims again in 1812, 1826, 1853, and 1874. The Caughnawagas, speaking for the Seven Nations again in 1812, denied that they had ever sold the land in question to the French or the English. Even when the English made settlements on it, the Indians continued to regard it as theirs, "and we shall claim it as long as the sun rolls from the East to the West." During a grand council held at Caughnawaga in the fall of 1827, before assembled representatives from the Algonquins, Nipissings, St. Regis, Lake of the Two Mountains, and Abenakis of St. Francis and Bécancour, the Caughnawaga chief reminded officers of the British Indian Department: "We had Lands at Otter River in the state of Vermont bordering upon Lake Champlain which are now in the hands of the Americans and We pray our Father to interest himself for their recovery for us." The Indians' British father evidently took little interest in their prayers, and the Vermont Legislature repeatedly dismissed their claims.[36]

The petitions raised again the conflicting claims of Mohawks and Abenakis to original occupancy of the eastern shore of Lake Champlain.[37] But in rejecting the Indians' claims out of hand, the Vermont legislature completed the process that British Indian agents had initiated in the 1760s after the conquest and that the Allens had perfected after the Revolution. By refusing to recognize the rights and sovereignty of the western Abenakis on the basis that those rights had been extinguished in previous treaties between other powers, they effectively deprived the Abenakis of any place in their homeland. By 1800, in the eyes of the new Vermonters, the western Abenakis were trespassing nomads with no present rights and no legitimate historical claim to the country that they had inhabited and continued to inhabit.

Chapter 13

Epilogue: Continuity and Survival

War and migration had taken a tremendous toll on western Abenaki society by 1800. Abenaki communities had suffered serious losses due to warfare and diseases. They had incorporated refugees from other displaced Indian populations and had adopted individual white captives. Abenakis had intermarried with non-Abenakis and, in some cases, with non-Indian neighbors. The western Abenakis had also seen their people scattered across northeastern North America. Some made new lives for themselves in mission villages along the St. Lawrence; some became members of new communities that were themselves products of the diaspora; others stayed in their ancient homelands. Nineteenth-century white America looked upon all Indians as members of a "vanishing race," doomed to disappear before the advance of "civilization," and the western Abenakis seemed to comply with this view. In an article entitled "The Last of the Pennacooks," the *Farmer's Monthly Visitor* recorded that after 1800 "there were but three Indians known to reside in, or upon the frontiers of, New Hampshire." Another writer predicted there would soon be a "last of the Abenaquis," just as there had been a "last of the Mohicans."[1] But the reported disappearance of Abenakis from Vermont and New Hampshire was illusory, and the notion that the sad remnants had moved en masse to Canada was a convenient distortion that belied the reality of Abenaki survivals behind the frontier. In the midst of disruption and diaspora there was continuity and survival.

When white commentators wrote romantically about the "last" of a tribe and the "passing of a race," what they more likely saw, or failed to see, was an Indian remnant group adjusting to new realities by old strategies of withdrawal. As the Abenakis have pointed out, "one must be careful not to confuse cultural humility, native quiet and an ancient flexibility with classical notions of tribal 'disappearance' and cultural disintegration held by the dominant society."[2]

Not only did Abenakis seem to have disappeared from Vermont, but those in exile also appeared to be on the road to disappearance. Writing to the Reverend Jedidiah Morse in 1811, John Wheelock described the St. Francis community as comprising "the remains of the Abenaquies, who formerly extended through the region from the eastern border of Champlain, & south of the St. Lawrence, toward the ocean." This supposed last remnant showed a steady decline—there were 505 in 1808; 320 in the 1820s—while the pressure on their remaining lands continued.[3]

By the 1830s, when the Reverend Peter Paul Wzokhilain, or Osunkerhine, returned from Dartmouth College as the first Congregationalist missionary to his people, St. Francis was a community of some 400 in dire straits. Wzokhilain attributed much of the community's poverty to the dominance of the Roman Catholic religion, the Abenakis' lack of industry, and their intemperance; the village, he said, was "altogether a very wicked place." But Wzokhilain's reports also identified the economic problems at the core of the community's poverty. The Abenakis were beginning to appreciate the need to pay more attention to farming than to their hunting and wandering life-style, if they were to "get along" in their new world, but they struggled to eke out an existence on "a small and poor tract of land" that would not produce enough crops for them to live on. Many families were compelled to "go somewhere to gain their living" during the winter, returning in the spring to sow and plant their meager fields. Some individuals traveled farther afield in search of a living: by the late 1820s there were Abenakis on the Pacific Northwest Coast in the employ of the Hudson's Bay Company.[4]

But the extended family band that had been the basic unit of western Abenaki subsistence continued to function as the basic

By 1800 many western Abenakis had migrated north and shared the life-style of the unidentified Indians of lower Canada in this Cornelius Krieghoff lithograph. (National Archives of Canada, C-41043)

unit of survival and community. Oral histories, supported by census data, genealogical research, and scattered fragments of evidence in town histories and other documents convey the picture of an Abenaki community of several hundred people surviving in northwestern New England after 1800. This community was not a single unit with one physical residence; it was a fluid network of family bands, of which only the edges were visible to non-Indian observers. Some of the Indians mentioned in local town histories were refugee Abenakis living north of the border who kept up a seasonal visitation of old hunting and fishing grounds or who came to the new American settlements to trade and peddle baskets. Others operated on the fringes of white communities but belonged to family bands who preferred to keep a low profile back in the hinterland. After 200 years, the strategy of withdrawal, dispersal, and cautious reappearance was still the basic means of dealing with white intruders, and it explains the periodic reports of small Indian bands throughout Vermont and northern New Hampshire.[5]

In 1825, four or five families of Abenakis pitched their wigwams near Swanton, where they remained for a year or two, making a living by fishing, hunting, and basket making, and "claimed the lands, as the Indians have done from the first."[6] Ten years later, a reporter from the *Green Mountain Democrat* interviewed a family band of fifteen Abenakis who had camped for the winter on the banks of the Connecticut River near Windsor, Vermont, on their way to enroll a member of the family at Dartmouth College. By talking with the Abenakis themselves, the reporter did not fall into the mistake of labeling them "St. Francis Indians" from Canada; these people, he said, were "part of the tribe of the Missisques, who live a wandering life on the eastern shore of Lake Champlain." That same year, a French priest from St. Joseph's Church in Burlington reported to his superior in France that he slept "in the poor cabins of the Indians" when he traveled along the east shore of Lake Champlain.[7]

Abenakis continued to return to the ancient Indian fishing site at Bellows Falls. Each spring, Abenaki families came in canoes down the Connecticut. While the men fished at the falls, the women sold baskets they had made during the winter to townspeople and tourists. "The Last Abenaqui Chief at Bellows Falls" visited as usual in 1856, apparently chose to die there, and was buried by citizens in the Rockingham town cemetery.[8] Captain Joe, who returned with his family to live in old hunting grounds on the upper Connecticut, died in Newbury in 1819 and was buried in the town cemetery. Years later the Daughters of the American Revolution erected a gravestone in memory of his services in the Revolution.[9] Metallak, "the last of the Coashaukes," was in Canada with the St. Francis Indians in 1781, lived for a time around Lake Umbagog, working as a guide and hunter, and returned in the 1830s to pass his final years around Stewartstown, New Hampshire. In his old age he became entirely blind and was a pauper at the charge of Coos County where he died in 1848 "at an advanced age, the last of the New Hampshire Indians, leaving no kith or kin to mourn his death."[10] In June 1850 two compan-

Gravestone of Indian Joe at Newbury, Vermont (Photograph by Colin G. Calloway)

ions walking in the Vale of Tempe, just north of Dartmouth College campus, came upon the remains of a recently abandoned Indian camp of three lodges. "By the side of one of the huts there was something suspended on a tree which we concluded was their medicine."[11]

Behind such "sightings" lay a network of Abenaki family bands pursuing their old ways of life as nineteenth-century America changed around them. Intermarrying as they had for centuries with French-speaking non-Indian neighbors, Abenakis survived in communities around Swanton, Highgate, St. Albans, the Champlain Islands, and St. Johns, as well as near Newbury and other river towns on both banks of the upper Connecticut. Some of these townships showed a growing Indian population as the nineteenth century progressed.[12]

Small groups and scattered campsites dotted the western Abenaki homeland, often close to white townships that provided the Indians seasonal and daily labor or a market for their baskets so that they might supplement the living they made by traditional subsistence activities. In the White Mountains near Winthrop, Maine, Edward Augustus Kendall encountered one such group in 1808 at the side of the Cobbosseeconte Stream: "A very trifling number of the Indians, of this river, are still in existence, and belong to the village of Saint Francais, where they bear the name of Cabbassaguntiac, that is, people of Cabbassaguntiquoke." Cowasucks from the upper Connecticut River living at St. Francis likewise retained their distinctive identity, calling themselves "*Cohâssiac*," even though the pines of their homeland from which they derived their name had long since been replaced by meadows.[13]

As in old times, movement and interaction between groups was common. Western Abenakis visited and mixed with Penobscots, Mohawks, and Caughnawagas, and Abenakis from the Missisquoi community kept up with relatives and friends at St. Francis and St. Regis. A network of long-standing social and kinship relations lay behind Edward Kendall's passing observation that "The Indians of Saint Francais and Becancourt still occasionally pass and repass between the St. Lawrence and the Penobscot and Saint-Johns."[14]

Many Abenaki families, such as this one at an Indian camp at Highgate Springs, Vermont, remained in their traditional homelands long after white settlers crowded into the area. (Courtesy Vermont Historical Society)

However, as their own hunting territories became increasingly depleted, Abenakis from St. Francis began to turn to north of the St. Lawrence, where the Algonquins from Three Rivers hunted. Despite Algonquin protests that it had always been agreed the Abenakis should hunt the lands south of the river, the Abenakis petitioned the government for new hunting lands. In 1830, the St. Francis Abenakis shifted their hunting and trapping activities to the region north of the St. Lawrence, and communication between St. Francis and Missisquoi seems to have diminished considerably after that time, although the two communities continued to share a fundamental connection in western Abenaki cultural tradition.[15]

About the same time, most of the Abenakis who had taken lands in Durham township seem to have become reabsorbed into the community at St. Francis. By the late 1820s, disputes arose between the Abenakis and neighboring white settlers. In August

1829 a group of Durham inhabitants sent a petition to Lieutenant Governor Sir James Kempt of Lower Canada, in which they claimed that "the late Captain Joseph Annance, alias Francis, Chief and Agent of the St. Francis Indians," and other Abenakis had leased them lands in the township. Increasing immigration from Britain brought an additional fifty or so families to the area, although they did not settle on Indian lands, and the petitioners pointed out they had made considerable improvements, including building a road and plans for an Episcopal church. Since Annance was dead, however, the Abenakis declared they would drive the petitioners off the land "as the improvements have become too extensive for their hunting purposes." The petitioners begged the lieutenant governor to intervene and arrange an exchange of lands with the Indians. Voicing the argument that had been used to justify dispossession of the Abenakis for generations, they claimed the Abenakis had scarcely made any improvements on their lands and it was a great waste to allow the Indians to hold "such a large tract in an unsettled, uncultivated state (their [*sic*] being now only two or three Indian Families in the Township)."[16]

The petition sparked controversy over whether the Abenakis had breached the conditions of the original grant by leasing the lands in question: if they had, the lands reverted to the Crown. Superintendent of Indian Affairs William McKay visited the Abenakis at St. Francis and Durham, and called a meeting of Indians and settlers at Durham to iron out the issues. In answer to his query whether they considered Annance authorized to lease the lands, the Abenakis replied they did, but "at the same time they thought that those lands were given to them by their Great Father at Quebec for ever and ever, for their own use and profit, and that when they became useless as hunting grounds that they had a right to make the most of them for their benefit." The Abenakis said that, when they demanded rents from the inhabitants, the settlers abused them and refused to pay, claiming they had no right to lease those lots. The settlers complained in turn that they were in a bad situation: having leased the lands in good faith and made improvements, they were now informed that the grants were not dependable and they might be ordered off at any moment. Realizing that the Indians and the inhabitants were never going to agree, the superintendent concluded that the government should take over the lands and compensate the Abenakis at Durham "who make little or no use of that fine township."[17]

Other reports from the Durham Abenakis indicated that Annance had had no authority to lease their lands and that only a handful of cases could be prosecuted for contravening the terms of the original grant. The Abenakis acknowledged that the petitioners obtained some lots on lease, but said they took possession of many others by force "and went so far as to drive off the Indians from their Fields by Main force and to harrow up the seed which had been sown." A memorandum from Canada's military secretary noted, "The Abenaquois Indians are so remarkably quiet and inoffensive in their manners, it appears extremely improbable that they would commit the outrages described in the Petition."[18]

The Abenakis wanted the government to intervene and to have justice done for them, but they complained that the Indian Department was unresponsive. The intruders had taken land by force and had beaten, bullied, and abused the Indians who tried to recover it. Not knowing where to turn, the Abenakis threatened to drive off the intruders by force. Their lands were vital to them as they could no longer live by hunting: "Those spots once rich in game, when trod by our ancestors, Lords of the soil, can no longer afford us subsistence."[19]

The affair dragged on through the 1830s. Finally in 1839 a Committee of the Whole Council decided the Indians had no right to lease or otherwise dispose of their lands and, in failing to occupy them, had forfeited their rights to them. The council recommended instituting legal proceedings for reverting the lands to the Crown, after which the government could negotiate with the current occupants and make arrangements beneficial to both parties.[20] The satellite Abenaki community at Durham had never developed. Originally settled by seventeen families, its numbers dwindled as many returned to the core community at St. Francis. Only a handful remained in the 1830s, opening the way for encroachment by settlers and forfeiture of their lands. Even so,

Plaque in English, French, and Abenaki commemorating 300 years of Abenaki-Sokoki residence at Odanak (St. Francis). (Photograph by Colin G. Calloway)

Peter Paul Wzokhilain found the Durham community a good source of converts: as late as 1842 a dozen Abenakis there came forward to embrace the Congregationalist faith.[21]

Calamity continued to haunt western Abenakis in Quebec and Vermont. After Rogers' Rangers put their village to the torch in 1759, the St. Francis Abenakis had built a small wooden church that housed the bell they had saved from the original church. In 1819, fire destroyed the second church, and the Abenakis built themselves a third church between 1828 and 1831. That church was struck by lightening in 1900, and the new century opened with the St. Francis Abenakis once again rebuilding their Catholic church. In Vermont, even as many families continued to live in the Abenaki way, poverty, prejudice, and dependence on the white economy characterized their lives and promoted the tendency to conceal one's Indian identity. Abenaki children who attended white schools exposed themselves to ridicule if they admitted they were Indian, and to punishment if they dared to speak their native language. In 1941 the Missisquoi Abenakis found their hunting and fishing further curtailed when the state set aside much of the marsh at the mouth of the Missisquoi River as a wildlife refuge. Meanwhile, periodic shifts in federal policy brought little improvement in the lives of Vermont Abenakis. Interfamily relations and mutual help saw the people through the hard times of the nineteenth and early twentieth centuries, as they had through the previous two hundred years.[22] But not until the 1970s, in a new era of social ferment and public awareness, did the Vermont Abenakis come back out into the open.

No longer afraid or ashamed of admitting their Indian identity, Abenakis in Vermont literally stood up to be counted. In 1980 the U.S. Census reported an Indian population of 983 in Vermont, with a further 1,297 living in New Hampshire.[23] Tired of resting at the bottom of the social and economic ladder, Vermont Abenakis took action to improve their community's well-being while preserving its cultural heritage. They formed a tribal council, reconstituted the St. Francis–Sokoki Band of the Abenaki Nation, and established headquarters in an old railroad depot in Swanton. They drew up a written constitution providing for elections to tribal offices and outlining the powers of the tribal council and chief. They established the Abenaki Self Help Association (ASHAI) to obtain resources and provide educational and other services to the community. In 1976, Canadian Abenakis living at St. Francis and Bécancour, followed by the Quebec Federation of Indians and the U.S. Regional Task Force, all recognized the Vermont Abenakis and urged the state of Vermont to do likewise. At Thanksgiving, 1976, Vermont Governor Thomas Salmon issued an executive order, recognizing the Abenakis as a tribe. Only a few months later, however, the new governor, Richard Snelling rescinded the order. Because the Bureau of Indian Affairs did not officially recognize the Vermont Abenakis as a tribe, and because the Abenakis had no treaties, statutes, or orders protecting their rights, the Indians had to base their claims to use and occupy lands in the Swanton-Highgate area—the old Missisquoi homeland—on the theory of aboriginal rights. In 1982 the Vermont Abenakis stepped out of their marginal and anonymous past and submitted a formal petition to the Bureau of Indian Affairs claiming federal recognition as the St. Francis/Sokoki Band of the Abenaki Nation.[24]

Federal recognition is an expensive, time-consuming, frustrating, and potentially divisive process. For the Vermont Abenakis, documentation of their uninterrupted historical presence in their homeland constitutes a vital factor in their case; it also presents something of a problem since the historical records are at best incomplete and sometimes silent on the subject. No decision has been reached at the time of this writing. In addition, the Abenaki community at Swanton has engaged in legal disputes with the state of Vermont, demanding the return of ancestral lands for burial grounds and asserting their claims to subsistence fishing rights on the Missisquoi River on the basis of aboriginal occupancy.[25] In 1988 Chief Homer St. Francis demanded that the U.S. Fish and Wildlife Service vacate the Missisquoi National Wildlife Refuge and return the land to the Abenakis. For native peoples seeking to assert and maintain their identity, subsistence is more than just survival. It represents an ancient way of life that ties them to the land, to the animal world, and to their past. The determination to preserve traditional values and practices inevitably brings Indians into conflict with state and federal laws that attempt to protect wildlife by restricting subsistence activities.

In September 1988, the New England Indian Task Force, an organization serving the collective will and direction of New England Native American communities, offered full support to the St. Francis–Sokoki Band of Abenakis and asked that the state of Vermont and the United States government work with the Abenaki leadership to reach "a proper resolution" of issues affecting the well-being of the Indian and non-Indian communities of Missisquoi and Vermont. In August 1989, a Vermont District Court judge ruled that the Vermont Abenakis retained their original fishing rights. He said that the state of Vermont had failed to prove that the Abenakis had "abandoned or ceded their Missisquoi homeland or that their aboriginal rights were extinguished by either an express act or an act clearly and unambiguously implying any sovereign's intent to extinguish those rights."[26]

After two centuries of dispersal and disruption, western Abenakis clung to their identity and preserved important strains of their ancient culture. The dialects of the Pocumtucks, Pigwackets, and others evidently disappeared in the chaos of movement and amalgamation that characterized much of New England Indian life in the seventeenth and eighteenth centuries, but, despite the incorporation of numerous refugees into the communities at Missisquoi and St. Francis, the western Abenaki language survived. At the time of this writing, Gordon M. Day, director emeritus of the Canadian Ethnology Service, is putting the finishing touches to a western Abenaki dictionary. Moreover, the traditions of the western Abenaki homeland have continued to exist even as the people adapted to new conditions. The survival of their language and of important cultural traditions constitutes a crucial element in the continuity of western Abenaki life.

Studies of cultural enclaves in other areas of North America and the world indicate that a continuity of common identity based on a unique historical experience can be more important, as a determinant of group survival and societal integrity, than blood quantum, separate language, unchanging culture, or even possession of a sacred homeland. All societies have a sense of their past, whether they preserve that sense in written documents or oral tradition, but in many American Indian societies the power of the past and the value of tradition give meaning to the present and shape the future, which are seen as continuous with what has gone before. Seen in this light, the western Abenakis' shared experience of a two-hundred-year diaspora ironically provides a sense of internal tribal solidarity and a stronger collective continuity of identity. In the words of anthropologist Edward Spicer, "In their sense of identity every people molds a vessel into which they pour from generation to generation the meanings of their historical experience." Individuals and groups may come and go, but, "As long as a core endures to preserve continuity, the people remains," and membership can always resurge.[27]

The western Abenaki "core" has always been the family band, which allowed the people to survive even in the face of dispersal and upheaval. Whatever the outcome of the current legal battles, western Abenakis will continue to inhabit northwestern Vermont and surrounding areas as they have for centuries, a dispersed human community linked by family ties, a common heritage, and their attachment to the land that Odzihózo created for his people in a time beyond memory.

Notes

List of Abbreviations and Short Titles

Baxter MSS.   James Phinney, ed. *Baxter Manuscripts: Documentary History of the State of Maine.* 24 vols. Portland: Maine Historical Society, 1869–1916.

BRH   *Bulletin des Recherches Historiques.* Quebec, 1895–.

CMNF   *Collection de manuscrits contenant lettres, mémoires, et autres documents historiques rélatifs à la Nouvelle-France.* 4 vols. Quebec: Imprimerie à côte et cie, 1883–85.

C.O.   Colonial Office Records, Public Records Office, Kew, England.

CSP   *Calendar of State Papers, Colonial Series, America and the West Indies, 1677–1733, Preserved in the Public Record Office.* 30 vols. London: His Majesty's Stationery Office, 1896–1939.

Johnson Papers   *The Papers of Sir William Johnson.* Edited by James Sullivan et al. 15 vols. Albany: University of the State of New York, 1921–65.

JR   Reuben G. Thwaites, ed. *The Jesuit Relations and Allied Documents: Travels and Explorations of the Jesuit Missionaries in New France 1610–1791.* 73 vols. Cleveland: Burrows Brothers Co., 1896–1901.

Levis Mss.   *Collection des Manuscripts du Maréchal de Lévis*, publié sous la direction de l'abbe H.R. Casgrain. 12 vols. Montreal-Quebec, 1889–1895.

Mass. Archives   Massachusetts State Archives, Boston.

Mass. Hist. Soc.   Massachusetts Historical Society, Boston.

NYCD   Edmund B. O'Callaghan, ed. *Documents Relative to the Colonial History of New York.* 15 vols. Albany: Weed, Parsons, 1869–1916.

PAC   Public Archives of Canada, Ottawa.

PCC   Papers of the Continental Congress, National Archives, Washington, D.C. Microfilm No. 247

RAPQ   *Rapport de l'Archiviste de la Province de Québec*, Quebec, 1920– .

VHG   Abbe Hemenway, ed., *The Vermont Historical Gazetteer.* 5 vols. Burlington, 1868–91.

Preface

1. The state of Vermont, of course, did not exist as a political entity for most of the era under discussion. Indian bands regarded rivers as highways and resources running through the center of their territories rather than as territorial boundaries, and for much of the eighteenth century New York and New Hampshire disputed ownership of the Vermont area, which was known as the "New Hampshire grants." In fact, modern state boundaries between Vermont, New Hampshire and Quebec cut through western Abenaki territory. However, the geographic features that made the state also make sense of using the modern political designation as a term of convenience to indicate the region that formed the core of the western Abenaki homeland. Likewise, modern town and place-names are sometimes employed to help locate events that occurred long before these names existed.

2. Alvin H. Morrison, "Dawnland Directors: Status and Role of Seventeenth Century Wabanaki Sagamores," in William Cowan, ed., *Papers of the Seventh Algonquian Conference* (Ottawa: Carleton University Press, 1976), 1–19.

Chapter 1. The Green Mountain Frontier: Conflict, Coexistence, and Migration

1. Frank W. Porter, III, ed., *Strategies for Survival: American Indians in the Eastern United States*, 19–20.

2. For convenient guides to the archaeology of Vermont, see William A. Haviland and Marjory W. Power, *The Original Vermonters: Native Inhabitants Past and Present*, chaps. 2–5; Peter A. Thomas, "Comments on Recent Trends in Vermont Archaeology," *Man in the Northeast* 19

(Spring 1980): 3–14, and other papers in that special issue, esp. Marjory W. Power, Frank L. Cowan, and James B. Petersen, "Artifact Variability at the Multi-Component Winooski Site," 43–55. M. Pamela Bumsted, "VT-CH-94: Vermont's Earliest Known Agricultural Experiment Station," 73–82 in the same issue, documented corn remains from a Winooski River site dated c. 1450 A.D., but recent investigations at the Skitchewaug site near Springfield indicate maize, beans, and squash may have been present as early as 1120 A.D. Michael J. Heckenberger and James B. Petersen, *Archaeological Investigations at the Skitchewaug Site: A Multicomponent Stratified Site in Springfield, Windsor County, Vermont* (Montpelier: Division of Historic Preservation, 1988) document human occupation at the site spanning 3,500 years. Marjory W. Power and James B. Petersen, *Seasons of Prehistory: 4000 Years at the Winooski Site* (Montpelier: Division of Historic Preservation, 1984) survey 4,000 years of habitation at the Winooski site. W. A. Ritchie, "A Probable Paleo-Indian Site in Vermont," *American Antiquity* 18 (1953): 249–58, provides the first description of a major Paleo-Indian site overlooking the Missisquoi River.

3. Gordon M. Day, "Western Abenakis," in Bruce G. Trigger, ed., *Northeast, Handbook of North American Indians.* vol. 15, *JR* 37:261, 46:67; *New Voyages to North-America by the Baron de Lahontan*, ed. Reuben G. Thwaites, 1:327–28. William Cronon, *Changes in the Land: Indians, Colonists, and the Ecology of New England*, 89; Dean R. Snow, *The Archaeology of New England*, 34; Haviland and Power, *Original Vermonters*, 155, 157. Neal Salisbury, *Manitou and Providence: Indians, Europeans, and the Making of New England, 1500–1643*, 27; Sherburne F. Cook, *The Indian Population of New England in the Seventeenth Century*, 15–16, 84.

4. Ted J. C. Brasser, "Group Identification along a Moving Frontier," *Proceedings of the 38th International Congress of Americanists* 2 (1968): 261–65; Harald E. L. Prins, "Amesokanti: Abortive Tribeformation on the Colonial Frontier," paper presented at the Annual Conference of the American Society for Ethnohistory, 1988, p.1.

5. Gordon M. Day, "The Identity of the Sokokis," *Ethnohistory* 12 (1965): 237–49; Day, *The Identity of the St. Francis Indians*, 14–15; "Journal of an Embassy from Canada to the United Colonies of New England in 1650, by Father Gabriel Druillettes," ed. John Gilmeary Shea, *Collections of the New York Historical Society*, 2d ser., 3, pt. 1: 316, 322; *JR*, 24:101, 36:101.

6. Haviland and Power, *The Original Vermonters*, 152. P. André Sévigny, *Les Abénaquis: Habitat et Migrations (17e et 18e siècles)*, 105–106, suggests that the mother tribe may have been the Pequot, or Niantic, of Connecticut; Walter Hill Crockett, *Vermont: The Green Mountain State* 1:41, believed they were refugees from the "Mohican confederation";

and George Sheldon, *A History of Deerfield, Massachusetts, . . . with a Special Study of the Indian Wars in the Connecticut Valley* 1:49, reckoned they were a fugitive band of Mahicans who became members of the Pocumtuck "confederacy." They may also have been a division of the Cowasucks.

7. Peter A. Thomas, "Squahkeag Ethnohistory," *Man in the Northeast* 5 (Spring 1973): 27–29; Gordon M. Day, "The Indian Occupation of Vermont," *Vermont History* 33 (July 1965): 373; Day, *Identity of the St. Francis Indians*, 13; *JR* 36:139–41; Thomas, "In the Maelstrom of Change: The Indian Trade and Cultural Process in the Middle Connecticut River Valley, 1635–1665," Ph.D. diss., University of Massachusetts, 1979, 363; Day, "Western Abenaki," in Trigger, ed., *Northeast*, 150; *NYCD* 13:308. Edward Augustus Kendall, *Travels through the northern parts of the United States in the years 1807 and 1808* 3:203–207, 209–215, 219–221, provided extensive discussion of the Indian sculptures at Bellows Falls and the West River, although he attributed them to "the whim of vacant moments."

8. Crockett, *Vermont: The Green Mountain State* 1: 47–49; Frederic P. Wells, *History of Newbury, Vermont, from the Discovery of the Coos Country to the Present Time*, 6–7, 30; *VHG* 2:917–18, 924.

9. Gordon M. Day, "The Western Abenaki Transformer," *Journal of the Folklore Institute* 13 (1976): 75–89; Day, "Abenakis in the Lake Champlain Valley," in Jennie G. Versteeg, ed., *Lake Champlain: Reflections on Our Past*, 288. Haviland and Power, *Original Vermonters*, 189–90; John C. Huden, *Indian Place Names in New England*, 117; George McAleer, *A Study of the Etymology of the Indian Place Name Missisquoi*. In 1750, Captain Peter Winne testified that he "hath seen the Indians as they pass'd near the Rock making offerings by throwing Pipes Tobacca or other things into the Lake near the Rock and calling upon the Name Rogeo." *Letters and Papers of Cadwallader Colden* 68 (1935): 67, and New York State Archives, Colonial MSS., 76:110; also, Enclosures of Governor Clinton's letter, 29 Aug. 1750, Public Record Office, Kew, England, C.O. 5/1063: 108–12, in *Iroquois Indians: A Documentary History*, reel 14. Some interpretations suggest Missisquoi means "the great grassy meadows."

10. Gordon Day, "English-Indian Contacts in New England," *Ethnohistory* 9 (1956): 29; Henry R. Schoolcraft, *Information Respecting the History, Condition, and Prospects of the Indian Tribes of the United States* 4:227; Frederic Kidder, "The Abenaki Indians: Their Treaties of 1713 and 1717, and a Vocabulary, with a Historical Introduction," *Collections of the Maine Historical Society* 6 (1859): 236: John C. Huden, "The Abenakis, the Iroquoians, and Vermont," *Vermont History* 24 (Jan. 1956); Huden, "Indian Groups in Vermont," *Vermont History* 26 (April 1958): 112–15; Snow, *Archaeology of New England*, 70; Bert Salwen, "Indians of

Southern New England and Long Island: Early Period," in Trigger, ed., *Northeast*, 169; cf., Daniel Gookin, *Historical Collections of the New England Indians* (reprint, Towtaid, 1970), 7n. Day, *Identity of the St. Francis Indians*, 16, identifies the Openangoes as Pennacooks. Day, *The Mots Loups of Father Mathevet*, 35–44.

11. Snow, *Archaeology of New England*, 66, and "Eastern Abenaki," 147, considers the Pigwackets eastern Abenakis.

12. Thomas, "In the Maelstrom of Change"; Sherburne F. Cook, *The Indian Population of New England in the Seventeenth Century*, 56; George Sheldon, "The Pocumtuck Confederacy," *History and Proceedings of the Pocumtuck Valley Memorial Association* 2 (1898): 390–408.

13. Ted J. Brasser, *Riding on the Frontier's Crest: Mahican Indian Culture and Culture Change*, 5, 9, 66; Brasser, "Mahican," in Trigger, ed., *Northeast*, 198, 200; Brasser, "Group Identification along a Moving Frontier," 261; Crockett, *Vermont: The Green Mountain State* 1 : 40; Alanson Skinner, "Notes on Mahikan Ethnology," *Bulletin of the Public Museum of the City of Milwaukee* 2 : 102; *The Papers of Sir William Johnson*, ed. James Sullivan et al., 8 : 256; John C. Huden, "Indian Groups in Vermont," 112–15; Haviland and Power, *Original Vermonters*, 144.

14. Gordon Day, "The Eastern Boundary of Iroquoia: Abenaki Evidence," *Man in the Northeast* 1 (1971): 7–8.

15. See, for example, *Letters and Papers of Cadwallader Colden* 9 : 89, 98–99; Eastern Indians' Letter to the Gouverneur, July 27, 1721, *Collections of the Massachusetts Historical Society*, 2d series, 8 (1826): 260; extract of a letter written to the court by M. Begon, 21 Apr. 1725, PAC., MGI C11A, 47 : 203–11, copy in Vermont Historical Society, Misc. File, 318 : 6. French Intendant M. Begon declared flatly in 1725 that the Connecticut River "never was the old boundary between the Abenakis and the Iroquois." Massachusetts Historical Society, Parkman Papers, 31 : 367. Gordon Day Tapes, Dartmouth College, Special Collections, reel 24, side 2.

16. Bernard Bailyn, "The Peopling of British North America: An Introduction," in *Perspectives in American History*, n.s., 2 (1985): 1–98; Bailyn, *Voyagers to the West: A Passage in the Peopling of America on the Eve of the Revolution*; D. W. Meinig, *The Shaping of America: A Geographical Perspective on 500 Years of History*, vol. 1, *Atlantic America, 1492–1800* (New Haven: Yale University Press, 1986).

17. "Les Registres du Fort St. Frédéric," in Pierre-Georges Roy, *Hommes et choses du Fort Saint-Frederic* (Montreal: Editions du Dix, 1946), 268–312.

18. Eric R. Wolf, *Europe and the People Without History* (Berkeley: University of California Press, 1982); Haviland and Power, *Original Vermonters*, chap. 1 and pp. 213–14; Aurelia C. Hucksoll, "Watercourses and Indian Population in the Northeast Kingdom," in George R. Clay,

ed., *Primitive Versus Modern: Contrasting Attitudes Toward Environment*, 5–10; Thomas, "In the Maelstrom of Change," Ph.D. diss., 396; John C. Huden, "Indian Trails Through Vermont, used by Indians and French, 1500?-1760," in *Indian Place Names in Vermont*, 31–32; Chester B. Price, "Historic Indian Trails of New Hampshire," *New Hampshire Archaeologist* 8 (March 1958): 2–13.

19. Francis Jennings, *The Ambiguous Iroquois Empire*, 31; Archer Butler Hulbert, ed., *The Crown Collection of Photographs of American Maps*. 1st Ser. 1: #s16–18 (cxxi.16); Henry N. Muller, III, "The Commercial History of the Lake Champlain–Richelieu River Route, 1760–1815," Ph.D. diss., University of Rochester, 1969, chap. 1.

20. Laurence M. Hauptman, "Refugee Havens: The Iroquois Villages of the Eighteenth Century," in Christopher Vecsey and Robert W. Venables, eds., *American Indian Environments: Ecological Issues in Native American History*, 139.

21. Cf. James H. Merrell, "The Indians' New World: The Catawba Experience," *William and Mary Quarterly*, 3d ser., 41 (Oct. 1984): 537–63.

22. "A Narrative of the Captivity of Mrs. Johnson," in *Indian Narratives*, 131, 140; Robert Rogers, *The Journals of Major Robert Rogers*, vi. John Moody, "The Native American Legacy," in Jane C. Beck, ed., *Always in Season: Folk Art and Traditional Culture in Vermont*, 58. Cf. Neal Salisbury, "Social Relationships on a Moving Frontier: Natives and Settlers in Southern New England, 1638–1675," *Man in the Northeast* 33 (Spring 1987): 89–99.

23. Charles E. Clark, *The Eastern Frontier: The Settlement of Northern New England, 1610–1763*, 263; Francis Chase, ed. *Gathered Sketches from the Early History of New Hampshire and Vermont*, 68.

24. Mary R. Cabot, comp. and ed., *Annals of Brattleboro, 1681–1895* 1:12. Myron O. Stachiw, *Massachusetts Officers and Soldiers, 1723–1743: Dummer's War to the War of Jenkins' Ear*, 67, 128, 164, 177, 185, 248, 252, 260. See also Walter L. Harrington, "Fort Dummer: An Archaeological Investigation of the First Permanent English Settlement in Vermont," in *New England Archaeology*, Dublin Seminar for New England Folklife Annual Proceedings (1977), 86–94.

25. Roy, *Hommes et choses du Fort St. Frédéric*, 224, 268ff., 288, 305.

26. Thomas, "In the Maelstrom of Change," 121.

27. Guy Omeron Coolidge, "The French Occupation of the Champlain Valley from 1609 to 1759," *Proceedings of the Vermont Historical Society*, n.s., 6 (1938): 309; Samuel Carter, "The Route of the French and Indian Army that sacked Deerfield, Feb. 29th, 1703–4 [O.S.] on their return march to Canada with the captives," *History and Proceedings of the Pocumtuck Valley Memorial Association* 2 (1898): 126–51. For the experi-

ence of captives in this area, see Colin G. Calloway, "An Uncertain Destiny: Indian Captivities on the Upper Connecticut River," *Journal of American Studies* 17 (1983), 189–210.

28. Alden T. Vaughan and Daniel K. Richter, "Crossing the Cultural Divide: Indians and New Englanders, 1605–1765," *Proceedings of the American Antiquarian Society* 90 (1980): esp. 53, 58–60.

29. Samuel Penhallow, *Penhallow's Indian Wars*, ed. Edward Wheelock, 13; "The Last of the Pennacooks," *Farmer's Monthly Visitor* 13, no. 10 (Oct. 1853): 293.

30. On the central importance of captive taking in Iroquois warfare, see Daniel K. Richter, "War and Culture: The Iroquois Experience," *William and Mary Quarterly*, 3d ser., 40 (Oct. 1983): 528–59; James Lynch, "The Iroquois Confederacy and the Adoption and Administration of Non-Iroquoian Individuals and Groups Prior to 1756," *Man in the Northeast* 30 (Fall 1985): 83–99; "At a Meeting of the Commissioners for Indian affairs, Sept. 21, 1754, Public Record Office, C.O. 5/926:289, in *Iroquois Indians: A Documentary History*, reel 16.

31. James Axtell, "The White Indians of Colonial America," *William and Mary Quarterly*, 3d ser., 32 (1975): 71–72; George Avery [Journal of the Royalton Raid, 1780], Dartmouth College Library, Ms. 780900.5, p. 7–8; "The Last of the Pennacooks," 297; "Captivity of Zadock Steele," in *Indian Narratives*, 221–22; "Narrative of the Captivity of Mrs. Johnson," 147–48; 156–57; Rev. Pierre F.X. de Charlevoix, *Journal of a Voyage to North America* 1:369–70; cf. "Letters relating to Mrs. Jemina Howe, who was taken by the Indians at Hinsdale, N.H., in July 1755," *Collections of the New Hampshire Historical Society* 5 (1837):257. Caleb Stark, ed., *Reminiscences of the French and Indian War*, 174.

32. For the story of Eunice Williams, see Alexander Medlicott, Jr., "Return to this Land of Light: A Plea to an Unredeemed Captive," *New England Quarterly* 38 (1965): 202–16; C. Alice Baker, *True Stories of New England Captives Carried to Canada During the Old French and Indian Wars*, 135–36; Mass. Archives, 2:67a; John Williams to Stephen Williams, May 14, 1716, Ayer Mss. 1004, Newberry Library.

33. Vaughan and Richter, "Crossing the Cultural Divide," 63–65; Erwin H. Ackernecht, "'White Indians': Psychological and Physiological Peculiarities of White Children Abducted and Reared by North American Indians," *Bulletin of the History of Medicine* 15 (1944): 15–36; Axtell, "White Indians," 81–82; "Journal of Captain Phineas Stevens' Journey to Canada, 1752," 314; *Narrative of Titus King of Northampton, Mass.: A Prisoner of the Indians in Canada, 1755–1758*, 17; "Narrative of Mrs. Johnson," 175.

34. Laurel Thatcher Ulrich, *Good Wives: Image and Reality in the Lives of Women in Northern New England, 1650–1750*, 205.

35. James Phinney Baxter, *Baxter Manuscripts* 23 (1916): 440; "Journal of Captain Phineas Stevens To and From Canada—1749," *Collections of the New Hampshire Historical Society* 5 (1837): 203; "Journal of Captain Phineas Stevens' Journey to Canada, 1752," in Newton D. Mereness, ed., *Travels in the American Colonies*, 311, 315; Massachusetts State Archives, Mass. Archives, 5:543–46; "Nathaniel Wheelwright's Canadian Journey," ed. Edward P. Hamilton. 277, 284.

36. Mass. Archives, 70:469, 525; John C. Huden, "The White Chief of the St. Francis Abenakis," *Vermont History* 24, July 1956, 199–210, Oct. 1956, 337–55; "Narrative of Mrs. Johnson," 158, 178; Henry L. Masta, "When the Abenaki Came to Dartmouth," *Dartmouth Alumni* 21 (1928–29): 303.

37. Abenaki Nation of Vermont, *Petition for Federal Recognition as an American Indian Tribe*, submitted by the Abenaki Nation of Vermont (Swanton, Vt., 1982), 27. Stephen William, however, included no one of that name in his list of "Names of the captives who were taken at the town of Deerfield," in Stephen W. Williams, *Biographical Memoir of the Rev. John Williams*, 100–101.

38. Axtell, *The Invasion Within: The Contest of Cultures in Colonial North America*, 212–13.

39. Vaughan and Richter, "Crossing the Cultural Divide," 51, 60–62, 84–85; Axtell, *Invasion Within*, chap. 12.

40. Cf. Colin G. Calloway, "Neither Red nor White: White Renegades on the American Indian Frontier," *Western Historical Quarterly* 17 (Jan. 1986): 43–66; James A. Clifton, *Being and Becoming Indian: Biographical Studies of North American Frontiers*.

41. Bruce J. Bourque, "Ethnicity on the Maritime Peninsula, 1600–1759," *Ethnohistory* 36 (Summer 1989): 257–84.

42. Charland, *Les Abenakis d'Odanak*, 100; Nathaniel Bouton, ed., *New Hampshire Provincial Papers* 6:236; *JR* 70:135.

43. In a dissertation completed about the same time as this manuscript, David L. Ghere independently reached similar conclusions about the continuity resilience, and adaptability of Abenaki social structures in Maine and New Hampshire. Ghere, "Abenaki Factionalism, Emigration, and Social Continuity: Indian Society in Northern New England, 1725 to 1765," Ph.D. diss., University of Maine, 1988.

2. Contagion and Competition

1. Muller, "The Commercial History of the Lake Champlain–Richelieu River Route," Ph.D. diss., 2; "The Exploration of the Merrimack River, in 1638 By Order of the General Court of Massachusetts, with a plan of the same," *Historical Collections of the Essex Institute* 14, no. 3 (July 1877): 153–71.

2. Henry F. Dobyns, *Native American Historical Demography*, 21–22; Dobyns, *Their Number Become Thinned: Native American Population Dynamics in Eastern North America*, esp. essay 2. Francis Jennings, *The Invasion of America: Indians, Colonialism, and the Cant of Conquest*, chap. 2. Scholars have questioned Dobyns's methodolgy and findings; one of the most critical is David Henige, "Primary Source by Primary Source? On the Role of Epidemics in New World Depopulation," *Ethnohistory* 33 (Summer 1986): 293–312. Dean R. Snow and Kim M. Lamphear, "European Contact and Indian Depopulation in the Northeast: The Timing of the First Epidemics," *Ethnohistory* 35 (Winter 1988): 15–33, question Dobyns's theory of pandemic disease and argue that there were no epidemics of consequence in the Northeast in the sixteenth century.

3. Dobyns, *Their Number Become Thinned*, 21, 23; Herbert U. Williams, "The Epidemic of the Indians of New England, 1616–1620," *Johns Hopkins Hospital Bulletin* 20 (1919): 340–49; Billie Hoornbeck, "An Investigation into the Cause or Causes of the Epidemic Which Decimated the Indian Population of New England, 1616–1619," *New England Archaeologist* 19 (1976–77): 35–46; Sherburne F. Cook, "The Significance of Disease in the Extinction of the New England Indians," *Human Biology* 45 (1973): 487–89; Arthur E. and Bruce D. Spiess, "New England Pandemic of 1616–1622: Cause and Archaeological Implication," *Man in the Northeast* 34 (Fall, 1987): 71–83, assert that the 1616 epidemic definitely was not smallpox. Daniel Gookin, "Historical Collections of the Indians in New England," *Collections of the Massachusetts Historical Society for 1792* (reprint, Towtaid, 1971), 9–12; Charles Francis Adams, Jr., ed., *The New England Canaan of Thomas Morton* (reprint, New York, 1967), 120, 133. Edward Johnson, *Johnson's Wonder-Working Providence, 1628–1651*, ed. J. Franklin Jameson, 39–42; Kenneth Morrison, "The People of the Dawn; The Abnaki and Their Relations with New England and New France, 1600–1727," Ph.D. diss., University of Maine, 1975, 78, 83.

4. Snow and Lamphear, "European Contact and Indian Depopulation in the Northeast"; Edward Johnson, *Johnson's Wonder-Working Providence*, 79–80; Bruce G. Trigger, *The Children of Aataentsic: A History of the Huron People to 1660*, 2:499–501, 603; Cook, "Significance of Disease," 491–93; William Bradford *Bradford's History of Plymouth Plantation, 1606–1646*, ed. William T. Davis, 312–13; *Winthrop's Journal: "History of New England,"* ed. James Kendall Hosmer, 1:111, 114–15, 118–19.

5. Trigger, *Children of Aataentsic* 2:588; Dobyns, *Their Number Become Thinned*, 15; *JR* 15:237, 16:53, 101, 155, 217–19.

6. *JR* 28:203, 31:185–87, 207; Kenneth M. Morrison, *The Embattled Northeast: The Elusive Ideal of Alliance in Abenaki-Euramerian Relations*, 80, 83.

7. Dobyns, *Their Number Become Thinned*, 15, 19, 20; Cook, "Significance of Disease," 500.

8. Dobyns, *Their Number Become Thinned*, 15; Ted J. Brasser, *Riding on the Frontier's Crest*, 23; Morrison, *Embattled Northeast*, 92.

9. Ghere, "Abenaki Factionalism, Emigration and Social Continuity," chap. 3; Dobyns, *Their Number Become Thinned*, 15, 17, 20, 22; Adriaen van der Donck, *A Description of the New Netherlands*, quoted in Snow and Lamphear, "European Contact and Indian Depopulation in the Northeast," 27.

10. James Mooney, "The Aboriginal Population of America North of Mexico," Smithsonian Institution, *Miscellaneous Collections* 80 (1928), was for years considered the accepted wisdom on the subject. For more recent investigations, see Dobyns, *Native American Historical Demography*; Wilbur R. Jacobs, "The Tip of an Iceberg: Pre-Columbian Indian Demography and Some Implications for Revisionism," *William and Mary Quarterly*, 3d ser., 31 (1974): 123–32; William M. Denevan, ed., *The Native Population of the Americas in 1492*, esp. chap. 1; Douglas H. Ubelaker, "Prehistoric New World Population Size: Historical Reviews and Current Appraisal of North American Estimates," *American Journal of Physical Anthropology* 43 (1977): 661–66; Russell Thornton, *American Indian Holocaust and Survival: A Population History since 1492*; S. Ryan Johansson, "The Demographic History of the Native Peoples of North America: A Selective Bibliography," *Yearbook of Physical Anthropology* 25 (1982): 133–52. Peter A. Thomas, "In the Maelstrom of Change," 25–28, 417–21, discusses Mooney's figures for New England.

11. Thomas, "In the Maelstrom of Change," 25–28; Dean Snow, *The Archaeology of New England*, 33, 38; Cronon, *Changes in the Land*, 42, 89; Salisbury, *Manitou and Providence*, 22–30. William J. Eccles, *France in America*, 34, 51, 88, 110, 120.

12. Snow, *Archaeology of New England*, 34; Snow and Lamphear, "European Contact and Indian Depopulation in the Northeast," 24, increases the pre-epidemic estimate of western Abenaki population to 12,000.

13. Haviland and Power, *The Original Vermonters*, 213–14.

14. Bruce G. Trigger, *Natives and Newcomers: Canada's "Heroic Age" Reconsidered*, 136; Dean Snow, "Abenaki Fur Trade in the Sixteenth Century," *Western Canadian Journal of Anthropology* 6, no. 1 (1976): 3–11; Bruce J. Bourque and Ruth Holmes Whitehead, "Tarrantines and the Introduction of European Trade Goods in the Gulf of Maine," *Ethnohistory* 32 (1985): 327–41.

15. Dean Snow, "The Ethnohistoric Baseline of the Eastern Abenakis," *Ethnohistory* 23 (1976): 291–306; Pauleena MacDougall Seeber,

"The European Influence on Abenaki Economics Before 1616," in William Cowan, ed., *Papers of the 15th Algonquian Conference*, 201–14.

16. Trigger, *Natives and Newcomers*, 177; Trigger, "The Mohawk-Mahican War, 1624–1628: The Establishment of a Pattern," *Canadian Historical Review* 52 (1971): 276–86; Ted J. Brasser, *Riding on the Frontier's Crest*, 11–16.

17. Sylvester Judd, "The Fur Trade on the Connecticut River in the Seventeenth Century," *New England Historical and Genealogical Register* 11 (1857): 217–19; Thomas, "In the Maelstrom of Change"; *Letters of John Pynchon, 1654–1700*, ed. Carl Bridenbaugh, xv.

18. Gordon M. Day, *The Identity of the St. Francis Indians*, 13; *JR* 36 : 139, 141; Peter A. Thomas, "Squakheag Ethnohistory," 27–29; Thomas, "In the Maelstrom of Change," 177, 363, 377–79, 389.

19. "Pennacook Papers," *Collections of the New Hampshire Historical Society* (Concord, N.H.), 3 (1832): 214–24; Cabot, ed., *Annals of Brattleboro, 1681–1895* 1 : 12; *VHG* 5 : 45.

20. *New Voyages to North-America by Baron de Lahontan* 1 : 90.

21. Thomas, "In the Maelstrom of Change," 387, 390–92, 412.

22. Patrick Mitchell Malone, "Indian and English Military Systems in New England in the Sevententh Century," Ph.D. diss., Brown University, 1971; *JR* 12 : 189, 27 : 273; PAC MG1 C11A, 122 : 201–202; Trigger, *Natives and Newcomers*, 262; Nathaniel Bouton, ed., *New Hampshire Provincial Papers* 1 : 343.

23. *JR* 28 : 225; James Axtell, *The Invasion Within: The Contest of Cultures in Colonial North America*, 248; Alaric and Gretchen Faulkner, *The French at Pentagoet, 1635–1674: An Archaeological Portrait of the Acadian Frontier* (The New Brunswick Museum and the Maine Historic Preservation Commission, 1987), 43.

24. "Traces of an Indian Legend," *Catholic World* 22 (Oct. 1875-March 1876): 278–81; *VHG* 4 : 1090; Thomas, "In the Maelstrom of Change," 375–77; Coolidge, "French Occupation of the Champlain Valley," 166–67, 482–83.

25. *JR* 60 : 133–39, 233;

26. Gordon M. Day, "Missisquoi: A New Look at an Old Village," *Man in the Northeast* 6 (Fall 1973): 53; *NYCD* 9 : 194; *JR* 62 : 161; Day, *Identity of the St. Francis Indians*, 22–23; PAC, MG1 C11A, 9 : 373.

27. PAC, NMC 6359, H3/900/1713 and NMC 6364, H3/900/1715.

28. The Abenaki wampum belt is still on display in the crypt at Chartres Cathedral. A replica of the statue of Notre-Dame de Sous-Terre is in the present Catholic church at Odanak. *VHG* 4: 956.

29. Axtell, *Invasion Within*, 222; Gookin, *Historical Collections of the Indians of New England*, 75–76; *Baxter MSS* 23 : 29; *CSP* (1700), 399,

401; "Indian Treaties," *Collections of the Maine Historical Society* 4 (1856): 129, 131.

30. *JR* 67:29, 95, 113, 197; PAC MG1 C11A, 11:315–17, 35:42; *NYCD* 9:878–79; Morrison, *Embattled Northeast*, chap. 3. The Caughnawaga statement is in *Johnson Papers* 2:379 and 9:220.

31. *JR* 31:207, 60:237; Morrison, *Embattled Northeast*, esp. chap. 3; Axtell, *Invasion Within*, chap. 6; Robert Conkling, "Legitimacy and Conversion in Social Change: The Case of French Missionaries and the Northeastern Algonkian," *Ethnohistory* 21 (Winter 1974): 1–24.

32. George R. Hamell, "Mythical Realities and European Contact in the Northeast During the Sixteenth and Seventeenth Centuries," *Man in the Northeast* 33 (Spring 1987): 68, 80. Calvin Martin, *Keepers of the Game: Indian-Animal Relationships and the Fur Trade* (Berkeley: University of California Press, 1978), provides a provocative and controversial discussion of the disintegration of such sanctions among the Abenakis' northern neighbors, the hunter-gatherers of eastern Canada. The essays in Sheperd Krech, III, ed., *Indians, Animals, and the Fur Trade: A Critique of Keepers of the Game*, comment on Martin's thesis.

33. *JR* 62:39; "Pennacook Papers," 214–15; PAC MG1 C11A, 12–2: 784–809, 4:211–13, 11:318–20; 39:198–205, 41:61–65; *JR* 67:39–41; Cornelius J. Jaenen, *The French Relationship with the Native Peoples of New France and Acadia*, 128–38.

34. *JR* 60:239; 63:71, 111; *NYCD* 9:441.

35. *NYCD* 9:441; *JR* 67:197, 60:135–37; Jacques Le Sueur, "History of the Calumet and of the Dance," *Contributions from the Museum of the American Indian, Heye Foundation* 12, no. 5 (1952): 1–22; Thomas M. Charland, *Abénakis d'Odanak*, 93–97.

36. Jaenen, *French Relationship with the Native Peoples of New France and Acadia*, 94–95, 98; John Webster Grant, *Moon of Wintertime: Missionaries and the Indians of Canada in Encounter since 1534*, 240, 245; Morrison, *Embattled Northeast*; Hamell, "Mythical Realities and European Contact in the Northeast," 80; *JR* 60:239. On the question of Indian conversion, see James Axtell, "Were Indian Conversions *Bona Fide?*" in *After Columbus: Essays in the Ethnohistory of Colonial America*, 100–21.

37. Cronon, *Changes in the Land*, chap. 3; Day, "Western Abenaki," in Trigger, ed., *Northeast*, 154; Thomas, "In the Maelstrom of Change," 11, 96–108. PAC, MG1 C11A, 22:226. Dean R. Snow, "Wabanaki Family Hunting Territories," *American Anthropologist* 70 (1968): 1143–51, summarizes the literature on the controversial question of whether "family hunting territories" among nonhorticultural Algonquians were precontact in origin or whether they represented adaptations to the European fur trade. Snow maintains that, while some northern Algonquians made

such an adaptation, the Abenakis and other eastern hunters had family-band hunting territories before European contact.

38. Thomas, "In the Maelstrom of Change," 339.

39. Peter A. Thomas, "Contrastive Subsistence Strategies and Land Use as Factors for Understanding Indian-White Relations in New England," *Ethnohistory* 23 (1976). Tallying fur returns in the Connecticut Valley between 1650 and 1670, Thomas also challenges the standard interpretation that overhunting and European encroachment undermined native societies in all situations. In "The Fur Trade, Indian Land, and the Need to Define Adequate 'Environmental' Parameters," *Ethnohistory* 28 (1981): 359–79, Thomas argues that Connecticut Valley tribes exchanged lands as part of a strategy to maintain social and cultural obligations.

40. Cronon, *Changes in the Land*, 55–57; Thomas, "Contrastive Subsistence Strategies," 4–5.

41. Cronon, *Changes in the Land*, 6; *Letters and Papers of Cadwallader Colden 9, Collections of the New York Historical Society* 68:214–15; Edward Augustus Kendall, *Travels* 3:191. For a broader discussion of the biological and ecological effects of European invasion, see Alfred W. Crosby, Jr., *The Columbian Exchange: Biological and Cultural Consequences of 1492* (Westport, Conn.: Greenwood Press, 1972), and, in a global context, Crosby, *Ecological Imperialism: The Biological Expansion of Europe, 900–1900*.

3. Relations with Algonquins and Iroquois, 1603–1669

1. Bacqueville de la Pothèrie, *Histoire de l'Amérique Septentrionale* 1:309.

2. Gordon Day, "The Ouragie War: A Case of History in Iroquois–New England Indian Relations," in Michael K. Foster, Jack Campisi, Marianne Mithun, eds., *Extending the Rafters: Interdisciplinary Approaches to Iroquoian Studies*, 37.

3. Richter, "War and Culture: The Iroquois Experience," 529–30; Roger Williams, *A Key into the Language of America* (London, 1643; edited by John T. Teunissen and Evelyn J. Hinz, Detroit: Wayne State University Press, 1973), 237.

4. *The Voyages of Jacques Cartier*, ed. H. P. Biggar, 141–73.

5. Bruce G. Trigger, *Natives and Newcomers*, 144–48, 173; James W. Bradley, *Evolution of the Onondaga Iroquois: Accommodating Change, 1500–1655* (Syracuse: Syracuse University Press, 1987), 83–89; *The Works of Samuel de Champlain* ed. H. P. Biggar, 1:125–57, 5:78; *JR* 22:207; Trigger, "Trade and Tribal Warfare on the St. Lawrence in the Sixteenth Century," *Ethnohistory* 9 (1962): 240–56. Marc Lescarbot: *The History*

of New France, ed. H. P. Biggar, 3:267–68; "A Brief Description of Laconia," *Collections of the Maine Historical Society,* (Portland), 2 (1847): 67; R. Cole Harris, *Historical Atlas of Canada,* vol. 1, pl. 33.

6. *JR* 22:215; Day, "Abenakis in the Lake Champlain Valley," 279; *Works of Champlain* 2:90.

7. *Works of Champlain* 2:93; Huden, "Indian Groups in Vermont," 112–15; Huden, *Indian Place Names in New England,* 215; Floyd Lounsbury, "Iroquois Place-Names in the Champlain Valley," in Hauptman and Campisi, eds., *Neighbors and Intruders,* 117–22, discredits the notion that the Mohawks referred to Lake Champlain as "the gateway to the country." Archer Butler Hulbert, ed., *The Crown Collection of Photographs of American Maps,* 1st ser., 1: #47 [cxxi.12]; D. P. Thompson, "The Aboriginal Inhabitants of Winooski Valley," in *History of the Town of Montpelier* (Montpelier: E. P. Walton, 1860), 304–305, 307; Henry R. Schoolcraft, *Information Respecting the History, Condition, and Prospects of the Indian Tribes of the United States* 4:226–27; Eastern Indians' Letter to the Governeur, July 17, 1721, *Collections of the Massachusetts Historical Society,* 2d ser., 8 (1826): 260; Vermont Historical Society, Misc. File #318, p. 6; Massachusetts Historical Society, Parkman Papers, 31:367.

8. Gordon Day, "The Eastern Boundary of Iroquoia: Abenaki Evidence," *Man in the Northeast* 1(1971): 7–8; Day, "Abenakis in the Lake Champlain Valley," 279; PAC, NMC H3/900/[1694]. Although Raffeix's map is dated 1694, the Jesuit's knowledge of the area went back almost 30 years, since he accompanied Courcelle on a campaign against the Iroquois in 1666 (*Dictionary of Canadian Biography* 2:540); *NYCD* 7:573, 576; Lewis Henry Morgan, *The League of the Ho-De'-No-Sau-Nee, or Iroquois* (reprint, Secaucus, N.J.: Citadel Press, 1972), 46.

9. Neal Salisbury, "Toward the Covenant Chain: Iroquois and Southern New England Algonquians, 1637–84," in Richter and Merrell, eds., *Beyond the Covenant Chain,* 61–62, 65–66; Eric P. Jackson, "Indian Occupation and Use of the Champlain Lowland," *Papers of the Michigan Academy of Science, Arts, and Letters* 14 (1940): 21, 115, 128, 155; Pierre F.X. de Charlevoix, *History and General Description of New France,* ed. John Gilmeary Shea, 2:246; *VHG* 4:942, 949; Vermont Historical Society, Misc. File #3; Dartmouth College, Special Collections, Gordon Day Tapes, reel 9, side 1, reel 30, side 1.

10. Trigger, *Natives and Newcomers,* 304–305; Trigger, "Champlain Judged by His Indian Policy: A Different View of Early Canadian History," *Anthropologia,* n.s., 13 (1971): 85–114; Jennings, *Ambiguous Iroquois Empire,* 41; *Works of Champlain* 2:71.

11. *Works of Champlain* 2:96–104; Wendell S. Hadlock, "War among the Northeastern Woodland Indians," *American Anthropologist,* n.s., 49

(1974): 204–21; Keith F. Otterbein, "Why the Iroquois Won: An Analysis of Iroquois Military Tactics," *Ethnohistory* 11 (Winter 1964): 56–63.

12. George T. Hunt, *The Wars of the Iroquois: A Study in Intertribal Trade Relations*, argued that exhaustion of beaver supplies in their own territory was the driving force behind Iroquois expansion. See also K. H. Schleiser, "Epidemics and Indian Middlemen: Rethinking the Wars of the Iroquois, 1609–1653," *Ethnohistory* 23 (Spring 1976): 129–45, and Trigger, *Natives and Newcomers*, 260–62.

13. On Mohawk-Mahican relations and the war see T. J. Brasser, *Riding on the Frontier's Crest*, 11–16, 19; Bruce G. Trigger, "The Mohawk-Mahican War, 1624–1628: The Establishment of a Pattern," *Canadian Historical Review* 52 (1971): 176–86; J. Franklin Jameson, ed., *Narratives of New Netherland, 1609–1664*, 89, 131; Thomas, "In the Maelstrom of Change," Ph.D. diss., 48–49. Brasser claims that Jameson mistranslated the Dutch records in referring to Mahicans taking refuge in the Connecticut Valley. *NYCD* 13:185. Walter Hill Crockett said that some Mahicans fled to the Great Oxbow at Cowass, journeying through the Battenkill Pass and over the Green Mountains to the Connecticut River, where, according to legend, their women cleared the Coos meadows and cultivated corn and beans. Crockett, *Vermont* 1:47. Day, "The Ouragie War," 39, cites the evidence for Pocumtuck and Sokoki involvement (*NYCD* 13:381).

14. Alden T. Vaughan, *New England Frontier: Puritans and Indians, 1620–1675*, chap. 5, and Jennings, *Invasion of America*, chap. 13, present diametrically opposed views of the Pequot War. See also Salisbury, *Manitou and Providence*, 215–25, and Adam J. Hirsch, "The Collision of Military Cultures in Seventeenth Century New England," *Journal of American History* 74 (March 1988): 1187–1212.

15. Jennings, *Ambiguous Iroquois Empire*, 50; Brasser, *Riding on the Frontier's Crest*, 18.

16. *JR* 8:27–29; Trigger, *Children of Aetaentsic* 2:609–10, 634–36, 653; *NYCD* 2:157, 9:194; *JR* 24:101; Jennings, *Ambiguous Iroquois Empire*, 78; Brasser, *Riding on the Frontier's Crest*, 18–21; Brasser, "Mahican," in Trigger, ed, *Northeast*, 203.

17. Thomas, "In the Maelstrom of Change," Ph.D. diss., 81; Day, Indian Occupation of Vermont," 373; *JR* 24: 183–85, 25:53, 31:85–87; Jameson, ed., *Narratives of New Netherland*, 246.

18. Trigger, *Children of Aataentsic* 2:653; *JR* 27:79, 28:277–79.

19. *JR* 28:275, 285; Charlevoix, *History of New France* 2:185.

20. *JR* 31:85.

21. Day, "Ouragie War," 39–41; Thomas, "In the Maelstrom of Change," Ph.D. diss., 204–14, 240, 396.

22. Eccles, *France in America*, 51; Trigger, *Natives and Newcomers*, 7.

23. *NYCD* 9:5–6; *Collections of the New York Historical Society*, 2d ser., 3, pt 1: 323; *CMNF* 1:127. "Druillettes Journal," 317–23; *JR* 36: 75–81, 101–05, 129, 227, 37: 77, 259; Day, "Ouragie War," 40.

24. *JR* 36:139–43.

25. *JR* 37:119, 97, 40:197; Alfred Goldsworthy, Bailey, *The Conflict of European and Eastern Algonkian Cultures, 1504–1700*, 29–30.

26. Trigger, *Children of Aetaentsic* 2:793; PAC, MG1 C11A, 1:321–26.

27. *JR* 40: 197; Gordon M. Day, "A Bibliography of the Saint Francis Dialect," *International Journal of American Linguistics* 27, no. 1 (Jan. 1961): 81.

28. Thomas, "In the Maelstrom of Change," Ph.D. diss., 231–36, 238.

29. Day, "Ouragie War," 41; *NYCD* 13:225; *JR* 47:279.

30. Brasser, "Mahican," 204; *JR* 47:107; 49:139–41; *NYCD* 2:371.

31. On Fort Hill see Thomas, "In the Maelstrom of Change," Ph.D. diss., 239–60 and passim.

32. Thomas, "In the Maelstrom of Change," Ph.D. diss., 245–46; *NYCD* 13:308–309. The "Message of the Indians of Agawam to the Dutch" is reprinted in *Letters of John Pynchon*, 45–46.

33. *NYCD* 13:298; Day, "Ouragie War," 42.

34. Thomas, "In the Maelstrom of Change," Ph.D. diss., 250; *NYCD* 13:355–56.

35. Day, *The Identity of the St. Francis Indians*, 15; Day, *The Mots Loups of Father Mathevet*, 38; Day, "Abenakis in the Lake Champlain Valley," 282; Charland, *Abénakis d'Odanak* 18–19.

36. Day, "Ouragie War," 42; *NYCD* 13:380–82; Thomas, "In the Maelstrom of Change," Ph.D. diss., 253–55. Cf. journal of commissioners to negotiate between Mohawks and Northern Indians (in Dutch), New York State Archives, Colonial MSS, 15:129–30, reproduced in *Iroquois Indians: A Documentary History*, reel 1.

37. Day, "Ouragie War," 42–43; *NYCD* 3:68, 13:389; Sheldon, *History of Deerfield* 1:68–69.

38. Thomas, "In the Maelstrom of Change," Ph.D. diss., 256; *Letters of John Pynchon*, 50; Day "Ouragie War," 45–48 (Day suggests this tradition refers to an attack launched in 1666).

39. Thomas, "In the Maelstrom of Change," Ph.D. diss., 259–60, 395.

40. Day, "Ouragie War," 43.

41. Gookin, *Historical Collections of the Indians in New England*, 34.

42. *NYCD* 3:118–19; Leder, ed., *The Livingston Indian Records, 1666–1723*, 33–35; Gov. Richard Nicolls to John Allyn, 19 Sept. 1666, Connecticut Historical Society, Hartford, Wyllys Papers, in *Iroquois Indians: A Documentary History*, reel 2; Day, "Ouragie War," 43–48; PAC, MG1 C11A, 3:505–11.

43. Richter, "War and Culture," 540.

44. Day, "Ouragie War," 44; Gookin, *Historical Collections*, 40–42; *JR* 53:137–53.

45. Brasser, *Frontier's Crest*, 21–22; Brasser, "Mahican," 204: *NYCD* 2:371–72; *JR* 51:83, 197; Peace Between Mohawks and Northern Indians, 14 May 1670, New York State Archives, Albany, Council Minutes, 31: 26–27; Peace Between the Mohawks and Mahicans, 22 Oct. 1670, Council Minutes, 31:33, in *Iroquois Indians: A Documentary History*, reel 2.

46. Day, "Ouragie War," 44.

47. Richter, "War and Culture," 544.

48. Temple and Sheldon, *History of the Town of Northfield, Massachusetts*, 55, 69–70.

49. *NYCD* 9:194; *JR* 62:157, 161; PAC, MG1 C11A, 6–1: 97–99, 101–105, 222–53.

50. E.g., Proposition of the Mohawk Tahaiadons, 5 Apr. 1678, in *Iroquois Indians: A Documentary History*, reel 3; *JR* 63:67; Jacques Paquin, "Mémoire sur l'Eglise du Canada," PAC, MSS, 220, cited by Charland, *Abénakis d'Odanak*, 21, and Gordon Day, "Abenakis in the Lake Champlain Valley," 284; *CMNF* 1:514, 589–90.

4. King Philip's War and the Great Dispersals, 1675–1677

1. Sévigny, *Abénaquis,* 126.

2. Thomas, "In the Maelstrom of Change," Ph.D. diss., 260; Temple and Sheldon, *History of the Town of Northfield*, 29–31; Gookin, *Historical Collections of the Indians in New England*, 40–42.

3. Thomas, "Squahkeag Ethnohistory," 29–30; Harry Andrew Wright, ed., *Indian Deeds of Hampden County*, 80–81; Temple and Sheldon, *History of Northfield*, 31, 35.

4. Temple and Sheldon, *History of Northfield*, 55, 69–70; Sheldon, *History of Deerfield* 1:129–30, 138.

5. "A New and Further Narrative of the State of New England, by N. S.," in Charles H. Lincoln, ed., *Narratives of the Indian Wars, 1675–1699*, 87–88; Day, "Missisquoi," 51.

6. Jennings, *Invasion of America*, 314–16; "A New and Further Narrative of the State of New England, by N. S.," 97. In March 1676 the New York authorities sent a party as far east as the Connecticut River to search for Metacom and demand the return of captives. *NYCD* 13:494.

7. Crockett, *Vermont* 1:44; Temple and Sheldon, *History of Northfield*, 83–87; "Narrative of the Captivity of Mary Rowlandson," in Lincoln, ed., *Narratives of the Indian Wars*, 133–34; Douglas Edward Leach, "The 'Whens' of Mary Rowlandson's Captivity," *New England Quarterly* 34

(1961): 352–63, attempts to reconstruct the chronology of events during Rowlandson's 83-day captivity in an effort to shed more light on the Indians' comings and goings during these months.

8. Douglas Edward Leach, *Flintlock and Tomahawk: New England in King Philip's War*, 200–204; Richard Slotkin and James K. Folsom, eds., *So Dreadful a Judgment: Puritan Responses to King Philip's War, 1676–1677*, 119; "A New and Further Narrative of the State of New England," 95–96; Jennings, *Invasion of America*, 319; *CSP* 9:406.

9. Kenneth M. Morrison, "The Bias of Colonial Law: English Paranoia and the Abenaki Arena of King Philip's War, 1675–1678," *New England Quarterly* 53 (1980): 363–87; Massachusetts State Archives, Mass. Archives, 69:46; and *Papers of John Pynchon*, 167.

10. Morrison, *Embattled Northeast*, 88–93; Sévigny, *Abénaquis*, 124–25; Day, *Identity of the St. Francis Indians*, 16–17; New York State Archives, Colonial MSS, 27:139, 143; *JR* 60:133, 233; Day, "Indian Occupation," 374; Day, *Mots Loups of Father Mathevet*, 40; Harris, ed., *Historical Atlas of Canada*, vol. 1, pl. 47.

11. Francis Parkman, *La Salle and the Discovery of the Great West* (New York: New American Library, 1963), 214, 221, 234, 254; Bacqueville de La Pothèrie, "History of the Savage Peoples Who are Allies of New France," in Emma Helen Blair, trans. and ed., *The Indian Tribes of the Upper Mississippi Valley and Region of the Great Lakes* 1:364–66, 372; La Pothèrie, *Histoire de l'Amerique Septentrionale* 2:135, 151, 180, 210; Charlevoix, *Histoire de la Nouvelle France* 5:141–43, *JR* 66:348n; Day, *Mots Loups of Father Mathevet*, 43; Brasser, "Group Identification along a Moving Frontier," 263; Brasser, *Riding on the Frontier's Crest*, 25; Helen Hornbeck Tanner, ed., *Atlas of Great Lakes Indian History*, 2, 29, and map 6; Jacques Le Sueur, "History of the Calumet and of the Dance," *Contributions from the Museum of the American Indian, Heye Foundation, New York* 12, no. 5 (1952): 1–22. The Indian peoples of the Great Lakes and Midwest were accustomed to accommodating refugees: Richard White, "Creating New Homelands: The Beaver Wars and Algonquian Migrations in the Seventeenth Century," paper delivered at the Ninety-ninth Annual Meeting of the American Historical Association, Chicago, Dec. 1984.

12. Thomas, "Squahkeag Ethnohistory," 31–35.

13. Day, *Identity of the St. Francis Indians*, 17, 21, 29; Sévigny, *Abénaquis*, 124–26, 203; Kidder, "The Abenaki Indians," 237; Mass. Archives, 30:178–79, 182, 204, 206b, 67:265a; Samuel Drake, *The History of the Indian Wars in New England* 1:49, 96, 2:133, 186–88; Bouton, ed., *New Hampshire Provincial Papers* 1:357–58; "Biography of Wanalancet," *Farmer's Monthly Visitor* 12, no. 9 (Sept. 1852): 260, 263; Colin G. Calloway, "Wanalancet and Kancamagus: Indian Strategy and Leadership on

the New Hampshire Frontier," *Historical New Hampshire* 43 (Winter 1988), 264–90.

14. *JR* 60:217; Day, "Western Abenaki," 151; Day, *Identity of the St. Francis Indians*, 23, 29–30; Leder, ed., *Livingston Indian Records*, 82; Crockett, *Vermont* 1:75; Sévigny, *Abénaquis*, 124, 126; "Biography of Kancamagus," *Farmer's Monthly Visitor* 13, no. 5 (May 1853): 130–32; Bouton, ed., *New Hampshire Provincial Papers* 1:583–89; Calloway, "Wanalancet and Kancamagus," Harris, ed., *Historical Atlas of Canada*, vol. 1, pl. 47.

15. Jennings, *Invasion of America*, chap. 18; Sévigny, *Abénaquis*, 111–12; Allen W. Trelease, *Indian Affairs in Colonial New York*, 326; Day, *Identity of the St. Francis Indians*, 19–20; Day, "Indian Occupation of Vermont," 370; *NYCD* 4:743, 902, 991, 13:496–97, 503; Egbert C. Smyth, "Papers Relating to the Construction and First Occupancy of Fort Dummer, and to a Conference with the Scatacook Indians Held There," *Proceedings of the Massachusetts Historical Society*, 2d ser., 6 (1891): 375–76; Brasser, *Riding on the Frontier's Crest*, 24; *CSP* 1700:571; Mass. Archives, 32:347–50; Harris, ed., *Historical Atlas of Canada*, vol. 1, pl. 47.

16. Leder, ed., *Livingston Indian Records*, 77–82, 95–96; *NYCD* 4:596–97, 743–45, 648–52, 902–903, 990–92, 5:222–23, 722, 798–99; 6:909, 9:66; Sévigny, *Abénaquis*, 112–13, 163; Day, "Missisquoi," 52–54.

17. Wells, *History of Newbury, Vermont*, 6–7, 30; Zadock Thompson, *History of Vermont*, pt. 2, 205; *VHG* 2:917–18, 924.

18. Day, "Indian Occupation of Vermont," 371, 374; Day, *Identity of the St. Francis Indians*, 49–50; *VHG* 4:944; Sévigny, *Abénaquis*, 159.

19. *NYCD* 13:511–12, and *Letters of John Pynchon*, 173–76n. On Ashpelon's raid see also Sheldon, *History of Deerfield* 1:180–83.

20. Sévigny, *Abénaquis*, 204–205; *Henry Tufts: The Autobiography of a Criminal*, edited by Edmund Pearson, 72; *VHG* 1:1028; "Mémoire Touchant les Sauvages Abénaquis de Sillery," *CMNF* 1:272–73, 3:194–95; *JR* 24:101.

21. Day, "Indian Occupation of Vermont," 369; Jackson, "Indian Occupation and Use of the Champlain Lowland," 125, 143; Crockett, *Vermont* 1:49–51, 76–77; Sévigny, *Abénaquis*, 161–62; Huden, "Indian Groups," 113–14; *VHG* 2:473, 1140, 4:944; "A New and Further Account of the State of New England," op. cit., 87–88; Day, "Missisquoi," 51; PAC, MG1, C11A, 9:f. 373; also in *NYCD* 9:795.

22. Day, "Indian Occupation of Vermont," 369; *NYCD* 9:194; *JR* 62:160.

23. Day, *Identity of the St. Francis Indians*, 22–23; *New Voyages to North-America by the Baron de Lahontan* 1:90. Thwaites identified the three tribes as Sokokis of Maine, Mohegans, and New Brunswick Algonquins, or Quoddy Indians, 90n. Lahontan probably referred to the 156 "North

Indians" who arrived at Schaghticoke that summer and to the group who visited their relatives at Pennacook; Leder, ed., *Livingston Indian Records*, 77–79, 82; *NYCD* 3:482. The Marquis de Denonville maintained that the "Loups" who left Chambly and went to the English did so to escape persecution by French traders to whom they had become indebted for "l'eau de vie"; *Rapport de l'Archiviste de la Province de Quebec* (hereafter RAPQ) (1939–40), 285.

24. John Moody, "Missisquoi: Abenaki Survival in Their Ancient Homeland"; Sévigny, *Abénaquis*, 205; Day, "Western Abenaki," 149; Day, *Identity of the St. Francis*, 58; Crockett, *Vermont* 1:74, 78.

25. Morrison, "People of the Dawn," 118; Morrison, *Embattled Northeast*, 168.

26. James P. Ronda, "The Sillery Experiment: A Jesuit Indian Village in New France, 1637–1663," *American Indian Culture and Research Journal* 3 no. 1 (1979): 1–8; *JR* 28:169, 60:133, 233; 62:25, 109, 63:10–11, 69–71; Charland, *Abénakis d'Odanak*, 12–13, 22; Massachusetts Historical Society, Parkman Papers, 29:407–408; *New Voyages to North-America by the Baron de Lahontan* 1:48.

27. La Pothèrie, *Histoire de l'Amérique Septentrionale* 1:309; Day, *Identity of the St. Francis*, 10, 12, 32, 59, 66, 111; Charland, *Abénakis d'Odanak*, 13, 16–17, 22; Sévigny, *Abénaquis*, 112, 165, 173; *JR* 65:187; *CMNF* 3:23.

28. Slotkin and Folsom, eds., *So Dreadful a Judgment*, 142.

29. Patrick Malone, "Indian and English Military Systems in New England in the Seventeenth Century," Ph.D. diss., Brown University, 1971, passim; Jennings, *Invasion of America*, chap. 9; Hirsch, "The Collision of Military Cultures in Seventeenth Century New England," *Journal of American History* 74 (March 1988): 1187–21; Slotkin and Folsom, eds., *So Dreadful a Judgment*, pt. 6.

5. Echoes of Distant Storms, 1688–1715

1. Richard R. Johnson, "The Search for a Usable Indian: An Aspect of the Defense of Colonial New England," *Journal of American History* 64 (1977): 623–51; Marcus A. McCorison, "Colonial Defense of the Upper Connecticut Valley," *Vermont History* 30 (1962): 50–62; Bouton, ed., *New Hampshire Provincial Papers* 1:499–500.

2. Charlevoix, *History of New France* 5:209–10, 279; Coolidge, "French Occupation of the Champlain Valley," 197–99; PAC, MG1 C11A, 11:328.

3. PAC, AC C11A, 3:123; *NYCD* 9:66, 441; PAC, MG1 C11A, 11:315–17.

4. Morrison, *Embattled Northeast*, esp. chap. 3; *JR* 67:101–103; New York State Archives, Colonial MSS, 39:174.

5. Temple and Sheldon, *History of Northfield*, 111–20; *CSP* (1685–88),

583, 588–92; *Letters of John Pynchon*, xxiv, 184–87; 202; *NYCD* 3:550–54, 557, 565; Examination of an Indian relative to certain Canada Indians coming to Deerfield and vicinity," Sept. 15, 1688, Mass. Archives, 30:310–11; also in *NYCD* 3:561–62.

6. Thomas, "Squakheag Ethnohistory," 32–35; Wright, ed. *Indian Deeds of Hampden County*, 105–107, 114–15.

7. PAC, NMC 10854, and Bruce J. Bourque, "Ethnicity on the Maritime Peninsula," 277; Charland, *Abénakis d'Odanak*, 18–19; Day, *Identity of the St. Francis Indians*, 84; *Baxter MSS* 23: 306.

8. *NYCD* 3:482; *CSP* (1688), 583; Bouton, ed. *New Hampshire Provincial Papers* 2:48–56; Cotton Mather, "Decennium Luctuosum" (1699), in Lincoln, ed., *Narratives of the Indian Wars*, 196; Benjamin Church, *The History of the Eastern Expeditions of 1689, 1690, 1692, 1696, and 1704 Against the Indians and French* (Boston: J. K. Wiggin and Wm. Parsons Lunt, 1897), 53–55, 62–64; *Baxter MSS* 5:162–66, 233–35; Calloway, "Wanalancet and Kancamagus," 21–24; C. E. Potter, *History of Manchester, New Hampshire* (Manchester: C. E. Potter, 1856), 97.

9. PAC, MG1, F3, 6–2:532–33; Charlevoix, *History of New France* 4:130–32; *NYCD* 9:471; La Pothèrie, *L'Amérique Septentrionale* 3:76–77; Francis Parkman, *Count Frontenac and New France under Louis XIV* (Toronto: George N. Morang, 1898), 218–45.

10. Charlevoix: *History of New France* 4:145n–47n, 188; La Pothèrie, *L'Amérique Septentrionale* 3:126; *NYCD* 9:513–14, and 513n for identification of the messenger as Sokoki. Journal, 14 July to 6 Sep. 1690, Public Records Office, Kew, England, C.O. 5/1039, in *Iroquois Indians: A Documentary History*, reel 4; PAC, MG1 C11A, 11:153–57, 280–84, 12–1:68–87, 12–2:422–68, *NYCD*, 3:800–05, 9:555–57.

11. *CMNF*, 1:514, 589–90; New York State Archives, Colonial MSS, 38:158; 49:149b; *NYCD* 9:539–40.

12. Submission and Agreement of the Eastern Indians, 11 Aug. 1693, *Baxter MSS* 10:7–11.

13. *NYCD* 9:550, 557–58, 650; Charlevoix, *History of New France*, 4:233, 5:13.

14. PAC, MG1 C11A, 14:239–42; MG1 C11A, 12–1:152–65; MG1 F3, 7:2–8; MG1 C11A, 14:200.

15. Mass. Archives, 30:358–59, 435–36. The payment of scalp bounties provides the context for Hannah Duston's celebrated killing and scalping of her Indian captors in 1697. *CSP* (1697–98), 84, 241.

16. Daniel K. Richter, "Rediscovered Links in the Covenant Chain: Previously Unpublished Transcripts of New York Indian Treaty Minutes, 1677–1691," *Proceedings of the American Antiquarian Society* 92, pt. 1 (1982):85; Trelease, *Indian Affairs in Colonial New York*, 326–27, 360–61, *CSP* (1689–92), 461, 470.

17. *NYCD* 4:248.

18. Cadwallader Colden, *History of the Five Indian Nations Depending on the Province of New-York in America*, 84; Mass. Archives, 30:425; *CSP* 16 (1697–98):431–32, 437–38, 449.

19. Mass. Archives, 30:368b.

20. Brasser, *Riding on the Frontiers Crest*, 23; *NYCD* 4:337; *CSP* (1697–98): 175, 430; "Table showing decrease of the Indians," 7 Nov. 1698, in *Iroquois Indians: A Documentary History*, reel 6.

21. *NYCD* 4:249; PAC, MG1 F3, 7:882; *JR* 67:183–95; Bourque, "Ethnicity on the Maritime Peninsula," 276n; Prins, "Amesokanti," 7, 13; Day, *Identity of the St. Francis Indians*, 26. Sévigny, *Abenaquis*, 111, 113, 147, suggests they were Mohegans.

22. Mass. Archives, 70:380.

23. *NYCD* 4:575–76; Day, *Identity of the St. Francis Indians*, 28. Day, "Indian Occupation of Vermont," 370; Crockett, *Vermont* 1:58. Cf. "Papers pertaining to councils involving the Five Nations," 14 Sept. 1698, Public Record Office, C.O. 5/1041, p. 15, in *Iroquois Indians: A Documentary History*, reel 6.

24. Jaenen, *French Relationship*, 164–65; William A. Starna has suggested that the Mohawks' pre-epidemic population may have been between 8,000 and 17,000. These estimates may be too high, but losses in battle, invasions by French armies, attacks by enemy tribes, and a steady exodus of Catholic converts to Canada took a drastic toll. In the 1640s the Mohawks could field 700 to 800 warriors, but they could raise only 130 in 1691. One count indicated that the Mohawks fell from 270 to 110 men during King William's War. Other Iroquois tribes suffered similar declines. William A. Starna, "Mohawk Iroquois Populations: A Revision," *Ethnohistory* 27 (Fall 1980): 371–82; cf. Gunther H. Michelson, "Iroquois Population Statistics," *Man in the Northeast* 14 (Fall 1977): 4, table 1; Richter, "War and Culture: The Iroquois Experience," 542–43, 547, 551; *NYCD* 4:337, 648–52; *CSP* (1697–98), 175; "Table showing decrease of Indians," 7 Nov. 1698, in *Iroquois Indians: A Documentary History*, reel 6.

25. Leroy V. Eid, "The Ojibwa-Iroquois War: The War the Iroquois Did Not Win," *Ethnohistory* 26 (Fall 1979): 297–324.

26. Richter, "War and Culture," 553–54; Richter and James H. Merrell, eds., *Beyond the Covenant Chain*, 26, 53; Richard Aquila, *The Iroquois Restoration: Iroquois Diplomacy on the Colonial Frontier* (Detroit: Wayne State University Press, 1983); *Iroquois Indians: A Documentary History*, reel 6, passim.

27. Willard Walker, Robert Conkling, and Gregory Buesing, "A Chronological Account of the Wabanaki Confederacy," in Ernest L. Schusky, ed., *Political Organization of Native North Americans*, 48–49.

28. Mass. Archives, 30:426; *NYCD* 4:619; *Baxter MSS* 10:53; Mass. Archives, 30:450; *CSP* (1700), 90–98, 179–87.

29. *NYCD* 4:637; *CSP* (1700), 186–87.

30. *Baxter MSS* 10:63–65; Mass. Archives, 30:459.

31. *Baxter MSS* 10:68–69; *CSP* (1700), 400.

32. Sévigny, *Abénaquis*, 112, 166; *NYCD* 4:662; *CSP* (1700), 276.

33. *NYCD* 4:743–45, 758–59, 834, 836, 903, 991–92; *CSP* (1700), 34, 185–86, 570–71, 590.

34. *Baxter MSS* 10:90. Prins, "Amesokanti," 9, identifies one Adeawando as a Pennacook who lived at Pigwacket before moving to St. Francis. Cf.n. 58 below.

35. *NYCD* 4:996–97; *CSP* (1702), 642–43.

36. E.g. Order in Council at Portsmouth, N.H., 23 Aug. 1703, Newberry Library, Ayer MSS, 621.

37. Leder, ed., *Livingston Indian Records*, 188–90.

38. Samuel Carter, "The Route of the French and Indian Army That Sacked Deerfield, Feb. 29th, 1703–4 [O.S.], on their return march to Canada with the captives," *History and Proceedings of the Pocumtuck Valley Memorial Association* 2 (1898): 126–51; Francis Parkman, *A Half Century of Conflict*, 2 vols. (Toronto: George N. Morang, 1898), 1:55–93. John Williams, *The Redeemed Captive Returning to Zion*, 8–25; "Account of the Captivity of the Rev. Doctor Stephen Williams, Written by Himself," *A Biographical Memoir of the Rev. John Williams* in Stephen W. Williams, (Greenfield, Mass.: C. J. J. Ingersoll, 1837), 103; *VHG* 4:950; PAC, MGI CIIA, 22:45–48, 50; *NYCD* 9:759.

39. Sheldon, *History of Deerfield* 1:319.

40. PAC, MGI CIIA, 21:15, 58, 22:16; PAC, MGI F3, 2–2:392–95, 627–28; *BRH* 38 (1932): 447–48, 569–72, 42 (1936): 610; Massachusetts Historical Society, Parkman Papers, 30:413–15; *NYCD* 9:762.

41. PAC, MGI CIIA, 21:14–15, 58, 22:16; "Counseil entre les Sauvages de Koessek et Monsieur le Marquis de Vaudreuil, 13 June 1704," PAC, MGI F3, 2–2:407–10; and *CMNF* 2:414–16; also in *BRH* 37 (1931): 598–60, and Massachusetts Historical Society, Parkman Papers, 30:417–419.

42. Samuel Penhallow, *Penhallow's Indian Wars*, 20–23; William Douglass, *A Summary, Historical and Political, of the first Planting, progressive Improvements, and present State of the British Settlements in North America*, 2 vols. (Boston, 1749–53), 1:557; "Account of the Captivity of Stephen Williams," 105–06; Day, *Identity of the St. Francis Indians*, 33–34, 49–50.

43. "Copy of Major Hilton's Journal, 1703–1704," *Baxter MSS* 9:142; Sévigny, *Abénaquis*, 153; Samuel Penhallow, *Penhallow's Indian Wars*, 48; cf. "Journal of Rev. John Pike," *Collections of the New Hampshire Histori-*

cal Society 3 (1832): 51, 58; Bouton, ed., *New Hampshire Provincial Papers* 2:565–66; Day, *Identity of the St. Francis Indians*, 63.

44. "Capt. Stoddard's Journal of his scout from Deerfield to Onion or French River in 1707," in Stephen Williams, *a Biographical Memoir of the Rev. John Williams*, 113. From the soldier's description, the Rev. John Williams thought the woman was Jehannah Ardanay, or Ardaway, a captive from the east, and the soldier "saith he thought it was she as soon as he saw her face." But Emma Lewis Coleman pointed out that if so, she made a good recovery, since Jeanne Ardaway gave birth to a child by a Bécancour Abenaki in 1710. Coleman, *New England Captives* 1:351.

45. *BRH* 38 (1932): 569–72.

46. PAC, MG1 C11A, 28:84–99, esp. 89; Coolidge, "French Occupation of the Champlain Valley," 211; PAC, MG1 C11A, 29:127–28. Caughnawaga warriors who turned out to join this expedition apparently refused to go any farther when they reached Lake Champlain because they said sickness had broken out among them; E. J. Devine, S. J., *Historic Caughnawaga* (Montreal: The Messenger Press, 1922), 162–63.

47. PAC, MG1 C11A, 30:2–21, 89–93, 31:82–84; *RAPQ* (1942–43), 399, 427; *BRH* 38 (1932), 569.

48. *CSP* (1706–1708), 511; *CSP* (1708–1709), 316; *Letters and Papers of Cadwallader Colden* 9:362, 364.

49. *NYCD* 9:831; *Penhallow's Indian Wars*, 48–49; Mass. Archives, 31:55–56; "Journal of Rev John Pike," 62; Massachusetts Historical Society, Manuscript notes and copies of letters . . . collected by Emma Lewis Coleman and C. A. Baker, 110–11, 121–22.

50. *NYCD* 5:222–23; New York State Archives, Colonial MSS 52:45, 51.

51. Charland, *Abénakis d'Odanak*, 51; *RAPQ* (1946–47), 433–36: James F. Kenney, "A British Secret Service Report on Canada, 1711," *Canadian Historical Review* 1 (1920): 52.

52. PAC, MG1, C11A, 32:132–50.

53. *CSP* (1710–11), 525; Mass. Hist. Soc., Belknap MSS, 61A50; *Penhallow's Indian Wars*, 61.

54. "Captain Thomas Baker's Scout," reprinted in Sheldon, *History of Deerfield* 1:379–80; "Carte du Canada avec partie des côtes de la Nouvelle Angleterre et de l'Acadie," PAC, N.M.C. 6359, H3/900/1713, and N.M.C. 6364, H3/900/1715; Day, *Identity of the St. Francis Indians*, 50.

55. A copy of the Abenaki letter is in the Musée des Abénakis at Odanak, Quebec.

56. *JR* 67:101–103; Henry L. Masta, "When the Abenaki Came to Dartmouth," *Dartmouth Alumni* 21 (1928–29): 303; Sévigny, *Abénaquis*, 127; Charland, *Abénakis d'Odanak*, 61.

57. Day, *Identity of the St. Francis Indians*, 50; *The New England His-*

torical and Geneaological Register for the Year 1866, 20:9; *Collections of the Maine Historical Society* 3 (1853): 355–58; Nathaniel Bouton, *History of Concord*, 40. Sévigny, *Abénaquis*, 202–203; Harris, ed., *Historical Atlas of Canada*, vol. 1, plate 47.

58. PAC MG CııA, 35:62–66; also in Mass. Hist. Soc., Parkman Papers, 31:189–91; Sévigny, *Abénaquis*, 154–55, 173; *JR* 67:31–35;, *CMNF* 3:23; Gordon Day favors Atecouando as the chief's name, *Identity of the St. Francis Indians*, 76; "Atecuando," *Dictionary of Canadian Biography* 2:25–26; Harris, ed., *Historical Atlas of Canada*, vol. 1, plate 47.

59. *Baxter MSS* 10:108–09; *CSP* (1710–11), 525

60. PAC, MGı, CııA, 35:42; *NYCD* 9:878–79; Brasser, *Riding on the Frontier's Crest*, 27.

61. Gordon M. Day, "Missisquoi," 51–52.

6. Grey Lock's War, 1723–1727

1. Douglas Edward Leach, *The Northern Colonial Frontier, 1607–1763*, 131–36; Frederic Kidder, "The Abenaki Indians; Their Treaties of 1713 and 1717, and a vocabulary: with a Historical Introduction," *Collections of the Maine Historical Society* 4 (1859): 229–63.

2. Governor Samuel Shulte's Proclamation, Boston, July 25, 1722, in *Penhallow's Indian Wars*, 88–91; Morrison, *Embattled Northeast*, 165–85.

3. Eastern Indians' Letter to the Governour, July 27, 1721, *Collections of the Massachusetts Historical Society*, 2d ser., 8 (1826): 259–63; *CSP* (1724–25), 428; PAC, MGı F3, 2–2:499–500, 502–507; PAC, MGı CııA, 124:284; *NYCD* 9:903–06; *Baxter MSS* 23:158–59; PAC, MGı CııA, 47:208. Also, Mass. Hist. Soc., Parkman Papers, 31:293–98, 303–304, 341–43; 53:211–17, 223–26.

4. Marcus A. McCorison, "Colonial Defence of the Upper Connecticut Valley," *Vermont History* 30 (Jan. 1962): 50–62.

5. PAC, MGı CııA, 43:266–34; 45: 5–6, 12:233–34; *NYCD* 9:936; Vaudreuil and Begon to Minister of Marine, Oct. 14, 1723, Archives Nationales, Paris, CııA, 45:18–20, in *Iroquois Indians: A Documentary History*, reel 9; Mémoire sur les sauvages Abénakis, 1725, Newberry Library, Ayer MSS, 592; *CSP* (1724–25), 432–35; Mass. Hist. Soc., Parkman Papers, 31:316, 322.

6. PAC, Indian Affairs, RG 10, Vol. 1819, Reel C-1220, 17a–42a, esp. 23a, 24, 31a-33; Mass. Archives 29:115, 170–71, 181 (also in *Baxter MSS* 23, esp. 131, 139–44); PAC, MGı CııA, 45:12; *NYCD* 5:723–25, 9:938; cf. *Penhallow's Indian Wars*, 94, 101–102, 107; *Baxter MSS* 23:182–83. See also *CSP* (1724–25), 198, 248, 270–71; Governor Burnet to the Board of Trade and Plantations, 7 Nov. 1724, Public Record Office, C.O. 5/1053, Burnet to Duke of Newcastle, 21 Nov. 1724, and enclosures, C.O. 5/1092, and Vaudreuil and Begon to Minister of Marine, 14 Oct. 1723, Archives

Nationales, CIIA, 45:12—22v, all in *Iroquois Indians: A Documentary History*, reel 9.

7. Gordon M. Day, "Gray Lock," *Dictionary of Canadian Biography* 3:265; Sheldon, *History of Deerfield* 1:397; Mass. Archives, 29:361; Temple and Sheldon, *History of the Town of Northfield*, 194.

8. Temple and Sheldon, *History of Northfield*, 194; Crockett, *Vermont: The Green Mountain State* 1:51; Charles Howard McIlwain, ed., *Peter Wraxall's Abridgment of New York Indian Records, 1678—1751*, 149.

9. Day, "Missisquoi," 52; Day, "Gray Lock," 265.

10. Temple and Sheldon, *History of Northfield* 1:195—96; *Penhallow's Indian Wars*, 97; Crockett, *Vermont* 1:84; *CSP* (1722—23), 422; Mass. Hist. Soc., Parkman Papers, 37:136—37.

11. PAC, RG 10, vol. 1819, Reel C-1220, 57.

12. PAC, RG 10, vol. 1819, Reel C-1220, 60; Temple and Sheldon, *History of Northfield*, 196; Mass. Hist. Soc., Parkman Papers, 31:322.

13. Joseph Kellogg was born in Hadley in 1691. Taken captive in the raid on Deerfield and carried off to Canada, he returned home in 1714. Temple and Sheldon, *History of Northfield* 1:196—97, 228; Mass. Archives, 46:32.

14. Wright to Dummer, Dec. 5, 1723, quoted in Temple and Sheldon, *History of Northfield*, 198—99.

15. Cabot, ed., *Annals of Brattleboro, 1681—1895* 1:8—10; Smyth, "Papers Relating to the Construction and First Occupancy of Fort Dummer . . . ," 359—71; Temple and Sheldon, *History of Northfield*, 199—201. Captain Dwight's son, born May 27, 1726, is said to have been the first white child born in Vermont.

16. Cf. John K. Mahon, "Anglo-American Methods of Indian Warfare, 1676—1794," *Mississippi Valley Historical Review* 45 (1958—59): 254—75; McCorison, "Colonial Defence of the Upper Connecticut Valley"; Cabot, ed., *Annals of Brattleboro* 1:11; Mass. Archives, 38A:70.

17. Mass. Archives, 51:4—5; Temple and Sheldon, *History of Northfield*, 203; PAC, RG 10, vol. 1819, Reel C-1220, 74.

18. Temple and Sheldon, *History of Northfield*, 204; Crockett, *Vermont* 1:85; *Penhallow's Indian Wars*, 102.

19. *Baxter MSS* 10:209—11; Temple and Sheldon, *History of Northfield*, 204—205.

20. Temple and Sheldon, *History of Northfield*, 205; Dummer to Goffe, July 27, 1724, Newberry Library, Chicago, Ayer MSS, 576.

21. PAC, RG 10, vol. 1819, Reel C-1220, 86a, 65—66a, 94a-96, 169; *NYCD* 5:721—22; New York State Archives, Albany, New York Council Minutes, 14:353—73 (Oct. 8, 1724), in *Iroquois Indians: A Documentary History*, reel 9; Mass. Archives, 29:160; Temple and Sheldon, *History of Northfield*, 203; McIlwain, ed., *Wraxall's Abridgement of the New York*

Indian Records, 149, 149n, 152. Wraxall noted that he came across several complaints from the Schaghticokes in the records about trade abuses and encroachments on their lands, "but as these Indians are now become a Scattered few I did not think it very necessary to take notice of their Affairs."

22. *CSP* (1722–23): 409: C.O. 5, pt. 1, reel 1, vol. 10, 155; *NYCD* 9:945–46; *CMNF*, 3:109; Charland, *Abénakis d'Odanak*, 64. In October 1722, "All the Numerous Families of Eastern Indians withdrew from Norridgewack and Wintered at the Town of Wawenack and St. Francis." James Phinney Baxter, *The Pioneers of New France in New England*, 322.

23. *Baxter MSS* 10:222, 227–29, reprinted in Temple and Sheldon, *History of Northfield*, 206; Cabot, ed., *Annals of Brattleboro* 1:11.

24. Temple and Sheldon, *History of Northfield*, 206–207; Crockett, *Vermont* 1:100–101.

25. Mass. Archives, 38A:86–88; *Penhallow's Indian Wars*, 110, 112–16. For an account of the delegation of Colonels William Dudley and Samuel Thaxter of Massachusetts and Theodore Atkinson of New Hampshire, see *NYCD* 9:941–45. The delegates endured great hardships in their journey, traveling over frozen Lake Champlain, and were gone four months. *Penhallow's Indian Wars*, 108–10. Temple and Sheldon, *History of Northfield*, 208–209.

26. PAC, RG 10, 1819:96; *NYCD* 5:723; Mass. Archives, 38A:93–94; Temple and Sheldon, *History of Northfield*, 209; Crockett, *Vermont* 1:86.

27. "A true Journal of our march from N-field to Mesixcouk bay under ye command of Benj. Wright Captain, begun July 27, A.D. 1725," reprinted in Temple and Sheldon, *History of Northfield*, 210–12; *Baxter MSS* 10:350–51.

28. *Baxter MSS* 10:334, 337; PAC, RG 10, vol. 1819, reel C-1220: 145a.

29. Arthur D. Woodrow, ed. and comp., *Metallak: The Last of the Cooashaukes;* "Memoir of the Sokokis or Pequaket Tribe of Indians," *Magazine of History, with Notes and Queries*, extra no. 5 (1909), 91; *VHG* 2:924. The Indians who remained in the White Mountains gave rise to the local legend of the curse of Chocorua, "the last Pegwacket," although in some versions he is a Sokoki. According to the legend, Chocorua refused to leave when the rest of his tribe retreated to Canada and coexisted peacfully for a time with the white settlers. Ultimately, however, he was dramatically killed on a mountaintop, invoking curses on the invaders of his homeland. See, for example, John Stephen English, *Indian Legends of the White Mountains*, 1–15, and Frederick W. Kilbourne, *Chronicles of the White Mountains* (Boston: Houghton Mifflin, 1916), 10–12.

30. Temple and Sheldon, *History of Northfield*, 213; *Penhallow's Indian Wars*, 122.

31. Temple and Sheldon, *History of Northfield*, 214; Mass. Hist. Soc., Parkman Papers, 31:367; *Penhallow's Indian Wars*, 122–27; 130–32; Morrison, *Embattled Northeast*, 187–90.

32. *CSP* (1726–27), 39; *Baxter MSS* 10:369.

33. Temple and Sheldon, *History of Northfield*, 214; Crockett, *Vermont* 1:88–89.

34. *NYCD* 5:798–99; see also *NYCD* 5:868–69, 969–70.

35. In 1740, Kellogg was appointed interpreter to the Indian Nations. Temple and Sheldon, *History of Northfield*, 215, 228.

36. PAC, RG 10, vol. 1819, Reel C-1220, 177a–78.

37. *Baxter MSS* 10:358.

38. *Baxter MSS* 10:359.

39. *Baxter MSS* 10:364–65.

40. PAC, RG 10, vol. 1819, reel C-1220, 177a–78; *Baxter MSS* 10:371–73.

41. *Baxter MSS* 10:381.

42. *NYCD* 9:940.

43. *Baxter MSS* 10:402.

44. PAC, MG1 F3, 2:457, 560–61; Morrison, *Embattled Northeast*, 189–90.

45. *New England Historical and Geneaological Register for the Year 1866*, 20:9; *Collections of the Maine Historical Society*, 3 (1853); 355–58; *Baxter MSS* 10:380, 392–93, 397.

46. *Baxter MSS* 10:378.

47. PAC, RG 10, vol. 1820, Reel C-1220, II291A–II292.

48. Day, "Missisquoi," 54; Day, "Gray Lock," 266; Roy, *Hommes et choses du Fort Saint-Frédéric*, 271.

49. PAC, RG 10, vol. 1820, reel C-1220, 308A.

50. Moody, "Missisquoi."

7. Peace in the Valleys, 1727–1744

1. Charles E. Clark, *The Eastern Frontier*, chaps. 8, 9, and 11; *CMNF*, 3:160–61; *Baxter Mss.* 10:380.

2. Ira Allen, *The Natural and Political History of the State of Vermont*, (reprint, Rutland, Vt.: Charles E. Tuttle Co., 1969), 18; *CMNF* 3:172; Charland, *Abénakis d'Odanak*, 64 and chap. 6, esp. pp. 69, 73, 76–78; Sévigny, *Abénaquis*, 205–207.

3. *BRH* 34 (1928): 541; *NYCD* 9:1052.

4. Coolidge, *French Occupation of the Champlain Valley*, 87–88, 115–25, *NYCD* 1:444, 9:1021; André Senecal, "Everyday Life at the French Settlements at Pointe la Chevelure and the Seigneurie de Hocquart," paper presented at the Dublin Seminar for New England Folklife, 1989.

5. Roy, *Hommes et choses du Fort Saint Frédéric*, 268 ff., 270–71.

6. *NYCD* 9:1002; Roy, *Hommes et choses du Fort Saint Frédéric*, 300.

7. Roy, *Hommes et choses du Fort Saint Frédéric*, 224–25, 276.

8. Coolidge, *French Occupation of the Champlain Valley*, 86–90; McIlwain, ed., *Wraxall's Abridgment of the New York Indian Records*, 213; Senecal, "Everyday Life at the French Settlements."

9. PAC, MG1 Series B, 78–1:148–49; Charland, *Abénakis d'Odanak*, 76–78; Day, *Mots Loups of Father Mathevet*, 47; PAC, MG1 C11A, 81: 31–32; Moody, "Missisquoi," 4.

10. PAC, RG 10, 1819:273–74, 307–308, 340–42, 1820–2: 46–47, 118–19, 195–96, 232–33; New York State Archives, Albany, New York Council Minutes, 15:282–308, in *Iroquois Indians: A Documentary History*, reel 10; *NYCD* 5:869–70; McIlwain, ed., *Wraxall's Abridgment of the New York Indian Records*, 175, 196, 207, 227–28.

11. Coolidge, *French Occupation of the Champlain Valley*, 82, 84; *Letters and Papers of Cadwallader Colden* 2:52–54, 4:202–203; Muller, "The Commercial History of the Lake Champlain–Richelieu River Route," Ph.D. diss., 14; Jean Lunn, "The Illegal Fur Trade Out of New France, 1713–1760," *Canadian Historical Association Report* (1939), 61–76; Jaenen, *French Relationship with the Native Peoples of New France and Acadia*, 142.

12. Cabot, ed., *Annals of Brattleboro* 1:11–12; Mass. Archives, 32: 360–61, 573, 628–29; Axtell, *Invasion Within*, 199–204; Meeting of the Commissioners for Indian Affairs at the Council Chamber in Boston, Aug. 16, 1734, Newberry Library, Ayer MSS, 570.

13. "Indian Treaties," *Collections of the Maine Historical Society* 4 (1856): 123–44.

14. "Indian Treaties," 129–30.

15. "Indian Treaties," 131–33.

16. "Indian Treaties," 133–34; letter from Captain Cunkapot to Nehemiah Bull, Feb. 5, 1734/5, Newberry Library, Ayer MSS, 205, and accompanying note. A Stockbridge Indian named John Konkapot attended Dartmouth College in the 1770s; Eric P. Kelly, "The Dartmouth Indians," *Dartmouth Alumni Magazine*" 22 (Dec. 1929): 123.

17. "Indian Treaties," 141–42.

18. Mass. Archives, Vol. 245, doc. 736, folio 145; *CMNF* 3:182–85.

19. Mass. Archives, 29:333–35, 38A:126.

20. *Letters and Papers of Cadwallader Colden* 3:149–51; 4:414.

21. Wright, ed., *Indian Deeds of Hampden County*, 125–27, 129–33. For identification of Pinawans and Wallenas, see Day, *Identity of the St. Francis Indians*, 78, 98.

22. Temple and Sheldon, *History of Northfield*, 234; Lyman S. Hayes, *The Connecticut River Valley in Southern Vermont and New Hampshire:*

Historical Sketches, 66; "Narrative of the Captivity of Mrs. Johnson," 131; John Moody, "The Native American Legacy," in Jane C. Beck, ed., *Always in Season*, 58.

23. Mass. Archives, 29:361–62; PAC, RG10, 1820–2:292A.

24. "Walter Bryant's Journal, 1741," in Albert Stillman Batchellor, ed., *New Hampshire Provincial Papers* 19 (1891): 508–509.

8. King George's War, 1744–1748

1. Samuel G. Drake, *A Particular History of the Five Years French and Indian war in New England and Parts Adjacent . . .* , 48.

2. PAC, MG1 Series B, 78–1:162; PAC, MG1 C11A, 81:42.

3. *NYCD* 6:276, 281; Drake, *History of the French and Indian War*, 34.

4. Bouton, ed., *New Hampshire Provincial Papers* 5:231, 713; "Papers Relating to Fort Dummer," *Collections of the New Hampshire Historical Society* 1:143–47; Drake, *History of the French and Indian War*, 47; Temple and Sheldon, *History of Northfield*, 239; Mass. Hist. Soc., Belknap MSS, 61B:23a; Petition of John Thomlinson, relating to Fort Dummer, 4 Jan. 1749, Newberry Library, Ayer MSS 886.

5. Sévigny, *Abénaquis*, 209; *CMNF* 3:464.

6. Day, *Identity of the St. Francis Indians*, 51.

7. Day, "Atecuando," *Dictionary of Canadian Biography* 2:26; *NYCD* 6:542; "Memoir of the Sokoki or Pequaket Tribe of Indians," *Magazine of History, with Notes and Queries*, extra no. 5, 2(1909): 91; Sévigny, *Abénaquis*, 202; A declaration of war against the Cape Sable and St. John's Indians, Oct. 19, 1744, Newberry Library, Ayer MSS, 578; Mass. Archives, 30:21, 31:494–94A, 507–508, 631–31A, 687, 32:20–23; Day, *Identity of the St. Francis Indians*, 42; Douglass, *A Summary, Historical and Political, of the first Planting, progressive Improvements, and present State of the British Settlements in North America* 1:394, 2:185.

8. *NYCD* 9:1110; Document presenting news brought . . . by Tecanancouassin, 19 Oct. 1744, Archives Nationales, Paris, C11A, 81:208–209; Account of what passed in Canada, 9 and 12 Aug. 1745, American Philosophical Society Library, Philadelphia, MSS, Class B, no. L82, 4:117, both in *Iroquois Indians: A Documentary History*, reel 12.

9. PAC, MG1 Series B, 78–1:148–49; Douglass, *Summary* 2:185; PAC, MG1 C11A, 81:32; PAC, MG1 Series B, 81:233; Memorandum from the King of France . . . , 28 Apr. 1745, Archives Nationales, Paris, General Correspondence, B Series, Canada, 3d part, Dispatches and Orders of the King 1745, 81:287–89, in *Iroquois Indians: A Documentary History*, reel 12.

10. PAC, RG 10, vol. 1820, reel C-1220, II291A–II292A. "Asschicantecook" was probably one of the variant forms of Arosaguntacook applied to the St. Francis Abenakis.

11. Mass. Archives, 31:520; Account of a treaty with the Six Nations at Albany, 27 Sept.–15 Oct. 1745, photocopy from Huntington Library, p. 12, in *Iroquois Indians: A Documentary History*, reel 12.

12. PAC, RG10, vol. 1820, reel C-1221, II308A.

13. Mass. Archives, 31:520.

14. PAC, MG1 C11A, 83:345.

15. Rev. Benjamin Doolittle, "A Short Narrative of the Mischief done by the French and Indian Enemy on the Western Frontiers of the Province of the Massachusetts Bay," *Magazine of History, with Notes and Queries*, extra no. 7, 2 (1909): 6; Drake, *History of the French and Indian War*, 77–78; Crockett, *Vermont* 1:102–103.

16. PAC, RG 10, vol. 1821, reel C-1221, 3:75; Mass. Archives, 29:401; *NYCD* 6:298.

17. Crockett, *Vermont* 1:103; Temple and Sheldon, *History of Northfield*, 240–41.

18. Doolittle, "Narrative," 6; Drake, *History of the French and Indian War*, 85–86; Temple and Sheldon, *History of Northfield*, 241–42; Crockett, *Vermont* 1:103; PAC, MG1 C11A, 83:141–43; Captain William Pote's Journal, Newberry Library, Ayer MSS, 733:181–82.

19. Francis Parkman, *A Half-Century of Conflict*, 2:217.

20. Mass. Archives, 53:193–96; PAC, MG1 C11A, 86:203–14; Doolittle, "Narrative," 7; Drake, *History of the French and Indian War*, 91; Mass. Hist. Soc., Belknap MSS, 161A:39; Captain William Pote's Journal, 128. All three captives wound up in the same prison as Nehemiah How, but eventually returned home.

21. Doolittle, "Narrative," 7; Drake, *History*, 93. Blake was redeemed the following winter.

22. *NYCD* 10:32; *CMNF* 3:275; Drake, *History*, 37.

23. *NYCD* 10:33; *CMNF* 3:278; PAC, MG1 C11A, 86:203–14; Drake, *History*, 38; McIlwain, ed., *Wraxall's Abridgment of the New York Indian Records*, 247.

24. *NYCD* 10:34; Roy, *Hommes et choses du Fort Saint Frédéric*, 300.

25. Doolittle, "Narrative," 7–9; Drake, *History*, 94–95, 100–101; Mass. Hist. Soc., Belknap MSS, 161A:39. Sartle later returned home and reported that five of the attackers died in the fight, and that the enemy left blankets, coats, and guns behind. Parkman, *Half Century of Conflict* 2:221.

26. Drake, *History*, 102.

27. Doolittle, "Narrative," 10–11; Drake, *History*, 104–105, 109, 111, 114–15; Crockett, *Vermont* 1:103; Mass. Hist. Soc., Belknap MSS, 161A:39; Jos. Savage to Richard Bradley, 13 Aug. 1746, and Account written by Richard Bradley, 1817, Bradley Family Papers, New Hampshire Historical Society.

28. Drake, *History*, 117ff.; Crockett, *Vermont* 1:103–104: The French account is in PAC, MGI CIIA, 89:265–73.

29. Letter from Joseph Ashley, 13 June 1746, Newberry Library, Ayer MSS, N.A. 34. The Reverend Jonathan Ashley evidently used the back of the letter to scribble notes for a sermon.

30. Drake, *History*, 132, 134–35; Bouton, ed., *New Hampshire Provincial Papers* 5:231, 374–75, 440. About this time, a Mohawk war party under Hendrick killed a Frenchman and captured another on Isle La Motte. Mass. Hist. Soc., Belknap MSS, 61C:88C.

31. Charland, *Abénakis d'Odanak*, 81; *CMNF* 3:327, 339.

32. Doolittle, "Narrative," 14–15.

33. Indian Petition to the General Assembly, Number 2 on Connecticut River, Apr. 1, 1747, Newberry Library, Ayer MSS, 423.

34. PAC, MGI CIIA, 85:385–91

35. Doolittle, "Narrative," 15; Crockett, *Vermont* 1:104; Drake, *History*, 140–41; "Captivity of Mrs. Johnson," 135. Stevens's account of the siege is in Mass. Hist. Soc., Belknap MSS, 161A:40; the French account is in *NYCD* 10:97.

36. Crockett, *Vermont* 1:104.

37. Doolittle, "Narrative," 18; Drake, *History*, 153–54; *NYCD* 10:147.

38. Mass. Hist. Soc., Belknap MSS, 161A:39; Drake, *History*, 155–56; Doolittle, "Narrative," 18–19; Crockett, *Vermont* 1:104. Doolittle repeated the complaint in the Belknap MSS almost verbatim.

39. "Journal of Captain Eleazar Melvin, with eighteen men in his command, in the Wilderness towards Crown Point—1748," *Collections of the New Hampshire Historical Society* 5 (1837): 207–11; Doolittle, "Narrative," 20–21.

40. Drake, *History*, 163; Crockett, *Vermont* 1:107; Doolittle, "Narrative," 21.

41. Drake, *History*, 163–65; Crockett, *Vermont* 1:107; Doolittle, "Narrative," 21–22. I am grateful to John Moody for identifying Jacques Sacket.

42. Drake, *History*, 168; Crockett, *Vermont* 1:108; Doolittle, "Narrative," 22–23.

43. Petition of John Thomlinson, 4 Jan. 1749, Newberry Library, Ayer MSS, 886.

44. *Baxter MSS,* 23(1916): 312, 314, 318–19; *BRH* 44 (1938): 376–77; "Journal of Capt. Phineas Stevens To and From Canada—1749," Mass. Archives, 38A:143, reprinted in *Collections of the New Hampshire Historical Society* 5 (1837), 201.

45. Doolittle, "Narrative," 24–27.

46. Huden, "The White Chief of the St. Francis Abenakis," 200–201; Tanner, ed., *Atlas of Great Lakes Indian History*, map 9.

47. Peter Kalm, *Travels into North America* 2:212.

48. *BRH* 44 (1938): 375–77; PAC, MG1 C11A, 93:198; Lampee, "The Missisquoi Loyalists," *Proceedings of the Vermont Historical Society*, n.s., 6 (June 1938): 101–102, 104; Hulbert, ed., *Crown Collection of Photographs of American Maps*, vol. 4, no. 10 (cxxviii, 52), vol. 1, nos. 16–18 (cxxi, 16); Day, *Mots Loups of Father Mathevet*, 63; Abenaki Nation of Vermont, *A Petition for Federal Recognition as an American Indian Tribe . . .* , 31–32.

49. PAC, MG1 Series B, 89:184; PAC, MG1 C11A, 93:336.

50. *BRH* 44(1938): 375–77.

9. The English, French, and Indian War, 1754–1760

1. Mass. Archives, 32:99, 38a:154–56.

2. "Journal of Captain Phineas Stevens," in Mereness, ed., *Travels in the American Colonies*, 315–16; *Baxter MSS* 23:361; Bouton, ed., *New Hampshire Provincial Papers* 6:236; "Phineas Stevens' Account Book, kept at Fort #4, 1752–1756," pp. 176–77, MS in Stevens Family Papers (box 1, folder 8), Bailey/Howe Library, University of Vermont, microfilm copy in the Silsby Library, Charlestown, N.H.

3. "Journal of Captain Phineas Stevens' Journey to Canada, 1752," 302–303, 311–15.

4. Chase, *Gathered Sketches from the History of Vermont and New Hampshire*, 63; Hayes, *Connecticut Valley in Southern Vermont and New Hampshire*, 67; Crockett, *Vermont* 1:166; C. Horace Hubbard and Justus Dartt, *History of the Town of Springfield, Vermont* (Boston: Geo. H. Walker and Co., 1895), 1. Abenakis had occupied the Springfield region for hundreds of years; Heckenberger and Petersen, *Archaeological Investigations at the Skitchewaug Site* (see chap. 1, n. 2).

5. Mass. Archives, 32:99, 113, 155; *Baxter MSS* 23:386, 398–99, 403–405.

6. Day, "Western Abenaki," 151; *NYCD* 10:252–54; Kidder, "Memoir of the Sokoki or Pequaket Tribe," 91; Mass. Archives, 32:468; *CMNF* 3:509–12; Thomas M. Charland, "Atecuando (Jerome)," *Dictionary of Canadian Biography* 3:20–21, finds no evidence to confirm that Jerome Atecuando was related to the Pigwacket chief who lived at St. Francis ca. 1706 to 1714.

7. Mass. Archives, 32:336–37, 351, 5:180; *VHG* 2:916; Frank G. Speck, "The Eastern Algonkian Wabanaki Confederacy," *American Anthropologist*, n.s., 17 (1915): 493–96; John R. Cuneo, *Robert Rogers of the Rangers*, 10–11.

8. C.O., 5, pt. 1, reel 1, 14:203ff.; *NYCD* 6:832–86; Mass. Archives, 5:186, 188–89; *NYCD* 2:354, 6:886; Bouton, ed., *New Hampshire Provincial Papers* 6:278; James De Lancey to Lords of Trade and Plantations,

22 July 1754, Public Record Office, C.O., 5/1066: 112, in *Iroquois Indians: A Documentary History*, reel 16.

9. C.O., 5. pt. 1, reel 1, 14:533; Grant Powers, *Historical Sketches of the Discovery, Settlement, and Progress of Events in the Coos Country*, 15–32; Bouton, ed., *New Hampshire Provincial Papers* 6:234.

10. C.O., 5. pt. 1, reel 1, 15:33–48; *NYCD* 2:343. On the question of whether a fort was ever built at Cowass and the dubious evidence of a map etched on a soldier's powder horn, see John R. Cuneo, "Mysterious Fort Wentworth," and Philip N. Guyol, "Fort Wentworth: The Mystery Compounded," *Historical New Hampshire* 17 (June 1962): 18–25, 26–48.

11. Mass. Archives, 5:182–84, 186, 4:522, 32:523–36, 547–50; C. E. Potter, *History of Manchester, New Hampshire* (Manchester: C. E. Potter, 1856), 279–84; Bouton, ed., *New Hampshire Provincial Papers* 6:25–28, 236, 264–65, 291; At a Meeting of the Commissioners for Indian Affairs at Albany, Sept. 21, 1754, C.O., 5/926:289–90, in *Iroquois Indians: A Documentary History*, reel 16; New York State Archives, Colonial MSS, 79:51; "Nathaniel Wheelwright's Canadian Journey, 1753–4," ed. Edward P. Hamilton, *Bulletin of the Fort Ticonderoga Museum* 10, no. 4 (Feb. 1960): 280–81, 283.

12. Mass. Archives, 8:289, 29:466–69; New York State Archives, Colonial MSS, 79:17–19, 22–24, 30–31, 37–38, 47, 48a; Bouton, ed., *New Hampshire Provincial Papers* 6:330–31; *Johnson Papers* 2:379, 9:220 (PAC, RG 10, 1819:75, for St. Francis Abenakis' granting power of negotiation to Caughnawagas in 1724).

13. Sévigny, *Abénaquis* 112–13; *NYCD* 2:349–50, 5:722, 6:880–81, 909; C.O., 5, pt. 1, reel 1, 14:543; Gov. James De Lancey to Board of Trade and Plantations, Oct. 8 1754, C.O., 5/1066:135–36, and At a Meeting of the Commissioners for Indian Affairs, Sept. 21 1754, both in *Iroquois Indians: A Documentary History*, reel 16; Mass. Archives, 32: 547–50; Declaration of James Johnson, Mass. Archives, 8:289, Bouton, ed., *New Hampshire Provincial Papers* 6:330–31; New York State Archives, Colonial MSS, 79:30, 49, 51. Dr. Ezra Stiles, "Indians on Connecticut River," *Collections of the Massachusetts Historical Society*, 1st ser., 10 (1809): 105, said about 12 families left Schaghticoke and incorporated with the St. Francis Indians. Harris, cd., *Historical Atlas of Canada*, I, plate 47.

14. Sévigny, *Abénaquis*, 204–205; Day, *Identity of the St. Francis Indians*, 51.

15. Day, *Identity of the St. Francis Indians*, 52; Hall, *History of Eastern Vermont*, 117–18.

16. Woodrow, ed. and comp., *Metallak: The Last of the Cooashaukes*, 11, 68. Cf. Charles M. Starbird, *The Indians of the Androscoggin Valley*

(Lewiston, Me.: Journal Printshop, 1928), for the continuing Indian presence in the Androscoggin Valley at this time.

17. *VHG* 4:955; Sévigny, *Abénaquis*, 206–207; PAC, NMC H 12/200; Hulbert, ed., *Crown Collection of Photographs of American Maps* 4:8 (cxxi gi); John C. Huden, ed., "An English Captive's Map," *Vermont History* 26 (Oct. 1958): 303–305.

18. Moody, "Missisquoi," 8; Roy, *Hommes et choses du Fort Saint-Frédéric*, 279–89, 303–305.

19. *BRH* 37 (1931): 412; Charland, *Abénakis d'Odanak*, 83–84.

20. Charland, *Abénakis d'Odanak*, 104–05; *RAPQ* (1923–24), 249, 261; *JR* 70:91; *Journal de Montcalm*, in *Lévis MSS* 7:146–47, 192, 335, 369.

21. Oral tradition supports the story of Soosap's presence at the battle. Powers, *Historical Sketches of the Coos Country*, related in Katherine Blaisdell, *Over the River and Through the Years*, book 2. (Bradford, Vt., and Woodsville, N.H., 1980), 99. An obituary of Captain John Vincent reported that he formed the ambush on Braddock, E. P. Walton, ed., *Records of the Governor and Council of the State of Vermont*, 8 vols. (Montpelier, Vt.: J. M. Poland, 1873–80), 5:25n.

22. *Collections of the New Hampshire Historical Society* 5 (1837): 255; Bouton, ed., *New Hampshire Provincial Papers* 6:412; Mass. Archives, 117:1, 3. Rev. Henry White, *The Early History of New England*, 8th ed. (Concord, N.H.: I. S. Boyd, 1843), 107–10; Chase, ed., *Gathered Sketches from the Early History of New Hampshire and Vermont*, 65–68.

23. Mass. Archives, 32:606; Shirley to Abercrombie, 27 June 1756, C.O., 5, pt. 3, reel 3, vol. 46; Rogers, *Journals*, 26, 31, 76, 125–31, 136.

24. Loudon to Henry Fox, April 22, 1756, C.O., 5, pt. 3, reel 2, vol. 48.

25. Hall, *History of Eastern Vermont* 1:84.

26. New York State Archives, Colonial MSS 77:147 (badly burned); Charland, "Atecuando," *Dictionary of Canadian Biography* 3:20–21; Mass. Archives, 38A:329; Louis Antoine de Bougainville, *Adventure in the Wilderness*, ed. Edward P. Hamilton, 42–44, 136, 198–99, 242, 267; "Diary Kept by Captain de Léry," *Bulletin of the Fort Ticonderoga Museum* 6, no. 4 (July 1942): 132, 138–39, 142; *JR* 70:90–203; *NYCD* 10:405, 287, 607, 674; *RAPQ* (1926–27), 380, 403; *RAPQ* (1923–24), 278, 287; *Journal de Montcalm*, in *Lévis MSS* 7:69, 71, 79–80, 139, 153, 264, 359, 407, 423, 427, 467, 471, 473, 562.

27. Bougainville, *Adventure in the Wilderness*, 42–44, 242; *JR* 70:195; *Journal de Montcalm*, in *Lévis MSS* 7:406; *NYCD* 10:316–18, 616–19, 633; Mass. Archives, 4:522; New York State Archives, Colonial MSS, 79:38; "Nathaniel Wheelwright's Canadian Journey," 280–81, 293 (cf. Mass. Hist. Soc., Parkman Papers, 31:166).

28. Chase, ed., *Gathered Sketches from the Early History of New Hampshire and Vermont*, 62–70, 75–90 (Jemina Howe's captivity narrative is also in Drake, ed., *Indian Captivities*, 156–60); White, *The Early History of New England*, 107–10. (In fact, Mrs. Howe lost *two* husbands killed by Indians; Crockett, *Vermont* 1 : 111–12.)

29. Mass. Archives, 5 : 226; Loudon to Pitt, 25 Apr. 1757, C.O., 5, pt. 3, reel 2, vol. 48; *RAPQ* (1923–24), 358; *Journal de Montcalm*, in *Lévis MSS* 7 : 440; Hall, *History of Eastern Vermont*, 86.

30. Bougainville, *Adventure in the Wilderness*, 199, 243, 247; *Lévis MSS* 5 : 217, 7 : 341.

31. C.O., 5, pt. 1, reel 3, 18 : 715–34.

32. C.O., 5, pt. 3, reel 3, 54 : 153–55, 263–64, 273–75; Rogers, *Journals*, 123.

33. C.O., 5, pt. 3, reel 3, 56 : 501–503.

34. *VHG* 4 : 956.

35. Charland, "The Lake Champlain Army and the Fall of Montreal," *Vermont History* 28 (1960): 296–97; Rogers, *Journals*, 144; *NYCD* 10 : 1033; *Lévis MSS* 4 : 255, 258, 266–67, 5 : 39–40, 8 : 89–91, 9 : 49–50, 10 : 46; *Journal de Montcalm*, in *Lévis MSS* 7 : 596–97.

36. Rogers, *Journals*, 146ff.; C.O., 5, pt. 3, reel 4, 57 : 1–16; Stark, ed., *Reminiscences of the French War*, 161; Mass. Archives, 38A : 329; *Lévis MSS* 8 : 119–20.

37. Charland, "The Lake Champlain Army and the Fall of Montreal," 298–99. The French account is in *RAPQ* (1928–29), 29–86, esp. 72–73, 79, 83–85; *NYCD* 10 : 1042; and *Lévis MSS* 1 : 223–24, 229, 5 : 47–49, 55, 76–77, 8 : 113, 116, 154.

38. Gordon M. Day, "Rogers' Raid in Indian Tradition," *Historical New Hampshire* 17 (June 1962): 3–17. Gordon Day Tapes, Dartmouth College, Special Collections, reel 29, side 1.

39. Charland, *Abénakis d'Odanak*, 117–18; Rev. Henry Saunderson, *History of Charlestown, New Hampshire*, 88.

40. Moody, "Missisquoi," 10–12; Rogers, *Journals*, 173–81; Cuneo, *Robert Rogers*, 120–22; Moody, "Missisquoi," 59n.

41. Charland, *Abénakis d'Odanak*, 117; *VHG* 4 : 961.

42. Jack A. Frisch, "The Abenakis among the St. Regis Mohawks," *Indian Historian* 4 (Spring 1971): 27–29.

43. *VHG* 4 : 956; PAC, NMC H2/300/1776.

44. Powers, *Historical Sketches*, 37, 179; *VHG* 2 : 924; Thompson, *Natural and Civil History*, 205; Vermont Historical Society, misc. file no. 717, p. 45.

10. Adjustment to Conquest, 1760–1775

1. Jaenen, *The French Relationship with the Native Peoples of New France and Acadia*, 34, 40–41; Clark, *Eastern Frontier*, chap. 20, pp. 352–59;

VHG 2:917; Crockett, *Vermont* 1:204–12; Ray Billington, *Westward Expansion*. 4th ed. (New York: Macmillan, 1967), 104; Muller, "The Commercial History of the Lake Champlain–Richelieu River Route, 1760–1815," Ph.D. diss., 15–21; Bailyn, *Voyagers to the West: A Passage in the Peopling of America on the Eve of the Revolution*, 10.

2. *American Husbandry* (London, 1775), 1:47, quoted in Frederick Jackson Turner, "The Old West," *Proceedings of the Wisconsin State Historical Society* (1908), 189; C.O., 5, pt.1, reel 1, 69:75–78; "A Journal of the Managers of the Scotch American Company of Farmers," in *The Upper Connecticut: Narratives of Its Settlement and Its Part in the American Revolution* 1:181–203, also 218, 220–21, 286; Bailyn, *Voyagers to the West*, 604–37; Crockett, *Vermont* 1:249–55; Lampee, "The Missisquoi Loyalists," 82–83.

3. Day, *The Identity of the St. Francis Indians*, 52.

4. Cronon, *Changes in the Land*, passim; Muller, "Commercial History of the Lake Champlain–Richelieu River Route," Ph.D. diss., 15–29, 318; Adam Shortt and Arthur G. Doughty, eds., *Documents Relating to the Constitutional History of Canada, 1759–1791* 1: 318; *Letters and Papers of Cadwallader Colden* 9: 214–16.

5. "The Last of the Pennacooks," *The Farmer's Monthly Visitor*, 13, no. 10 (Oct. 1853): 289; Powers, *Historical Sketches of the Discovery, Settlement, and Progress of Events in the Coos Country*, 37; *VHG* 2:918; "Reminiscences of Colonel Frye Bayley," in *The Upper Connecticut* 2:29.

6. PAC, RG 10, 1827–28:85–87, reel C-1222; *Abenaki Petition*, 39, 42; *Johnson Papers* 12:841–42.

7. Haldimand Papers, British Museum, Add. MSS, 21667: 25, 36; Claus Papers, PAC, MG 19 F1, 1:124.

8. Day, *Identity of the St. Francis Indians*, 47.

9. Ibid., 46–47; *Johnson Papers* 8:553.

10. *Johnson Papers* 12:622.

11. *NYCD* 1:24, 7:582.

12. Charland, *Abénakis d'Odanak*, 122–25; *Johnson Papers* 3:281, 660, 10:409–11, 431; PAC, RG 10, 1824:188–90; Père Roubaud to Sir William Johnson, Feb. 16, 1761(?), Chicago Historical Society.

13. *Johnson Papers* 10:412–14, 448, 792–94; PAC, RG 10, 1827:190–93, reel C-1222.

14. *Johnson Papers* 3:554–56, 346, 395, 578; *JR* 70:90–203; Jane Lape, "Père Roubaud, Missionary Extraordinary," *Bulletin of the Fort Ticonderoga Museum* 12, no. 1 (March 1966): 63–71.

15. Charland, *Abénakis d'Odanak*, 132, 134 (Haldimand to Barton, 25 Nov. 1763, PAC B9: 23–24); *NYCD* 7:544–45.

16. Moody, "Missisquoi: Abenaki Survival in their Ancient Homeland," 15.

17. *Johnson Papers* 4:790.

18. *NYCD* 8:237; Shortt and Doughty, eds., *Documents Relating to the Constitutional History of Canada, 1759–1791* 1:20, 33; PAC, NMC H2/ 300/1776; *Johnson Papers* 4:811. Lester J. Cappon, ed., *Atlas of Early American History: The Revolutionary Era, 1760–1790* (Princeton: Princeton University Press, 1976), 15, indicates vagaries in the proclamation line along the Green Mountain chain; cf Tanner, ed. *Atlas of Great Lakes Indian History,* 54–55.

19. Moody, "Missisquoi," 12, 14; Leonard Woods Labaree, ed., *Royal Instructions to British Colonial Governors, 1670–1776* 2:467–68, 476–78; Charland, *Abénakis d'Odanak,* 172; J. Goldtrap to Collins and Lieut. Scott, 29 March 1765, PAC, RG4, C2, 1:3(3), reel C-10462.

20. The Robertson lease is reprinted in *VHG* 1:454–55 and 4:962; a typed copy is in the Vermont Historical Society, Misc. File #914. Day, "Missisquoi," 55; cf. Moody, "Missisquoi," 13–16, and *Abenaki Petition,* 38.

21. *Johnson Papers* 12:172; Vermont Historical Society, Misc. File #719. Jennings, *Ambiguous Iroquois Empire,* passim. Successive generations of Iroquois petitioned the Vermont legislature for redress for loss of the lands that they had claimed without success.

22. PAC, reel C-11, 888, 3:328–30. Other versions and copies of the Missisquois' speech are in *Johnson Papers* 12:173; Vermont Historical Society, Misc. File #719; *Vermont History* 26 (Jan. 1958): 38–39; PAC, RG 10, 1827–28:84–87, reel C-1222. See also PAC, reel C-11, 888, 3:393–94, and Vermont Historical Society, Misc. File # 719, for Guy Carleton's report on the Abenakis' concern about liquor traders.

23. Moody, "Missisquoi," 16–17; *New York Land Patents* 16:38–43, 66–73.

24. *Johnson Papers* 12:1027. The same document in mutilated form is in *Johnson Papers* 8:840. See also *Johnson Papers* 13:617.

25. Day, *Identity of the St. Francis Indians,* 47–48.

26. *Johnson Papers* 12:571; PAC, RG 10, 1827–28: 85–87, reel C-1222; 1822–26:38–41, reel C-1223; Day, *Identity of the St. Francis Indians,* 47.

27. *Johnson Papers* 7:109–12; Jack A. Frisch, "The Abenakis among the St. Regis Mohawks," *Indian Historian* 4 (Spring 1971): 27–29. Claus's report of his conversation with Carleton about the issue is in *Johnson Papers* 7:126–28.

28. Proceedings of a treaty . . . held near German Flats, 15–24 July 1770, Public Record Office, C.O., 5/71, pt. 2, 24, in *Iroquois Indians: A Documentary History,* reel 30; Huden, "The White Chief of the St. Francis Abenakis," 204.

29. *Johnson Papers* 7:818–19.

30. *Johnson Papers* 12:840–41 (also in PAC, RG 10, 1827–28: 100–111, reel C-1222.

31. *Johnson Papers* 12:843–44, 846.

32. *Johnson Papers* 12:845–46, 7:897; Day, *Identity of the St. Francis Indians*, 48.

33. *Johnson Papers* 7:923, 928–29, 8:212–14; Claus Papers, PAC, MG 19 F1, 1:123–26; Moody, "Missisquoi," 69–70.

34. Frisch, "The Abenakis among the St. Regis Mohawks," 28–29; Day, *Identity of the St. Francis Indians*, 48; *BRH* 67:20, 23, 29; Moody, "Missisquoi," 69–75

35. *Henry Tufts: The Autobiography of a Criminal*, 63–64, 69–72, 78; Gordon Day, "Henry Tufts as a Source on the Eighteenth Century Abenakis," *Ethnohistory* 21 (Summer 1974): 189–97.

36. Day, *Identity of the St. Francis Indians*, 52; *VHG* 2:936.

37. Day, *Identity of the St. Francis Indians*, 61–62; *Abenaki Petition*, 69–71.

11. Western Abenakis and the American Revolution, 1775–1783

1. Letter from Henry Young Brown, May 16, 1775, U.S. Revolution Collection, American Antiquarian Society, Worcester, Mass.; Peter Force, ed. *American Archives*, 4th ser., 2:621.

2. E.g. Thomas Chittenden, *The Public Papers of Governor Thomas Chittenden*, edited by John A. Williams, 17:70, 246, 413, 513; Vermont State Archives, Stevens Papers, 1:363–64, 2:273–75, 289–90.

3. Force, ed., *American Archives*, 4th ser., 3:51; Crockett, *Vermont* 1:492; Vermont State Archives, Stevens Papers, 1:363–64; Abenaki *Nation, Petition*, 44.

4. Vermont State Archives, Stevens Papers, 1:409–10.

5. Force, ed., *American Archives*, 4th ser., 2:339, 976–78, 1041–42, 1048, 1594–96, 1734–35; Charles A. Jellison, *Ethan Allen, Frontier Rebel*, 136–37, 151–52; K. G. Davies, ed., *Documents of the American Revolution, 1770–1783* 9:142–43: PCC, reel 166, item 152, 2:379–81; reel 172, item 153, 1:41–44, 75, 176–77, 2:206; reel 183, item 166, 397; W. C. Ford, ed., *Journals of the Continental Congress* 3 (1775) (Washington, D.C.: Government Printing Office, 1905), 401; George Washington, *The Writings of George Washington* 5:221, 251, 261–62, 403–404, 6:236, 434–36; *Baxter MSS* 24 (1916): 165–95; "A Short Acco. of a Tour undertaken 9th March 1775 from Dartmo College to Canada," New York Public Library, Schuyler Papers, reel 7, box 13. For detailed discussion of the disposition of the Canadian and other tribes in the early years of the war, see Paul L. Stevens, "His Majesty's 'Savage' Allies: British Policy and the Northern Indians during the Revolutionary War: The Carleton Years, 1774–1778," Ph.D. diss., State University of New York at Buffalo, 1984.

6. *Writings of Washington* 3:423–24, 436–39; Day, *The Identity of the St. Francis Indians*, 53; William Allen, comp., "A Journal of the Expedition to Quebec in 1775," *Collections of the Maine Historical Society* 1st ser., 1 (1831): 394, 397; John Joseph Henry, *Account of Arnold's Campaign Against Quebec* (Albany: Joel Munsell, 1887), 31–32, 74–75; "Colonel Thomas Johnson's Letters," in *Upper Connecticut* 2:94–95; "Memoir of the Sokokis or Pequaket Tribe of Indians," *Magazine of History with Notes and Queries*, extra no. 5 (2) (1909), 93; Woodrow, ed., *Metallak*, 16, 65–66.

7. *PCC*, reel 172, 1:200, 2:206; Day, *Identity of the St. Francis Indians*, 53; Vermont State Archives, Stevens Papers, 1:467–68; *VHG* 1:861, 875, 4:973. Maurault, *Histoire des Abénakis*, recounted Abenaki participation in the defense of Quebec, but Stevens, "His Majesty's 'Savage' Allies," 511, 2036, n. 20, suspects that Abenakis later fabricated the story to make life easier for themselves in British Canada.

8. Davies, ed., *Documents of the American Revolution* 11:166; Bouton, ed., *New Hampshire Provincial Papers* 7:547; "A Short Acco. of a Tour undertaken 9th March 1775 from Dartmo College to Canada," New York Public Library, Schuyler Papers.

9. Vermont State Archives, Stevens Papers, 2:267–68, 273–75, 289–91; "Colonel Thomas Johnson's Letters," in *Upper Connecticut* 2:91; John Sullivan, *Letters and Papers of Major-General John Sullivan*, ed. by Otis G. Hammond, 1:285–86; Force, ed., *American Archives*, 5th ser., 1:190–91, 2:231.

10. Manuscript account by Jonathan Elkins, Vermont Historical Society MSS, 774940, 1–2. Elkins' journal is reprinted in *Upper Connecticut* 1:263–89.

11. "Reminiscences of Colonel Frye Bayley," in *Upper Connecticut* 2:38; *PCC*, reel 183, item 166, 63; reel 70, item 157, 81–83; reel 173, item 153, 3:36: *Collections of the New York Historical Society* 12 (1879): 59; Vermont State Archives, Stevens Papers, 2:283, 286, 395–97; "Report of Colonel Bedel," Henry Stevens Papers (copies from New York State Library, Albany, in Vermont State Archives), box 90, folder 12; *VHG* 2:936; Bouton, ed., *New Hampshire State Papers* 8 (1874): 405, 510; Force, ed., *American Archives*, 5th ser., 3:1081. Bedel's efforts are recorded in Col. Timothy Bedel's Account, Jan. 1777–Jan. 1778, New York Public Library, Schuyler Papers, reel 7, box 14.

12. *PCC*, reel 77, item 63, 86; *Collections of the New York Historical Society* 12 (1879): 17–18, 13 (1880): 102–103; Vermont State Archives, Stevens Papers, 3:337–38; *Public Papers of Governor Thomas Chittenden* 17:76.

13. Vermont State Archives, Stevens Papers, 3:618; *PCC*, reel 70, item 157, 52.

14. Brian Burns, "Massacre or Muster? Burgoyne's Indians and the Militia at Bennington," *Vermont History* 45 (Summer 1977): 133–44; Davies, ed., *Documents of the American Revolution* 14:121.

15. Davies, ed., *Documents of the American Revolution* 15:223; Ida H. and Paul A. Washington, *Carleton's Raid*, 13, 33.

16. Wynn Underwood, "Indian and Tory Raids on the Otter Valley, 1777–1782," *Vermont Quarterly*, n.s., 15 (Oct. 1947): 195–221; *Public Papers of Governor Thomas Chittenden* 17:51, 61, 246, 267–70, 397, 413–15, 513.

17. John C. Huden, "The White Chief of the St. Francis Abenakis," *Vermont History* 24 (1956): 205–206, 339; Bouton, ed., *New Hampshire Provincial Papers* 7:547; *Letters and Papers of Major-General John Sullivan* 1:287; Eric P. Kelly, "The Dartmouth Indians," *Dartmouth Alumni Magazine* 22, no. 2 (Dec. 1929): 123; Gordon M. Day, "Dartmouth and St. Francis," *Dartmouth Alumni Magazine* 52 (Nov. 1959): 28–30. Gill's son, Anthony, left Dartmouth in 1777: Rev. Eleazar Wheelock explained to his father, "he don't love books, but loves play & idleness much better," Wheelock to Sachim Gill, Dartmouth College MS 777601. Memorial of John Wheelock, 3 Jan. 1780, *PCC*, reel 52, item 10, 423–24; reel 172, item 1, 42. By 1808, Edward Augustus Kendall found little trace of the school's original purpose of affording education to Indian children, although it still drew funds on that basis. Kendall, *Travels Through the Northern Part of the United States* 3:195–98.

18. Wes Herwig, "Indian Raid on Royalton," *Vermont Life*, Autumn 1964, 16–21; Crockett, *Vermont* 2:265–67; "The Destruction of Royalton, 16 Octr. 1780," Dartmouth College, MS 780566; George Avery's Journal, Dartmouth College, MS 780900.5, p. 7; Vermont State Archives, Manuscript Vermont State Papers, 19:107, 128, 147; John K. Alexander, ed., "Journal of an American Naval Prisoner of War and Vermont Indian Fighter," *Vermont History* 36 (Spring 1968): 89; "Captivity of Zadock Steele," in *Indian Narratives*, 216–17, 273–74.

19. Haldimand Papers, British Museum, Add. MSS, 21705, 44–47; 21714, 46; 21773, 165; 21774, 156.

20. Day, *Identity of the St. Francis Indians*, 53; Woodrow, ed., *Metallak*, 12; "The Last of the Pennacooks," 293; Vermont Historical Society, MS 781210.

21. Elkins's journal, Vermont Historical Society, MS 774940:3.

22. "J. Sullivan's Journal to Penobscot, May–June [1770s?]," U.S. Revolution Collection, American Antiquarian Society; Huden, "The White Chief of the St. Francis Abenakis," 337; W. Greening, "Historic Odanak and the Abenaki Nation," *Canadian Geographic Journal* 73 (1966): 92–97; Isaac W. Hammond, ed., *New Hampshire State Papers* 17 (1889): 265, 276, 281–82, 328, 350; Vermont State Archives, Stevens Papers,

3:669; *PCC*, reel 170, item 152, 8:159; reel 159, item 147, 4:301; reel 24, item 14, 327; reel 183, item 166, 481–83; *Writings of Washington* 17:68–69, 82–83.

23. Vermont State Archives, Stevens Papers, 3:75–76, 81–82; Hammond, ed., *New Hampshire State Papers* 17 (1889): 128–31.

24. Vermont State Archives, Stevens Papers, 3:667; *PCC*, reel 183, item 166, 63; "Report of Colonel Bedel"; "Col. Timothy Bedel's Account" and "List of St. Francis Indians, June 5, 1778," Schuyler Papers, reel 7, box 14; Hammond, ed., *New Hampshire State Papers* 17 (1889): 152–53, 218–19.

25. Day, *Identity of the St. Francis Indians*, 54; "Report of Colonel Bedel"; Vermont State Archives, Stevens Papers, 3:81–82; Hammond, ed., *New Hampshire State Papers* 17 (1889): 242.

26. Vermont State Archives, Stevens Papers, 3:99; *Baxter MSS* 15 (1910): 241–42.

27. Haldimand Papers, 21777, 67–68.

28. Walton, ed., *Records of the Governor and Council of the State of Vermont* 5:24–26n; "Muster Roll of Captain John Vincent's Company of Indian Rangers," in Wells, *History of Newbury*, 409; "Colonel Johnson's Letters," in *Upper Connecticut* 2:94–95. According to Walter Hill Crockett, Vincent was a Caughnawaga; *Vermont* 2:595–96. Woodrow, ed., *Metallak*, 16. Tradition holds that Captain Joe was a member of a Nova Scotia tribe that scattered when he was a child, and he came to Cowass as a young man after being raised at St. Francis; *VHG* 2:924. See also Lois Goodwin Greer, "Indian Joe: Revolutionary Scout," *The Vermonter* 27 (1922): 257–59.

29. Huden, "The White Chief of the St. Francis Abenakis," 337. For events at St. Francis during this period, see Charland, *Abénakis d'Odanak*, chap. 10.

30. Huden, "White Chief," 340.

31. Haldimand Papers, 21777, 34; Davies, ed., *Documents of the American Revolution* 15:221.

32. Haldimand Papers, 21777, 34–35.

33. Haldimand Papers, 21777, 67; Hammond, ed., *New Hampshire State Papers* 17 (1889): 281–82, 328; Huden, "White Chief," 340.

34. Huden, "White Chief," 341–42; Haldimand Papers, 21777, passim, e.g., 67, 180, 184; "Col. Timothy Bedel's Account."

35. Haldimand Papers, 21777, 107–11, 117, 137–38; *Writings of Washington* 17:155; *PCC* reel 183, item 166, 343.

37. Haldimand Papers, 21777, 168.

37. Ibid., 271.

38. Ibid., 250; Huden, "White Chief," 343; *PCC*, reel 24, item 14, 327; reel 159, item 147, 4:301.

39. Haldimand Papers, 21777, 269–71.

40. Haldimand Papers, 21772, 2–4; Huden, "White Chief," 343–44. Antoine was the son who had been captured by Rogers' Rangers.

41. Haldimand Papers, 21772, 6–7, 12, 46–50, 62, 150; 21773, 173–75, 183–85; 21774, 242; Charland, *Abénakis d'Odanak*, 166–67.

42. *PCC*, reel 172, item 153, 1:31, 71–72, 98; Moody, "Missisquoi," 17–18, 22; Day, *Identity of the St. Francis Indians*, 55; "Reminiscences of Colonel Frye Bayley," in *Upper Connecticut* 2:31, 57.

43. Moody, "Missisquoi," 19–20; Force, ed., *American Archives*, 4th ser., 2:1734; 5th ser., 2:533; "Account of Capts Louis Cook and Jean Vincent, Dec. 30, 1777," *PCC*, reel 70, item 157, 83; Major Clement Gosselin to Ira Allen, Aug. 18, 1786, Vermont State Archives, Stevens Papers, Misc. Correspondence, 1780–89.

44. PAC, NMC H2/300/17776, NMC 6/310-Champlain/1778; Day, *Identity of the St. Francis Indians*, 55; *VHG* 4:972–74; Rev. Townshend, "The First Settlement of Clarenceville Village and Vicinity," Fifth Report of the Missisquoi County Historical Society (1850), 46.

45. "Petition of Joseph Shausequeth," Vermont State Archives, Manuscript Vermont State Papers, 22:26–27; Walton, ed., *Records of the Governor and Council of the State of Vermont* 2:127–28, 3:180, 200, 5:82; John C. Huden, "Indians in Vermont," *Vermont History* 23 (Jan. 1955): 26–28; "The Naming of Marshfield, Vermont," ibid., 56–57; *VHG* 4:197; cf. *PCC*, reel 50, item 41, 4:435; reel 73, item 59, 3:211–12.

12. Exiles in Their Own Land

1. Day, *The Identity of the St. Francis Indians*, 56.

2. *VHG* 2:523.

3. Muller, "The Commercial History of the Lake Champlain–Richelieu River Route," 67–69; *VHG* 4–994–96; Moody, "Missisquoi," 31–32.

4. Lampee, "The Missisquoi Loyalists," 81–139 (quote on p. 125). For registers of the Missisquoi loyalists, see PAC, reel C-1475, esp. 105:166–70; for lists of loyalists who petitioned to settle around Missisquoi Bay, PAC, reel C-2559, 171:83379–80.

5. Crockett, *Vermont* 1:241; Haviland and Power, *Original Vermonters*, 243–44. An account of the disputes surrounding Abenaki lands on the Missisquoi River and the Allens' acquisition of lands there is in "The Annals of the Indians at Missisquoi down to 1790," in John B. Perry Papers, Special Collections, University of Vermont, Bailey/Howe Library, box 3, folder 3, 192–204.

6. University of Vermont, Allen Family Papers, 6–75 (copy in Vermont Historical Society, Misc. File #575); "Reminiscences of Col. Frye Bayley," in *Upper Connecticut* 2:31.

7. Allen Family Papers, 6–75.

8. Vermont Historical Society, Misc. File #575, Allen Family Papers, 6–78; Charland, *Abénakis d'Odanak*, 173–74; Haldimand Papers, 21772: 249.

9. *VHG* 4:994, 972; Clement Gosselin to Ira Allen, 18 Aug. 1786, Vermont State Archives, Stevens Papers, Misc. Correspondence, 1780–89.

10. *VHG* 4:998–99.

11. *VHG* 4:999-1000.

12. University of Vermont, Stevens Family Papers, 9:1; *VHG* 4:999. Moody, "Missisquoi," 44, n. 36, suggests that Outalamagouine may have been a descendant of Grey Lock.

13. Chambly Catholic Church register, cited in Moody, "Missisquoi," 15.

14. Henry Lorne Masta, *Abenaki Indian Legends, Grammar, and Place Names*, 32; Day, *Identity of the St. Francis Indians*, 57, questions the date of this tradition.

15. Hulbert, ed., *Crown Collection of American Maps*, 1st ser., #2 (cxix, 43.2).

16. *VHG* 2:371, 255, 4:1001; "Annals of the St. Francis Indians," John Perry MSS, Special Collections, University of Vermont, Bailey/Howe Library, box 3, folder 3, 241.

17. PAC, Indian Records Series 2, 4:242, cited in Charland, *Abénakis d'Odanak*, 175–76, and Day, *Identity of the St. Francis Indians*, 60.

18. *VHG* 4:1000; Moody, "Missisquoi," 33, 43.

19. Charland, *Abénakis d'Odanak*, 325–26; *VHG* 3:313.

20. Peter Shea, "A New and Accurate Map of Philip's Grant," *Vermont History* 53 (Winter 1985): 36–42; Jeremiah Eames, Plan of Philip's Grant 1796, New Hampshire Historical Society; Payment of account due to Thomas Eames by Philip Indian Company, and Letters of Samuel Bradley, Aug. 17 and Aug. 31, 1804, in Bradley Family Papers, New Hampshire Historical Society; Day, *Identity of the St. Francis Indians*, 59; *Collections of the New Hampshire Historical Society*, 11:11–12; Woodrow, *Metallak*, 17, suggested this Philip might have been the son of Captain John Soosap.

21. Day, *Identity of the St. Francis Indians*, 59; Day, "Henry Tufts as a Source on the Eighteenth Century Abenakis," *Ethnohistory* 21, no. 3 (Summer 1974): 189–97.

22. *VHG* 2:924–47, 3:315; Woodrow, *Metallak*, 16–17; Catherine S-C. Newell, *Molly Ockett* (Bethel, Me: Bethel Historical Society, 1981).

23. Vermont, Secretary of State, *State Papers of Vermont* 9:452–53, 15:119; Walton, ed., *Records of the Governor and Council of the State of Vermont*, 4:36, 205, 311, 5:262, 270, 6:138, 199.

24. Walton, ed., *Records of the Governor and Council of the State of Vermont* 5 : 24–25, 38, 40, 132, 155, 193, 203, 271.

25. PAC, reel 2559, 172 : 83659–83728, passim, esp. 83662–63, 83667–74, 83679, 83698, 83704–5, 83716, 83725; PAC, MG 11, Q Series, vol. 79, pt. 1 : 200, vol. 94 : 9–10, 13; Charland, *Abénakis d'Odanak*, 175–76, 200; Day, *Identity of the St. Francis Indians*, 60–61, 111; Day, "Western Abenaki," 152.

26. *Abenaki Petition*, 58–59; *Addendum to the Abenaki Petition*, pt. 2, 171–72, 319.

27. Moody, "Missisquoi," 46; *Johnson Papers* 12 : 173.

28. *VHG* 2 : 37; Charland, *Abénakis d'Odanak*, 325–26.

29. Henry K. Adams, *A Centennial History of St. Albans, Vermont* (St. Albans: Wallace Printing Co., 1899), 1; Lewis Cass Aldrich, *History of Franklin and Grand Isle Counties* (New York: D. Mason and Co., 1891), 28.

30. E.g., *VHG* 4 : 1001. Cf. "The Last of the Pennacooks," 298.

31. Moody, "Native American Legacy," 59; "Annals of the St. Francis Indians," Bailey/Howe Library, University of Vermont, 242.

32. Vermont State Archives, Manuscript Vermont State Papers, 30 : 348, 367; Timothy P. Redfield, *Report on the Claim of the Iroquois Indians upon the State of Vermont for their "Hunting Ground"* (Montpelier, Vt.: E. P. Walton, 1854), 14–20; Walton, ed., *Records of the Governor and Council of the State of Vermont* 8 : 312–61.

33. Redfield, *Report on the Claim of the Iroquois Indians*, 21–22. The Seven Nations Treaty with New York is in *American State Papers: II, Indian Affairs* 4 (Washington, D.C.: Gales and Seaton, 1832), 616–20.

34. Redfield, *Report*, 24–25.

35. Redfield, *Report*, 25–26.

36. Redfield, *Report*, 30; Proceedings of a grand council at Caughnawaga, 5 Oct. 1827, Scottish Record Office, Edinburgh, Dalhousie Muniments, GD 45/3/510, 261 (cited by permission of the Rt. Hon. The Earl of Dalhousie), and PAC, RG 10, vol. 663, both in *Iroquois Indians: A Documentary History*, reel 46.

37. E.g., Gordon Day Tapes, reel 24, side 2.

13. Epilogue: Continuity and Survival

1. "The Last of the Pennacooks," 298; "Annals of the St. Francis Indians," Bailey/Howe Library, University of Vermont, 246.

2. E.g., Woodrow, ed., *Metallak*, 11–15; *Abenaki Petition Addendum*, pt. B, 130.

3. Wheelock to Morse, Feb. 25, 1811, Dartmouth College, MS 811175.1; PAC, RG 10, vol. 11, 10003–4, 10006, reel C-11000; vol. 15, 11918–20, 11924, 11928, reel C-11002; vol. 7, 3733–45, reel C-10999.

4. *Missionary Herald* 30 (1834): 141, 32 (1836): 29, 33 (1837): 79, *Peter Skene Ogden's Snake Country Journal, 1826–27*, ed. K. G. Davies (London: Hudson's Bay Record Society, 1961), 174n.

5. *Abenaki Petition*, 6–7, 10, 27, 52–99, passim; *Petition Addendum*, pt. B, 175, 303–5, 315.

6. *VHG* 4:1001

7. *Green Mountain Democrat* (Fayetteville, Vt.), April 3, 1835, quoted in *Petition Addendum*, pt. B, 308–9; letter from Amable Petithomme to Father Coudrian, July 28, 1835, Archives of the Sacred Heart of Jesus and Mary, Vatican, cited in *Petition Addendum*, pt. B, 313.

8. Hayes, *Connecticut River Valley*, 61–64.

9. *VHG* 2:926.

10. Woodrow, ed., *Metallak*, 11–16, 19–21; "The Last of the Penna-cooks," 298–99.

11. Thomas Burns Mack, Journal at .Dartmouth, 1850, Dartmouth College, Special Collections, 2:1.

12. Moody, "Native American Legacy," 58; Moody, "Missisquoi," 50, 54.

13. Kendall, *Travels* 3:124, 191. The Cobbosseecontee area Abenakis seem to have formed a group at St. Francis known as "the Sturgeon Folk," Ghere, "Abenaki Factionalism, Emigration, and Social Continuity," 68–69.

14. Kendall, *Travels* 3:67; Moody, "Missisquoi," 67–74.

15. Charland, *Abénakis d'Odanak*, 325–27; Day, *Identity of the St. Francis Indians*, 61; *Abenaki Petition*, 4, 6, 8, 15–16, 41–42.

16. PAC, reel C-2559, 172:83787–9; 83794–5.

17. PAC, reel C-2559, 172:83791–2, 83796–9; 83800–3.

18. PAC, reel C-2559, 172:83804–5, 83846–7, 83851–3, 83859, 83867–8.

19. PAC, reel C-2559, 172:83867–8

20. PAC, reel C-2559, 172:83876–8.

21. *Missionary Herald* 38 (July 1842): 301.

22. *Abenaki Petition*, E.g., 87–102; *Petition Addendum*, pt. B, 128, 152–53.

23. *1980 Census of Population, Supplementary Reports: Race of the Population by States*, 1980, table 1.

24. Christine Doremus, "Jurisdiction over Adjudications Involving the Abenaki Indians of Vermont," *Vermont Law Review* 10 (Fall 1985): 417–35; Haviland and Powers, *Original Vermonters*, chap. 7; *Abenaki Petition*, 103–113.

25. E.g., *New York Times*, Sept. 7, 1987, Oct. 2, 1988.

26. New England Indian Task Force, "Statement of Support from the Indian Leadership of New England," Abenaki Archives, Swanton, Vt.;

State of Vermont vs. *Harold St. Francis et al.*, Vt. Dist. Court, Franklin Circuit, Unit #2, 1989, quote at 92.

27. George Pierre Castile and Gilbert Kushner, eds., *Persistent Peoples: Cultural Enclaves in Perspective*, esp. xvi-xxi; Edward H. Spicer, *The Yaquis: A Cultural History* (Tucson: University of Arizona Press, 1980), chaps. 6–7, quote at p. 360; Howard L. Harrod, *Renewing the World: Plains Indian Religion and Morality* (Tucson: University of Arizona Press, 1987), 38–39.

Glossary of Indian Groups and Communities

ABENAKI. Related tribes of the Algonquian language family inhabiting Vermont, New Hampshire, Maine, and southeastern Quebec. Became part of the WABANAKI CONFEDERACY.

AGAWAM. Indian village on the Connecticut River near Springfield, Massachusetts. Communities of the same name were located at Ipswich and at Wareham, Massachusetts.

AKWESASNE. See ST. REGIS.

ALGONQUIAN. Language family that includes the majority of the Indian peoples living in the northeastern United States and eastern Canada.

ALGONQUIN. Algonquian-speaking tribe that inhabited the Ottawa Valley and adjacent regions of eastern Canada.

AMESOKANTI. A subdivision of the KENNEBEC INDIANS.

AROSAGUNTACOOK. See ANDROSCOGGIN.

ANDROSCOGGIN. Abenaki inhabitants of the Androscoggin River drainage. Also referred to as Arosaguntacook (by some writers) and Amariscoggin. The name Arosaguntacook was often applied to the ST. FRANCIS INDIANS.

ASSCHINCANTECOOK. Probably a synonym for Arosaguntacook.

BÉCANCOUR (Wôlinak). Mission village, established in 1704, inhabited primarily by Wawenocks and other eastern Abenaki refugees.

CAUGHNAWAGA (Kahnawake, Sault St. Louis). Mission village of Catholic Mohawks close to Montreal, established 1676.

CAYUGA. Member tribe of the Five (later Six) Nations of the IROQUOIS CONFEDERACY.

CHEROKEE. Iroquoian-speaking tribe that originally inhabited northern Georgia, eastern Tennessee, and the western Carolinas.

CHIPPEWA. See OJIBWA.

COWASS. "The place of the pines"; a western Abenaki community on the upper Connecticut River, centered around present-day Newbury, Vermont.

COWASUCK. The Abenaki people of COWASS and the vicinity.

DELAWARE. An eastern Algonquian people that originally occupied the Delaware River Valley but underwent piecemeal westward migration in the face of white contact in the eighteenth and nineteenth centuries.

ERIE. A northern Iroquoian people on the south shore of Lake Erie. Cultural and linguistic relatives of the HURON, the Eries were displaced by the IROQUOIS CONFEDERACY in the midseventeenth century.

FOX. An Algonquian tribe originally located in lower Michigan, the Foxes migrated to the Green Bay area, probably under pressure from the Iroquois, and were on the Wolf River in Wisconsin at the time of early white contacts. They subsequently moved south to the Fox River in Illinois and, in the eighteenth century, to Iowa on the west bank of the Mississippi. After their wars with the French in the 1730s, the Foxes were absorbed by the SAUK tribe.

HASSANAMESETT. An Indian "praying town" established at Grafton, Massachusetts, in 1654.

HOCHELAGA. Populous Iroquoian town at the site of Montreal, visited by Jacques Cartier in 1535.

HURON. A confederacy of northern Iroquoian tribes living around Georgian Bay on the northeast shore of Lake Huron; dispersed by Iroquois attacks during the midseventeenth century.

IROQUOIS. The original Five Nations of the IROQUOIS CONFEDERACY of upstate New York were from east to west the MOHAWK, the ONEIDA, the ONONDAGA, the CAYUGA, and the SENECA. They were joined early in the eighteenth century by Tuscarora refugees from the Carolinas.

KAHNAWAKE. See CAUGHNAWAGA.

KENNEBEC. Eastern Abenaki group inhabiting the Kennebec Valley, with their major village at NORRIDGEWOCK.

KIKHESIPIRINI. An ALGONQUIN band centered around Morrison's (Allumette) Island in the Ottawa River, the Kikhesipirini were middlemen in the fur trade.

LAKE OF TWO MOUNTAINS (Oka). A mission village near Montreal in 1663, inhabited by ALGONQUIN, NIPISSING, and IROQUOIS people.

LORETTE. A mission village of Hurons near Quebec, established by refugees after the IROQUOIS CONFEDERACY attacks of the midseventeenth century.

LOUP. The French name for MAHICAN; occasionally applied to PENNACOOK, SOKOKI, and other groups.

MAHICAN. Algonquian tribe inhabiting the upper Hudson Valley and stretching into southwestern Vermont and western Massachusetts. Related to, but distinct from, the MOHEGAN tribe of Connecticut.

MALECITE (Maliseet). Eastern Algonquian people living along the St. John River in Maine and New Brunswick; closely related to the PASSAMAQUODDY and the MICMAC.

MENOMINEE. Known as the "Wild Rice People," the Menominees were a central Algonquian tribe living in Wisconsin.

MIAMI. An Algonquian group including about a half-dozen tribes. Originally living on the southwest shore of Lake Michigan, the Miamis had moved to the Fox-Wisconsin river region by the time of contact, and in the eighteenth century moved into the Indiana region.

MICMAC. In the sixteenth century the Micmac tribe occupied the region south and west of the Gulf of St. Lawrence in New Brunswick and Nova Scotia. They later joined the WABANAKI CONFEDERACY.

MISSISQUOI. The "place of the flint"; the core community and central village of the Abenakis who inhabited the area between Lake Champlain and the headwaters of the Missisquoi River.

MOHAWK (*Fr*.: Agniers, Anniehronnons; Maquas). The easternmost tribe of the Iroquois Confederacy, with villages in the Mohawk Valley.

MOHEGAN. Southern Connecticut tribe living around the Thames River.

MONTAGNAIS. This northern Algonquian people living in the uplands north of the lower St. Lawrence River were trappers and traders in the French fur trade.

NARRAGANSETT. An eastern Algonquian people of Rhode Island, the Narragansetts were hard hit in King Philip's War, and many of the survivors were driven into exile among the Abenakis and Mahicans.

NASHAWAY. (Nashua). An Indian community on the upper Nashua River near Lancaster, Massachusetts.

NEUTRAL. Small confederacy of allied northern Iroquoian groups who lived between the HURON and the IROQUOIS CONFEDERACIES, between Lake Ontario and the Grand River.

NIPISSING. An Algonquian-speaking people living around Lake Nipissing, Ontario, the Nipissings formed a major component of the LAKE OF TWO MOUNTAINS mission village and operated as middlemen in the French fur trade.

NATICK. Indian "praying town" southwest of Boston, founded in 1650 under the supervision of John Eliot.

NIPMUC(K). A group of Indian villages and bands inhabiting central Massachusetts.

NONOTUCK. Algonquian village on the Connecticut River near Northampton, Massachusetts.

NORRIDGEWOCK. The last surviving village of the eastern Abenakis of the Kennebec Valley, destroyed by the English in 1724.

NORWOTTUCK. (Nalvotogy, Norwootuc). Connecticut Valley Algonquian group around South Hadley, Massachusetts.

ODANAK. See ST. FRANCIS

ONEIDA. Member tribe of the IROQUOIS CONFEDERACY.

ONONDAGA. The central tribe and central council fire of the IROQUOIS CONFEDERACY.

OJIBWA. A numerous central Algonquian people occupying an extensive area north of Lakes Superior and Huron and spreading into Ontario, Michigan, Wisconsin, and Minnesota after contact with whites.

OSSIPEE. Small western Abenaki group living near Lake Ossipee, New Hampshire.

OSWEGATCHIE. Mission established at La Presentation on the upper St. Lawrence River by Sulpician missionaries after 1748; mainly inhabited by ONONDAGA Indians, as well as some of the CAYUGA and ONEIDA tribes.

OTTAWA. Central Algonquian tribe located around the Great Lakes. Closely associated with the OJIBWA and POTAWATOMI tribes, the Ottawas were middlemen in the seventeenth-century French fur trade.

PANIS. Originally applied to the Pawnee, by the eighteenth century this French term had come to denote any Indian slave, since so many slaves were taken in raids on the Pawnees.

PASCATAWAY. (Piscataqua). Small tribe connected with the PENNACOOK, living near Dover on the Piscataqua River, which divides Maine and New Hampshire. (Piscataway refers to an Indian group in Maryland.)

PASSAMAQUODDY. An eastern Algonquian group on the coast of Maine and New Brunswick, closely associated with the MALECITE.

PAWTUCKET. The Pawtuckets, often called Pennacooks, inhabited the coast of New England from north of Massachusetts Bay into Maine.

PENNACOOK. This western Abenaki tribe inhabited the Merrimack Valley and adjacent regions of New Hampshire, with their main village at Concord.

PENOBSCOT. (*Fr.*: Pentagouet). An eastern Abenaki tribe on the Penobscot drainage in Maine.

PEQUOT. An offshoot of the Mohegan tribe of southern Connecticut. The main Pequot village was destroyed in the Pequot War of 1637.

PIGWACKET. (Pequawket; *Fr.*: Peguaki). Abenaki group inhabiting the headwaters of the Saco River.

POCUMTUCK. Algonquian community, or communities, on the middle Connecticut River, with their main village at Deerfield, Massachusetts.

POTAWATOMI. Central Algonquian tribe of the southern Great Lakes, closely connected with the OJIBWA and OTTAWA tribes.

QUABOAG. (Quabaug). Indian community in south central Massachusetts.

RIVER INDIANS. Name applied to the MAHICAN tribe as well as to refugees from various New England tribes who settled at SCHAGHTICOKE and elsewhere on the Hudson River.

ST. FRANCIS (Odanak). A mission village in Quebec on the south bank of the St. Lawrence River, peopled by refugees of the SOKOKI and ABENAKI tribes, as well as remnants from other tribes in western New England. Today the reserve at Odanak is the largest community of Abenakis in Quebec.

ST. JOHNS. The name usually refers to the MALECITE people of the St. John River in New Brunswick, but may occasionally apply to a group of western Abenakis living near St. Johns, Quebec.

ST. REGIS (Akwesasne). Mission village established for Catholic Mohawks in 1755 on the St. Lawrence River at the present U.S.-Canadian border.

SCHAGHTICOKE. Community of refugee Indians from New England settled by Governor Edmund Andros of New York on the Hoosac River near its confluence with the Hudson, during and after King Philip's War. Like the MAHICANS, the Schagticokes were sometimes referred to as RIVER INDIANS.

SAUK (SAC). The Sauks originally were central Algonquian tribes located near Green Bay, Wisconsin. In the 1730s they absorbed FOX refugees from their wars with the French, and the two tribes became intermixed.

SENECA. The westernmost tribe of the IROQUOIS CONFEDERACY.

SEVEN NATIONS OF CANADA. Seven mission communities along the St. Lawrence, including CAUGHNAWAGA, LAKE OF TWO MOUNTAINS, ST. FRANCIS, BÉCANCOUR, OSWEGATCHIE, LORETTE, and ST. REGIS.

SHAWNEE. An Algonquian people with a long history of migration and dispersal, usually associated with Kentucy and Ohio.

SILLERY. A short-lived Jesuit mission established near Quebec in 1637. Sillery catered mainly to the ALGONQUIN and MONTAGNAIS tribes, along with some ABENAKI people after King Philip's War. It was deserted in the 1680s.

SIOUX. Extensive and loosely related tribes originally found on the upper Mississippi River. Divided into the Santee (eastern), Yankton (middle), and Teton (western) branches, the Sioux Indians eventually spread onto the Great Plains.

SQUAKHEAG. A SOKOKI community near Northfield, Vermont, on the Connecticut River.

SOKOKI (Sokwaki). A Western Abenaki group originally situated in the middle and upper Connecticut Valley.

STADACONA. An Indian community visited by Jacques Cartier in 1535 at the site of Quebec City.

STOCKBRIDGE. A village on the Housatonick River in western Massachusetts, mainly composed of MAHICAN tribesmen who moved there in 1664 after MOHAWK attacks. Stockbridge became the "fireplace" of the Mahican nation in the eighteenth century.

THREE RIVERS. A trading post and mission village of the ALGONQUIN and MONTAGNAIS tribes on the north bank of the St. Lawrence.

WABANAKI CONFEDERACY. A confederation that developed in the eighteenth century, involving ABENAKI, PASSAMAQUODDY, MALECITE, and MICMAC Indians.

WAMPANOAG (Pokanoket). A group of allied Algonquian villages in eastern Rhode Island and southern Massachusetts, including Cape Cod and Martha's Vineyard.   .

WINNEBAGO. A Siouan-speaking tribe who inhabited west central Wisconsin before migrating south and west in the eighteenth and nineteenth centuries.

WINOOSKI. Western Abenaki community on the Winooski River.

WORONOKE (Waranoke, Woronoco). Indian community on the Westfield River in Massachusetts.

WYANDOT. Refugee HURON Indians who fled west after the onslaught of the IROQUOIS CONFEDERACY on Huronia in the midseventeenth century.

Bibliography

Manuscripts

American Antiquarian Society, Worcester, Massachusetts
J. Sullivan's Journal to Penobscot, May–June [1770s?], U.S. Revolution Collection. Letter from Henry Young Brown, May 16, 1775, U.S. Revolution Collection.

British Museum, London
Haldimand Papers. Correspondence and Papers of Governor-General Sir Frederick Haldimand, 1758–1791; Additional Mss., 21661–892 on microfilm.

Chicago Historical Society
Pierre Joseph Antoine Roubaud to Sir William Johnson, Feb. 16, 1761.

Dartmouth College Archives, Baker Library, Hanover, New Hampshire
Avery, George. Journal of the Royalton Raid, 1780. Ms. 780900.5.
Day, Gordon. Abenaki Journal. Gordon Day Tapes.
The Destruction of Royalton, 16 Oct. 1780. MS 780566.
Thomas Burns Mack, Journal at Dartmouth. 1850. 4 vols.
Eleazar Wheelock to Sachim Gill, Nov. 1, 1777, MS 777601.
John Wheelock to Rev. Jedidiah Morse, Feb. 25, 1811, MS 811175.1.

Massachusetts Historical Society, Boston
Belknap Manuscripts, esp. 61, and two letters of Phineas Stevens, 161A, 39–40.
Manuscript notes and copies of letters and documents concerning Indian captivities collected by Emma Lewis Coleman and C.A. Baker. 1 box.
Parkman Papers. Esp. vols 29–31: Historical Documents relating to Acadia, the Commonwealth of Massachusetts, the French Colonial Gov-

ernment, and the Abenaquis, copied from the originals in the Archives of France by Ben: Perley Poore, for Francis Parkman, Esq.

Massachusetts State Archives, Boston
Mass. Archives. Esp. vols. 5, 29–34, 38A, 51, 70–71.

National Archives, Washington, D.C.
Papers of the Continental Congress, 1774–1789. Microcopy no. 247.

Newberry Library, Chicago. Ayer Manuscripts

34 Letter from Joseph C. Ashley to Jonathan Ashley, Fort Dummer, June 13, 1746.

205 Letter from Captain Cunkapot to Nehemiah Bull, Housatunuck, Feb. 5, 1734/5.

423 Indian Petition to the House of Representatives. Number 2 on Connecticut River, April 1, 1747.

570 Meeting of the Commissioners for Indian Affairs at the Council Chamber in Boston, Aug. 16, 1734.

578 A declaration of war against the Cape Sable and St. John's Indians, Boston, Oct. 19, 1744.

591 Eleazar Melvin's Account of Lovewell's fight at Pequaket, May 8, 1725.

592 Mémoire pour M. Le Cardinal sur les sauvages Abenakis, Canada, 1723.

593 [Mémoire sur les] Sauvages Abenaquise, 1718–1726 [excerpts from letters].

621 Minutes of a Council held at Portsmouth, Aug. 23, 1703.

733 Captain William Pote's Journal during his captivity among the French and Indians, May 17, 1745–Aug. 1747.

886 John Thomlinson's Petition to the king in council concerning boundary disputes of New Hampshire and Massachusetts and support of Fort Dummer, Jan. 4, 1749.

1004 Letter of John Williams to Stephen Williams, Deerfield, May 14, 1716.

New Hampshire Historical Society, Concord
Bedel Papers.
Bradley Family Papers.
Jeremiah Eames' Plan of Philip's Grant, 1796.

New York Public Library, New York City
Philip Schuyler Papers: Indian Affairs, reel 7, boxes 13–14.

New York State Archives, Albany
New York Colonial Manuscripts.

New York State Library, Albany
Henry Stevens Papers (copies in Vermont State Archives).

Public Archives of Canada, Ottawa
Claus Papers, MG 19 F1, vol. 1, reel C-1478
France: Archives des Colonies, AC.
France: Archives des Colonies, Correspondence générale, MG1 C11A.
France: Archives des Colonies, Collection Moreau Saint Méry, MG1 F3
Lower Canada Land Papers, reel C-2559; vols. 170–73, esp. St. Francis
    Abenaqui Indians, vol. 172, 83659–83883.
Ordres et dépêches du Roi, MG1 Series B
National Map Collection, NMC
Records Relating to Indian Affairs, RG 10: esp. Commission des Affairs
    indiennes, Albany 1677–1748, vols. 1819–39; reels C-1220–C-1221; Su-
    perintendent's Office Correspondence, vols. 1827–28, reel C-1222; and
    Minutes of Indian Affairs, 1755–90, vols. 1822;–26, reel C-1223.

Public Records Office, Kew, England
American Manuscript Maps in British Repositories, 1763–83, from the
    Public Record Office. Microfilm. 4 reels. London: Her Majesty's Sta-
    tionery Office, 1980.
Records of the British Colonial Office, Class 5 Microfilm, edited by Ran-
    dolph Boehm. Her Majesty's Stationery Office. Frederick, Maryland:
    University Publications of America, 1972. (Part 1: Westward Expan-
    sion; Part 3: The French and Indian War, 1754–1763).

University of Vermont, Bailey/Howe Library
Allen Family Papers.
"The Annals of the Indians at Missisquoi down to 1790," John B. Perry
    Papers, box 3, folder 3, 192–204.
"The Annals of the St. Francis Indians," John B. Perry Papers, 24–46.
"Lease of certain lands on the Missisquoi River by Abenakis of Missis-
    quoi to James Robertson." Stevens Family Papers, 9:1 (copy from
    Public Archives of Canada).
"Phineas Stevens Account Book kept at Fort #4, Charlestown, N.H.,
    1752–1756," Stevens Family Papers (Box 1, folder 8); microfilm copy at
    the Silsby Library, Charlestown, N.H.
"Purport of a Declaration made by Louis Outalamagouine, an Abenaqui
    Indian of Missiskoui. September 11, 1788." Stevens Family Papers, 9:1.

Vermont Historical Society, Montpelier
[Elkins, Jonathan] Reminiscences, 1774–1783. MS 774940
MS 781210 [Letter, March 10, 1781].
Miscellaneous Files #s 3, 318, 575, 717, 719, 913.

Vermont State Archives, Montpelier
Manuscript Vermont State Papers
Henry Stevens Papers (copies from the New York State Library, Albany)
Stevens Papers. 3 vols.

Dissertations

Ghere, David Lynn. "Abenaki Factionalism, Emigration, and Social Continuity: Indian Society in Northern New England, 1725 to 1760." Ph.D. diss., University of Maine, 1988.

Malone, Patrick M. "Indian and English Military Systems in New England in the Seventeenth Century." Ph.D. diss., Brown University, 1971.

Melvoin, Richard Irwin, "New England Outpost: War and Society in Colonial Frontier Deerfield, Massachusetts." Ph.D. diss., University of Michigan, 1983.

Morrison, Alvin Hamblen. "Dawnland Decisions: Seventeenth-Century Wabanaki Leaders and Their Responses to the Differential Contact Stimuli in the Overlap Area of New France and New England." Ph.D. diss., University of New York at Buffalo, 1974.

Morrison, Kenneth M. "The People of the Dawn: The Abnaki and Their Relations with New England and New France, 1600–1727." Ph.D. diss., University of Maine, 1975.

Muller, Henry N., III. "The Commercial History of the Lake Champlain–Richelieu River Route, 1760–1815." Ph.D. diss., University of Rochester, 1969.

Richter, Daniel K. "The Ordeal of the Longhouse: Change and Persistence on the Iroquois Frontier, 1609–1720." Ph.D. diss., Columbia University, 1984.

Stevens, Paul Lawrence. "His Majesty's 'Savage' Allies: British Policy and the Northern Indians During the Revolutionary War: The Carleton Years, 1774–1778. Ph.D. diss., State University of New York at Buffalo, 1984.

Thomas, Peter Allen. "In the Maelstrom of Change: The Indian Trade and Cultural Process in the Middle Connecticut River Valley, 1635–1665," Ph.D., diss., University of Massachusetts, 1979.

Published Primary Sources

Adams, Charles Francis, Jr., ed. *The New England Canaan of Thomas Morton*. Reprint, New York, 1967.

Allen, Ira. *The Natural and Political History of the State of Vermont*. Reprint, Rutland, Vt.: Charles E. Tuttle Co., 1969.

Allen, William, comp. "A Journal of the Expedition to Quebec in 1775." *Collections of the Maine Historical Society* 1, 1st. ser., 1 (1831): 387–416.

Batchellor, Albert Stillman, ed. *The New Hampshire Grants, being transcripts of The Charters of Townships and minor grants of lands made by the Provincial Government of New Hampshire, within the present boundaries of the State of Vermont, from 1749 to 1764.* State Papers of New Hampshire, vol. 3. Concord, 1895.

Baxter, James Phinney, ed., *Baxter Manuscripts: Documentary History of the State of Maine.* 24 vols. Portland: Maine Historical Society, 1869–1916.

Bougainville, Louis Antoine de. *Adventure in the Wilderness: The American Journals of Louis Antoine de Bougainville, 1756–1760.* Edited by Edward P. Hamilton. Norman: University of Oklahoma Press, 1964.

Bouton, Nathaniel, ed. *New Hampshire Provincial Papers: Documents Relating to the Province of New Hampshire.* 7 vols. Concord, Nashua, Manchester, 1867–73.

Bradford, William. *Bradford's History of Plymouth Plantation, 1606–1646.* Edited by William T. Davis. New York, 1908.

Bulletin des Recherches Historiques. 70 vols. Levis, Quebec: George Roy et Antoine Roy, 1895–1965.

Cabot, Mary R., comp. and ed. *Annals of Brattleboro, 1681–1895.* 2 vols. Brattleboro, Vt.: E. L. Hildreth and Co., 1921–22.

Calendar of State Papers, Colonial Series, America and the West Indies, 1677–1733, preserved in the Public Record Office. 30 vols. London: His Majesty's Stationery Office, 1896–1939; reprint, New York: Kraus Reprint Ltd., 1964.

Carpenter, Jonathan Alexander. "Jonathan Carpenter and the American Revolution: The Journal of an American Prisoner of War and Vermont Indian Fighter." *Vermont History* 36 (Spring, 1968): 74–90.

Cartier, Jacques. *The Voyages of Jacques Cartier.* Edited by H. P. Biggar. Ottawa: Publications of the Public Archives of Canada, 1924.

Casgrain, Abbé H.-R., ed. *Collection des Manuscripts du Maréchal de Lévis.* 12 vols. Montreal-Quebec: publié sous la direction de l'Abbé H.-R. Casgrain. 1889–95.

Champlain, Samuel de. *The Works of Samuel de Champlain.* Edited by H. P. Biggar. 6 vols. Toronto: Champlain Society, 1922–36.

Charlevoix, Rev. Pierre F. X. de. *History and General Description of New France by the Reverend P. F. X. de Charlevoix, S.J.* Edited and translated by John Gilmeary Shea. 6 vols. Reprint, Chicago: Loyola University Press, 1962.

———. *Journal of a Voyage to North America.* 2 vols. Ann Arbor: University Microfilms, 1966.

Chase, Francis, ed. *Gathered Sketches from the Early History of New Hampshire and Vermont.* Claremont, N.H.: Tracy, Kenney and Co., 1856.

Chittenden, Thomas. *The Public Papers of Governor Thomas Chittenden,*

1778–1789; 1790–1797. Edited by John A. Williams. Vol. 17. Montpelier: State Papers of Vermont, 1969.

Church, Benjamin. *The History of the Eastern Expeditions of 1689, 1690, 1692, 1696 and 1704 against the Indians and the French.* Boston: J. K. Wiggin and Wm. Parsons Lunt, 1897.

Colden, Cadwallader. *History of the Five Indian Nations Depending on the Province of New-York in America.* London, 1727. Ithaca: Cornell University Press, 1973.

———. *The Letters and Papers of Cadwallader Colden.* 9 vols. in *Collections of the New York Historical Society* 50–56 (1917–23), 67–68 (1934–35).

Collection de Manuscrits contenant Lettres, Mémoires, et Autres Documents Historiques Rélatifs à La Nouvelle-France. 4 vols. Quebec: Imprimerie à côté et cie, 1883–85.

Davies, K.G., ed. *Documents of the American Revolution 1770–1783 (Colonial Office Series).* 20 vols. Shannon: Irish University Press, 1972–79.

Doolittle, Rev. Benjamin. "A Short Narrative of Mischief done by the French and Indian Enemy on the Western Frontiers of the Province of the Massachusetts Bay." *Magazine of History with Notes and Queries,* extra no. 7 (2), 1909.

Douglass, William. *A Summary, Historical and Political, of the First Planting, progressive Improvements, and present State of the British Settlements in North-America.* 2 vols. Boston, 1749–53.

Drake, Samuel, ed. *The History of the Indian Wars in New England from the First Settlement to the Termination of the War with King Philip in 1677, from the Original Work by the Rev. William Hubbard.* 2 vols. Reprint, New York: Burt Franklin, 1971.

———. *Indian Captivities, or Life in the Wigwam; being true narratives of captives who have been carried away by Indians, from the frontier settlements of the United States, from the earliest period to the present time.* Auburn: Derby and Miller, 1852.

Druillettes, Gabriel. "Journal of an Embassy from Canada to the United Colonies of New England in 1650, by Father Gabriel Druillettes." Edited by John Gilmeary Shea. *Collections of the New York Historical Society,* 2d ser., 3, pt. 1.

"The Exploration of the Merrimack River, in 1638 By Order of the General Court of Massachusetts, with a plan of the same." *Historical Collections of the Essex Institute* 14, no. 3 (July 1877): 153–71.

Fletcher, Ebenezer. *A Narrative of the Captivity and Sufferings of Ebenezer Fletcher.* New Ipswich, N.H., 1813.

Force, Peter, ed. and comp. *American Archives.* 9 vols. Washington, D.C., 1837–53.

Gookin, Daniel. *Historical Collections of the Indians in New England.* Collections of the Massachusetts Historical Society for 1792; reprint, Towtaid, 1970.

Hammond, Isaac W., ed. *New Hampshire State Papers*. Vol. 17. Concord, 1889.

Hanson, Elizabeth. *The Remarkable Captivity and Surprising Deliverance of Elizabeth Hanson*. 3d ed. Dover, N.H., 1824.

Hulbert, Archer Butler, ed. *The Crown Collection of Photographs of American Maps*. Ser. 1, 5 vols. Cleveland: Arthur H. Clark Co., 1907.

"Indian Treaties." *Collections of the Maine Historical Society* 4 (1856): 118–84.

Iroquois Indians: A Documentary of the Diplomacy of the Six Nations and Their League. Edited by Francis Jennings, William Fenton, et al. Microfilm publication, 50 reels. Woodbridge, Conn.: Research Publications, 1984.

Jameson, J. Franklin, ed. *Narratives of New Netherland, 1609–1664*. New York: Barnes & Noble, 1959.

Johnson, Edward. *Johnson's Wonder-Working Providence, 1628–1651*. Edited by J. Franklin Jameson. New York, 1910.

Johnson, Susanna Willard. "A Narrative of the Captivity of Mrs. Johnson." Pp. 128–82 in *Indian Narratives*. Claremont, N.H.: Tracy and Brothers, 1854.

Johnson, Sir William. *The Papers of Sir William Johnson*. Edited by James Sullivan et al. 15 vols. Albany: State University of New York Press, 1921–65.

Kalm, Peter. *Travels into North America*. . . . 3 vols. London, 1772.

Kendall, Edward Augustus. *Travels through the northern parts of the United States in the years 1807 and 1808*. 3 vols. New York: I. Riley, 1809.

Kenney, James F., ed. "A British Secret Service Report on Canada, 1711." *Canadian Historical Review* 1 (1920): 48–54.

King, Titus. *Narrative of Titus King of Northampton, Mass. A Prisoner of the Indians in Canada 1755–1758*. Hartford: Connecticut Historical Society, 1938.

Labaree, Leonard Woods, ed. *Royal Instructions to British Colonial Governors, 1670–1776*. New York: D. Appleton Century Co., 1935.

Lahontan, Louis Armand de Lom d'Arce, Baron de. *New Voyages to North-America by Baron de Lahontan*. Edited by Reuben Gold Thwaites. 2 vols. Chicago: A. C. McClurg and Co., 1905.

La Pothèrie, Bacqueville de. *Histoire de l'Amérique Septentrionale*. 4 vols. Paris: Jean-Luc Nion, 1722.

———. "History of the Savage Peoples Who are Allies of New France." In Emma Helen Blair, trans. and ed., *The Indian Tribes of the Upper Mississippi Valley and Region of the Great Lakes*. Cleveland: The Arthur H. Clark Co., 1911.

Leder, Lawrence H., ed., *The Livingston Indian Records, 1666–1723*. Gettysburg: Pennsylvania Historical Association, 1956.

Léry, Captain de. "Diary Kept by Captain de Léry, 1756." *Bulletin of the Fort Ticonderoga Museum* 6, no. 4 (July 1942): 128–44.

Lescarbot, Marc. *Marc Lescarbot: The History of New France*. Edited by H. P. Biggar. 3 vols. Toronto: Champlain Society, 1907–14.

"Letters relating to Mrs. Jemina How, who was taken by the Indians at Hinsdale, N.H., in July 1755." *Collections of the New Hampshire Historical Society* 5 (1837): 256–58.

Lincoln, Charles H., ed. *Narratives of the Indian Wars, 1675–1699*. New York: Charles Scribner's Sons, 1913.

McIlwain, C. H., ed. *Peter Wraxall's Abridgement of the New York Indian Records*. Cambridge, Mass.: Harvard University Press, 1915.

Mary Ellery, the Indian Captive. Montpelier: Vermont Historical Society, n.d.

Melven, Eleazar. "Journal of Capt. Eleazar Melven, with eighteen men in his command, in the Wilderness towards Crown Point—1748." *Collections of the New Hampshire Historical Society*, 5 (1837): 207–11.

"Memoir of the Sokokis or Pequaket Tribe of Indians." *Magazine of History, with Notes and Queries*, extra no. 5 (2), ·909.

Missionary Herald, containing the Proceedings at Large of the American Board of Commissioners for Foreign Missions.

Montcalm, Louis Joseph. *Journal du Marquis de Montcalm durant ses campagnes en Canada de 1756 à 1759*. In *Collections des Manuscripts du Maréchal de Lévis*, vol. 7.

O'Callaghan, E. B., ed. *The Documentary History of the State of New York*. 4 vols. Albany: Weed, Parsons and Co., 1850.

———. *Documents Relative to the Colonial History of New York*. 15 vols. Albany: Weed, Parsons, 1855–61.

"Papers Relating to Fort Dummer." *Collections of the New Hampshire Historical Society* 1 : 143–47.

Penhallow, Samuel. *Penhallow's Indian Wars: A Facsimile Reprint of the First Edition, 1726*. Edited by Edward Wheelock. Freeport, N.Y.: Books for Libraries Press, 1971.

"Pennacook Papers." *Collections of the New Hampshire Historical Society* 3 (1832): 214–24.

Pennacook/Sokoki Inter Tribal Nation, comps. *Historical Indian-Colonial Relations of New Hampshire*. Manchester: Pennacook/Sokoki Inter-Tribal Nation, New Hampshire Indian Council Inc., 1977.

Pike, John. "Journal of Rev. John Pike." *Collections of the New Hampshire Historical Society* 3 (1832).

Powers, Grant. *Historical Sketches of the Discovery, Settlement, and Progress of Events in the Coos Country*. Haverhill, N.H.: J. F. C. Hayes, 1841.

Pynchon, John. *The Pynchon Papers, Vol. 1: Letters of John Pynchon, 1654–1700*. Edited by Carl Bridenbaugh. Boston: Colonial Society of Massachusetts, 1982.

Rapport de l'Archiviste de la Province de Québec. Quebec, 1920–.

Redfield, Timothy P. *Report on the Claim of the Iroquois Indians upon the State of Vermont for their "Hunting Ground."* Montpelier, Vt.: E. P. Walton, 1854.

Rogers, Robert. *The Journals of Major Robert Rogers*. London, 1765. Readex Microprint facsimile edn., 1966.

Roy, Pierre-Georges, *Hommes et choses du Fort Saint-Frédéric*. Montreal: Les Editions du Dix, 1946.

Sanders, D. C. *A History of the Indian Wars with the First Settlers of the United States, Particularly in New England*. Montpelier, Vt.: Wright and Sibley, 1812.

Shortt, Adam, and Arthur G. Doughty, eds. *Documents Relating to the Constitutional History of Canada, 1759–1791*. 2 vols. Ottawa: The Historical Documents Publication Board, 1918.

Slotkin, Richard, and James K. Folsom, eds. *So Dreadful a Judgment: Puritan Responses to King Philip's War, 1676–1677*. Middletown, Conn.: Wesleyan University Press, 1978.

Smyth, Egbert C., ed. "The construction and first occupancy of Fort Dummer and a conference with the Scatacook Indians held there." *Proceedings of the Massachusetts Historical Society*, 2d ser., 6 (March 1891): 359–81.

Stachiw, Myro O. *Massachusetts Offices and Soldiers, 1723–1743: Dummer's War to the War of Jenkin's Ear*. Boston: New England Historic Genealogical Society, 1979.

Stark, Caleb, ed. *Reminiscences of the French War: containing Rogers' expeditions with the New England rangers . . . [and] an account of the life and military services of Maj. Gen. John Stark*. Concord: Luther Roby, 1831.

Steele, Zadock. "Captivity of Zadock Steele." Pp. 209–76 in *Indian Narratives. . . .* Claremont, N.H.: Tracy and Brothers, 1854.

Stevens, Phineas. "Journal of Capt. Phineas Stevens to and from Canada—1749." *Collections of the New Hampshire Historical Society* 5 (1837): 199–205.

———. "Journal of Captain Phineas Stevens' Journey to Canada, 1752." In Newton D. Mereness, ed., *Travels in the American Colonies*. New York: Macmillan Co., 1916.

Stiles, Dr. Ezra. "Indians on Connecticut River." *Collections of the Massachusetts Historical Society*, 1st ser., 10 (1809): 104–105.

Stockwell, John. *The Account of John Stockwell of Deerfield, Massachusetts. Being a Faithful Narrative of His Experiences in the Hands of the Wachusett Indians—1677–1678*. Somerville, N.J.: Clark S. Yowell, 1928.

Sullivan, John. *Letters and Papers of Major-General John Sullivan.* Edited by Otis G. Hammond. 3 vols. Concord: New Hampshire Historical Society, 1930–39.

Thwaites, Reuben Gold, ed. *The Jesuit Relations and Allied Documents: Travels and Explorations of the Jesuit Missionaries in New France, 1610–1791.* 73 vols. Cleveland: Burrows Brothers Co., 1896–1901.

Tufts, Henry. *Henry Tufts: The Autobiography of a Criminal.* Edited by Edmund Pearson. New York: Duffield and Co., 1930.

———. *A Narrative of the Life, Adventures, Travels and Sufferings of Henry Tufts.* Dover, N.H.: Samuel Bragg, Jr., 1807.

The Upper Connecticut: Narratives of Its Settlement and Its Part in the American Revolution. 2 vols. Montpelier: Vermont Historical Society, 1943.

Vaughan, Alden T., and Edward W. Clark, eds. *Puritans among the Indians: Accounts of Captivity and Redemption, 1676–1724.* Cambridge, Mass.: Belknap Press of Harvard University Press, 1981.

Vermont. Secretary of State. *State Papers of Vermont.* 17 vols. Montpelier: Secretary of State's Office, 1918–69.

Walton, E. P., ed. *Records of the Governor and Council of the State of Vermont.* 8 vols. Montpelier: J. M. Poland, 1813–80.

Washington, George. *The Writings of George Washington.* Edited by John C. Fitzpatrick. 39 vols. Washington, D.C.: Government Printing Office, 1931–44.

Wheelwright, Nathaniel. "Nathaniel Wheelwright's Canadian Journey, 1753–4." Edited by Edward P. Hamilton. *Bulletin of the Fort Ticonderoga Museum* 10, no. 4 (Feb. 1960): 259–96.

Williams, John. *The Redeemed Captive Returning to Zion, or a Faithful History of Remarkable Occurrences in the Captivity and Deliverance of Mr. John Williams.* 1707. Ann Arbor, Mich.: University Microfilms, 1966.

Williams, Samuel. *The Natural and Civil History of Vermont.* Walpole, N.H.: Isaiah Thomas and David Carlisle, 1794.

Williams, Stephen. *A Biographical Memoir of the Rev. John Williams.* Greenfield, Mass: C. J. J. Ingersoll, 1837.

Winthrop, John. *Winthrop's Journal: "History of New England."* Edited by James Kendall Hosmer. 2 vols. Reprint, New York, 1966.

Wright, Harry Andrew, ed. *Indian Deeds of Hampden County.* Springfield, Mass., 1905.

Secondary Sources

Abenaki Nation of Vermont. *A Petition for Federal Recognition as an American Indian Tribe by the Abenaki Nation of Vermont.* Swanton, 1982.

———. *Addendum to the Petition for Federal Recognition as an American Indian Tribe*, Part B. Swanton, Vt., 1986.

Aquila, Richard. *The Iroquois Restoration: Iroquois Diplomacy on the Colonial Frontier, 1701–1754.* Detroit: Wayne State University Press, 1983.

Auger, Leonard, A. "St. Francis Through the Years." *Vermont History* 27, no. 4 (Oct. 1959): 287–304.

Axtell, James. *The European and the Indian: Essays in the Ethnohistory of Colonial North America.* New York: Oxford University Press, 1981.

———. *The Invasion Within: The Contest of Cultures in Colonial North America.* New York: Oxford University Press, 1985.

———. "Were Indian Conversions *Bona Fide?*" In Axtell, *After Columbus: Essays in the Ethnohistory of Colonial America,* 100–121. New York: Oxford University Press, 1988.

———. "The White Indians of Colonial North America." *William and Mary Quarterly,* 3d ser., 32 (Jan. 1975): 55–88.

Bailey, Alfred Goldsworthy. *The Conflict of European and Eastern Algonkian Cultures, 1504–1700.* 2d ed. Toronto: University of Toronto Press, 1969.

Bailyn, Bernard. *Voyagers to the West: A Passage in the Peopling of America on the Eve of the Revolution.* New York: Vintage, 1988.

Baker, C. Alice. *True Stories of New England Captives Carried to Canada During the Old French and Indian Wars.* Cambridge: E. A. Hall and Co., 1897.

Ballard, Edward. "Character of the Penacooks." *Collections of the New Hampshire Historical Society* 8 (1866): 428–45.

Baxter, James Phinney, *The Pioneers of New France in New England.* Albany: Joel Munsell's Sons, 1894.

Bayreuther, William A. "Environmental Diversity as a Factor in Modeling Prehistoric Settlement Patterns: Southeastern Vermont's Black River Valley." *Man in the Northeast* 19 (Spring 1980): 83–93.

Belknap, Jeremy. *The History of New Hampshire.* 3 vols. Dover: Stevens and Ela and Wadleigh, 1831.

"Biography of Kancamagus." *The Farmer's Monthly Visitor* (Manchester, N.H.), 13, no. 5 (May 1853): 129–38.

"Biography of Passaconaway." *The Farmer's Monthly Visitor,* 12, no. 2 (Feb. 1852): 33–40.

"Biography of Wanalancet." *The Farmer's Monthly Visitor* 12, no. 9 (Sept. 1852): 259–65.

Bouton, Nathaniel. *The History of Concord . . . with a History of the Ancient Penacooks.* Concord, N.H.: B. W. Sanborn, 1856.

Bourque, Bruce J. "Ethnicity on the Maritime Peninsula, 1600–1759." *Ethnohistory* 36 (Summer 1989): 257–84.

Bourque, Bruce J. and Ruth Holmes Whitehead. "Tarrantines and the

Introduction of European Trade Goods in the Gulf of Maine." *Ethnohistory* 32 (1985): 327–41.

Brasser, Ted J. "Group Identification along a Moving Frontier." *Proceedings of the 38th International Congress of Americanists* 2 (1968): 261–65.

———. "Mahican." In Trigger, ed., *Northeast*, 198–212, *Handbook of North American Indians* 15.

———. *Riding on the Frontier's Crest: Mahican Indian Culture and Culture Change*. Publications in Ethnology, no. 13. Ottawa: National Museum of Man, 1974.

Bumsted, M. Pamela. "VT-CH-94: Vermont's Earliest Known Agricultural Experiment Station." *Man in the Northeast* 19 (Spring 1980): 73–82.

Burns, Brian. "Massacre or Muster? Burgoyne's Indians and the Militia at Bennington." *Vermont History* 45, no. 3 (Summer 1977): 133–44.

Calloway, Colin G. "The Conquest of Vermont: Vermont's Indian Troubles in Context." *Vermont History* 52 (Summer 1984): 161–79.

———. "Gray Lock's War." *Vermont History* 55 (Fall 1987): 212–27.

———. "Green Mountain Diaspora: Indian Population Movements in Vermont, C. 1600–1800." *Vermont History*, 54 (Fall 1986), 197–228.

———. "Survival Through Dispersal: Vermont Abenakis in the Eighteenth Century." *Proceedings of the American Historical Association, 1987*.

———. "An Uncertain Destiny: Indian Captivities on the Upper Connecticut River." *Journal of American Studies* 17 (Aug. 1983): 189–210.

———. "Wanalancet and Kancagamus: Indian Strategy and Leadership on the New Hampshire Frontier." *Historical New Hampshire* 43 (Winter 1988): 264–90.

Carter, Samuel. "The Route of the French and Indian army that sacked Deerfield Feb. 29th, 1703–4 [O.S.], on their return march to Canada with the captives." *History and Proceedings of the Pocumtuck Valley Memorial Association* 2 (1898): 126–151.

Castile, George Pierre, and Gilbert Kushner, eds. *Persistent Peoples: Cultural Enclaves in Perspective*. Tucson: University of Arizona Press, 1981.

Charland, Thomas M. *Les Abénakis d'Odanak: Histoire des Abénakis d'Odanak, 1675–1937*. Montreal: Editions du Levrier, 1964.

———. "Atecuando (Jerome)." *Dictionary of Canadian Biography*. 3: 20–21. Toronto: University of Toronto Press, 1966–.

———. "Joseph Louis Gill." *Dictionary of Canadian Biography* 4: 293–94.

———. "The Lake Champlain Army and the Fall of Montreal. *Vermont History*. 28 (1960): 293–301.

———. "Un Village d'Abénaquis sur la Rivière Missisquoi," *Revue d'Histoire de l'Amérique Français* 15, no. 3 (1961): 319–22. (Translation by Grace Huden in Vermont Historical Society Library.)

Clark, Charles E. *The Eastern Frontier: The Settlement of Northern New England, 1610–1763*. New York: Alfred A. Knopf, 1970.

Clifton, James A. *Being and Becoming Indian: Biographical Studies of North American Frontiers*. Chicago: Dorsey Press, 1989.

Colby, Solon B. *Colby's Indian History: Antiquities of the New Hampshire Indians and Their Neighbors*. Exeter, N. H., 1975.

Coleman, Emma L. *New England Captives Carried to Canada Between 1677 and 1760 during the French and Indian Wars*. 2 vols. Portland, Me.: Southwourth Press, 1925.

Conkling, Robert. "Legitimacy and Conversion in Social Change: The Case of French Missionaries and the Northern Algonkian." *Ethnohistory* 21, no. 1 (Winter 1974): 1–24.

Cook, Sherburne F. *The Indian Population of New England in the Seventeenth Century*. Berkeley: University of California Press, 1976.

———. "Interracial Warfare and Population Decline among the New England Indians." *Ethnohistory* 20, no. 1 (Winter 1973): 1–24.

———. "The Significance of Disease in the Extinction of the New England Indian." *Human Biology* 45 (1973): 485–508.

Coolidge, Guy Omeron. "The French Occupation of the Champlain Valley from 1609 to 1759." *Proceedings of the Vermont Historical Society*, n.s., 6, no. 3 (Sept. 1938): 143–313. Reprint, Harrison, N.Y.: Harbor Hill Books, 1979.

Crockett, Walter Hill. *Vermont: The Green Mountain State*. 5 vols. New York: Century History Co., 1921.

Cronon, William. *Changes in the Land: Indians, Colonists, and the Ecology of New England*. New York: Hill and Wang, 1983.

Crosby, Alfred W., Jr. *The Columbian Exchange: Biological and Cultural Consequences of 1492*. Westport, Conn.: Greenwood Press, 1972.

———. *Ecological Imperialism: The Biological Expansion of Europe, 900–1900*. New York: Cambridge University Press, 1986.

———. "Virgin Soil Epidemics as a Factor in the Aboriginal Depopulation in America." *William and Mary Quarterly*, 3rd ser., 33 (April 1976): 289–99.

Cuneo, John R. *Robert Rogers of the Rangers*. New York: Oxford University Press, 1959.

Daniels, Thomas E. *Vermont Indians*. Poultney, Vt.: Journal Press, 1963.

Day, Gordon M. "Abenaki Place-Names in the Champlain Valley." *International Journal of Applied Linguistics* 47, no. 2 (1981): 143–71.

———. "Abenakis in the Lake Champlain Valley." In Jennie G. Versteeg, ed., *Lake Champlain: Reflections in Our Past*, 277–88. Burlington: University of Vermont, Center for Research on Vermont, 1987.

———. "Arosagunticook and Androscoggin." In William Cowan, ed.,

Papers of the 10th Algonquian Conference, 10–15. Ottawa: Carleton University Press, 1979.

————. "Atecuando." *Dictionary of Canadian Biography* 2:25–26.

————. "Dartmouth and St. Francis." *Dartmouth Alumni Magazine* 52 (Nov. 1959): 28–30.

————. "The Eastern Boundary of Iroquoia: Abenaki Evidence." *Man in the Northeast* 1 (March 1971): 7–13.

————. "English-Indian Contacts in New England." *Ethnohistory* 9, no. 1 (Winter 1962): 24–40.

————. "Henry Tufts as a Source on the Eighteenth Century Abenakis." *Ethnohistory* 21, no. 3 (Summer 1974): 189–97.

————. *The Identity of the St. Francis Indians*. Canadian Ethnology Service Paper no. 71. Ottawa: National Museums of Canada, 1981.

————. "The Identity of the Sokokis." *Ethnohistory* 12, no. 3 (Summer 1965): 237–49.

————. "The Indian Occupation of Vermont." *Vermont History* 33 (July 1965): 365–74.

————. "Missisquoi: A New Look at an Old Village." *Man in the Northeast* 6 (Fall 1973): 51–57.

————. *The Mots Loups of Father Mathevet*. Publications in Ethnology, no. 8. Ottawa: National Museums of Canada, 1975.

————. "The Ouragie War: A Case History in Iroquois–New England Indian Relations." in Michael K. Foster, Jack Campisi, Marianne Mithun, eds., *Extending the Rafters: Interdisciplinary Approaches to Iroquoian Studies*. Albany: State University of New York Press, 1984.

————. "Rogers' Raid in Indian Tradition." *Historical New Hampshire* 17 (June 1962): 3–17.

————. "Western Abenaki." In Trigger, ed., *Northeast*, 148–59, *Handbook of North American Indians* 15.

————. "The Western Abenaki Transformer." *Journal of the Folklore Institute* 13 (1976): 75–89.

Denevan, William., ed. *The Native Population of the Americas in 1492*. Madison: University of Wisconsin Press, 1976.

Devine, E. J., S.J. *Historic Caughnawaga*. Montreal: Messenger Press, 1922.

Dobyns, Henry. *Native American Historical Demography*. Bloomington: Indiana University Press, 1976.

————. *Their Number Become Thinned: Native American Population Dynamics in Eastern North America*. Knoxville: University of Tennessee Press, 1983.

Doremus, Christine A. "Jurisdiction over Adjudications Involving the Abenaki Indians of Vermont." *Vermont Law Review* 10 (1985): 417–35.

Drake, Samuel Adams. *The Border Wars of New England. Commonly*

Called King William's and Queen Anne's Wars. New York: Charles Scribner's Sons, 1897.

———. *A Particular History of the Five Years French and Indian War in New England and Parts Adjacent. . . .* Reprint, Freeport, N.Y.: Books for Libraries Press, 1970.

Eccles, William J. *The Canadian Frontier, 1534–1760*. New York: Holt, Rinehart, and Winston, 1969.

———. *France in America*. New York: Harper and Row, 1972.

English, John Stephen. *Indian Legends of the White Mountains*. Boston: Rand Avery, 1915.

Fitzhugh, William W., ed. *Cultures in Contact: The European Impact on Native Cultural Institutions in Eastern North America, A.D. 1000–1800*. Washington: Smithsonian Institution Press, 1985.

Follette, Clara E. "The Iroquoian Claim on Vermont." *Vermont History* 23 (Jan. 1955): 54–55.

Frisch, Jack A. "The Abenakis among the St. Regis Mohawks." *Indian Historian* 4 (Spring 1971): 27–29.

Gale, John E. "Northern Neighbors of the Pocumtucks." *History and Proceedings of the Pocumtuck Valley Memorial Association* 9 (1939): 22–30.

Graffagnino, J. Kevin. *The Shaping of Vermont: From the Wilderness to the Centennial, 1749–1887*. Rutland and Bennington: Vermont Heritage Press and Bennington Museum, 1983.

Grant, John Webster. *Moon of Wintertime: Missionaries and the Indians of Canada in Encounter since 1534*. Toronto: University of Toronto Press, 1984.

Greening, W. "Historic Odanak and the Abenaki Nation." *Canadian Geographic Journal* 73 (1966): 92–97.

Hadlock, Wendell S. "War among the Northeastern Woodland Indians." *American Anthropologist*, n.s., 49, (1947): 204–21.

Hall, Benjamin H. *History of Eastern Vermont from the Earliest Settlement to the Close of the Eighteenth Century*. New York: D. Appleton and Co., 1858. Albany, N.Y.: J. Munsell, 1865.

Hall, Hiland. *The History of Vermont*. Albany: Joel Munsell, 1868.

Hamell, George R. "Mythical Realities and European Contact in the Northeast during the Sixteenth and Seventeenth Centuries." *Man in the Northeast* 33 (Spring 1987): 63–87.

Harrington, Walter L. "Fort Dummer: An Archaeological Investigation of the First Permanent English Settlement in Vermont." In *New England Archaeology*, Dublin Seminar for New England Folklife, Annual Proceeedings (1977), 86–94.

Harris, R. Cole, ed. *Historical Atlas of Canada, I: From the Beginning to 1800*. Toronto: University of Toronto Press, 1987.

Hauptman, Laurence M. "The Dispersal of the River Indians: Frontier Expansion and Indian Dispossession in the Hudson Valley." In Hauptman and Campisi, eds., *Neighbors and Intruders*, 244–60.

———. "Refugee Havens: The Iroquois Villages of the Eighteenth Century." In Christopher Vecsey and Robert W. Venables, eds., *American Indian Environments: Ecological Issues in Native American History*, 128–39. Syracuse: Syracuse University Press, 1980.

——— and Jack Campisi, eds. *Neighbors and Intruders: An Ethnohistorical Exploration of the Indians of Hudson's River*. Ottawa: National Museum of Man Mercury Series, 1978.

Haviland, William A., and Marjory W. Power. *The Original Vermonters: Native Inhabitants, Past and Present*. Hanover, N.H.: University Press of New England, 1981.

Hayes, Lyman S. *The Connecticut River Valley in Southern Vermont and New Hampshire: Historical Sketches*. Rutland, Vt.: Charles E. Tuttle Co., 1929.

Hemenway, Abby, ed. *The Vermont Historical Gazeteer*. 5 vols. Burlington, 1868–91.

Herwig, Wes. "Indian Raid on Royalton." *Vermont Life*, Autumn 1964, 16–21.

Hirsch, Adam J. "The Collision of Military Cultures in Seventeenth Century New England." *Journal of American History* 74 (March 1988): 1187–212.

Hobart, Frances L. *The Early Indian Tribes of Vermont and Their Relics* N.d., 8 p. Vermont Hist. Soc. MS 27#68.

Hoornbeck, Billie. "An Investigation into the Cause or Causes of the Epidemic which Decimated the Indian Population of New England, 1616–1619." *New England Archaeologist* 19 (1976–77): 35–46.

Hucksoll, Aurelia C. "Watercourses and Indian Population in the Northeast Kingdom." In George R. Clay, ed., *Primitive Versus Modern: Contrasting Attitudes Toward Environment*. Occasional Paper no. 2. Bennington: Vermont Academy of Arts and Sciences.

Huden, John C. "The Abenakis, the Iroquoians, and Vermont." *Vermont History* 24 (Jan. 1956): 21–25.

———. "Frontier Dangers, 1781–1784." *Vermont History* 27 (Oct. 1959): 352–53; 28 (Jan. 1960): 81–91.

———. "Indian Groups in Vermont." *Vermont History* 26 (April 1958): 112–15.

———. Indian Place Names in Vermont. Burlington: privately published 1957.

———. *Indian Place Names of New England*. New York: Museum of the American Indian, Heye Foundation, 1962.

———. "Indians in Vermont—Present and Past." *Vermont History* 23 (Jan. 1955): 25–28.

————. "Indian Troubles in Vermont." *Vermont History* 25 (Oct. 1957): 288–91; 26 (Jan. 1958): 38–41; 26 (July 1958): 206–7.

————. "Iroquois Place Names in Vermont." *Vermont History* 25 (Jan. 1957): 66–80.

————. "The Problem—Indians and White Men in Vermont—When and Where (1550–?)." *Vermont History* 24 (April 1956): 110–20.

————. "The White Chief of the St. Francis Abenakis—Some Aspects of Border Warfare: 1690–1790." *Vermont History* 24 (July 1956): 199–219; 24 (Oct. 1956): 337–55.

Hunt, George T. *The Wars of the Iroquois: A Study in Intertribal Trade Relations*. Madison: University of Wisconsin Press, 1940, 1972.

Jackson, Eric P. "Indian Occupation and Use of the Champlain Lowland." *Papers of the Michigan Academy of Science, Arts, and Letters* 14 (1931): 113–60.

Jaenen, Cornelius. *The French Relationship with the Native Peoples of New France and Acadia*. Ottawa: Research Branch, Indian and Northern Affairs Canada, 1984.

————. "French Sovereignty and Native Nationhood during the French Regime." *Native Studies Review* 2 (1986): 83–113.

————. *Friend and Foe: Aspects of French-Amerindian Cultural Contact in the Sixteenth and Seventeenth Centuries*. New York: Columbia University Press, 1976.

Jellison, Charles A. *Ethan Allen, Frontier Rebel*. Taftsville, Vt.: Countryman Press, 1969.

Jennings, Francis. *The Ambiguous Iroquois Empire: The Covenant Chain Confederation of Indian Tribes with English Colonies from Its Beginnings to the Lancaster Treaty of 1744*. New York: W. W. Norton, 1984.

————. *Empires of Fortune: Crowns, Colonies, and Tribes in the Seven Years War*. New York: W. W. Norton, 1988.

————. *The Invasion of America: Indians, Colonialism, and the Cant of Conquest*. Chapel Hill: University of North Carolina Press, 1975; paperback, New York: W. W. Norton, 1976.

Johansson, S. Ryan. "The Demographic History of the Native Peoples of North America: A Selective Bibliography." *Yearbook of Physical Anthropology* 25 (1982): 133–52.

Johnson, Richard R. "The Search for a Usable Indian: An Aspect of the Defense of Colonial New England." *Journal of American History* 64 (1977): 623–51.

Judd, Sylvester. "The Fur Trade on the Connecticut River in the Seventeenth Century." *New England Historical and Genealogical Register* 11 (1857): 217–19.

Kelly, Eric P. "The Dartmouth Indians." *Dartmouth Alumni Magazine* 22 (Dec. 1929): 122–25.

Kidder, Frederic. "The Abenaki Indians: Their Treaties of 1713 and 1717, and a Vocabulary, with a Historical Introduction." *Collections of the Maine Historical Society* 6 (1859): 250–62.

———. *The Expeditions of Capt. John Lovewell and His Encounters with the Indians*. Boston: Bartlett and Halliday, 1865. In *The Magazine of History with Notes and Queries*, extra no. 5, 1909.

Lampee, Thomas C. "The Missisquoi Loyalists." *Proceedings of the Vermont Historical Society*, n.s., 6 (June 1938): 80–140.

Lape, Jane M. "Père Roubaud, Missionary Extraordinary." *Bulletin of the Fort Ticonderoga Museum* 12, no. 1 (March 1966): 63–71.

"The Last of the Pennacooks." *The Farmer's Monthly Visitor* 13, no. 9 (Sept. 1853): 257–67; 13, no. 10 (Oct. 1853): 289–99.

Laurent, Stephen. "The Abenakis: Aborigines of Vermont." *Vermont History* 23 (Oct. 1955): 286–95; 24 (Jan. 1956): 3–11.

Leach, Douglas Edward. *Arms for Empire: A Military History of the British Colonies in North America, 1607–1763*. New York: Macmillan, 1973.

———. *Flintlock and Tomahawk: New England in King Philip's War*. New York: W. W. Norton, 1966.

———. *The Northern Colonial Frontier, 1607–1763*. New York: Holt, Rinehart and Winston, 1966; reprint, Albuquerque: University of New Mexico Press, 1974.

———. "The 'Whens' of Mary Rowlandson's Captivity." *New England Quarterly* 34 (1961): 352–63.

Le Sueur, Jacques. "History of the Calumet and of the Dance," *Contributions from the Museum of the American Indian, Heye Foundation* 12, no. 5 (1952): 1–22.

Lounsbury, Floyd G. "Iroquois Place–Names in the Champlain Valley." in Hauptman and Campisi, eds., *Neighbors and Intruders*, 103–49.

Lunn, Jean. "The Illegal Fur Trade Out of New France, 1713–1760." *Canadian Historical Association Report* (1939), 61–76.

Lynch, James. "The Iroquois Confederacy and the Adoption and Administration of Non-Iroquoian Individuals and Groups prior to 1756." *Man in the Northeast* 30 (Fall 1985): 83–99.

McAleer, George. *A Study of the Etymology of the Indian Place Name Missisquoi*. Worcester, Mass: Blanchard Press, 1906.

McCorison, Marcus A. "Colonial Defence of the Upper Connecticut Valley." *Vermont History* 30 (Jan. 1962): 50–62.

McEwan, Alice Clark. *Excerpts from "The Burning of Royalton."* Dartmouth College MS 965900, 1965.

Malone, Patrick M. "Changing Military Technology among the Indians of Southern New England, 1600–1677." *American Quarterly* 25 (1973): 48–63.

Man in the Northeast 19 (Spring 1980) Special issue of papers on Vermont archaeology.

Masta, Henry Lorne. *Abenaki Indian Legends, Grammar, and Place Names*. Victoriaville, P.Q.: La Voix des Bois-Francs, 1932.

———. "When the Abenaki Came to Dartmouth," *Dartmouth Alumni* 21 (1928–29): 302–303.

Maurault, Joseph P. A. *Histoire des Abénakis, depuis 1605 jusqu'à nos jours*. Sorel, Quebec: L'Atelier typographique de la Gazette de Sorel, 1866.

Medlicott, Alexander, Jr. "Return to This Land of Light: A Plea to an Unredeemed Captive." *New England Quarterly* 38 (1965): 202–16.

Merrell, James H. "The Indians' New World: The Catawba Experience." *William and Mary Quarterly*, 3d ser., 41 (Oct. 1984): 537–65.

Moody, John. "Missisquoi: Abenaki Survival in their Ancient Homeland." Manuscript on file with the author, Sharon, Vt., 1978..

———. "The Native American Legacy." In Jane C. Beck, ed., *Always in Season: Folk Art and Traditional Culture in Vermont*, 54–65. Montpelier: Vermont Council on the Arts, 1982.

Morrison, Alvin H. "Dawnland Directors: Status and Role of Seventeenth Century Wabanaki Sagamores." In William Cowan, ed., *Papers of the Seventh Algonquian Conference*. Ottawa: Carleton University Press, 1976.

Morrison, Kenneth M. "The Bias of Colonial Law: English Paranoia and the Abenaki Arena of King Philip's War, 1675–1678." *New England Quarterly* 53 (Sept. 1980): 363–87.

———. *The Embattled Northeast: The Elusive Ideal of Alliance in Abenaki-Euramerican Relations*. Berkeley: University of California Press, 1984.

Naroll, Raoul. "The Causes of the Fourth Iroquois War," *Ethnohistory* 16, (Winter 1969): 51–81.

Nelson, Eunice. *The Wabanaki: An Annotated Bibliography*, Cambridge, Mass.: American Friends Service Committee, 1982.

Newell, Catherine S-C. *Molly Ockett*. Bethel, Me.: Bethel Historical Society, 1981.

Norton, Thomas Elliott. *The Fur Trade in Colonial New York, 1686–1776*. Madison: University of Wisconsin Press, 1974.

Otterbein, Keith F. "Why the Iroquois Won: An Analysis of Iroquois Military Tactics." *Ethnohistory* 11 (Winter 1964): 56–63.

Parkman, Francis. *Count Frontenac and New France under Louis XIV*. Toronto: George N. Morang, 1898.

———. *A Half-Century of Conflict*. 2 vols. Toronto: George N. Morang, 1898.

———. *Pioneers of France in the New World*. Toronto: George N. Morang, 1898.

——. *The Jesuits in North America in the Seventeenth Century*. Toronto: George N. Morang, 1898.

Pierce, Ken. *A History of the Abenaki People*. Burlington: University of Vermont Instructional Development Center, 1977.

Porter, Frank W., III, ed. *Strategies for Survival: American Indians in the Eastern United States*. Westport, Conn.: Greenwood Press, 1986.

Power, Marjory, and James B. Petersen. *Seasons of Prehistory: 4000 Years at the Winooski Site*. Montpelier: Vermont Division of Historic Preservation, 1984.

Price, Chester B. "Historic Indian Trails of New Hampshire." *New Hampshire Archaeologist* 8 (1956): 2–13.

Prins, Harald E. L. "Amesokanti: Abortive Tribeformation on the Colonial Frontier." Paper presented at the Annual Meeting of the American Society for Ethnohistory, 1988.

Prins, Harald E. L., and Bruce J. Bourque. "Norridgewock: Village Translocation on the New England-Acadian Frontier." *Man in the Northeast* 33 (Spring 1987): 137–58.

Ramenofsky, Ann F. *Vectors of Death: The Archaeology of European Contact*. Albuquerque: University of New Mexico Press, 1987.

Richter, Daniel K. "Cultural Brokers and Intercultural Politics: New York-Iroquois Relations, 1664–1701." *Journal of American History* 75 (June 1988): 40–67.

——. "Rediscovered Links in the Covenant Chain: Previously Unpublished Transcripts of New York Indian Treaty Minutes, 1677–1691." *Proceedings of the American Antiquarian Society* 92, pt. 1 (1982).

——. "War and Culture: The Iroquois Experience." *William and Mary Quarterly*, 3d ser., 40 (Oct. 1983): 528–59.

Richter, Daniel K., and James H. Merrell, eds. *Beyond the Covenant Chain: The Iroquois and their Neighbors in Indian North America, 1600–1800*. Syracuse: Syracuse University Press, 1987.

Ritchie, W. A. "A Probable Paleo-Indian Site in Vermont," *American Antiquity* 18 (1953): 249–58.

Ronda, James P. "The Sillery Experiment: A Jesuit Indian Village in New France, 1637–1663," *American Indian Culture and Research Journal* 3, no. 1 (1979): 1–8.

Russell, Howard S. *Indian New England before the Mayflower*. Hanover, N.H.: University Press of New England, 1980.

Salisbury, Neal. *Manitou and Providence: Indians, Europeans, and the Making of New England, 1500–1643*. New York: Oxford University Press, 1982.

——. "Social Relationships on a Moving Frontier: Natives and Settlers in Southern New England, 1638–1675." *Man in the Northeast* 33 (Spring 1987): 89–99.

———. "Toward the Covenant Chain: Iroquois and Southern New England Algonquians, 1637–1684." In Richter and Merrell, eds., *Beyond the Covenant Chain*, 61–73.

Saunderson, Rev. Henry H. *History of Charlestown, New Hampshire, The Old No. 4, embracing the part borne by its inhabitants in the Indian, French and Revolutionary Wars, and the Vermont Controversy.* Claremont, N.H.: 1876.

Schleiser, K. H. "Epidemics and Indian Middlemen: Rethinking the Wars of the Iroquois, 1609–1653." *Ethnohistory* 23 (Spring 1976): 129–45.

Schoolcraft, Henry R. *Information Respecting the History, Condition and Prospects of the Indian Tribes of the United States.* Philadelphia: Lippincott, Grambo and Co., 1854–60.

Seeber, Pauleena MacDougall. "The European Influence on Abenaki Economics before 1615." In William Cowan, ed., *Papers of the 15th Algonquian Conference*, 201–14. Ottawa: Carleton University, 1984.

Sévigny, P.-André. *Les Abénaquis: Habitat et Migrations (17e et 18e siècles).* Montreal: Editions Bellarmin, 1976.

Shea, Peter. "A New and Accurate Map of Philip's Grant." *Vermont History* 53 (Winter 1985): 36–42.

Sheldon, George. *A History of Deerfield, Massachusetts . . . with a Special study of the Indian Wars in the Connecticut Valley.* 2 vols. Deerfield: E. A. Hall and Co., 1895–96.

———. "The Pocumtuck Confederacy." *History and Proceedings of the Pocumtuck Valley Memorial Association* 2 (1898): 390–408.

Simmons, William S. "Cultural Bias in the New England Puritans' Perception of Indians." *William and Mary Quarterly*, 3d ser., 38 (Jan. 1981): 56–72.

———. *Spirit of the New England Tribes: Indian History and Folklore, 1620–1984.* Hanover, N.H.: University Press of New England, 1986.

Skinner, Alanson. "Notes on Mahikan Ethnology." *Bulletin of the Public Museum of the City of Milwaukee* 2.

Smith, Robinson V. "New Hampshire Persons Taken as Captives by the Indians." *Historical New Hampshire* 8 (October 1952): 24–31.

Snow, Dean R. "Abenaki Fur Trade in the Sixteenth Century." *Western Canadian Journal of Anthropology* 6, no. 1 (1976): 3–11.

———. *The Archaeology of New England.* New York: Academic Press, 1980.

———. "Eastern Abenaki." In Trigger, ed., *Northeast*, 137–47. *Handbook of North American Indians* 15.

———. "The Ethnohistoric Baseline of the Eastern Abenakis." *Ethnohistory* 23 (1976): 291–306.

———. "Wabanaki Family Hunting Territories." *American Anthropologist*, n.s., 70 (1968): 1143–51.

Snow, Dean R., and Kim M. Lamphear. "European Contact and Indian

Depopulation in the Northeast: The Timing of the First Epidemics." *Ethnohistory* 35 (Winter 1988): 15–33.

Speck, Frank G. "The Eastern Algonkian Wabanaki Confederacy." *American Anthropologist*, n.s., 17 (1915): 492–508.

Spiess, Arthur E., and Bruce D. "New England Pandemic of 1616–1622: Cause and Archaeological Implication." *Man in the Northeast* 34 (Fall 1987): 71–83.

Tanguay, Cyprien. *Dictionnaire Genealogique des Familles Canadiennes.* 7 vols. Montreal: Eusebe Senecal, 1871–90.

Tanner, Helen Hornbeck, ed. *Atlas of Great Lakes Indian History.* Norman: University of Oklahoma Press, 1987.

Temple, Josiah, and George Sheldon. *History of the Town of Northfield, Massachusetts, for 150 Years, with an Account of the Prior Occupation of the Territory by the Squakheags.* Albany: Joel Munsell, 1875.

Thomas, Peter A. "Bridging the Cultural Gap: Indian/White Relations." In John W. Ifkovic and Martin Kaufman, eds., *Early Settlement in the Connecticut Valley.* Historic Deerfield, Institute for Massachusetts Studies, Westfield College, 1984.

———. "Comments on Recent Trends in Vermont Archaeology." *Man in the Northeast* 19 (Spring 1980): 3–14.

———. "Contrastive Subsistence Strategies and Land Use as Factors for Understanding Indian-White Relations in New England." *Ethnohistory* 23 (Winter 1976): 1–18.

———. "The Fur Trade, Indian Land, and the Need to Define Adequate 'Environmental' Parameters." *Ethnohistory* 28 (1981): 359–79.

———. "Squakheag Ethnohistory: A Preliminary Study of Culture Conflict on the Seventeenth Century Frontier." *Man in the Northeast* 5 (Spring 1973): 27–36.

Thompson, Zadock. *History of Vermont, Natural, Civil, and Statistical.* . . . Burlington, Vt.: C. Goodrich, 1842.

Thornton, Russell. *American Indian Holocaust and Survival: A Population History since 1492.* Norman: University of Oklahoma Press, 1987.

"Traces of an Indian Legend." *The Catholic World* 22 (Oct. 1875–March 1876): 277–81.

Trelease, Allen W. *Indian Affairs in Colonial New York: The Seventeenth Century.* Ithaca, N.Y.: Cornell University Press, 1960.

Trigger, Bruce G. "Champlain Judged by His Indian Policy: A Different View of Early Canadian History." *Anthropologia*, n.s., 13 (1971): 85–114.

———. *The Children of Aataentsic: A History of the Huron People to 1660.* 2 vols. Montreal: McGill-Queen's University Press, 1976.

———. "The Mohawk-Mahican War (1624–28): The Establishment of a Pattern." *Canadian Historical Review* 52 (1971): 276–86.

————. *Natives and Newcomers: Canada's "Heroic Age" Reconsidered.* Kingston and Montreal: McGill-Queens University Press, 1985.

————. "Trade and Tribal Warfare on the St. Lawrence in the Sixteenth Century." *Ethnohistory* 9, no. 3 (Summer 1962): 240–256.

————, ed. *Northeast. Handbook of North American Indians,* edited by William C. Sturtevant, vol. 15. Washington, D.C.: Smithsonian Institution Press, 1978.

Trumbull, James Russell. *History of Northampton, Massachusetts, from its settlement in 1654.* 2 vols. Northampton, 1898–1902.

Ulrich, Laurel Thatcher. *Good Wives: Image and Reality in the Lives of Women in Northern New England, 1650–1750.* New York: Knopf, 1982.

Underwood, Wynn. "Indian and Tory Raids on the Otter Valley, 1777–1782." *Vermont Quarterly*, n.s., 15, no. 4 (Oct. 1947): 195–221.

Vaughan, Alden T. *New England Frontier: Puritans and Indians, 1620–1675.* Rev. ed. New York: W. W. Norton and Co., 1979.

Vaughan, Alden, and Daniel Richter. "Crossing the Cultural Divide: Indians and New Englanders, 1605–1763." *Proceedings of the American Antiquarian Society* 90, pt. 1 (Oct. 1980): 23–99.

Walker, Willard, Robert Conkling, and Gregory Buesing. "A Chronological Account of the Wabanaki Confederacy." In Ernest L. Schusky, ed., *Political Organization of Native North Americans.* Washington, D.C.: University Press of America, 1980.

Washington, Ida H., and Paula A. *Carleton's Raid.* Canaan, N.H.: Phoenix Publishing, 1977.

Wells, Frederic P. *History of Newbury, Vermont, from the Discovery of the Coos Country to the Present Time.* St. Johnsbury, Vt.: The Caledonian Co., 1902.

White, Rev. Henry. *The Early History of New England.* 8th ed. Concord, N.H.: I. S. Boyd, 1843.

Williams, Herbert U. "The Epidemic of the Indians of New England, 1616–1620." *Johns Hopkins Hospital Bulletin* 20 (1919): 340–49.

Willoughby, Charles C. *Antiquities of the New England Indians.* Cambridge, Mass.: Peabody Museum of American Archaeology and Ethnology, 1935.

Woodrow, Arthur D., ed. and comp. *Metallak: The Last of the Cooashaukes.* Rumford, Me.: Rumford Publishing Co., 1928.

Index